∴ ∴∴ ∴∴ sustainability

 Other titles in this
series include:

Culture: A Reader for Writers,
John Mauk
(ISBN: 9780199947225)

Language: A Reader for Writers,
Gita DasBender
(ISBN: 9780199947485)

Identity: A Reader for Writers,
John Scenters-Zapico
(ISBN: 9780199947461)

Globalization: A Reader for Writers,
Maria Jerskey
(ISBN: 9780199947522)

sustainability

A READER *for* WRITERS

Carl G. Herndl
University of South Florida

New York Oxford
Oxford University Press

Oxford University Press, publishes works that further Oxford University's
objective of excellence in research, scholarship, and education.

Oxford   New York
Auckland   Cape Town   Dar es Salaam   Hong Kong   Karachi
Kuala Lumpur   Madrid   Melbourne   Mexico City   Nairobi
New Delhi   Shanghai   Taipei   Toronto

With offices in
Argentina   Austria   Brazil   Chile   Czech Republic   France   Greece
Guatemala   Hungary   Italy   Japan   Poland   Portugal   Singapore
South Korea   Switzerland   Thailand   Turkey   Ukraine   Vietnam

Published by Oxford University Press.
198 Madison Avenue, New York, New York 10016
http://www.oup.com

Oxford is a registered trademark of Oxford University Press

Library of Congress Cataloging-in-Publication Data
Herndl, Carl George.
 Sustainability : a reader for writers / Carl Herndl, University of South Florida. -- First Edition.
   pages cm
 Includes bibliographical references and index.
 ISBN 978-0-19-994750-8 (pbk.)
 1. English language--Rhetoric. 2. Report writing. 3. Creative writing. 4. College readers.
 5. Readers--Nature. 6. Readers--Ecology. I. Title.
 PE1408.H469 2013
 808'.0427--dc23
                          2013037170
Printing number: 9 8 7 6 5 4 3 2
Printed in the United States of America
on acid-free paper

brief table of contents

preface   xxii

1   Us: How We Live With Each Other
    & With the World   1

2   Trash: The Costs of Throwing "Stuff" Away   47

3   Food: A Different View of the Food Chain   115

4   Climate Change: What It Is, How It Affects Us,
    & Why We Argue About It So Much   155

5   Energy: Supply, Demand, & Invisible
    Consequences   229

6   Soil and Water: Resources We Take for Granted   307

appendix   377

index   417

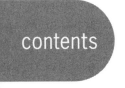

contents

preface   xxii

1 Us: How We Live With Each Other & With the World   1

Rachel Carson, **"The Obligation to Endure"** *Silent Spring*   4

"Such thinking, in the words of the ecologist Paul Shepard, 'idealizes life with only its head out of water, inches above the limits of toleration of the corruption of its own environment . . . Why should we tolerate a diet of weak poisons, a home in insipid surroundings, a circle of acquaintances who are not quite our enemies, the noise of motors with just enough relief to prevent insanity? Who would want to live in a world which is just not quite fatal?'"

Aldo Leopold, **"Thinking Like a Mountain"** *Sand County Almanac*   12

"I now suspect that just as a deer herd lives in mortal fear of its wolves, so does a mountain live in mortal fear of its deer."

Jared Diamond, **"The World as Polder: What Does It Mean to Us Today"** *Collapse: How Societies Choose to Fail or Succeed*   15

"In the Netherlands, we have another expression, 'You have to be able to get along with your enemy, because he may be the person operating the neighboring pump in your polder.' And we're all down in the polders together."

Garrett Hardin, **"Tragedy of the Commons"** *Science*   28

"Ruin is the destination toward which all men rush, each pursuing his own best interest in a society that believes in the freedom of the commons. Freedom in a commons brings ruin to all."

2   Trash: The Costs of Throwing "Stuff" Away   47

Annie Leonard, **"The Story of Stuff: Electronics"** Story of Stuff
    Project   50

"So let's get our brains working on sending that old design for the dump mentality to the dump where it belongs and instead building an electronics industry and a global society that's designed to last."

Annie Leonard, **"The Story of Stuff: Bottled Water"** Story of Stuff
    Project   62

"These bottled water companies say they're just meeting consumer demand—But who would demand a less sustainable, less tasty, way more expensive product, especially one you can get almost free in your kitchen?"

Chris Caroll, **"High Tech Trash"** National Geographic Magazine   78

"We in the developed world get the benefit from these devices," says Jim Puckett, head of Basel Action Network, or BAN, a group that opposes hazardous waste shipments to developing nations. "But when our equipment becomes unusable, we externalize the real environmental costs and liabilities to the developing world."

Luke W. Cole and Sheila R. Foster, **"We Speak for Ourselves: The
    Struggle of Kettleman City"** From the Ground Up: Environmental
    Racism and the Rise of the Environmental Justice Movement   88

"The story is a classic David-and-Goliath tale, in which a small farm-worker town took on the largest toxic waste dumping company in the world—and won."

Emily Fontaine, **"Where Did Our Clothes Come From?"** Le Quaintrelle
    Blog   97

"It all comes down to realizing that each purchase you make is like a vote. . . . But if you vote to buy domestic, or even foreign goods, as long as either are from companies that have fair wages, and acceptable work environments, then you are showing that that is what you want and what you expect from companies."

Lucy Siegle, **"Why It's Time to End Our Love Affair With Cheap
    Fashion"** The Observer Newspaper   103

"The nation's penchant for 'McFashion'—as one-night-only T-shirts and skinny jeans have been dubbed—was found to translate into more than three million tons of carbon dioxide emissions."

Gay Hawkins, **"Worm Stories"** *The Ethics of Waste: How We Relate to Rubbish*   108

"Worms are the penultimate loss managers, and they give us a powerful example of how quotidian and inevitable change is. . . . You have to live with your waste a little more carefully so as to facilitate its effective transition by worms, and in these habits a calmer acceptance of your own transience might be nurtured."

3   Food: A Different View of the Food Chain   115

Jeff Opperman, **"Getting to Know Your Bacon: Hogs, Farms, and Clean Water"** The Nature Conservancy Blog   118

"I mostly eat bacon that comes from pigs that I can visit. Pigs that lounge happily in sun-dappled mud puddles. Pigs that forage for acorns and hickory nuts and stand proudly on the edge of a meadow like some porcine version of Elsa (the lion from *Born Free*). I've directly witnessed all of these piggish pursuits during annual visits to 'our' farm in Wayne County, Ohio."

Sarah Lozanova, **"Starbucks Coffee: Green or Greenwashed?"** GreenBiz.com Blog   121

"Starbucks is frequently targeted by environmentalists for unsustainable practices, but do they deserve this? The nature of the coffee industry is unsustainable in many ways, but Starbucks has helped lead the industry towards greener practices."

Stephanie Wear, **"Finding Nemo on Your Plate"** The Nature Conservancy Blog   126

"From the predator to the grazer (herbivore) to the very picky eaters (specialists), each fish plays an important part in the coral reef 'city.' . . . In the case of coral reefs, the fish that are now landing on the dinner plate, the grazers, are extremely important for keeping coral competitors in check (namely, seaweed)."

Dan Charles, **"How Community-Supported Agriculture Sprouted in China"** *The Salt*, National Public Radio Blog   130

"Little Donkey, being organic, uses only manure and compost for fertilizer, but most Chinese farmers abandoned those methods over the past forty years. They're now among the world's biggest users of synthetic fertilizer, and it's helped them boost their food production dramatically."

Michael Pollan, **"The Genius of the Place"** *Omnivore's Dilemma*   132

"This is an astounding cornucopia of food to draw from a hundred acres of pasture, yet what is perhaps still more astonishing is the fact that this pasture will be in no way diminished by the process—in fact, it will be the better for it, lusher, more fertile, even springier underfoot (this thanks to the increased earthworm traffic)."

Deborah Whitman, **"Genetically Modified Foods: Harmful or Helpful?"** ProQuest   140

"The world population has topped 6 billion people and is predicted to double in the next 50 years. Ensuring an adequate food supply for this booming population is going to be a major challenge in the years to come.... Most concerns about GM foods fall into three categories: environmental hazards, human health risks, and economic concerns."

Paul Epstein, **"Food Security and Climate Change: The True Cost of Carbon"** *The Atlantic*   147

"While the fossil fuel industry continues its well-funded, well-orchestrated campaign to keep up a drum beat of doubt on climate change, the impacts are becoming self evident, and nowhere are they more pronounced than with the emergence of food insecurity."

4   Climate Change: What It Is, How It Affects Us, & Why We Argue About It So Much   155

Ralph Cicerone, **"Finding Climate Change and Being Useful"** National Council for Science and the Environment   158

"As important as it is to have detected contemporary climate change and to develop a theoretical understanding of why it is changing, there is a great deal more that scientists can do to be useful to society."

National Research Council, **"Advancing the Science of Climate Change"** *Advancing the Science of Climate Change*   183

"Scientific research will never completely eliminate uncertainties about climate change and its risks to human health and well-being, but it can provide information that can be helpful to decision makers who must make choices in the face of risks."

Terry Cannon, **"Gender and Climate Hazards in Bangladesh"** *Gender and Development*   197

"The principal climatic hazards affecting Bangladesh—floods and cyclones—are likely to increase in frequency, intensity, duration, and extent. . . . If there is no serious progress in reducing poverty, then it can be assumed that women will become increasingly affected by the impact of intensified hazards, in terms of their ability to resist and recover from them."

Roman Krznaric, **"Empathy and Climate Change: A Proposal for a Revolution of Human Relationships"** *Future Ethics: Climate Change and Apocalyptic Imagination*   206

"How can we close the gap between knowledge and action on climate change?"

New Evangelical Partnership for the Common Good, **"Climate Change: An Evangelical Call to Action"** Evangelical Climate Initiative Webpage   216

"But now we have seen and heard enough to offer the following moral argument related to the matter of human-induced climate change. We commend the four simple but urgent claims offered in this document to all who will listen, beginning with our brothers and sisters in the Christian community, and urge all to take the appropriate actions that follow from them."

5 Energy: Supply, Demand, & Invisible Consequences   229

National Research Council, **"Energy Supply and Use"** *Advancing the Science of Climate Change*   233

"This chapter focuses on what is already known about energy and climate change and about what more needs to be known. . . . this chapter provides only a brief summary of critical knowledge and research needs in the energy sector"

Liz Barratt-Brown, **"It Is All About the Framing: How Polls and the Media Misrepresent the Keystone XL[Tar Sands] [Oil] Pipeline"** National Resources Defense Council Blog   253

"So, without context, what do you think most Americans would first think of when asked about a pipeline? Jobs and the economy. And that is just the framing they have also been hearing again and again from the media."

Climate Guest Blogger, **"'Thinking Big' on Efficiency Could Cut U.S. Energy Costs up to $16 Trillion and Create 1.9 Million Net Jobs by 2050"**   258

"The new report outlines three scenarios under which the U.S. could either continue on its current path or cut energy consumption by the year 2050 almost 60 percent, add nearly two million net jobs in 2050, and save energy consumers as much as $400 billion per year (the equivalent of $2600 per household annually)."

Vandana Shiva, **"Food for Cars or People: Biofuels a False Solution to Climate Change and a Threat to Food Security"** *Soil Not Oil*   262

"Subsidization of biofuels is creating a deep impact on demand for foodstuffs from the United States. . . . The rising price of food is good for producers. It is dreadful, however, for consumers, particularly for those in poor, food-importing countries."

Thomas L. Friedman, **"The Age of Noah: Biodiversity"** *Hot, Flat and Crowded: Why We Need a Green Revolution and How It Can Renew America*   273

"The Energy-Climate Era is about more than just addressing soaring energy demand, drastic climate change, and proliferating petrodictatorships. It is also about dealing with another effect of a world that is hot, flat, and crowded—the threat to the earth's biodiversity, as more and more plant and animal species are endangered or go extinct."

Evan I. Schwartz, **"How Not to Make Energy Decisions: Lessons From the Battle Over Cape Wind"** *Technology Review MIT*   283

"America's first offshore wind farm promises to be a picture of ugliness, . . . Or it promises to be a vision of beauty . . . The turbines, spread out over an area as large as Manhattan, will be visible from the coastline for miles."

Willett Kempton, **"The Offshore Power Debate: Views From Cape Cod"** *Coastal Management*   288

"The Nantucket proposal, upon which this article focuses, seems almost a textbook case of environmental policy debates and environmental mobilization."

Christopher Bateman, **"A Colossal Fracking Mess"** *Vanity Fair*   296

"According to Theo Colborn, a noted expert on water issues and endocrine disruptors, at least half of the chemicals known to be present in fracking fluid are toxic; many of them are carcinogens, neurotoxins, endocrine disruptors, and mutagens. But Colborn estimates that a third of the chemicals in fracking fluid remain unknown to the public."

6   Soil & Water: Resources We Take for Granted   307

David Montgomery, **"Good Old Dirt"** Dirt: the Erosion of Civilization   309

"In our accelerated modern lives it is easy to forget that fertile soil still provides the foundation for supporting large concentrations of people on our planet."

Monday Creek Restoration Project, **"Upstream Rock Run Coal Mine Remediation"** from Up the Creek, Fall 2010 1.1 Newsletter   317

"The goal of this project is to construct a healthy functioning riparian corridor, restore water quality, create an integrated land management strategy, while increasing species diversity and abundance of fish and other aquatic organisms in the streams by improving overall watershed condition."

Sandra Steingraber, **"The Case for Gardening as a Means to Curb Climate Change"** Raising Elijah: Protecting Our Children in an Age of Environmental Crisis   320

"[B]ecause it serves as fertilizer for the garden, compost obviates the need to purchase synthetic fertilizers, which are manufactured from fossil fuels, and which, when used as directed, add a second noxious greenhouse gas to the air: nitrous oxide (whose heat-trapping powers are 300 times more potent than carbon dioxide; it is also a precursor of smog)."

Bryan Walsh, **"Nature: A Major Company Puts a Value on the Environment"** Time Blog "Science and Space"   324

"Ask yourself a simple question: if nature weren't available to provide a service that human beings need, how much would it cost to provide that service artificially?"

Dan Charles, **"Putting Farmland on a Fertilizer Diet"** National Public Radio Blog, "The Salt"   328

"In the United States, the best-known casualties of nutrient pollution include the Chesapeake Bay and a portion of the Gulf of Mexico called the 'dead zone.'"

Louisiana Universities Marine Consortium, **"About Hypoxia"**
"Hypoxia in the Northern Gulf of Mexico" Webpage   331

"Hypoxia, or oxygen depletion, is an environmental phenomenon where the concentration of dissolved oxygen in the water column decreases to a level that can no longer support living aquatic organisms."

Cynthia Barnett, **"The Illusion of Water Abundance"** *Blue Revolution: Unmaking America's Water Crisis*   337

"But water is much more important to our future than oil. That's because there are no alternatives to it, no new substitute for life's essential ingredient being cooked from corn, french fry grease, or algae."

Michael Specter, **"Why Sewers Should EXCITE Us"** "We Are All Downstream." water.org   347

"Clean water has done more for the health of humanity than any medicine of scientific achievement. . . . If we did nothing other than provide access to clean water, without any other medical intervention, we could save 2 MILLION lives each YEAR."

Lisa Stiffler, **"All You Need to Know About Storm Water Runoff"** Sightline Daily, Blog of the Sightline Institute   353

"Stormwater doesn't match the traditional image of pollution. . . . Polluted runoff long ago surpassed industry as the number one source for petroleum and other toxic chemicals that wash into the Northwest's water bodies."

Elizabeth Kolbert, **"The Darkening Sea"** *The New Yorker*   362

"Humans have, in this way, set in motion change on a geologic scale. The question that remains is how marine life will respond."

appendix   377

index   417

analogy

Jared Diamond, **"The World as Polder: What Does It Mean to Us Today"**
Collapse: How Societies Choose to Fail or Succeed 15

Emily Fontaine, **"Where Did Our Clothes Come From?"** Le Quaintrelle
Blog 97

Stephanie Wear, **"Finding Nemo on Your Plate"** The Nature
Conservancy blog 126

Thomas L. Friedman, **"The Age of Noah: Biodiversity"** *Hot, Flat and Crowded:
Why We Need a Green Revolution and How It Can Renew America* 273

argument and persuasion

Rachel Carson, **"The Obligation to Endure"** *Silent Spring* 4

Garrett Hardin, **"Tragedy of the Commons"** *Science* 28

Annie Leonard, **"The Story of Stuff: Electronics"** *Story of Stuff Project* 50

Annie Leonard, **"The Story of Stuff: Bottled Water"** *Story of Stuff Project* 62

Chris Caroll, **"High Tech Trash"** *National Geographic Magazine* 78

Stephanie Wear, **"Finding Nemo on Your Plate"** The Nature Conservancy
Blog 126

Paul Epstein, **"Food Security and Climate Change: The True Cost
of Carbon"** *The Atlantic* 147

Ralph Cicerone, **"Finding Climate Change and Being Useful"** National
Council for Science and the Environment 158

National Research Council, **"Advancing the Science of Climate Change"** *Advancing the Science of Climate Change* 183

Terry Cannon, **"Gender and Climate Hazards in Bangladesh"** *Gender and Development* 197

New Evangelical Partnership for the Common Good, **"Climate Change: An Evangelical Call to Action"** Evangelical Climate Initiative Webpage 216

Liz Barratt-Brown, **"It Is All About the Framing: How Polls and the Media Misrepresent the Keystone XL[tar sands] [oil] Pipeline"** National Resources Defense Council Blog 253

Climate Guest Blogger, **"'Thinking Big' on Efficiency Could Cut U.S. Energy Costs up to $16 Trillion and Create 1.9 Million Net Jobs by 2050"** 258

Vandana Shiva, **"Food for Cars or People: Biofuels a False Solution to Climate Change and a Threat to Food Security"** *Soil Not Oil* 262

Thomas L. Friedman, **"The Age of Noah: Biodiversity"** *Hot, Flat and Crowded: Why We Need a Green Revolution and How It Can Renew America* 273

Evan I. Schwartz, **"How Not to Make Energy Decisions: Lessons From the Battle Over Cape Wind"** *Technology Review MIT* 283

Willett Kempton, **"The Offshore Power Debate: Views From Cape Cod"** *Coastal Management* 288

Christopher Bateman, **"A Colossal Fracking Mess"** *Vanity Fair* 296

Sandra Steingraber, **"The Case for Gardening as a Means to Curb Climate Change"** *Raising Elijah: Protecting Our Children in an Age of Environmental Crisis* 320

Cynthia Barnett, **"The Illusion of Water Abundance"** *Blue Revolution: Unmaking America's Water Crisis* 337

Michael Specter, **"Why Sewers Should EXCITE Us"** **"We Are All Downstream"** water.org 347

cause-and-effect analysis

Aldo Leopold, **"Thinking Like a Mountain"** *Sand County Almanac* 12

Garrett Hardin, **"Tragedy of the Commons"** *Science* 28

Lucy Siegle, **"Why It's Time to End Our Love Affair With Cheap Fashion"** *The Observer* Newspaper 103

Paul Epstein, **"Food Security and Climate Change: The True Cost of Carbon"** *The Atlantic* 147

Ralph Cicerone, **"Finding Climate Change"** National Council for Science and the Environment 158

National Research Council, **"Advancing the Science of Climate Change"** *Advancing the Science of Climate Change* 183

Terry Cannon, **"Gender and Climate Hazards in Bangladesh"** *Gender and Development* 197

Liz Barratt-Brown, **"It Is All About the Framing: How Polls and the Media Misrepresent the Keystone XL[tar sands] [oil] Pipeline"** National Resources Defense Council Blog 253

Vandana Shiva, **"Food for Cars or People: Biofuels a False Solution to Climate Change and a Threat to Food Security"** *Soil Not Oil* 262

Thomas L. Friedman, **"The Age of Noah: Biodiversity"** *Hot, Flat and Crowded: Why We Need a Green Revolution and How It Can Renew America* 273

Christopher Bateman, **"A Colossal Fracking Mess"** *Vanity Fair* 296

David Montgomery, **"Good Old Dirt"** *Dirt: The Erosion of Civilization* 309

Dan Charles, **"Putting Farmland on a Fertilizer Diet"** National Public Radio Blog, "The Salt." 328

Louisiana Universities Marine Consortium, **"About Hypoxia"** *Hypoxia in the Northern Gulf of Mexico* Webpage 331

Lisa Stiffler, **"All You Need to Know About Storm Water Runoff"** Sightline Daily, Blog of the Sightline Institute 353

Elizabeth Kolbert, **"The Darkening Sea"** *The New Yorker* 362

comparison and contrast

Jared Diamond, **"The World as Polder: What Does It Mean to Us Today"** *Collapse: How Societies Choose to Fail or Succeed* 15

Jeff Opperman, **"Getting to Know Your Bacon: Hogs, Farms, and Clean Water"** The Nature Conservancy Blog 118

Sarah Lozanova, **"Starbucks Coffee: Green or Greenwashed?"** GreenBiz.com Blog 121

Deborah Whitman, **"Genetically Modified Foods: Harmful or Helpful?"** ProQuest 140

Willett Kempton, **"The Offshore Power Debate: Views From Cape Cod"** *Coastal Management* 288

Michael Specter, **"Why Sewers Should EXCITE Us"** "We Are All Downstream." water.org 347

definition

Garrett Hardin, **"Tragedy of the Commons"** *Science* 28

Sarah Lozanova, **"Starbucks Coffee: Green or Greenwashed?"** GreenBiz.com Blog 121

Deborah Whitman, **"Genetically Modified Foods: Harmful or Helpful?"** ProQuest 140

Terry Cannon, **"Gender and Climate Hazards in Bangladesh"** *Gender and Development* 197

Roman Krznaric, **"Empathy and Climate Change: A Proposal for a Revolution of Human Relationships"** *Future Ethics: Climate Change and Apocalyptic Imagination* 206

National Research Council, **"Energy Supply and Use"** *Advancing the Science of Climate Change* 233

Christopher Bateman, **"A Colossal Fracking Mess"** *Vanity Fair* 296

Bryan Walsh, **"Nature: A Major Company Puts a Value on the Environment"** *Time* Blog "Science and Space" 324

Louisiana Universities Marine Consortium, **"About Hypoxia"** "Hypoxia in the Northern Gulf of Mexico" Webpage 331

Lisa Stiffler, **"All You Need to Know About Storm Water Runoff"** Sightline Daily, Blog of the Sightline Institute 353

Elizabeth Kolbert, **"The Darkening Sea"** *The New Yorker* 362

description

Aldo Leopold, **"Thinking Like a Mountain"** *Sand County Almanac* 12

Chris Caroll, **"High Tech Trash"** *National Geographic Magazine* 78

Jeff Opperman, **"Getting to Know Your Bacon: Hogs, Farms, and Clean Water"** The Nature Conservancy blog 118

Dan Charles, **"How Community-Supported Agriculture Sprouted in China"** *The Salt*, National Public Radio Blog 130

Michael Pollan, **"The Genius of the Place"** *Omnivore's Dilemma* 132

Evan I. Schwartz, **"How Not to Make Energy Decisions: Lessons From the Battle Over Cape Wind"** *Technology Review MIT* 283

Willett Kempton, **"The Offshore Power Debate: Views From Cape Cod"**
Coastal Management 288

Christopher Bateman, **"A Colossal Fracking Mess"** *Vanity Fair* 296

Sandra Steingraber, **"The Case for Gardening as a Means to Curb
Climate Change"** *Raising Elijah: Protecting Our Children in an Age of
Environmental Crisis* 320

Cynthia Barnett, **"The Illusion of Water Abundance"** *Blue Revolution:
Unmaking America's Water Crisis* 337

Lisa Stiffler, **"All You Need to Know About Storm Water Runoff"**
Sightline Daily, Blog of the Sightline Institute 353

Elizabeth Kolbert, **"The Darkening Sea"** *The New Yorker* 362

Monday Creek Restoration Project. **"Upstream Rock Run Coal Mine
Remediation"** from *Up the Creek*, Fall 2010 1.1 Newsletter 317

division and classification

Emily Fontaine, **"Where Did Our Clothes Come From?"** Le Quaintrelle
Blog 97

Terry Cannon, **"Gender and Climate Hazards in Bangladesh"**
Gender and Development 197

Roman Krznaric, **"Empathy and Climate Change: A Proposal for a
Revolution of Human Relationships"** *Future Ethics: Climate Change and
Apocalyptic Imagination* 206

National Research Council, **"Advancing the Science of Climate Change"**
Advancing the Science of Climate Change 183

Thomas L. Friedman, **"The Age of Noah: Biodiversity"** *Hot, Flat and Crowded:
Why We Need a Green Revolution and How It Can Renew America* 273

example and illustration

Aldo Leopold, **"Thinking Like a Mountain"** *Sand County Almanac* 12

Jared Diamond, **"The World as Polder: What Does It Mean to Us Today"**
Collapse: How Societies Choose to Fail or Succeed 15

Annie Leonard, **"The Story of Stuff: Electronics"** Story of Stuff Project 50

Annie Leonard, **"The Story of Stuff: Bottled Water"** Story of Stuff
Project 62

Chris Caroll, **"High Tech Trash"** *National Geographic Magazine* 78

Lucy Siegle, **"Why It's Time to End Our Love Affair With Cheap Fashion"** *The Observer* Newspaper 103

Michael Pollan, **"The Genius of the Place"** *Omnivore's Dilemma* 132

Deborah Whitman, **"Genetically Modified Foods: Harmful or Helpful?"** ProQuest 140

Ralph Cicerone, **"Finding Climate Change"** National Council for Science and the Environment 158

Liz Barratt-Brown, **"It is All About the Framing: How Polls and the Media Misrepresent the Keystone XL[tar sands] [oil] Pipeline"** National Resources Defense Council Blog 253

Vandana Shiva, **"Food for Cars or People: Biofuels a False Solution to Climate Change and a Threat to Food Security"** *Soil Not Oil* 262

Christopher Bateman, **"A Colossal Fracking Mess"** *Vanity Fair* 296

David Montgomery, **"Good Old Dirt"** *Dirt: the Erosion of Civilization* 309

Sandra Steingraber, **"The Case for Gardening as a Means to Curb Climate Change"** *Raising Elijah: Protecting Our Children in an Age of Environmental Crisis* 320

Bryan Walsh, **"Nature: A Major Company Puts a Value on the Environment"** *Time* Blog "Science and Space" 324

Cynthia Barnett, **"The Illusion of Water Abundance"** *Blue Revolution: Unmaking America's Water Crisis* 337

narration

Aldo Leopold, **"Thinking Like a Mountain"** *Sand County Almanac* 12

Annie Leonard, **"The Story of Stuff: Electronics"** Story of Stuff Project 50

Annie Leonard, **"The Story of Stuff: Bottled Water"** Story of Stuff Project 62

Chris Caroll, **"High Tech Trash"** *National Geographic Magazine* 78

Luke W. Cole and Sheila R. Foster, **"We Speak for Ourselves: The Struggle of Kettleman City"** *From the Ground Up: Environmental Racism and the Rise of the Environmental Justice Movement* 88

Emily Fontaine, **"Where Did Our Clothes Come From?"** Le Quaintrelle Blog 97

Jeff Opperman, **"Getting to Know Your Bacon: Hogs, Farms, and Clean Water"** The Nature Conservancy Blog 118

Stephanie Wear, **"Finding Nemo on Your Plate"** The Nature Conservancy Blog 126

Dan Charles, **"How Community-Supported Agriculture Sprouted in China"** *The Salt*, National Public Radio Blog 130

Michael Pollan, **"The Genius of the Place"** *Omnivore's Dilemma* 132

Roman Krznaric, **"Empathy and Climate Change: A Proposal for a Revolution of Human Relationships"** *Future Ethics: Climate Change and Apocalyptic Imagination* 206

Thomas L. Friedman, **"The Age of Noah: Biodiversity"** *Hot, Flat and Crowded: Why We Need a Green Revolution and How It Can Renew America* 273

Evan I. Schwartz, **"How Not to Make Energy Decisions: Lessons From the Battle Over Cape Wind"** *Technology Review MIT* 283

David Montgomery, **"Good Old Dirt"** *Dirt: the Erosion of Civilization* 309

Sandra Steingraber, **"The Case for Gardening as a Means to Curb Climate Change"** *Raising Elijah: Protecting Our Children in an Age of Environmental Crisis* 320

Cynthia Barnett, **"The Illusion of Water Abundance"** *Blue Revolution: Unmaking America's Water Crisis* 337

Elizabeth Kolbert, **"The Darkening Sea"** *The New Yorker* 362

process analysis

Garrett Hardin, **"Tragedy of the Commons"** *Science* 28

Chris Caroll, **"High Tech Trash"** *National Geographic Magazine* 78

Stephanie Wear, **"Finding Nemo on Your Plate"** The Nature Conservancy Blog 126

Michael Pollan, **"The Genius of the Place"** *Omnivore's Dilemma* 132

David Montgomery, **"Good Old Dirt"** *Dirt: the Erosion of Civilization* 309

Dan Charles, **"Putting Farmland on a Fertilizer Diet"** National Public Radio Blog, "The Salt" 328

Louisiana Universities Marine Consortium, **"About Hypoxia"** "Hypoxia in the Northern Gulf of Mexico" Webpage 331

Elizabeth Kolbert, **"The Darkening Sea"** *The New Yorker* 362

Making the Invisible Visible

Talk about sustainability and "going green" is everywhere. Starbucks has green products and takes 10 cents off the cost of coffee when customers bring in their own cups to reduce waste. You can go to the grocery store and buy "sustainably harvested" seafood. National Public Radio's "Marketplace" has a "sustainability desk" that provides daily reports on sustainability in business and economics. Former Vice President Al Gore made the movie "An Inconvenient Truth" and won a Nobel Peace prize for his work on climate change but also provoked a serious backlash. Universities are now rated by how sustainable or green they are, and they are opening schools and colleges of sustainability with their own programs and degrees. The debate over climate change, no matter which side you are on, has made sustainability and our response to environmental threats part of everyday popular culture.

If you Google the term "sustainability," you will find a series of links to all things sustainable. You will also find a list of other searches related to sustainability, including "environmental sustainability," "sustainability definition," "sustainability topics," "business sustainability," "food sustainability," "corporate sustainability," "sustainability jobs," and, last but not least, "sustainability defined." As you might expect, it is not easy to define a concept that has so many applications. It is equally difficult to define "freedom" in a way that makes everyone happy and captures all the fine distinctions of the concept. But few of us would want to dump the idea of freedom just because it is complicated or hard to define.

Here is how the U.S. Environmental Protection Agency (EPA) defines "sustainability":

> Sustainability is based on a simple principle: Everything that we need for our survival and well-being depends, either directly or indirectly, on our natural environment. Sustainability creates and maintains the conditions under which humans and nature can exist in productive harmony, that permit fulfilling the social, economic and other requirements of present and future generations.

The EPA definition includes most of the crucial elements of sustainability. This definition reflects the common expression that sustainability is a "three-legged stool"; it is held up by ecological, economic, and social "legs." To be sustainable, an activity has to protect the natural resources upon which we depend, be economically successful, and promote social equality and prosperity. The EPA definition also includes the crucial issue of time because sustainability applies to our present needs and activities but also to the future conditions our actions will create. A sustainable activity has to provide for people living today but also provide a healthy, productive world for our grandchildren and their grandchildren.

In the *New York Times* bestseller *Collapse: How Societies Choose to Fail or Succeed*, Jared Diamond identifies five factors that he says can contribute to the decline or collapse of individual societies. The first four factors are environmental damage, hostile neighbors, climate change, and friendly trading partners. According to Diamond, these are not always important to the decline of a society and its quality of life. The last factor, however, is a society's response to its environmental problems, and he says that it is always important in a society's success or failure. As he discusses the collapse of the Easter Island society in the South Pacific, Diamond asks, "What were the Easter Islanders saying as they cut down the last tree on the island?" One popular theory for why the Easter Island society died out is that cutting all the trees on the island led to an ecological collapse that the islanders could not survive. When Diamond asks what they were saying to each other, he suggests a core issue for writing and the motivation for this book: What we say about physical and social environment and how we say it has lasting consequences for the long-term sustainability of our society. Writing matters.

The many challenges to sustainability that come up in the readings in this book have an upside and a downside. These problems are caused by human activity. That's the downside. The upside is, it is within our power to change the scenario or storyline and its outcome. But to change the scenario, writers need to help people see and understand these issues and convince them to change. To do that, writers have to make the invisible visible. For example, in the debate over building a huge "wind farm" of electric turbines in the waters of Nantucket Sound off Cape Cod, Massachusetts, researchers point out that it is easy to see the turbines, but you can't see the benefit they create. People can see the huge towers and blades, but they can't see the reduction in greenhouse gas the wind power provides or the marginal slowing of climate change we get from using clean energy. This is frequently the problem facing people writing about sustainability; the drawbacks are concrete and visible and people can feel them. Resetting thermostats and limiting the amount we drive can be uncomfortable. The advantages that justify change are often much harder to see and feel. Anyone trying to change the status quo has a harder task than the person who argues for the status quo. That is why in a court "the burden of proof" is on the prosecution; someone is innocent until proven guilty. Much the same tends to be true with sustainability.

There are three ways that sustainability can be invisible. The first is simply **time**; we can't see the future. Since sustainability involves preserving resources for future generations, we have to know (and care) what the future will look like. The consequences of our actions are often too far removed in time to seem real. Unfortunately, those consequences are too far into the future to bother many people. Sustainability science uses models and precise notions of uncertainty to make different possible futures visible, but many people don't trust models or understand uncertainty. That is one reason people challenge sustainability science.

The second way sustainability can be invisible is that the consequences of action are often far removed in **space** rather than in time. In an interconnected system, the consequences of action can occur across the continent or across the planet, and the connections between pieces of the system can be hard to see. The dead zone in the Gulf of Mexico (Chapter 6) seems pretty removed from a Midwestern cornfield or the day-to-day lives of people in those farming communities. Similarly, the increasing flooding of low-lying countries in the developing world caused by climate change and sea level rise is a long way from home for most of us in the developed world. It is difficult to see, and it does not affect the community where we live or anyone we know. It is hard to identify with the conditions of people living half a world away.

Finally, sustainability can be invisible because it is so **ordinary**, so small and so taken for granted. Water is a good example of this here on the "blue planet." Unless their water bill is really high, few people worry about watering their lawn. We like nice green grass. Researchers estimate that Americans use as much as 19 trillion gallons of water on their lawns every year. That is about as much water as England uses for everything they do. Our supply of water isn't inexhaustible, either, though it may seem so because all we have to do is turn on a tap. Similarly, when you go to the grocery store and pick up a piece of fruit, often it was grown and shipped across the globe. If it is perishable, it was probably shipped in an airplane that uses huge amounts of fossil fuels compared to a cargo train or a ship. Watering the grass and buying fruit and flowers from other continents seem like such small things. They are such a part of our everyday routine that we no longer see them.

To write successfully about sustainability, you have to be able to make these distant or overlooked realities visible. And there is no silver bullet, no single solution or strategy that will always get the job done. It is better to think of a silver shotgun shell, full of lots of small silver pellets. And even then, there are no guarantees, only options and strategies. Convincing people of things and motivating them to act is a risky business. You won't always succeed.

Despite the difficulty of writing persuasively about sustainability, all of the writers whose work appears here share a commitment to sustainability. It is dangerous to make sweeping statements about writing, but I'll suggest three things that seem true of the essays in this book and of writing generally. First, people write well when they care about the topic and find it compelling. If you have a reason and purpose for writing, it is easier and usually turns out better. Second, people usually write in response to something someone else has said or written. Writing that is in some kind of dialog with other writing, that is part of a conversation, is usually more engaging. Finally, writing can be surprising and even enjoyable when you are genuinely engaged in the process. Try to write in ways you enjoy.

Sustainability: A Reader for Writers is part of a series of brief single-topic readers from Oxford University Press designed for today's college writing courses. Each reader in this series approaches a topic of contemporary conversation from multiple perspectives:

- **Timely** Most selections were originally published in 2010 or later.
- **Global** Sources and voices from around the world are included.
- **Diverse** Selections come from a range of nontraditional and alternate print and online media, as well as representative mainstream sources.

In addition to the rich array of perspectives on topical (even urgent) issues addressed in each reader, each volume features an abundance of different genres and styles—from the academic research paper to the pithy Twitter argument. Useful but non-intrusive pedagogy includes:

- **Chapter introductions** that provide a brief overview of the chapter's theme and a sense of how the chapter's selections relate both to the overarching theme and to each other.
- **Headnotes** introduce each reading by providing concise information about its original publication and pose an open-ended question that encourages students to explore their prior knowledge of (or opinions about) some aspect of the selection's content.
- **"Analyze" and "Explore" questions** after each reading scaffold and support student reading for comprehension as well as rhetorical considerations, providing prompts for reflection, classroom discussion, and brief writing assignments.
- **"Forging Connections" and "Looking Further" prompts** after each chapter encourage critical thinking by asking students to compare perspectives and strategies among readings both within the chapter and with readings in other chapters, suggesting writing assignments that engage students with larger conversations in the academy, the community, and the media.
- **An appendix on researching and writing about sustainability** guides student inquiry and research in a digital environment. Co-authored by a research librarian, a writing program director, and the book's editor, this appendix provides real-world, transferable strategies for locating, assessing, synthesizing, and citing sources in support of an argument. This appendix also contains a sample student essay, "Climate Change and Sea Level Rise," written by students in an undergraduate course on sustainability and climate change.

about the author

Carl G. Herndl directs the applied rhetoric of science and sustainability initiative in the University of South Florida's Patel College of Global Sustainability, where he teaches a graduate course, "Communicating the Value of Sustainability," and serves as associate dean. He is also a professor in the English Department at USF, where he directs the graduate program in rhetoric and composition. His expertise is in the rhetoric of science, professional communication, and rhetorical theory, and he studies the public discourse on sustainability and sustainable technology development. He has participated in a number of interdisciplinary research teams working on sustainable agroecosystem management and sustainable biofuel development. He was also a faculty affiliate of the Los Alamos National Laboratory in experimental statistics. He has authored white papers for new research centers at Iowa State University; led workshops at the National Conference on Science Policy and the Environment; co-authored research proposals for NSF, USDA, and USAID; and co-authored articles in refereed science journals. He has published articles in many edited collections in rhetoric and in most of the major rhetoric journals. In 1996 he published *Green Culture: Environmental Rhetoric in Contemporary America*, which won the National Council of Teachers of English award for the best collection in the rhetoric of science and technology.

acknowledgments

I would like to thank the Patel College of Global Sustainability for providing a research assistant to make this book possible. More important to me, however, is the commitment to making the world more sustainable and more livable that animates everyone in the college. My colleagues at the Patel College and in sustainable agriculture at Iowa State University have taught me a great deal about science, sustainability, and the pleasures of working together and with the members of concerned communities. I especially thank my colleagues Kalanithy Vairavamoorthy, Micheal Burkhardt, Mathew Leibman, and Rick Cruse. I also thank the many students with whom I have worked in writing courses on sustainability over the years. They have given me a broader and more practical perspective on writing about sustainability. Thanks as well to all who provided reviews for this book: Olivia Chadha, University of Colorado, Boulder; Sharon Williams, Hamilton College; Julie Sparks, San Jose State University; Laura Dubek, Middle Tennessee State University; Anne Withey, Chatham University; Dawnelle Jager, State of New York College of Environmental Science and Forestry; Robert Brown, University of Minnesota; Morgan Reitmeyer, Regis University; Mark O'Gorman, Maryville College; Keely McCarthy, Chestnut Hill College; Kerri Morris, Governors State University; Kelsi Matwick, University of Florida; Cheryl Fish, Borough of Manhattan Community College; Carol Kushner, Dutchess Community College; Veronica House, University of Colorado, Boulder; Sue Whatley, Stephen F. Austin State University; Carol McFrederick, Miami-Dade College; Frances Chamberlain, Southern Connecticut State University; Deborah Miller, University of Georgia; Violet Dutcher, Eastern Mennonite University; and Gesa Kirsch, Bentley University. And, finally, I thank my research assistant Lauren Cutlip, who worked long and hard helping me gather and select materials and who constructed much of the pedagogical material in the book.

Us: How We Live With Each Other & With the World

Flooded polder in the Netherlands

In the field of urban planning, where city planners and regulators make decisions about what to build and where to build it, people recognize what they call "wicked" problems. These are problems for which there is no perfect solution. With wicked problems, there are only trade-offs between different values and different costs or conflicts between the interests of some individuals and the interests of the community. For example, every city needs a sewer treatment plant, but who wants one in their neighborhood? Wicked. In "Tragedy of the Commons," Garrett Hardin describes overpopulation as a "no technical solution problem" because it does not have a purely technical solution. Instead it requires "change in human values or ideas of morality" (1243).

Many of the problems in sustainability are like this. Dealing with them involves tradeoffs, tough decisions, and a negotiation over values. As individuals and as a society or planet, we face a tradeoff between short-term gains and long-term benefits, between the freedom and interests of individuals and the health or survival of the community. We face difficult conflicts between cherished values such as freedom, autonomy, equality, and fairness. In the chapter "The World as Polder" excerpted below, Jared Diamond captures the basic ethical issue of sustainability nicely when he writes that "we can't advance our interests at the expense of others" (519). Hardin addresses this challenge with a much more direct and much harsher response. "What," he asks, "is the meaning of freedom?" After his analysis of the tragedy of the commons he defines freedom, quoting the German philosopher Hegel, as "the recognition of necessity."

These wicked, no-technical-solution problems can be described as ethical issues of responsibility. But in a globalized world where money, people, and goods, and also pollution, disease, climate change, and resource destruction, cross national borders every day, it is also a practical matter of prosperity and survival. Scholars who study water resources like those in Chapter 6, like to say that "we all live downstream." That is, our situation is always affected by the actions of people who live "upstream." In turn, our actions always affect the situation for people downstream of us. In his analysis of how whole societies prosper or decline and sometimes collapse, Diamond says, "we are all in a polder." He explains that a polder is a large area in the Netherlands that is below sea level and surrounded by dikes. The polders require constant pumping to keep out the seawater that seeps in; that is why the Dutch invented windmills so long ago. Faced with the real possibility of deadly flooding, every citizen in the polder depends on every other citizen for his or her survival.

These ethical issues are a moral extension of the scientific notion of an interconnected ecosystem. As Aldo Leopold suggests in his beautiful essay below, the health of the whole mountain community depends on the balance between all of its members. Like a polder, a mountain is a metaphor for a system where actions in one place have multiple consequences elsewhere in the system. This is certainly true in Rachel Carson's case, where using lethal insecticides to kill "pests" has huge consequences up the food chain, all the way to human beings. One of the difficult challenges of sustainability is that the notion requires us to expand our understanding of who and what belongs to our community.

A second important scientific concept that runs throughout the readings in this chapter and in the book generally is that of time scales. As Carson points out, we produce about 500 new chemical poisons every year (and this was 1962), but it can take hundreds of years for species and the environment to adapt to these new chemicals. Humans create change at a rate so much faster than the natural world can cope with it that it can cause disasters. This leads scholars like Carson or David Montgomery (Chapter 6) to formulate a general principle that says that systems that mold human activity to nature are sustainable, but systems that try to mold nature to human activity are not.

But how do you get people to accept the "freedom of necessity"? If you write well and develop useful metaphors like Diamond's "polder" or Leopold's "mountain," you might succeed in getting readers to see the interconnected system of which we are all a part. But how do you get them to really care or, harder still, to act? I know I should lose 15 pounds, but I've been saying that for a long time now; I just bought pants with a bigger waist. Ethics are important, and most people recognize their responsibility to act ethically. But it is hard: it often requires tradeoffs and personal change. There is no single or simple answer to this rhetorical problem. All the writers in this chapter and in this book develop different strategies to motivate readers to change, some more successful than others. But I'll leave you with one odd observation by way of a suggestion. Few readers like to hear about "sacrifice." It just sounds painful. But the very notion of a sacrifice involves giving up one thing you may want in order to get something else you want more.

Rachel Carson
"The Obligation to Endure"

Rachel Carson is one of the most famous environmental writers of the 20th century, and her book *Silent Spring*, from which our excerpt "The Obligation to Endure" is taken, is widely recognized as the beginning of the environmental movement in America. The publication of *Silent Spring* led to a special investigation by President Kennedy's Science Advisory Committee and, eventually, to the founding of the Environmental Protection Agency. Born in 1907, Carson received a master's degree in marine zoology from Johns Hopkins University in 1932 and spent her early career as a writer and later chief publications editor for the U.S. Fish and Wildlife Service. She published *Under the Sea Wind* (1941), *The Sea Around Us* (1951), *The Edge of the Sea* (1955), and *Silent Spring* (1962), a book that has been continuously in print since its publication. The first chapter of *Silent Spring*, "A Fable for Tomorrow," describes a fictitious future in which deadly chemicals have killed all the insects and the birds that eat them and then sickened the animals higher on the food chain, including humans. It is an environmental "worst-case-scenario" story. "The Obligation to Endure" is based on, among other things, the fact that we develop deadly pesticides much faster than natural processes of adaptation. Because we have an obligation to future generations, Carson argues, we have a right to know the truth about these pesticides.

The history of life on earth has been a history of interaction between living things and their surroundings. To a large extent, the physical form and the habits of the earth's vegetation and its animal life have been molded by the environment. Considering the whole span of earthly time, the opposite effect, in which life actually modifies its surroundings, has been relatively slight. Only within the moment of time represented by the present century has one species—man—acquired significant power to alter the nature of his world.

During the past quarter century this power has not only increased to one of disturbing magnitude but it has changed in character. The most alarming of all man's assaults upon the environment is the contamination of air, earth, rivers, and sea with dangerous and even lethal materials. This pollution is for the most part irrecoverable; the chain of evil it initiates not only in the world that must support life but in living tissues is for the most part irreversible. In this now universal contamination of the environment, chemicals are the sinister and little-recognized partners of radiation in changing the very nature of the world—the very nature of its life. Strontium 90, released through nuclear explosions into the air, comes to earth in rain or drifts down as fallout, lodges in soil, enters into the grass or corn or wheat grown there, and in time takes up its abode in the bones of a human being, there to remain until his death. Similarly, chemicals sprayed on croplands or forests or gardens lie long in soil, entering into living organisms, passing from one to another in a chain of poisoning and death. Or they pass mysteriously by underground streams until they emerge and, through the alchemy of air and sunlight, combine into new forms that kill vegetation, sicken cattle, and work unknown harm on those who drink from once pure wells. As Albert Schweitzer has said, 'Man can hardly even recognize the devils of his own creation.'

It took hundreds of millions of years to produce the life that now inhabits the earth—eons of time in which that developing and evolving and diversifying life reached a state of adjustment and balance with its surroundings. The environment, rigorously shaping and directing the life it supported, contained elements that were hostile as well as supporting. Certain rocks gave out dangerous radiation; even within the light of the sun, from which all life draws its energy, there were short-wave radiations with power to injure. Given time—time not in years but in millennia—life adjusts, and a balance has been reached. For time is the essential ingredient; but in the modern world there is no time.

The rapidity of change and the speed with which new situations are created follow the impetuous and heedless pace of man rather than the deliberate pace of nature. Radiation is no longer merely the background radiation of rocks, the bombardment of cosmic rays, the ultraviolet of the sun that have existed before there was any life on earth; radiation is now the unnatural creation of man's tampering with the atom. The chemicals to which life is asked to make its adjustment are no longer merely the calcium and silica and copper and all the rest of the minerals washed out of the rocks and carried in rivers to the sea; they are the synthetic creations of man's inventive mind, brewed in his laboratories, and having no counterparts in nature.

To adjust to these chemicals would require time on the scale that is nature's; it would require not merely the years of a man's life but the life of generations. And even this, were it by some miracle possible, would be

5

futile, for the new chemicals come from our laboratories in an endless stream; almost five hundred annually find their way into actual use in the United States alone. The figure is staggering and its implications are not easily grasped—500 new chemicals to which the bodies of men and animals are required somehow to adapt each year, chemicals totally outside the limits of biologic experience.

Among them are many that are used in man's war against nature. Since the mid-1940s over 200 basic chemicals have been created for use in killing insects, weeds, rodents, and other organisms described in the modern vernacular as 'pests'; and they are sold under several thousand different brand names.

These sprays, dusts, and aerosols are now applied almost universally to farms, gardens, forests, and homes—nonselective chemicals that have the power to kill every insect, the 'good' and the 'bad', to still the song of birds and the leaping of fish in the streams, to coat the leaves with a deadly film, and to linger on in soil—all this though the intended target may be only a few weeds or insects. Can anyone believe it is possible to lay down such a barrage of poisons on the surface of the earth without making it unfit for all life? They should not be called 'insecticides', but 'biocides'.

The whole process of spraying seems caught up in an endless spiral. Since DDT was released for civilian use, a process of escalation has been going on in which ever more toxic materials must be found. This has happened because insects, in a triumphant vindication of Darwin's principle of the survival of the fittest, have evolved super races immune to the particular insecticide used, hence a deadlier one has always to be developed—and then a deadlier one than that. It has happened also because, for reasons to be described later, destructive insects often undergo a 'flareback', or resurgence, after spraying, in numbers greater than before. Thus the chemical war is never won, and all life is caught in its violent crossfire.

Along with the possibility of the extinction of mankind by nuclear war, the central problem of our age has therefore become the contamination of man's total environment with such substances of incredible potential for harm—substances that accumulate in the tissues of plants and animals and even penetrate the germ cells to shatter or alter the very material of heredity upon which the shape of the future depends.

10   Some would-be architects of our future look toward a time when it will be possible to alter the human germ plasm by design. But we may easily be doing so now by inadvertence, for many chemicals, like radiation, bring about gene

mutations. It is ironic to think that man might determine his own future by something so seemingly trivial as the choice of an insect spray.

All this has been risked—for what? Future historians may well be amazed by our distorted sense of proportion. How could intelligent beings seek to control a few unwanted species by a method that contaminated the entire environment and brought the threat of disease and death even to their own kind?

Yet this is precisely what we have done. We have done it, moreover, for reasons that collapse the moment we examine them. We are told that the enormous and expanding use of pesticides is necessary to maintain farm production. Yet is our real problem not one of overproduction? Our farms, despite measures to remove acreages from production and to pay farmers not to produce, have yielded such a staggering excess of crops that the American taxpayer in 1962 is paying out more than one billion dollars a year as the total carrying cost of the surplus-food storage program. And is the situation helped when one branch of the Agriculture Department tries to reduce production while another states, as it did in 1958, 'It is believed generally that reduction of crop acreages under provisions of the Soil Bank will stimulate interest in use of chemicals to obtain maximum production on the land retained in crops.'

All this is not to say there is no insect problem and no need of control. I am saying, rather, that control must be geared to realities, not to mythical situations, and that the methods employed must be such that they do not destroy us along with the insects.

The problem whose attempted solution has brought such a train of disaster in its wake is an accompaniment of our modern way of life. Long before the age of man, insects inhabited the earth—a group of extraordinarily varied and adaptable beings. Over the course of time since man's advent, a small percentage of the more than half a million species of insects have come into conflict with human welfare in two principal ways: as competitors for the food supply and as carriers of human disease.

Disease-carrying insects become important where human beings are crowded together, especially under conditions where sanitation is poor, as in time of natural disaster or war or in situations of extreme poverty and deprivation. Then control of some sort becomes necessary. It is a sobering fact, however, as we shall presently see, that the method of massive chemical control has had only limited success, and also threatens to worsen the very conditions it is intended to curb.

Under primitive agricultural conditions the farmer had few insect problems. These arose with the intensification of agriculture—the devotion of immense acreages to a single crop. Such a system set the stage for explosive increases in specific insect populations. Single-crop farming does not take advantage of the principles by which nature works; it is agriculture as an engineer might conceive it to be. Nature has introduced great variety into the landscape, but man has displayed a passion for simplifying it. Thus he undoes the built-in checks and balances by which nature holds the species within bounds. One important natural check is a limit on the amount of suitable habitat for each species. Obviously then, an insect that lives on wheat can build up its population to much higher levels on a farm devoted to wheat than on one in which wheat is intermingled with other crops to which the insect is not adapted.

The same thing happens in other situations. A generation or more ago, the towns of large areas of the United States lined their streets with the noble elm tree. Now the beauty they hopefully created is threatened with complete destruction as disease sweeps through the elms, carried by a beetle that would have only limited chance to build up large populations and to spread from tree to tree if the elms were only occasional trees in a richly diversified planting.

Another factor in the modern insect problem is one that must be viewed against a background of geologic and human history: the spreading of thousands of different kinds of organisms from their native homes to invade new territories. This worldwide migration has been studied and graphically described by the British ecologist Charles Elton in his recent book *The Ecology of Invasions*. During the Cretaceous Period, some hundred million years ago, flooding seas cut many land bridges between continents, and living things found themselves confined in what Elton calls 'colossal separate nature reserves'. There, isolated from others of their kind, they developed many new species. When some of the land masses were joined again, about 15 million years ago, these species began to move out into new territories—a movement that is not only still in progress but is now receiving considerable assistance from man.

The importation of plants is the primary agent in the modern spread of species, for animals have almost invariably gone along with the plants, quarantine being a comparatively recent and not completely effective innovation. The United States Office of Plant Introduction alone has introduced almost 200,000 species and varieties of plants from all over the world. Nearly half of the 180 or so major insect enemies of plants in the United States are accidental imports from abroad, and most of them have come as hitchhikers on plants.

In new territory, out of reach of the restraining hand of the natural enemies that kept down its numbers in its native land, an invading plant or animal is able to become enormously abundant. Thus it is no accident that our most troublesome insects are introduced species.

These invasions, both the naturally occurring and those dependent on human assistance, are likely to continue indefinitely. Quarantine and massive chemical campaigns are only extremely expensive ways of buying time. We are faced, according to Dr. Elton, 'with a life-and-death need not just to find new technological means of suppressing this plant or that animal'; instead we need the basic knowledge of animal populations and their relations to their surroundings that will 'promote an even balance and damp down the explosive power of outbreaks and new invasions.'

> "Who would want to live in a world which is just not quite fatal?"

Much of the necessary knowledge is now available but we do not use it. We train ecologists in our universities and even employ them in our governmental agencies but we seldom take their advice. We allow the chemical death rain to fall as though there were no alternative, whereas in fact there are many, and our ingenuity could soon discover many more if given opportunity.

Have we fallen into a mesmerized state that makes us accept as inevitable that which is inferior or detrimental, as though having lost the will or the vision to demand that which is good? Such thinking, in the words of the ecologist Paul Shepard, 'idealizes life with only its head out of water, inches above the limits of toleration of the corruption of its own environment. . . Why should we tolerate a diet of weak poisons, a home in insipid surroundings, a circle of acquaintances who are not quite our enemies, the noise of motors with just enough relief to prevent insanity? Who would want to live in a world which is just not quite fatal?'

Yet such a world is pressed upon us. The crusade to create a chemically sterile, insect-free world seems to have engendered a fanatic zeal on the part of many specialists and most of the so-called control agencies. On every hand there is evidence that those engaged in spraying operations exercise a ruthless power. 'The regulatory entomologists . . . function as prosecutor, judge and jury, tax assessor and collector and sheriff to enforce their own orders,' said

Connecticut entomologist Neely Turner. The most flagrant abuses go unchecked in both state and federal agencies.

25   It is not my contention that chemical insecticides must never be used. I do contend that we have put poisonous and biologically potent chemicals indiscriminately into the hands of persons largely or wholly ignorant of their potentials for harm. We have subjected enormous numbers of people to contact with these poisons, without their consent and often without their knowledge. If the Bill of Rights contains no guarantee that a citizen shall be secure against lethal poisons distributed either by private individuals or by public officials, it is surely only because our forefathers, despite their considerable wisdom and foresight, could conceive of no such problem.

I contend, furthermore, that we have allowed these chemicals to be used with little or no advance investigation of their effect on soil, water, wildlife, and man himself. Future generations are unlikely to condone our lack of prudent concern for the integrity of the natural world that supports all life.

There is still very limited awareness of the nature of the threat. This is an era of specialists, each of whom sees his own problem and is unaware of or intolerant of the larger frame into which it fits. It is also an era dominated by industry, in which the right to make a dollar at whatever cost is seldom challenged. When the public protests, confronted with some obvious evidence of damaging results of pesticide applications, it is fed little tranquilizing pills of half truth. We urgently need an end to these false assurances, to the sugar coating of unpalatable facts. It is the public that is being asked to assume the risks that the insect controllers calculate. The public must decide whether it wishes to continue on the present road, and it can do so only when in full possession of the facts. In the words of Jean Rostand, 'The obligation to endure gives us the right to know.'

Analyze

1. According to Carson's explanation, why do humans need to develop ever more toxic materials? In other words, why does a "flareback" often occur after spraying for insects?
2. In this selection, Carson emphasizes the importance of *time*. She argues that "in the modern world there is no time." What is the significance of time in relationship to pesticides that Carson lays out?

3. Does Carson say that we should never use chemicals to kill insects no matter what?

Explore

1. To make her argument effective, Carson must present her information in a way that is both factual and persuasive. One way she does this is by trying to reach her audience on an emotional level. Take another look at the following line:

> "To adjust to these chemicals would require time on the scale that is nature's; it would require not merely the years of a man's life but the life of generations."

   Consider the feelings that the author might have been trying to evoke through her choice of wording here. How might the use of the words "man," "life," and "generations" affect a reader? What kinds of thoughts, images, or feelings does this line bring up for you? Bonus: Read through the rest of the piece with a rhetorical eye, and identify other sections that might likewise be attempting to evoke an emotional response in the reader.

2. Carson describes a number of ways in which chemicals deposited in soil far away from humans still end up in human systems. One process by which this occurs is through the food chain. Go through the article again and identify at least one other chain of events described by Carson that result in human contamination. Then, write a fictional narrative that brings this chain of events to life in the form of a story, similarly to the way Carson brought the issue of pesticide poisoning to life in "A Fable for Tomorrow," as described in the prelude to this reading. Alternatively, create a visual representation of the whole chain and the process through which chemical contamination ends up in human bodies.

3. Carson refers to a number of instances in which chemicals released into the environment have been found later to be hazardous to human health. As a homework assignment, fact-check at least five of the claims she makes—for example, the claim that chemicals and radiation can cause mutations in genes. Using your library's research databases or another search engine, create a bibliography of at least 10 articles for each that discuss and support the claims made by the author.

Aldo Leopold
"Thinking Like a Mountain"

Aldo Leopold was an ecologist and forester who taught wildlife management at the University of Wisconsin and was one of the foremost nature writers in America. One of the founders of the Wilderness Society, Leopold was an early proponent of what he called a "land ethic," a concept that has influenced many subsequent writers. In *A Sand County Almanac*, from which our selection is taken, Leopold articulated his notion of our ethical relation to the natural world: "A thing is right when it tends to preserve the integrity, beauty and stability of the biotic community. It is wrong when it tends otherwise" (262). Where philosophers write in academic terms about ethics and abstract principles, Leopold writes in the first person and tells beautiful stories about his engagement with the natural world. In "Thinking Like a Mountain," Leopold tells the story of the first time he watched a wolf die and wonders what the mountain knows that few men ever realize.

A deep chesty bawl echoes from rimrock to rimrock, rolls down the mountain, and fades into the far blackness of the night. It is an outburst of wild defiant sorrow, and of contempt for all the adversities of the world. Every living thing (and perhaps many a dead one as well) pays heed to that call. To the deer it is a reminder of the way of all flesh, to the pine a forecast of midnight scuffles and of blood upon the snow, to the coyote a promise of gleanings to come, to the cowman a threat of red ink at the bank, to the hunter a challenge of fang against bullet. Yet behind these obvious and immediate hopes and fears there lies a deeper meaning, known only to the mountain itself. Only the mountain has lived long enough to listen objectively to the howl of a wolf.

Those unable to decipher the hidden meaning know nevertheless that it is there, for it is felt in all wolf country, and distinguishes that country from all other land. It tingles in the spine of all who hear wolves by night, or who scan their tracks by day. Even without sight or sound of wolf, it is implicit in a hundred small events: the midnight whinny of a pack horse, the rattle of rolling rocks, the bound of a fleeing deer, the way shadows lie under the spruces. Only the ineducable tyro can fail to sense the presence or absence of wolves, or the fact that mountains have a secret opinion about them.

My own conviction on this score dates from the day I saw a wolf die. We were eating lunch on a high rimrock, at the foot of which a turbulent river elbowed its way. We saw what we thought was a doe fording the torrent, her breast awash in white water. When she climbed the bank toward us and shook out her tail, we realized our error: it was a wolf. A half-dozen others, evidently grown pups, sprang from the willows and all joined in a welcoming melee of wagging tails and playful maulings. What was literally a pile of wolves writhed and tumbled in the center of an open flat at the foot of our rimrock.

In those days we had never heard of passing up a chance to kill a wolf. In a second we were pumping lead into the pack, but with more excitement than accuracy: how to aim a steep downhill shot is always confusing. When our rifles were empty, the old wolf was down, and a pup was dragging a leg into impassable slide-rocks.

We reached the old wolf in time to watch a fierce green fire dying in her eyes. I realized then, and have known ever since, that there was something new to me in those eyes—something known only to her and to the mountain. I was young then, and full of trigger-itch; I thought that because fewer wolves meant more deer, that no wolves would mean hunters' paradise. But after seeing the green fire die, I sensed that neither the wolf nor the mountain agreed with such a view.

Since then I have lived to see state after state extirpate its wolves. I have watched the face of many a newly wolfless mountain, and seen the south-facing slopes wrinkle with a maze of new deer trails. I have seen every edible bush and seedling browsed, first to anaemic desuetude, and then to death. I have seen every edible tree defoliated to the height of a saddlehorn. Such a mountain looks as if someone had given God a new pruning shears, and forbidden Him all other exercise. In the end the starved bones of the hoped-for deer herd, dead of its own too-much, bleach with the bones of the dead sage, or molder under the high-lined junipers.

I now suspect that just as a deer herd lives in mortal fear of its wolves, so does a mountain live in mortal fear of its deer. And perhaps with better cause, for while a buck pulled down by wolves can be replaced in two or three years, a range pulled down by too many deer may fail of replacement in as many decades. So also with cows. The cowman who cleans his range of wolves does not realize that he is taking over the wolf's job of trimming the herd to fit the range. He has not learned to think like a mountain. Hence we have dustbowls, and rivers washing the future into the sea.

We all strive for safety, prosperity, comfort, long life, and dullness. The deer strives with his supple legs, the cowman with trap and poison, the statesman with pen, the most of us with machines, votes, and dollars, but it all comes to the same thing: peace in our time. A measure of success in this is all well enough, and perhaps is a requisite to objective thinking, but too much safety seems to yield only danger in the long run. Perhaps this is behind Thoreau's dictum: In wildness is the salvation of the world. Perhaps this is the hidden meaning in the howl of the wolf, long known among mountains, but seldom perceived among men.

Analyze

1. What does the author mean when he suggests that the deer died "of its own too-much"?
2. Why did people like Leopold kill wolves? Are there reasons why we should not?
3. According to the author, what does it mean to think like a mountain?

Explore

1. In this essay, Leopold personifies the mountain, giving it human capabilities like listening and experiencing, as well as characteristics like wisdom. In the introduction to this chapter, you read that each of these readings has its own strategy for inspiring people to change the way they interact with nature. As a class, discuss Leopold's strategy here. What kind of effect does it have? How is it both different from and similar to Rachel Carson's strategy of outlining "man's war against nature"? Is one more effective than the other?
2. "Even without sight or sound of wolf, it is implicit in a hundred small events: the midnight whinny of a pack horse, the rattle of rolling rocks, the bound of a fleeing deer, the way shadows lie under the spruces." This line describes the way that the presence of the wolf can be sensed through the effects that it has on other parts of the environment. This idea of ripple-effects is a recurring theme found across this book and is central to an understanding of sustainability. To demonstrate your own understanding of this concept, choose an organism, event, or natural phenomenon and, in a group, create a list of effects that its

presence produces beyond the initially observable. Share your observations with the class.

3. As a homework assignment, research an instance in which "too much" of something ended in disaster. You can use any type of situation or event that you like. Then, using both text and images, create an advertisement that uses the event you researched as an analogy for sustainability, with the purpose of persuading your audience of the dangers of "too much."

Jared Diamond
"The World as Polder: What Does It Mean to Us Today"

Jared Diamond is a scientist and author of six books and numerous articles on environmental history and the development of human societies. Diamond has a B.A. from Harvard University and a Ph.D. in physiology from Cambridge University. He was a professor of physiology in the UCLA Medical School and is currently a professor of geography at UCLA. His many awards include a McArthur Foundation Fellowship, a Pulitzer Prize for *Guns, Germs and Steel*, and a National Medal of Science. In *Collapse: How Societies Choose to Succeed or Fail*, from which our selection is taken, Diamond compares the success or failure of past civilizations and what factors contributed to their endurance or decline to see what lessons we can draw from the past. Diamond opens this last chapter of his book with a list of 12 serious environmental problems facing us today—problems of resource destruction, of resource limits, of toxic and dangerous products, and of population growth. Despite this seemingly overwhelming list of problems, however, Diamond concludes that he is a "cautious optimist." Because these problems are caused by human activity, they are also within our control to change. As with other readings in this chapter, the change Diamond hopes for will require a change in our values and how we live among others.

Are the parallels between the past and present sufficiently close that the collapses of the Easter Islanders, Henderson Islanders, Anasazi, Maya, and Greenland Norse could offer any lessons for the modern world? At first, a critic, noting the obvious differences, might be tempted to object, "It's ridiculous to suppose that the collapses of all those ancient peoples could have broad relevance today, especially to the modern U.S. Those ancients didn't enjoy the wonders of modern technology, which benefits us and which lets us solve problems by inventing new environment-friendly technologies. Those ancients had the misfortune to suffer from effects of climate change. They behaved stupidly and ruined their own environment by doing obviously dumb things, like cutting down their forests, over-harvesting wild animal sources of their protein, watching their topsoil erode away, and building cities in dry areas likely to run short of water. They had foolish leaders who didn't have books and so couldn't learn from history, and who embroiled them in expensive and destabilizing wars, cared only about staying in power, and didn't pay attention to problems at home. They got overwhelmed by desperate starving immigrants, as one society after another collapsed, sending floods of economic refugees to tax the resources of the societies that weren't collapsing. In all those respects, we moderns are fundamentally different from those primitive ancients, and there is nothing that we could learn from them. Especially we in the U.S., the richest and most powerful country in the world today, with the most productive environment and wise leaders and strong loyal allies and only weak insignificant enemies—none of those bad things could possibly apply to us."

Yes, it's true that there are big differences between the situations of those past societies and our modern situation today. The most obvious difference is that there are far more people alive today, packing far more potent technology that impacts the environment, than in the past. Today we have over 6 billion people equipped with heavy metal machinery such as bulldozers and nuclear power, whereas the Easter Islanders had at most a few tens of thousands of people with stone chisels and human muscle power. Yet the Easter Islanders still managed to devastate their environment and bring their society to the point of collapse. That difference greatly increases, rather than decreases, the risks for us today.

A second big difference stems from globalization. Leaving out of this discussion for the moment the question of environmental problems within the First World itself, let's just ask whether the lessons from past collapses might apply anywhere in the Third World today. First ask some ivory-tower academic ecologist, who knows a lot about the environment but never reads a newspaper and has no interest in politics, to name the overseas countries facing some of the worst problems of environmental stress, over-population, or both. The ecologist would answer: "That's a no-brainer, it's obvious. Your list of environmentally stressed or overpopulated countries should surely include Afghanistan, Bangladesh, Burundi, Haiti, Indonesia, Iraq, Madagascar, Mongolia, Nepal, Pakistan, the Philippines, Rwanda, the Solomon Islands, and Somalia, plus others".

Then go ask a First World politician, who knows nothing and cares less about the environment and population problems, to name the world's worst trouble spots: countries where state government has already been over-whelmed and has collapsed, or is now at risk of collapsing, or has been wracked by recent civil wars; and countries that, as a result of those problems of their own, are also creating problems for us rich First World countries, which may end up having to provide foreign aid for them, or may face illegal immigrants from them, or may decide to provide them with military assistance to deal with rebellions and terrorists, or may even have to send in our own troops. The politician would answer, "That's a no-brainer, it's obvious. Your list of political trouble spots should surely include Afghanistan, Bangladesh, Burundi, Haiti, Indonesia, Iraq, Madagascar, Mongolia, Nepal, Pakistan, the Philippines, Rwanda, the Solomon Islands, and Somalia, plus others."

Surprise, surprise: the two lists are very similar. The connection between the two lists is transparent: it's the problems of the ancient Maya, Anasazi, and Easter Islanders playing out in the modern world. Today, just as in the past, countries that are environmentally stressed, overpopulated, or both become at risk of getting politically stressed, and of their governments collapsing. When people are desperate, undernourished, and without hope, they blame their governments, which they see as responsible for or unable to solve their problems. They try to emigrate at any cost. They fight each other over land. They kill each other. They start civil wars. They figure that they have nothing to lose, so they become terrorists, or they support or tolerate terrorism.

The results of these transparent connections are genocides such as the ones that already exploded in Bangladesh, Burundi, Indonesia, and Rwanda; civil wars or revolutions, as in most of the countries on the lists; calls for the dispatch of First World troops, as to Afghanistan, Haiti, Indonesia, Iraq, the Philippines, Rwanda, the Solomon Islands, and Somalia; the collapse of central government, as has already happened in Somalia and the Solomon Islands; and overwhelming poverty, as in all of the countries on these lists. Hence the best predictors of modern "state failures"—i.e., revolutions, violent regime change, collapse of authority, and genocide—prove to be measures of environmental and population pressure, such as high infant mortality, rapid population growth, a high percentage of the population in their late teens and 20s, and hordes of unemployed young men without job prospects and ripe for recruitment into militias. Those pressures create conflicts over shortages of land (as in Rwanda), water, forests, fish, oil, and minerals. They create not only chronic internal conflict, but also emigration of political and economic refugees, and wars between countries arising when authoritarian regimes attack neighboring nations in order to divert popular attention from internal stresses.

In short, it is not a question open for debate whether the collapses of past societies have modern parallels and offer any lessons to us. That question is settled, because such collapses have actually been happening recently, and others appear to be imminent. Instead, the real question is how many more countries will undergo them.

As for terrorists, you might object that many of the political murderers, suicide bombers, and 9/11 terrorists were educated and moneyed rather than uneducated and desperate. That's true, but they still depended on a desperate society for support and toleration. Any society has its murderous fanatics; the U.S. produced its own Timothy McVeigh and its Harvard educated Theodore Kaczinski. But well-nourished societies offering good job prospects, like the U.S., Finland, and South Korea, don't offer broad support to their fanatics.

The problems of all these environmentally devastated, overpopulated, distant countries become our own problems because of globalization. We are accustomed to thinking of globalization in terms of us rich advanced First Worlders sending our good things, such as the Internet and Coca-Cola, to those poor backward Third Worlders. But globalization means nothing more than improved worldwide communications, which can convey many things in either direction; globalization is not restricted to good things carried only from the First to the Third World.

10   Among bad things transported from the First World to developing countries, we already mentioned the millions of tons of electronic garbage intentionally transported each year from industrialized nations to China. To grasp the worldwide scale of unintentional garbage transport, consider

the garbage collected on the beaches of tiny Oeno and Ducie Atolls in the Southeast Pacific Ocean uninhabited atolls, without freshwater, rarely visited even by yachts, and among the world's most remote bits of land, each over a hundred miles even from remote uninhabited Henderson Island. Surveys there detected, for each linear yard of beach, on the average one piece of garbage, which must have drifted from ships or else from Asian and American countries on the Pacific Rim thousands of miles distant. The commonest items proved to be plastic bags, buoys, glass and plastic bottles (especially Suntory whiskey bottles from Japan), rope, shoes, and light-bulbs, along with oddities such as footballs, toy soldiers and airplanes, bike pedals, and screwdrivers.

A more sinister example of bad things transported from the First World to developing countries is that the highest blood levels of toxic industrial chemicals and pesticides reported for any people in the world are for Eastern Greenland's and Siberia's Inuit people (Eskimos), who are also among the most remote from sites of chemical manufacture or heavy use. Their blood mercury levels are nevertheless in the range associated with acute mercury poisoning, while the levels of toxic PCBs (polychlorinated bi-phenyls) in Inuit mothers' breast milk fall in a range high enough to classify the milk as "hazardous waste." Effects on the women's babies include hearing loss, altered brain development, and suppressed immune function, hence high rates of ear and respiratory infections.

Why should levels of these poisonous chemicals from remote industrial nations of the Americas and Europe be higher in the Inuit than even in urban Americans and Europeans? It's because staples of the Inuit diet are whales, seals, and seabirds that eat fish, molluscs, and shrimp, and the chemicals become concentrated at each step as they pass up this food chain. All of us in the First World who occasionally consume seafood are also ingesting these chemicals, but in smaller amounts. (However, that doesn't mean that you will be safe if you stop eating seafood, because you now can't avoid ingesting such chemicals no matter what you eat.)

Still other bad impacts of the First World on the Third World include deforestation, Japan's imports of wood products currently being a leading cause of deforestation in the tropical Third World; and overfishing, due to fishing fleets of Japan, Korea, Taiwan and the heavily subsidized fleets of the European Union scouring the world's oceans. Conversely, people in the Third World can now, intentionally or unintentionally, send us their own bad things: their diseases like AIDS, SARS, cholera, and West Nile fever, carried inadvertently by passengers on transcontinental airplanes; unstoppable numbers of legal and illegal immigrants arriving by boat, truck, train, plane, and on foot; terrorists; and other consequences of their Third World problems. We in the U.S. are no longer the isolated Fortress America to which some of us aspired in the 1930s; instead, we are tightly and irreversibly connected to overseas countries. The U.S. is the world's leading importer nation: we import many necessities (especially oil and some rare metals) and many consumer products (cars and consumer electronics), as well as being the world's leading importer of investment capital. We are also the world's leading exporter, particularly of food and of our own manufactured products. Our own society opted long ago to become interlocked with the rest of the world.

That's why political instability anywhere in the world now affects us, our trade routes, and our overseas markets and suppliers. We are so dependent on the rest of the world that if, 30 years ago, you had asked a politician to name the countries most geopolitically irrelevant to our interests because of their being so remote, poor, and weak, the list would surely have begun with Afghanistan and Somalia, yet they subsequently became recognized as important enough to warrant our dispatching U.S. troops. Today the world no longer faces just the circumscribed risk of an Easter Island society or Maya homeland collapsing in isolation, without affecting the rest of the world. Instead, societies today are so interconnected that the risk we face is of a worldwide decline. That conclusion is familiar to any investor in stock markets: instability of the U.S. stock market, or the post-9/11 economic downturn in the U.S., affects overseas stock markets and economies as well, and vice versa. We in the U.S. (or else just affluent people in the U.S.) can no longer get away with advancing our own self-interests, at the expense of the interests of others.

15   A good example of a society minimizing such clashes of interest is the Netherlands, whose citizens have perhaps the world's highest level of environmental awareness and of membership in environmental organizations. I never understood why, until on a recent trip to the Netherlands I posed the question to three of my Dutch friends while driving through their countryside (Plates 39,40). Their answer was one that I shall never forget:

> "Just look around you here. All of this farmland that you see lies below sea level. One-fifth of the total area of the Netherlands is below sea level, as much as 22 feet below, because it used to be shallow bays,

and we reclaimed it from the sea by surrounding the bays with dikes and then gradually pumping out the water. We have a saying, 'God created the Earth, but we Dutch created the Netherlands.' These reclaimed lands are called 'polders.' We began draining them nearly a thousand years ago. Today, we still have to keep pumping out the water that gradually seeps in. That's what our windmills used to be for, to drive the pumps to pump out the polders. Now we use steam, diesel, and electric pumps instead. In each polder there are lines of pumps, starting with those farthest from the sea, pumping the water in sequence until the last pump finally pumps it out into a river or the ocean. In the Netherlands, we have another expression, 'You have to be able to get along with your enemy, because he may be the person operating the neighboring pump in your polder.' And we're all down in the polders together. It's not the case that rich people live safely up on tops of the dikes while poor people live down in the polder bottoms below sea level. If the dikes and pumps fail, we'll all drown together. When a big storm and high tides swept inland over Zeeland Province on February 1, 1953, nearly 2,000 Dutch people, both rich and poor, drowned. We swore that we would never let that happen again, and the whole country paid for an extremely expensive set of tide barriers. If global warming causes polar ice melting and a world rise in sea level, the consequences will be more severe for the Netherlands than for any other country in the world, because so much of our land is already under sea level. That's why we Dutch are so aware of our environment. We've learned through our history that we're all living in the same polder, and that our survival depends on each other's survival."

That acknowledged interdependence of all segments of Dutch society contrasts with current trends in the United States, where wealthy people increasingly seek to insulate themselves from the rest of society, aspire to create their own separate virtual polders, use their own money to buy services for themselves privately, and vote against taxes that would extend those amenities as public services to everyone else. Those private amenities include living inside gated walled communities, relying on private security guards rather than on the police, sending one's children to well-funded private schools with small classes rather than to the underfunded crowded public schools, purchasing private health insurance or medical care, drinking bottled water instead of municipal water, and (in Southern California) paying to drive on toll roads competing with the jammed public freeways. Underlying such privatization is a misguided belief that the elite can remain unaffected by the problems of society around them: the attitude of those Greenland Norse chiefs who found that they had merely bought themselves the privilege of being the last to starve.

Throughout human history, most peoples have been connected to some other peoples, living together in small virtual polders. The Easter Islanders comprised a dozen clans, dividing their island polder into a dozen territories, and isolated from all other islands, but sharing among clans the Rano Raraku statue quarry, the Puna Pau pukao quarry, and a few obsidian quarries. As Easter Island society disintegrated, all the clans disintegrated together, but nobody else in the world knew about it, nor was anybody else affected. Southeast Polynesia's polder consisted of three interdependent islands, such that the decline of Mangareva's society was disastrous also for the Pitcairn and Henderson Islanders but for no one else. To the ancient Maya, their polder consisted at most of the Yucatan Peninsula and neighboring areas. When the Classic Maya cities collapsed in the southern Yucatan, refugees may have reached the northern Yucatan, but certainly not Florida. In contrast today our whole world has become one polder, such that events anywhere affect Americans. When distant Somalia collapsed, in went American troops; when the former Yugoslavia and Soviet Union collapsed, out went streams of refugees over all of Europe and the rest of the world; and when changed conditions of society, settlement, and lifestyle spread new diseases in Africa and Asia, those diseases moved over the globe. The whole world today is a self-contained and isolated unit, as Tikopia Island and Tokugawa Japan used to be. We need to realize, as did the Tikopians and Japanese, that there is no other island/other planet to which we can turn for help, or to which we can export our problems. Instead, we need to learn, as they did, to live within our means.

I introduced this section by acknowledging that there are important differences between the ancient world and the modern world. The differences that I then went on to mention—today's larger population and more potent destructive technology, and today's interconnectedness posing the risk of a global rather than a local collapse—may seem to suggest a pessimistic outlook. If the Easter Islanders couldn't solve their milder local problems in the past, how can the modern world hope to solve its big global problems?

People who get depressed at such thoughts often then ask me, "Jared, are you optimistic or pessimistic about the world's future?" I answer, "I'm a cautious optimist." By that, I mean that, on the one hand, I acknowledge the seriousness of the problems facing us. If we don't make a determined effort to solve them, and if we don't succeed at that effort, the world as a whole within the next few decades will face a declining standard of living, or perhaps something worse. That's the reason why I decided to devote most of my career efforts at this stage of my life to convincing people that our problems have to be taken seriously and won't go away otherwise. On the other hand, we shall be able to solve our problems—if we choose to do so. That's why my wife and I did decide to have children 17 years ago: because we did see grounds for hope.

One basis for hope is that, realistically, we are not beset by insoluble   20
problems. While we do face big risks, the most serious ones are not ones beyond our control, like a possible collision with an asteroid of a size that hits the Earth every hundred million years or so. Instead, they are ones that we are generating ourselves. Because we are the cause of our environmental problems, we are the ones in control of them, and we can choose or not choose to stop causing them and start solving them. The future is up for grabs, lying in our own hands. We don't need new technologies to solve our problems; while new technologies can make some contribution, for the most part we "just" need the political will to apply solutions already available. Of course, that's a big "just." But many societies did find the necessary political will in the past. Our modern societies have already found the will to solve some of our problems, and to achieve partial solutions to others.

Another basis for hope is the increasing diffusion of environmental thinking among the public around the world. While such thinking has been with us for a long time, its spread has accelerated, especially since the 1962 publication of *Silent Spring*. The environmental movement has been gaining adherents at an increasing rate, and they act through a growing diversity of increasingly effective organizations, not only in the United States and Europe but also in the Dominican Republic and other developing countries. At the same time as the environmental movement is gaining strength at an increasing rate, so too are the threats to our environment. That's why I referred earlier in this book to our situation as that of being in an exponentially accelerating horse race of unknown outcome. It's neither impossible, nor is it assured, that our preferred horse will win the race.

What are the choices that we must make if we are now to succeed, and not to fail? There are many specific choices, of which I discuss examples in the Further Readings section, that any of us can make as individuals. For our society as a whole, the past societies that we have examined in this book suggest broader lessons. Two types of choices seem to me to have been crucial in tipping their outcomes towards success or failure: long-term planning, and willingness to reconsider core values. On reflection, we can also recognize the crucial role of these same two choices for the outcomes of our individual lives.

One of those choices has depended on the courage to practice long-term thinking, and to make bold, courageous, anticipatory decisions at a time when problems have become perceptible but before they have reached crisis proportions. This type of decision-making is the opposite of the short-term reactive decision-making that too often characterizes our elected politicians—the thinking that my politically well-connected friend decried as "90-day thinking," i.e., focusing only on issues likely to blow up in a crisis within the next 90 days. Set against the many depressing bad examples of such short-term decision-making are the encouraging examples of courageous long-term thinking in the past, and in the contemporary world of NGOs, business, and government. Among past societies faced with the prospect of ruinous deforestation, Easter Island and Mangareva chiefs succumbed to their immediate concerns, but Tokugawa shoguns, Inca emperors, New Guinea highlanders, and 16th-century German landowners adopted a long view and reafforested. China's leaders similarly promoted reafforestation in recent decades and banned logging of native forests in 1998. Today, many NGOs exist specifically for the purpose of promoting sane long-term environmental policies. In the business world the American corporations that remain successful for long times (e.g., Procter and Gamble) are ones that don't wait for a crisis to force them to reexamine their policies, but that instead look for problems on the horizon and act before there is a crisis. I already mentioned Royal Dutch Shell Oil Company as having an office devoted just to envisioning scenarios decades off in the future.

Courageous, successful, long-term planning also characterizes some governments and some political leaders, some of the time. Over the last 30 years a sustained effort by the U.S. government has reduced levels of the six major air pollutants nationally by 25%, even though our energy consumption and population increased by 40% and our vehicle miles driven increased by 150% during those same decades. The governments of

Malaysia, Singapore, Taiwan, and Mauritius all recognized that their long-term economic well-being required big investments in public health to prevent tropical diseases from sapping their economies; those investments proved to be a key to those countries' spectacular recent economic growth. Of the former two halves of the overpopulated nation of Pakistan, the eastern half (independent since 1971 as Bangladesh) adopted effective family planning measures to reduce its rate of population growth, while the western half (still known as Pakistan) did not and is now the world's sixth most populous country. Indonesia's former environmental minister Emil Salim, and the Dominican Republic's former president Joaquin Balaguer, exemplify government leaders whose concern about chronic environmental dangers made a big impact on their countries. All of these examples of courageous long-term thinking in both the public sector and the private sector contribute to my hope.

The other crucial choice illuminated by the past involves the courage to make painful decisions about values. Which of the values that formerly served a society well can continue to be maintained under new changed circumstances? Which of those treasured values must instead be jettisoned and replaced with different approaches? The Greenland Norse refused to jettison part of their identity as a European, Christian, pastoral society, and they died as a result. In contrast, Tikopia Islanders did have the courage to eliminate their ecologically destructive pigs, even though pigs are the sole large domestic animal and a principal status symbol of Melanesian societies. Australia is now in the process of reappraising its identity as a British agricultural society. The Icelanders and many traditional caste societies of India in the past, and Montana ranchers dependent on irrigation in recent times, did reach agreement to subordinate their individual rights to group interests. They thereby succeeded in managing shared resources and avoiding the tragedy of the commons that has befallen so many other groups. The government of China restricted the traditional freedom of individual reproductive choice, rather than let population problems spiral out of control. The people of Finland, faced with an ultimatum by their vastly more powerful Russian neighbor in 1939, chose to value their freedom over their lives, fought with a courage that astonished the world, and won their gamble, even while losing the war. While I was living in Britain from 1958 to 1962, the British people were coming to terms with the outdatedness of cherished long-held values based on Britain's former role as the world's dominant political, economic, and naval power. The French, Germans, and other European countries have advanced even further in subordinating to the European Union their national sovereignties for which they used to fight so dearly.

All of these past and recent reappraisals of values that I have just mentioned were achieved despite being agonizingly difficult. Hence they also contribute to my hope. They may inspire modern First World citizens with the courage to make the most fundamental reappraisal now facing us: how much of our traditional consumer values and First World living standard can we afford to retain? I already mentioned the seeming political impossibility of inducing First World citizens to lower their impact on the world. But the alternative, of continuing our current impact, is more impossible. This dilemma reminds me of Winston Churchill's response to criticisms of democracy: "It has been said that Democracy is the worst form of government except all those other forms that have been tried from time to time." In that spirit, a lower-impact society is the most impossible scenario for our future—except for all other conceivable scenarios.

Actually, while it won't be easier to reduce our impact, it won't be impossible either. Remember that impact is the product of two factors: population, multiplied times impact per person. As for the first of those two factors, population growth has recently declined drastically in all First World countries, and in many Third World countries as well—including China, Indonesia, and Bangladesh, with the world's largest, fourth largest, and ninth largest populations respectively. Intrinsic population growth in Japan and Italy is already below the replacement rate, such that their existing populations (i.e., not counting immigrants) will soon begin shrinking. As for impact per person, the world would not even have to decrease its current consumption rates of timber products or of seafood: those rates could be sustained or even increased, if the world's forests and fisheries were properly managed.

My remaining cause for hope is another consequence of the globalized modern world's interconnectedness. Past societies lacked archaeologists and television. While the Easter Islanders were busy deforesting the highlands of their overpopulated island for agricultural plantations in the 1400s, they had no way of knowing that, thousands of miles to the east and west at the same time, Greenland Norse society and the Khmer Empire were simultaneously in terminal decline, while the Anasazi had collapsed a few centuries earlier, Classic Maya society a few more centuries before that, and Mycenean Greece 2,000 years before that. Today, though, we turn on our television sets or radios or pick up our newspapers, and we see, hear, or read about what happened in Somalia or Afghanistan a few hours earlier.

Our television documentaries and books show us in graphic detail why the Easter Islanders, Classic Maya, and other past societies collapsed. Thus, we have the opportunity to learn from the mistakes of distant peoples and past peoples. That's an opportunity that no past society enjoyed to such a degree. My hope in writing this book has been that enough people will choose to profit from that opportunity to make a difference.

Analyze

1. According to Diamond, how does population size affect a society's risk of collapse?
2. Briefly summarize why Diamond suggests the world's most environmentally devastated areas are also the world's most politically unstable areas.
3. How does the concept of globalization as Diamond uses it here relate to the concept of "living downstream" described in the introduction to this chapter? Put another way, how might the environmental problems of one country affect another?

Explore

1. Do you think that people commonly associate the environment with politics? Alternatively, what connotations do you think are more commonly associated with words like "sustainability"? Do you think that Diamond makes a strong argument for the connection between sustainability and social and political unrest? In a group, discuss ways that the public at large might begin to think about sustainability as a means not just of protecting the environment but also of protecting societal stability.
2. Diamond does not use the word "sustainability" in this selection, and yet issues of sustainability are discussed throughout his writing. While it may be unusual to attribute governmental collapse, civil war, or genocide to issues of sustainability, strong connections between them can be made. Using a search engine, research the conditions that brought about a major recent humanitarian crisis (e.g., a massive drought) and compose a short list that links that crisis to issues of sustainability.
3. Using your school's library databases in addition to online search engines, research one of the collapsed civilizations discussed in this selection to determine how the issue of sustainability contributed to its

collapse. Use your findings to craft a "Did You Know" editorial for your school's newspaper that educates readers on the historical importance of sustainability (using your research to provide examples) and how it relates to us today.

Garrett Hardin
"Tragedy of the Commons"

Garrett Hardin was an ecologist, philosopher, and author who published nine books and numerous articles on ecology, population growth, and ethics. Hardin earned a B.S. in ecology from the University of Chicago and a Ph.D. in microbiology from Stanford University and taught as a professor of human ecology at the University of California, Santa Barbara. Hardin is most famous for his essay "Tragedy of the Commons" (reprinted below), which was published in the journal *Science* in 1968. In this controversial essay Hardin describes the "social dilemma" of how individuals seek their self-interest at the cost of the common good. The "commons" refers to any publicly held resource, such as land, air, or oceans, that we all share and on which we depend. The question, however, is: How do we share it? How do we balance individual interests and rights against the long-term good of the community? Hardin was concerned about population growth and the "carrying capacity" of the planet (the number of people the Earth can support in reasonable standards of living), but his analysis of the tragedy of the commons applies to a wide range of problems and gets to the very heart of the ethics and politics of sustainability.

At the end of a thoughtful article on the future of nuclear war, Wiesner and York (1) concluded that: "Both sides in the arms race are . . . confronted by the dilemma of steadily increasing military power and steadily decreasing national security. *It is our considered professional judgment that this dilemma has no technical solution.* If the great powers continue to look for solutions in the area of science and technology only, the result will be to worsen the situation."

I would like to focus your attention not on the subject of the article (national security in a nuclear world) but on the kind of conclusion they reached, namely that there is no technical solution to the problem. An implicit and almost universal assumption of discussions published in professional and semipopular scientific journals is that the problem under discussion has a technical solution. A technical solution may be defined as one that requires a change only in the techniques of the natural sciences, demanding little or nothing in the way of change in human values or ideas of morality.

In our day (though not in earlier times) technical solutions are always welcome. Because of previous failures in prophecy, it takes courage to assert that a desired technical solution is not possible. Wiesner and York exhibited this courage; publishing in a science journal, they insisted that the solution to the problem was not to be found in the natural sciences. They cautiously qualified their statement with the phrase, "It is our considered professional judgment. . . ." Whether they were right or not is not the concern of the present article. Rather, the concern here is with the important concept of a class of human problems which can be called "no technical solution problems," and, more specifically, with the identification and discussion of one of these. It is easy to show that the class is not a null class.

Recall the game of tick-tack-toe. Consider the problem, "How can I win the game of tick-tack-toe?" It is well known that I cannot, if I assume (in keeping with the conventions of game theory) that my opponent understands the game perfectly. Put another way, there is no "technical solution" to the problem. I can win only by giving a radical meaning to the word "win." I can hit my opponent over the head; or I can drug him; or I can falsify the records. Every way in which I "win" involves, in some sense, an abandonment of the game, as we intuitively understand it. (I can also, of course, openly abandon the game—refuse to play it. This is what most adults do.)

The class of "No technical solution problems" has members. My thesis is that the "population problem," as conventionally conceived, is a member of this class. How it is conventionally conceived needs some comment. It is fair to say that most people who anguish over the population problem are trying to find a way to avoid the evils of overpopulation without relinquishing any of the privileges they now enjoy. They think that farming the seas or developing new strains of wheat will solve the problem— technologically. I try to show here that the solution they seek cannot be found. The population problem cannot be solved in a technical way, any more than can the problem of winning the game of tick-tack-toe.

What Shall We Maximize?

Population, as Malthus said, naturally tends to grow "geometrically," or, as we would now say, exponentially. In a finite world this means that the per capita share of the world's goods must steadily decrease. Is ours a finite world?

A fair defense can be put forward for the view that the world is infinite; or that we do not know that it is not. But, in terms of the practical problems that we must face in the next few generations with the foreseeable technology, it is clear that we will greatly increase human misery if we do not, during the immediate future, assume that the world available to the terrestrial human population is finite. "Space" is no escape (2). A finite world can support only a finite population; therefore, population growth must eventually equal zero. (The case of perpetual wide fluctuations above and below zero is a trivial variant that need not be discussed.) When this condition is met, what will be the situation of mankind? Specifically, can Bentham's goal of "the greatest good for the greatest number" be realized?

No—for two reasons, each sufficient by itself. The first is a theoretical one. It is not mathematically possible to maximize for two (or more) variables at the same time. This was clearly stated by von Neumann and Morgenstern (3), but the principle is implicit in the theory of partial differential equations, dating back at least to D'Alembert (1717–1783).

The second reason springs directly from biological facts. To live, any organism must have a source of energy (for example, food). This energy is utilized for two purposes: mere maintenance and work. For man, maintenance of life requires about 1600 kilocalories a day ("maintenance calories"). Anything that he does over and above merely staying alive will be defined as work, and is supported by "work calories" which he takes in. Work calories are used not only for what we call work in common speech; they are also required for all forms of enjoyment, from swimming and automobile racing to playing music and writing poetry. If our goal is to maximize population it is obvious what we must do: We must make the work calories per person approach as close to zero as possible. No gourmet meals, no vacations, no sports, no music, no literature, no art . . . I think that everyone will grant, without argument or proof, that maximizing population does not maximize goods. Bentham's goal is impossible.

10   In reaching this conclusion I have made the usual assumption that it is the acquisition of energy that is the problem. The appearance of atomic energy

has led some to question this assumption. However, given an infinite source of energy, population growth still produces an inescapable problem. The problem of the acquisition of energy is replaced by the problem of its dissipation, as J. H. Fremlin has so wittily shown (4). The arithmetic signs in the analysis are, as it were, reversed; but Bentham's goal is still unobtainable.

The optimum population is, then, less than the maximum. The difficulty of defining the optimum is enormous; so far as I know, no one has seriously tackled this problem. Reaching an acceptable and stable solution will surely require more than one generation of hard analytical work—and much persuasion.

We want the maximum good per person; but what is good? To one person it is wilderness, to another it is ski lodges for thousands. To one it is estuaries to nourish ducks for hunters to shoot; to another it is factory land. Comparing one good with another is, we usually say, impossible because goods are incommensurable. Incommensurables cannot be compared.

Theoretically this may be true; but in real life incommensurables are commensurable. Only a criterion of judgment and a system of weighting are needed. In nature the criterion is survival. Is it better for a species to be small and hideable, or large and powerful? Natural selection commensurates the incommensurables. The compromise achieved depends on a natural weighting of the values of the variables.

Man must imitate this process. There is no doubt that in fact he already does, but unconsciously. It is when the hidden decisions are made explicit that the arguments begin. The problem for the years ahead is to work out an acceptable theory of weighting. Synergistic effects, nonlinear variation, and difficulties in discounting the future make the intellectual problem difficult, but not (in principle) insoluble.

Has any cultural group solved this practical problem at the present time, even on an intuitive level? One simple fact proves that none has: there is no prosperous population in the world today that has, and has had for some time, a growth rate of zero. Any people that has intuitively identified its optimum point will soon reach it, after which its growth rate becomes and remains zero.   15

Of course, a positive growth rate might be taken as evidence that a population is below its optimum. However, by any reasonable standards, the most rapidly growing populations on earth today are (in general) the most miserable. This association (which need not be invariable) casts doubt on the optimistic assumption that the positive growth rate of a population is evidence that it has yet to reach its optimum.

We can make little progress in working toward optimum population size until we explicitly exorcize the spirit of Adam Smith in the field of practical demography. In economic affairs, *The Wealth of Nations* (1776) popularized the "invisible hand," the idea that an individual who "intends only his own gain," is, as it were, "led by an invisible hand to promote . . . the public interest" (5). Adam Smith did not assert that this was invariably true, and perhaps neither did any of his followers. But he contributed to a dominant tendency of thought that has ever since interfered with positive action based on rational analysis, namely, the tendency to assume that decisions reached individually will, in fact, be the best decisions for an entire society. If this assumption is correct it justifies the continuance of our present policy of laissez-faire in reproduction. If it is correct we can assume that men will control their individual fecundity so as to produce the optimum population. If the assumption is not correct, we need to reexamine our individual freedoms to see which ones are defensible.

Tragedy of Freedom in a Commons

The rebuttal to the invisible hand in population control is to be found in a scenario first sketched in a little-known pamphlet (6) in 1833 by a mathematical amateur named William Forster Lloyd (1794–1852). We may well call it "the tragedy of the commons," using the word "tragedy" as the philosopher Whitehead used it (7): "The essence of dramatic tragedy is not unhappiness. It resides in the solemnity of the remorseless working of things." He then goes on to say, "This inevitableness of destiny can only be illustrated in terms of human life by incidents which in fact involve unhappiness. For it is only by them that the futility of escape can be made evident in the drama."

The tragedy of the commons develops in this way. Picture a pasture open to all. It is to be expected that each herdsman will try to keep as many cattle as possible on the commons. Such an arrangement may work reasonably satisfactorily for centuries because tribal wars, poaching, and disease keep the numbers of both man and beast well below the carrying capacity of the land. Finally, however, comes the day of reckoning, that is, the day when the long-desired goal of social stability becomes a reality. At this point, the inherent logic of the commons remorselessly generates tragedy.

As a rational being, each herdsman seeks to maximize his gain. Explicitly or implicitly, more or less consciously, he asks, "What is the utility *to me* of adding one more animal to my herd?" This utility has one negative and one positive component.   20

1. The positive component is a function of the increment of one animal. Since the herdsman receives all the proceeds from the sale of the additional animal, the positive utility is nearly +1.
2. The negative component is a function of the additional overgrazing created by one more animal. Since, however, the effects of overgrazing are shared by all the herdsmen, the negative utility for any particular decision-making herdsman is only a fraction of −1.

Adding together the component partial utilities, the rational herdsman concludes that the only sensible course for him to pursue is to add another animal to his herd. And another; and another.... But this is the conclusion reached by each and every rational herdsman sharing a commons. Therein is the tragedy. Each man is locked into a system that compels him to increase his herd without limit—in a world that is limited. Ruin is the destination toward which all men rush, each pursuing his own best interest in a society that believes in the freedom of the commons. Freedom in a commons brings ruin to all.

Some would say that this is a platitude. Would that it were! In a sense, it was learned thousands of years ago, but natural selection favors the forces of psychological denial (8). The individual benefits as an individual from his ability to deny the truth even though society as a whole, of which he is a part, suffers.

Education can counteract the natural tendency to do the wrong thing, but the inexorable succession of generations requires that the basis for this knowledge be constantly refreshed.

A simple incident that occurred a few years ago in Leominster, Massachusetts, shows how perishable the knowledge is. During the Christmas shopping season the parking meters downtown were covered with red plastic bags that bore tags reading: "Do not open until after Christmas. Free parking courtesy of the mayor and city council." In other words, facing the prospect of an increased demand for already scarce space, the city fathers reinstituted the system of the commons. (Cynically, we suspect that they gained more votes than they lost by this retrogressive act.)

25   In an approximate way, the logic of commons has been understood for a long time, perhaps since the discovery of agriculture or the invention of private property in real estate. But it is understood mostly only in special cases which are not sufficiently generalized. Even at this late date, cattlemen leasing national land on the western ranges demonstrate no more than an ambivalent understanding, in constantly pressuring federal authorities to increase the head count to the point where overgrazing produces erosion and weed-dominance. Likewise, the oceans of the world continue to suffer from the survival of the philosophy of the commons. Maritime nations still respond automatically to the shibboleth of the "freedom of the seas." Professing to believe in "the inexhaustible resources of the oceans," they bring species after species of fish and whales closer to extinction (9).

The National Parks present another instance of the working out of the tragedy of the commons. At present, they are open to all, without limit. The parks themselves are limited in extent—there is only one Yosemite Valley—whereas population seems to grow without limit. The values that visitors seek in the parks are steadily eroded. Plainly, we must soon cease to treat the parks as commons or they will be of no value to anyone.

What shall we do? We have several options. We might sell them off as private property. We might keep them as public property, but allocate the right to enter them. The allocation might be on the basis of wealth, by the use of an auction system. It might be on the basis of merit, as defined by some agreed-upon standards. It might be by lottery. Or it might be on a first-come, first-served basis, administered to long queues. These, I think, are all the reasonable possibilities. They are all objectionable. But we must choose—or acquiesce in the destruction of the commons that we call our National Parks.

Pollution

In a reverse way, the tragedy of the commons reappears in problems of pollution. Here it is not a question of taking something out of the commons, but of putting something in—sewage, or chemical, radioactive, and heat wastes into water; noxious and dangerous fumes into the air, and distracting and unpleasant advertising signs into the line of sight. The calculations of utility are much the same as before. The rational man finds that his share of the cost of the wastes he discharges into the commons is less than the cost of purifying his wastes before releasing them. Since this is true for everyone, we are locked into a system of "fouling our own nest," so long as we behave only as independent, rational, free-enterprises.

The tragedy of the commons as a food basket is averted by private property, or something formally like it. But the air and waters surrounding us cannot readily be fenced, and so the tragedy of the commons as a cesspool must be prevented by different means, by coercive laws or taxing devices that make it cheaper for the polluter to treat his pollutants than to discharge them untreated. We have not progressed as far with the solution of this problem as we have with the first. Indeed, our particular concept of private property, which deters us from exhausting the positive resources of the earth, favors pollution. The owner of a factory on the bank of a stream— whose property extends to the middle of the stream, often has difficulty seeing why it is not his natural right to muddy the waters flowing past his door. The law, always behind the times, requires elaborate stitching and fitting to adapt it to this newly perceived aspect of the commons.

The pollution problem is a consequence of population. It did not much   30 matter how a lonely American frontiersman disposed of his waste. "Flowing water purifies itself every 10 miles," my grandfather used to say, and the myth was near enough to the truth when he was a boy, for there were not too many people. But as population became denser, the natural chemical and biological recycling processes became overloaded, calling for a redefinition of property rights.

How to Legislate Temperance?

Analysis of the pollution problem as a function of population density uncovers a not generally recognized principle of morality, namely: *the morality of an act is a function of the state of the system at the time it is performed* (10). Using the commons as a cesspool does not harm the general public under frontier conditions, because there is no public; the same behavior in a metropolis is unbearable. A hundred and fifty years ago a plainsman could kill an American bison, cut out only the tongue for his dinner, and discard the rest of the animal. He was not in any important sense being wasteful. Today, with only a few thousand bison left, we would be appalled at such behavior.

In passing, it is worth noting that the morality of an act cannot be determined from a photograph. One does not know whether a man killing an elephant or setting fire to the grassland is harming others until one knows the total system in which his act appears. "One picture is worth a thousand words," said an ancient Chinese; but it may take 10,000 words to validate it. It is as tempting to ecologists as it is to reformers in general to try to persuade others by way of the photographic shortcut. But the essence of an argument cannot be photographed: it must be presented rationally—in words.

That morality is system-sensitive escaped the attention of most codifiers of ethics in the past. "Thou shalt not . . ." is the form of traditional ethical directives which make no allowance for particular circumstances. The laws of our society follow the pattern of ancient ethics, and therefore are poorly suited to governing a complex, crowded, changeable world. Our epicyclic solution is to augment statutory law with administrative law. Since it is practically impossible to spell out all the conditions under which it is safe to burn trash in the back yard or to run an automobile without smog-control, by law we delegate the details to bureaus. The result is administrative law, which is rightly feared for an ancient reason— *Quis custodiet ipsos custodes*? "Who shall watch the watchers themselves?" John Adams said that we must have a government of laws and not men." Bureau administrators, trying to evaluate the morality of acts in the total system, are singularly liable to corruption, producing a government by men, not laws.

Prohibition is easy to legislate (though not necessarily to enforce); but how do we legislate temperance? Experience indicates that it can be accomplished best through the mediation of administrative law. We limit possibilities unnecessarily if we suppose that the sentiment of *Quis custodiet* denies us the use of administrative law. We should rather retain the phrase as a perpetual reminder of fearful dangers we cannot avoid. The great challenge facing us now is to invent the corrective feedbacks that are needed to keep custodians honest. We must find ways to legitimate the needed authority of both the custodians and the corrective feedbacks.

Freedom to Breed Is Intolerable

35   The tragedy of the commons is involved in population problems in another way. In a world governed solely by the principle of "dog eat dog"— if indeed there ever was such a world—how many children a family had

would not be a matter of public concern. Parents who bred too exuberantly would leave fewer descendants, not more, because they would be unable to care adequately for their children. David Lack and others have found that such a negative feedback demonstrably controls the fecundity of birds (11). But men are not birds, and have not acted like them for millenniums, at least.

If each human family were dependent only on its own resources; if the children of improvident parents starved to death; *if*, thus, overbreeding brought its own "punishment" to the germ line—*then* there would be no public interest in controlling the breeding of families. But our society is deeply committed to the welfare state (12), and hence is confronted with another aspect of the tragedy of the commons.

In a welfare state, how shall we deal with the family, the religion, the race, or the class (or indeed any distinguishable and cohesive group) that adopts overbreeding as a policy to secure its own aggrandizement (13)? To couple the concept of freedom to breed with the belief that everyone born has an equal right to the commons is to lock the world into a tragic course of action.

Unfortunately this is just the course of action that is being pursued by the United Nations. In late 1967, some 30 nations agreed to the following (14):

> The Universal Declaration of Human Rights describes the family as the natural and fundamental unit of society. It follows that any choice and decision with regard to the size of the family must irrevocably rest with the family itself, and cannot be made by anyone else.

It is painful to have to deny categorically the validity of this right; denying it, one feels as uncomfortable as a resident of Salem, Massachusetts, who denied the reality of witches in the 17th century. At the present time, in liberal quarters, something like a taboo acts to inhibit criticism of the United Nations. There is a feeling that the United Nations is "our last and best hope," that we shouldn't find fault with it; we shouldn't play into the hands of the archconservatives. However, let us not forget what Robert Louis Stevenson said: "The truth that is suppressed by friends is the readiest weapon of the enemy." If we love the truth we must openly deny the validity of the Universal Declaration of Human Rights, even though it is promoted by the United Nations. We should also join with Kingsley Davis (15) in attempting to get planned Parenthood-World Population to see the error of its ways in embracing the same tragic ideal.

Conscience Is Self-Eliminating

40   It is a mistake to think that we can control the breeding of mankind in the long run by an appeal to conscience. Charles Galton Darwin made this point when he spoke on the centennial of the publication of his grandfather's great book. The argument is straightforward and Darwinian.

People vary. Confronted with appeals to limit breeding, some people will undoubtedly respond to the plea more than others. Those who have more children will produce a larger fraction of the next generation than those with more susceptible consciences. The difference will be accentuated, generation by generation.

In C. G. Darwin's words: "It may well be that it would take hundreds of generations for the progenitive instinct to develop in this way, but if it should do so, nature would have taken her revenge, and the variety *Homo contracipiens* would become extinct and would be replaced by the variety *Homo progenitivus*" (16).

The argument assumes that conscience or the desire for children (no matter which) is hereditary—but hereditary only in the most general formal sense. The result will be the same whether the attitude is transmitted through germ-cells, or exosomatically, to use A. J. Lotka's term. (If one denies the latter possibility as well as the former, then what's the point of education?) The argument has here been stated in the context of the population problem, but it applies equally well to any instance in which society appeals to an individual exploiting a commons to restrain himself for the general good—by means of his conscience. To make such an appeal is to set up a selective system that works toward the elimination of conscience from the race.

Pathogenic Effects of Conscience

The long-term disadvantage of an appeal to conscience should be enough to condemn it; but has serious short-term disadvantages as well. If we ask a man who is exploiting a commons to desist "in the name of conscience," what are we saying to him? What does he hear?—not only at the moment but also in the wee small hours of the night when, half asleep, he remembers not merely the words we used but also the nonverbal communication cues we gave him unawares? Sooner or later, consciously or subconsciously, he senses that he has received two communications, and that they are contradictory: (i) (intended communication) "If you don't do as we ask, we will openly condemn you for not acting like a responsible citizen"; (ii) (the unintended communication) "If you do behave as we ask, we will secretly condemn you for a simpleton who can be shamed into standing aside while the rest of us exploit the commons."

Everyman then is caught in what Bateson has called a "double bind." 45 Bateson and his co-workers have made a plausible case for viewing the double bind as an important causative factor in the genesis of schizophrenia (17). The double bind may not always be so damaging, but it always endangers the mental health of anyone to whom it is applied. "A bad conscience," said Nietzsche, "is a kind of illness."

To conjure up a conscience in others is tempting to anyone who wishes to extend his control beyond the legal limits. Leaders at the highest level succumb to this temptation. Has any President during the past generation failed to call on labor unions to moderate voluntarily their demands for higher wages, or to steel companies to honor voluntary guidelines on prices? I can recall none. The rhetoric used on such occasions is designed to produce feelings of guilt in noncooperators.

For centuries it was assumed without proof that guilt was a valuable, perhaps even an indispensable, ingredient of the civilized life. Now, in this post-Freudian world, we doubt it.

Paul Goodman speaks from the modern point of view when he says: "No good has ever come from feeling guilty, neither intelligence, policy, nor compassion. The guilty do not pay attention to the object but only to themselves, and not even to their own interests, which might make sense, but to their anxieties" (18).

One does not have to be a professional psychiatrist to see the consequences of anxiety. We in the Western world are just emerging from a dreadful two-centuries-long Dark Ages of Eros that was sustained partly by prohibition laws, but perhaps more effectively by the anxiety-generating mechanisms of education. Alex Comfort has told the story well in *The Anxiety Makers* (19); it is not a pretty one.

Since proof is difficult, we may even concede that the results of anxiety 50 may sometimes, from certain points of view, be desirable. The larger question we should ask is whether, as a matter of policy, we should ever encourage the use of a technique the tendency (if not the intention) of which is psychologically pathogenic. We hear much talk these days of responsible parenthood; the coupled words are incorporated into the titles of some organizations devoted to birth control. Some people have proposed massive propaganda campaigns to instill responsibility into the nation's (or the world's) breeders. But what is the meaning of the word responsibility in this context? Is it not merely a synonym for the word conscience? When we use the word responsibility in the absence of substantial sanctions are we not trying to browbeat a free man in a commons into acting against his own interest? Responsibility is a verbal counterfeit for a substantial *quid pro quo*. It is an attempt to get something for nothing.

If the word responsibility is to be used at all, I suggest that it be in the sense Charles Frankel uses it (20). "Responsibility," says this philosopher, "is the product of definite social arrangements." Notice that Frankel calls for social arrangements—not propaganda.

Mutual Coercion Mutually Agreed Upon

The social arrangements that produce responsibility are arrangements that create coercion, of some sort. Consider bank-robbing. The man who takes money from a bank acts as if the bank were a commons. How do we prevent such action? Certainly not by trying to control his behavior solely by a verbal appeal to his sense of responsibility. Rather than rely on propaganda we follow Frankel's lead and insist that a bank is not a commons; we seek the definite social arrangements that will keep it from becoming a commons. That we thereby infringe on the freedom of would-be robbers we neither deny nor regret.

The morality of bank-robbing is particularly easy to understand because we accept complete prohibition of this activity. We are willing to say "Thou shalt not rob banks," without providing for exceptions. But temperance also can be created by coercion. Taxing is a good coercive device. To keep downtown shoppers temperate in their use of parking space we introduce parking meters for short periods, and traffic fines for longer ones. We need not actually forbid a citizen to park as long as he wants to; we need merely make it increasingly expensive for him to do so. Not prohibition, but carefully biased options are what we offer him. A Madison Avenue man might call this persuasion; I prefer the greater candor of the word coercion.

Coercion is a dirty word to most liberals now, but it need not forever be so. As with the four-letter words, its dirtiness can be cleansed away by exposure to the light, by saying it over and over without apology or embarrassment. To many, the word coercion implies arbitrary decisions of distant and irresponsible bureaucrats; but this is not a necessary part of its meaning. The only kind of coercion I recommend is mutual coercion, mutually agreed upon by the majority of the people affected.

To say that we mutually agree to coercion is not to say that we are   55 required to enjoy it, or even to pretend we enjoy it. Who enjoys taxes? We all grumble about them. But we accept compulsory taxes because we recognize that voluntary taxes would favor the conscienceless. We institute and (grumblingly) support taxes and other coercive devices to escape the horror of the commons.

An alternative to the commons need not be perfectly just to be preferable. With real estate and other material goods, the alternative we have chosen is the institution of private property coupled with legal inheritance. Is this system perfectly just? As a genetically trained biologist I deny that it is. It seems to me that, if there are to be differences in individual inheritance, legal possession should be perfectly correlated with biological inheritance—that those who are biologically more fit to be the custodians of property and power should legally inherit more. But genetic recombination continually makes a mockery of the doctrine of "like father, like son" implicit in our laws of legal inheritance. An idiot can inherit millions, and a trust fund can keep his estate intact. We must admit that our legal system of private property plus inheritance is unjust—but we put up with it because we are not convinced, at the moment, that anyone has invented a better system. The alternative of the commons is too horrifying to contemplate. Injustice is preferable to total ruin.

It is one of the peculiarities of the warfare between reform and the status quo that it is thoughtlessly governed by a double standard. Whenever a reform measure is proposed it is often defeated when its opponents triumphantly discover a flaw in it. As Kingsley Davis has pointed out (21), worshippers of the status quo sometimes imply that no reform is possible without unanimous agreement, an implication contrary to historical fact. As nearly as I can make out, automatic rejection of proposed reforms is based on one of two unconscious assumptions: (i) that the status quo is perfect; or (ii) that the choice we face is between reform and no action; if the proposed reform is imperfect, we presumably should take no action at all, while we wait for a perfect proposal.

But we can never do nothing. That which we have done for thousands of years is also action. It also produce evils. Once we are aware that status quo is action, we can then compare its discoverable advantages and disadvantages with the predicted advantages and disadvantages of the proposed reform, discounting as best we can for our lack of experience. On the basis of such a comparison, we can make a rational decision which will not involve the unworkable assumption that only perfect systems are tolerable.

Recognition of Necessity

Perhaps the simplest summary of this analysis of man's population problems is this: the commons, if justifiable at all, is justifiable only under conditions of low-population density. As the human population has increased, the commons has had to be abandoned in one aspect after another. First we abandoned the commons in food gathering, enclosing farm land and restricting pastures and hunting and fishing areas. These restrictions are still not complete throughout the world.

60   Somewhat later we saw that the commons as a place for waste disposal would also have to be abandoned. Restrictions on the disposal of domestic sewage are widely accepted in the Western world; we are still struggling to close the commons to pollution by automobiles, factories, insecticide sprayers, fertilizing operations, and atomic energy installations.

In a still more embryonic state is our recognition of the evils of the commons in matters of pleasure. There is almost no restriction on the propagation of sound waves in the public medium. The shopping public is assaulted with mindless music, without its consent. Our government is paying out billions of dollars to create supersonic transport which will disturb 50,000 people for every one person who is whisked from coast to coast 3 hours faster. Advertisers muddy the airwaves of radio and television and pollute the view of travelers. We are a long way from outlawing the commons in matters of pleasure. Is this because our Puritan inheritance makes us view pleasure as something of a sin, and pain (that is, the pollution of advertising) as the sign of virtue?

Every new enclosure of the commons involves the infringement of somebody's personal liberty. Infringements made in the distant past are accepted because no contemporary complains of a loss. It is the newly proposed infringements that we vigorously oppose; cries of "rights" and "freedom" fill the air. But what does "freedom" mean? When men mutually agreed to pass laws against robbing, mankind became more free, not less so. Individuals locked into the logic of the commons are free only to bring on universal ruin; once they see the necessity of mutual coercion, they become free to pursue other goals. I believe it was Hegel who said, "Freedom is the recognition of necessity."

The most important aspect of necessity that we must now recognize, is the necessity of abandoning the commons in breeding. No technical solution can rescue us from the misery of overpopulation. Freedom to breed will bring ruin to all. At the moment, to avoid hard decisions many of us are tempted to propagandize for conscience and responsible parenthood. The temptation must be resisted, because an appeal to independently acting consciences selects for the disappearance of all conscience in the long run, and an increase in anxiety in the short.

The only way we can preserve and nurture other and more precious freedoms is by relinquishing the freedom to breed, and that very soon. "Freedom is the recognition of necessity"—and it is the role of education to reveal to all the necessity of abandoning the freedom to breed. Only so, can we put an end to this aspect of the tragedy of the commons.

References

J. B. Wiesner and H. F. York, *Sci. Amer.* 211 (No. 4). 27 (1964).

G. Hardin, J. Hered. **50**, 68 (1959); S. von Hoernor, *Science* **137**, 18 (1962).

J. von Neumann and O. Morgenstern, *Theory of Games and Economic Behavior* (Princeton Univ. Press, Princeton, N.J., 1947), p. 11.

J. H. Fremlin. *New Sci.*, No. 415 (1964), p. 285.

A. Smith, *The Wealth of Nations* (Modern Library, New York, 1937), p. 423.

W. F. Lloyd, *Two Lectures on the Checks to Population* (Oxford Univ. Press, Oxford, England, 1833), reprinted (in part) in *Population, Evolution, and Birth Control,* G. Hardin. Ed. (Freeman, San Francisco, 1964), p. 37.

A. N. Whitehead, *Science and the Modern World* (Mentor, New York, 1948), p. 17.

G. Hardin, Ed. *Population, Evolution, and Birth Control* (Freeman, San Francisco, 1964). p. 56.

S. McVay, *Sci. Amer.* **216** (No. 8), 13 (1966).

J. Fletcher, *Situation Ethics* (Westminster, Philadelphia, 1966).

D. Lack, *The Natural Regulation of Animal Numbers* (Clarendon Press, Oxford, 1954).

H. Girvetz, *From Wealth to Welfare* (Stanford Univ. Press, Stanford, Calif., 1950).

G. Hardin, *Perspec. Biol. Med.* **6**, 366 (1963).

U. Thant, Int. *Planned Parenthood News,* No. 168 (February 1968), p. 3.

K. Davis, *Science* 158, 730 (1967).

S. Tax, Ed., *Evolution after Darwin* (Univ. of Chicago Press, Chicago, 1960), vol. 2, p. 469.

G. Bateson, D. D. Jackson, J. Haley, J. Weakland, *Behav. Sci.* **1**. 251 (1956).

P. Goodman, New York Rev. Books **10** (8), 22 (23 May 1968).

A. Comfort, *The Anxiety Makers* (Nelson, London, 1967).

C. Frankel, *The Case for Modern Man* (Harper, New York, 1955), p. 203.

J. D. Roslansky, *Genetics and the Future of Man* (Appleton-Century-Crofts, New York, 1966). p. 177.

Analyze

1. What does Hardin mean by "the greatest good for the greatest number"? Why does he claim that this is an unobtainable goal?

2. Why does Hardin argue that an appeal to people's conscience is not a solution to the population problem? What does he suggest, instead, is a potential solution?

3. What does the term *laissez-faire* mean, and where does it come from?

Explore

1. In your class, hold a debate in which groups represent both sides of the argument over whether the world is infinite. In your debate, address questions like: Are there some resources that cannot be replaced? Are humans capable of replacing resources or of coming up with new technologies that remove our needs for those resources?

2. Hardin makes a shocking claim about freedom when he states, "Therein is the tragedy. Each man is locked into a system that compels him to increase his herd without limit—in a world that is limited. Ruin is the destination toward which all men rush, each pursuing his own best interest in a society that believes in the freedom of the commons. Freedom in a commons brings ruin to all." Using concepts from at least three readings from this chapter, construct a poster or flyer that conveys Hardin's argument about the dangers of too much freedom. Think about how your viewer might initially view such a poster. Don't people usually consider freedom to be important? How might you convince someone to see "freedom" in this new light?

3. In his discussion of possibilities for restricting the National Parks as commons, Hardin makes the following argument:

> "We have several options. We might sell them off as private property. We might keep them as public property, but allocate the right to enter them. The allocation might be on the basis of wealth, by the use of an auction system. It might be on the basis of merit, as defined by some agreed-upon standards. It might be by lottery. Or it might be on a first-come, first-served basis, administered to long queues. These, I think, are all the reasonable possibilities. They are all objectionable. But we must choose—or acquiesce in the destruction of the commons that we call our National Parks."

Talk to people in your area or use an online search engine to locate a commons near you that in some way restricted public access. How has the right to enter the commons been allocated? Do you think the system is fair? What are the benefits and drawbacks of this system? Share and discuss your findings with your class.

Forging Connections

1. In "Tragedy of the Commons," Garrett Hardin claims that "most people who anguish over the population problem are trying to find a way to avoid the evils of overpopulation without relinquishing any of the privileges they now enjoy." This idea of relinquishing what we have—of sacrifice—is an important component of sustainability and has been an underlying concept throughout the readings in this chapter.

Sustainable use of resources requires sacrifice, but as the introduction to this chapter points out, sacrifice means not just giving something up, but getting something more important in return. Using these readings to inform your writing, construct an argument in which you persuade your reader that the benefits of a sustainable use of resources outweigh the sacrifice.

2. These readings have tended to use specific examples of past events or hypothetical situations to draw parallels between events that are occurring today or that may occur in the future. Aldo Leopold described wolves on a mountain; Jared Diamond discussed the collapse of past civilizations; and Garrett Hardin talked about livestock in a pasture. Looking back over these readings, synthesize these writers' arguments into an essay that describes their common warning about the way that people should be living today and in the future. Then, research some current events that demonstrate whether or not you see these warnings being heeded and integrate these observations into your essay. Based on your research and your understanding of these readings, conclude your paper by making some recommendations for the future.

Looking Further

1. Garrett Hardin's concept of the tragedy of the commons is central to almost any notion of sustainability, and in one form or another it applies to every chapter in this book. The relation of each individual to his or her community is at the core of Hardin's concept. Review some of the readings in other chapters, such as those on climate change, soil loss, and water scarcity, keeping in mind the idea of the individual and his or her relation to community. How should we as a society approach this "wicked" problem?

2. The readings in this chapter focus on people and our obligation to other humans. Readings in other chapters focus on the natural world, its resources, and our use of those resources. Using material or examples from other chapters, develop a visual—a diagram, chart, cartoon, collage, etc.—that helps people see the connection between our use of natural resources and our obligation to other people.

2

Trash: The Costs of Throwing "Stuff" Away

Ghana: digital dumping ground. Courtesy of Peter Klein, School of Journalism, University of British Columbia.

In almost any contemporary discussion of sustainability, you will hear the catch phrase "reduce, reuse, and recycle." Reducing the amount of resources you consume, reusing resources, and recycling resources when possible are part of "going green." Conserving resources applies to all the issues in this book, but it is especially appropriate to the question of trash. The story of "stuff," as Annie Leonard calls it (below), tells a narrative of waste, of hidden costs, and of ethics. As Gay Hawkins (below) writes, we live in a culture of "disposal, distance and denial" in which we put waste or trash not only out of sight and out of mind but also out of our economic, social, and ethical calculations. Most of us just don't think about it. Like many writers concerned with sustainability, the writers in this chapter are trying to change our "waste sensibilities." In Chapter 1, Aldo Leopold and Jared Diamond wrote about the human appreciation for nature and how sustainable living could enrich our lives. The readings in this chapter examine simple things that are everywhere in our daily lives—bottled water, clothes, electronic devices like cell phones and computers, even human waste—and they ask how these things link us to others. As Hawkins says, once you pay attention and notice these throwaway objects, you are placed in new networks of relationship. What we do, even in these simple actions, has consequences for others.

When we go shopping, most of us look at something like a new piece of electronics or a new piece of clothing and weigh just how much we want it and how much it costs. When an economist or engineer concerned with sustainability considers that object, he or she thinks about the "externalized costs" and about "life cycle analysis." If we examine an object from cradle to grave through its whole life cycle, we get a better picture of its real cost, its environmental impacts, and its effects on the people who make and dispose of our stuff. The children's movie "Wall·E" is a fantasy dystopia, an image of the worst-case scenario, that shows us a planetary trash-magedon. In "Wall·E" the culture of disposal, distance, and denial plays out to its extreme. The "Story of Stuff: Bottled Water" shows us how drinking bottled water became so popular and talks about the life cycle of plastic bottles. "High Tech Trash" shows us where computers go to die and the human costs of "e-waste" in vivid detail.

Life cycle analysis tends to be a technical analysis of energy, production costs, materials, and the costs of using and disposing of something. But as the readings about e-waste and the story of Kettleman City make plain, trash and waste are also a matter of environmental justice and of ethics. City planners and regulators talk about "NIMBY" or *Not In My Back Yard*. No one wants a toxic waste dump in their neighborhood or an incinerator next door. As some of these readings demonstrate, however, these dangerous and unwanted disposal sites where our trash all too often ends up are usually located in areas where the poor live or in developing countries where there are few if any regulations and safety standards to protect citizens from the toxic effects of disposal. The story of Kettleman City is a story of citizen action and democracy where a minority community triumphed over a huge international waste disposal company. But waste, like water, flows in the direction of least resistance and always away from power.

Trash involves complex technical and ethical issues, but few readers enjoy being preached at. Reading something too heavy-handed isn't pleasant and usually turns readers off. And making readers feel guilty is not a good rhetorical strategy; it rarely changes people's behavior. As you read these essays, think about how the writers get you to see the issue of trash and to care about the consequences. How do they use the first-person narrative to tell a story and, perhaps, get you to identify with them or the people in the story? How do vivid details of children foraging on garbage dumps appeal to your emotions and sense of decency? How do Annie Leonard's portrait of large corporations and her tone of voice make you feel about bottled water or computers that you have to replace every 18 months because they go out of date so fast? What's the best way to talk trash?

Annie Leonard
"The Story of Stuff: Electronics"

Annie Leonard co-created the Global Alliance for Incinerator Alternatives and is a member of the International Forum for Globalization and the Environmental Health Fund. In 2008, Leonard initiated the Story of Stuff Project, a collection of short, animated films that detail the complicated relationships between humans, their stuff, and the environment. These stories are available either in film or script version, and the script versions are supplemented with heavy footnotes to guide readers to additional information. The following piece is the script version of "The Story of Stuff: Electronics," which explores the massive environmental and human impacts that result from the design of modern electronics—designs that result in products with extremely short lifespans and, consequently, in a huge amount of electronics piling up in waste sites. Leonard contends that this "e-waste" has a high degree of toxicity, which threatens both the environment and the individuals involved in the maintenance of this e-waste. She concludes her piece by suggesting that a reconceptualization of the design of electronics, so as to maximize reusability and minimize the toxins involved in their production, is in order.

The other day, I couldn't find my computer charger. My computer is my lifeline to my work, my friends, my music.

So I looked everywhere, even in that drawer where this lives. I know you have one too, a tangle of old chargers, the sad remains of electronics past.

How did I end up with so many of these things? It's not like I'm always after the latest gadget. My old devices broke or became so obsolete I couldn't use them anymore. And not one of these old chargers fits my computer. Augh. This isn't just bad luck. It's bad design.[1] I call it "designed for the dump."

5   "Designed for the dump" sounds crazy, right? But when you're trying to sell lots of stuff, it makes perfect sense. It's a key strategy of the companies that make our electronics.[2] In fact it's a key part of our whole unsustainable materials economy.

> "Today's electronics are hard to upgrade, easy to break, and impractical to repair."

Designed for the dump means making stuff to be thrown away quickly. Today's electronics are hard to upgrade, easy to break, and impractical to repair. My DVD player broke and I took it to a shop to get fixed. The repair guy wanted $50 just to look at it! A new one at Target costs $39.[3]

In the 1960s, Gordon Moore, the giant brain and semiconductor pioneer, predicted that electronics designers could double processor speed every 18 months. So far he's been right. This is called Moore's Law.[4] But somehow the bosses of these genius designers got it all twisted up. They seem to think Moore's Law means every 18 months we have to throw out our old electronics and buy more.

Problem is, the 18 months that we use these things are just a blip in their entire lifecycle. And that's where these dump designers aren't just causing a pain in our wallets. They're creating a global toxic emergency!

See, electronics start where most stuff starts, in mines[5] and factories. Many of our gadgets are made from more than 1,000 different materials, shipped from around the world to assembly plants.[6]

There, workers turn them into products, using loads of toxic chemicals, like PVC, mercury, solvents and flame retardants.[7]

Today this usually happens in far off places that are hard to monitor.[8]   10 But it used to happen near my home, in Silicon Valley, which thanks to the electronics industry is one of the most poisoned communities in the U.S.[9]

IBM's own data revealed that its workers making computer chips had 40% more miscarriages and were significantly more likely to die from blood, brain and kidney cancer.[10] The same thing is starting to happen all around the world.[11] Turns out the high tech industry isn't as clean as its image.

So, after its toxic trip around the globe, the gadget lands in my hands. I love it for a year or so and then it starts drifting further from its place of honor on my desk or in my pocket. Maybe it spends a little time in my garage before being tossed out.[12]

And that brings us to disposal, which we think of as the end of its life. But really it's just moved on to become part of the mountains of e-waste we make every year.[13]

Remember how these devices were packed with toxic chemicals? Well there's a simple rule of production: toxics in, toxics out. Computers, cell phones, TVs, all this stuff, is just waiting to release all their toxics when we throw them away. Some of them are slowly releasing this stuff even while we're using them.[14] You know those fat, old TVs that people are chucking for high-def flat screens? They each have about 5 pounds of lead in them.[15] Lead! As in lead poisoning![16]

15   So almost all this e-waste either goes from my garage to a landfill or it gets shipped overseas to the garage workshop of some guy in Guiya, China whose job it is to recycle it.[17]

I've visited a bunch of these so-called recycling operations. Workers, without protective gear, sit on the ground, smashing open electronics to recover the valuable metals inside and chucking or burning the parts no one will pay them for. So while I'm on to my next gadget, my last gadget is off poisoning families. In Guida or India or Nigeria.

Each year we make 25 million tonnes of e-waste which gets dumped, burned or recycled.[18] And that recycling is anything but green. So are the geniuses who design these electronics actually . . . evil geniuses? I don't think so, because the problems they're creating are well hidden even from them.

You see, the companies they work for keep these human and environmental costs out of sight and off their accounting books. It's all about externalizing the true costs of production.[19] Instead of companies paying to make their facilities safe the workers pay with their health. Instead of them paying to redesign using less toxics villagers pay by losing their clean drinking water. Externalizing costs allows companies to keep designing for the dump—they get the profits and everyone else pays.

When we go along with it, it's like we're looking at this toxic mess and saying to companies "you made it, but we'll deal with it." I've got a better idea. How about "you made it, you deal with it"? Doesn't that make more sense?

20   Imagine that instead of all this toxic e-waste piling up in our garages and the streets of Guiyu, we sent it to the garages of the CEOs who made it. You can bet that they'd be on the phone to their designers demanding they stop designing for the dump.

Making companies deal with their e-waste is called Extended Producer Responsibility or Product Takeback.[20] If all these old gadgets were their problem, it would be cheaper for them to just design longer lasting, less toxic, and more recyclable products in the first place. They could even make them modular, so that when one part broke, they could just send us a new piece, instead of taking back the whole broken mess.[21]

Already takeback laws are popping up all over Europe and Asia.[22] In the U.S. many cities and states are passing similar laws—these need to be protected and strengthened.[23]

It's time to get these brainiacs working on our side. With takeback laws and citizen action to demand greener products, we are starting a race to the top, where designers compete to make long-lasting, toxic-free products. So, let's have a green Moore's law. How about: the use of toxic chemicals will be cut in half every 18 months? The number of workers poisoned will decline at an even faster rate?

We need to give these designers a challenge they can rise to and do what they do best—innovate. Already, some of them are realizing they're too smart to be dump designers and are figuring out how to make computers without PVC or toxic flame retardants.[24] Good job guys.

But we can do even more.   25

When we take our e-waste to recyclers, we can make sure they don't export it to developing countries.[25] And when we do need to buy new gadgets, we can choose greener products.[26]

But the truth is: we are never going to just shop our way out of this problem because the choices available to us at the store are limited by choices of designers and policymakers outside of the store. That's why we need to join with others to demand stronger laws on toxic chemicals and on banning e-waste exports.[27]

There are billions of people out there who want access to the incredible web of information and entertainment electronics offer. But it's the access they want, not all that toxic garbage. So let's get our brains working on sending that old design for the dump mentality to the dump where it belongs and instead building an electronics industry and a global society that's designed to last.

NOTES

1. It may seem crazy, but many of these products are actually designed to break after a certain amount of time. This concept is known as "planned obsolescence" or "designed for the dump." Planned obsolescence is designing and producing products with limited lifespans—so that they stop functioning or become undesirable within a specific time period. And it isn't just electronics, products may be designed for obsolescence either through function, like a paper coffee cup or a machine with breakable parts, or through "desirability," like a piece of clothing made for this year's fashion and then replaced by something totally different next year.

2. For many years, designers and consumers have advocated for electronic products that are truly modular, so that consumers can simply swap one "obsolete" part for a newer part without having to discard an entire product. While there has been some progress in this regard, such as hard drives and disk drives that are easier to replace, electronics companies have been wary of the "modular model" since they prefer to sell new, whole units. Likewise, many

have advocated for a "thin client" model of information delivery, where consumers access data on the Internet—or "the cloud"—using quite simple hardware and software, but again, the large computer companies often see this model as a threat to their commodity sales. For more information, see http://www.geek.com/articles/chips/fully-modular-computers-20040312/ and http://www.computerweekly.com/Articles/2008/09/01/232086/Thin-client-computing-smartens-up.htm

3. And it's not just DVD players—it's this way with all sorts of electronic gadgets. Think about that printer cartridge replacement that costs more than a new printer, the iPod battery that you can't replace, the cell phone charger that snaps. The list of electronics that are prohibitively expensive to upgrade or just plain impossible to repair goes on and on.

4. Moore's Law is named after Intel co-founder Gordon Moore. In 1965, he stated that the number of transistors that can be placed on a computer chip will double every year. This translates into increases in processor speed, more memory, and other performance improvements. In 1975, Moore revised it to doubling every 2 years. Over time, the concept was shortened from 2 years to 18 months by others at Intel. This trend has continued for over 40 years. To learn more check out: ftp://download.intel.com/museum/Moores_Law/Video-transcripts/Excepts_A_Conversation_with_Gordon_Moore.pdf

5. Most of our electronics contain precious metals and minerals, some of which are referred to as "conflict minerals." A particularly egregious example is coltan—or columbite-tantalite—a metallic ore that gets refined into tantalum, as well as tin, tungsten, and gold, all used in consumer electronics such as cell phones, DVD players, computers, and games consoles. The extraction and export of these four minerals from Africa have helped fuel environmental and social disruption, brutal violence and war in the Congo. See: http://www.nytimes.com/2010/06/27/opinion/27kristof.html?_r=2 and http://www.youtube.com/enoughproject#p/a/u/0/5Ycih_jMObQ

6. Over 1,000 materials, including solvents, brominated flame retardants, PVC, heavy metals, plastics and gases, are used to make electronic products and their components—semiconductor chips, circuit boards, and disk drives. A clunky CRT monitor can contain between four and eight pounds of lead alone (see Footnote 15). Big screen CRT TVs contain even more than that. Flat panel TVs and monitors contain less lead, but use lamps with mercury, which is very toxic in very small quantities. An EPA commissioned study noted that "approximately 70 percent of the heavy metals in municipal solid waste landfills are estimated to come from electronics discards. Heavy metals such as lead and mercury are highly toxic substances that can cause well documented adverse health effects, particularly to children and developing fetuses." http://www.epa.gov/oig/reports/2004/20040901-2004-P-00028.pdf

These toxicants are released during the production, use, and disposal of electronic products, with the greatest impact at end-of-life, particularly when they are exported to developing nations. Harmful chemicals released from incinerators and leached from landfills can contaminate air and groundwater. The burning of plastics at the waste stage releases dioxins and furans, known developmental and reproductive toxins that persist in the environment and concentrate up the food-chain. Some of the worst end-of-life toxic impacts occur when e-waste is exported to developing nations, where crude, unsafe "processing" methods result in significant exposures. The plastics are burned in uncontrolled outdoor waste piles, emitting dioxin into residential areas; circuit boards are "cooked" to melt the lead solder, emitting toxic lead fumes; and acids are used to extract precious metals. http://www.ban.org/E-Waste/technotrashfinalcomp.pdf

During the use phase, electronics can off-gas brominated flame retardants (BFRs), a group of toxic chemicals added to plastic casings. To read specifically on BFRs, see Footnote 14.

The production phase of electronics is the most chemically intensive, particularly in the manufacture of semiconductors and other components, which use very toxic solvents such as methylene chloride, toluene, glycol ethers, xylene and trichloroethylene (TCE), which have been linked to elevated rates of cancers, including blood cancers, brain cancers, reproductive problems and birth defects among electronics workers and their offspring. http://www.ehjournal .net/content/5/1/30

7. See Footnote 6 and http://www.electronicstakeback.com/problem/toxics_ problem.htm

8. Most electronics are manufactured in Asia, not by the companies whose brand names you know and go on the products, but by many contract manufacturing firms, sometimes called Electronics Manufacturing Services. Some of the largest of these include Foxconn, Flextronics, Quanta, Sanmina-SCI, Solectron, Celestica, and Jabil Circuit. There are also thousands of component manufacturers that make the individual components that get assembled into the final products. It's practically impossible for any brand name company to provide any significant oversight of the workplace or environmental conditions in this complex supply chain. Many companies in the electronics industry support a voluntary code of conduct for workplace and environmental conditions, created by a group called the Electronics Industry Citizenship Coalition, or EICC. But working conditions at contract giant Foxconn's plant in Shenzen, China, are so bad that 13 employees committed suicide in 2010 alone; mostly by jumping from the windows of the plant or dormitories. The company's response was to install "anti-suicide nets" around the plant. http://www.dailytech.com/Report+Only+Escape+From+ Hellish+Apple+iPhone+Factory+Was+Suicide/article18428.htm http://www .law.stanford.edu/publications/stanford_lawyer/issues/79/pdfs/sl79_kinks.pdf http://ehstoday.com/mag/ehs_imp_70124/ http://www.nytimes.com/2010/ 06/07/business/global/07suicide.html http://www.todayonline.com/World/ EDC101013-0000091/New-allegations-against-Foxconn

9. When the semiconductor industry emerged in the 1970's in Silicon Valley, it was touted as a new, clean industry. But over time, it came to light that these

companies were using very toxic chemicals, like the solvent TCE, to produce computer chips. These chemicals were sometimes dumped, or leaked out of underground storage tanks, into the groundwater. The polluted water led to exposure of the surrounding communities and resulted in miscarriages and birth defects. Now, most of these companies have moved their production off-shore to developing nations, leaving behind polluted "Superfund" sites that will cost millions to clean up. Silicon Valley is home to 29 toxic EPA "Super-fund" sites—the highest concentration in the country. The Silicon Valley Toxics Coalition (SVTC) has a map of the sites at http://www.svtc.org/site/PageServer?pagename=svtc_ silicon_valley_toxic_tour.

10. For decades IBM kept its own Corporate Mortality File (CMF), a concealed database tracking cause of death of all its employees. IBM workers were unaware of the CMF or what was in it until a lawsuit by IBM workers led to its release in 2000. Dr. Richard Clapp, from the Boston University School of Public Health, analyzed the data, and concluded that IBM workers involved in manufacturing (where they were exposed to solvents and other chemicals) have an increased risk of dying of cancer, especially cancers of the brain, blood, and kidneys.

Over 300 IBM workers in the US, who were exposed to toxic chemicals at work, sued IBM and its chemical suppliers alleging their chemical expo-sures caused cancers, birth defects in offspring, and other chronic diseases. All but two of these claims were settled prior to trial under confidentiality orders that were insisted upon by IBM and the chemical companies.

Two claims went to trial by IBM workers sick with cancer. Despite the fact that the trial was about fraudulent concealment claims, the judge did not allow the jury to hear any mention of IBM's Corporate Mortality File, let alone Dr. Clapp's analysis of its contents. The trial ended with no finding at all on the cause of the two workers' cancers. To read Dr. Clapp's report see: "Mortality among US employees of a large computer manufacturing company: 1969–2001", Dr. Richard Clapp, 19 Oct 2006, http://www.ehjournal.net/content/5/1/30 Also see: http://www.nyupress.org/product_info.php?products_id=3002 and http://www.salon.com/technology/feature/2001/07/30/almaden1

11. Attending a recent meeting on occupational health and safety issues in Asia, science writer Elizabeth Grossman described the following scene:

Women from China who have worked at a plant assembling cell phones— producing as many as 300 to 400 an hour—report that miscarriages and men-strual problems are common among their colleagues. We hear the same from Indonesian and Korean women. Similar stories come from the Philippines. Men who work in factories assembling automotive electronics and DVD players report co-workers who have died of cancer—lung cancer and brain tumors. Two young Indonesian women who work in electronics factories ask me if chemicals related to their work or perhaps to the "instant food" they all eat may have caused their co-workers' breast cancers. Occupational health advocates working on behalf of Samsung workers in Korea have now documented 96 cases of cancer—about a third of these fatal—among employees of the company's semiconductor plants. Many of these are young people. To read the full article see http://scienceblogs .com/thepumphandle/2010/08/apha_ohs_section_awards_honor.php

12. Consumers typically use cell phones for an average of 18 months before disposing of them, a much shorter period than the lifecycle of older phones. See http://www.enviroliteracy.org/article.php/1119. html

    And the situation isn't much different with computers. According to the EPA, laptops are used for only 2 to 3 years by the initial purchasers. See page 22 of http://www.epa.gov/wastes/conserve/materials/ecycling/docs/app-2.pdf

13. In the US alone, we chuck over 400 million electronic gadgets in a single year and that number is continuing to grow. See http://www.electronicstakeback .com/problem/problem_index2.htm

14. Brominated flame retardants (BFRs) are in a considerable percentage of electronics. A 2005 report released by Health Care Without Harm called Brominated Flame Retardants: Rising Levels of Concern, has this to say:

    Whereas flame resistant products save lives and prevent property damage, there are increasing concerns about the environmental and health effects of flame retardants such as BFRs. Overall, the available literature on BFR toxicology is incomplete. Based on the available data, however, we know that BFRs are associated with several health effects in animal studies, including neurobehavioral toxicity, thyroid hormone disruption, and possibly cancer. Additionally, there are data gaps but some evidence that BFRs can cause developmental effects, endocrine disruption, immunotoxicity, reproductive, and long-term effects, including second-generation effects. http://www.noharm.org/lib/downloads/bfrs/ BFRs_Rising_Concern.pdf

    We are exposed to BFRs in many ways. We ingest it via meat and dairy products, where it's been absorbed into the food chain and is found widely in the environment and animal tissues. Also, many studies have found BFRs in samples of household dust and indoor air, suggesting that some of the BFRs found in our bodies comes from inhaling it in dust. Because BFRs are used in multiple products, such as electronics, furniture and textiles, some studies have not attributed each product's contribution to the totals found.

    - One dust study in Indonesia found that BFR levels were higher in living rooms with computers than in living rooms without computers: http:// www.terrapub.co.jp/onlineproceedings/ec/02/pdf/ERA15.pdf

    - Another study was able to associate the high levels of one type of BFR (deca-BDE) in dust collected in certain homes with the same BFR found in televisions in those homes: http://pubs.acs.org /doi/abs/10.1021/es702964a

    - And in the lab, electronics have been determined to emit flame retardants, with emissions increasing as much as 500 times as the temperature increased: http://bit.ly/cZHSlG

    - To read more about BFRs in dust see the following papers by EWG and SVTC: http://www.ewg.org/reports/inthedust and http://www.svtc .org/site/PageServer?pagename=svtc_bfrs_in_electronics

15. Old-style TVs and computers contain a large glass Cathode Ray Tube (CRT). The glass contains lead, both to shield against radiation and to improve the optical quality of the picture, and it does a lot of other nasty things too (see Footnote 16). Also, it's not just old TVs and computers, lead is present in

solder used in many electronic products. To learn more check out: http://computer.howstuffworks.com/question678.htm

16. Lead exposure can cause many health effects, particularly damage to the nervous system. Kids are especially vulnerable to lead exposures, which can cause brain damage and death at high levels. Studies link lead exposure in children to lower IQs, higher incidents of ADHD, hearing and balance problems. http://www.atsdr.cdc.gov/csem/lead/pbphysiologic_effects2.html

17. E-waste is growing two to three times faster than other types of municipal waste. While most e-waste in the US still goes into the trash, the amount going to recyclers is increasing. However, 50 to 80 percent of the e-waste that is collected by recyclers is shipped overseas to developing countries in Asia and Africa where our outdated electronics are creating a global toxic emergency. Once exported, e-waste is typically smashed and burned in backyard operations with little to no health and safety precautions. The burning and dismantling of toxic electronic products under these conditions has led to widespread air and water pollution from toxic metals, dioxins, and other serious health hazards. Scientists have documented high levels of these pollutants in the local environments, and they have also found them in test samples from children and other residents of these communities. For example, health researchers showed that children living in Guiyu had significantly higher blood lead levels than those living in another community that was not polluted from e-waste. http://www.ban.org/E-Waste/technotrashfinalcomp.pdf http://www.ban.org/Library/TheDigitalDump.pdf http://www.ncbi.nlm.ih.gov/pmc/articles/PMC1913570 http://www.mitpressjournals.org/doi/abs/10.1162/glep.2004.4.4.76 http://www.gao.gov/new.items/d081044.pdf http://ngm.nationalgeographic.com/geopedia/E-Waste http://www.svtc.org/site/PageServer?pagename=citizensatrisk

18. 25 million metric tonnes per year or, in US measurement, roughly 27 tons. http://www.greenpeace.org/international/Global/international/planet-2/report/2010/2/toxic-transformers-briefing.pdf

19. Externalized costs, also known as "hidden costs," are any kind of loss or damage such as illness, environmental degradation, or economic disruption caused by industries engaged in natural resource extraction, production, distribution, and disposal, but not paid for by those industries. Externalized costs are most often borne by workers, community members and the environment, rather than by industries and corporations.

20. Extended Producer Responsibility (EPR, also called "Producer Takeback") is a product and waste management system in which manufacturers—not the consumer or government—take responsibility for the collection and environmentally safe management of their product when it is no longer useful or is discarded. When manufacturers take responsibility for the recycling of their own products they no longer pass the cost of disposal on to the government and taxpayer, but build it into the price of the product (internalizing the cost). This gives them a financial incentive to use environmentally safer

materials in the production process; design the product to be more recyclable; create safer recycling systems; and to keep waste costs down. http://www .electronicstakeback.com/legislation/about_epr.htm http://www.electronics takeback.com/legislation/about_epr.htm http://www.miller-mccune.com/ business-economics/the-smoldering-trash-revolt-7306

21. There are two ways in which modularity would be really helpful—for repairs and for upgrades. There has been some headway made in this arena, but we still have a long way to go. Electronics manufacturer ASUS developed a proto- type for a modular computer a few years ago, that was like a shelf onto which you stack modules (hard drive, battery, card reader, etc.) the size of CDs. But the parts—motherboards, CPU's, energy supplies—that would need to be upgraded to keep up with technology—like new software, faster processors, energy savings—were not designed to be simple to replace for average com- puter user (making it a computer-geek-only option).

 Currently, the release of a new operating system is what prompts many PC users to purchase their next computer, since the existing design of these electronics makes it easier to replace an entire computer rather than upgrading it. Adopting modular design elements that make it easy to upgrade a computer in order to keep up with advancing technology would exponentially prolong its lifespan and keep these electronics out of the dump and on our desks.

22. Europe has led the way with the passage of the Waste Electrical and Electronic Directive in 2003, which established the first major takeback requirements throughout Europe. Other countries have followed suit, including Japan and China. http://ec.europa.eu/environment/waste/weee/index_en.htm

23. Twenty-three states have already passed e-waste legislation and New York City passed an e-waste law but it was recently pre-empted by a statewide law in New York. To see an updated list of states with e-waste legislation, check out: http://www.electronicstakeback.com/legislation/state_legislation.htm   and http://www.electronicstakeback.com/index.htm

24. Some leading companies have been working with their suppliers to find safer alternatives to bromine and chlorine. High volume uses of bromine and chlo- rine in flame retardants and plastic resins like polyvinyl chloride (PVC) gained worldwide attention when scientific studies documented their link to the formation of dioxin, one of the most toxic chemicals around. Dioxins and other harmful chemicals are released into the environment during the burn- ing and smelting of electronic waste. Even the most sophisticated incineration facilities generate low levels of dioxin, but the most significant dioxin contri- bution occurs in developing countries whose facilities are not designed to handle toxic materials.

 Apple has phased out the use of brominated and chlorinated flame retar- dants, in addition to PVC, mercury, arsenic, and lead. All new models of Nokia mobile phones are free of PVC, brominated and chlorinated com- pounds and antimony trioxide. New Sony Ericsson products are 99.9% free from all halogenated flame retardants. For more resources, see Footnote 26.

25. To ensure that your e-waste is recycled responsibly and not exported overseas, make sure that your recycler is a certified E-Steward. E-Stewards are recyclers who voluntarily adhere to the highest standards in the recycling industry: not to export e-waste to developing nations, not to send it to prison recycling, not to landfill/incinerate it. This program was developed by the non-profit Basel Action Network (BAN) as a voluntary pledge program—but it has recently been expanded into a rigorous certification program, with independent, accredited auditors. To find an E-Steward in your area go to: http://e-stewards.org/.

26. Two good sources to use are the Greenpeace Guide to Greener Electronics, and the ETBC Recycling report card, which grades companies on their efforts to take back and recycle their old products. http://www.electronicstakeback .com/reportcard.htm http://www.greenpeace.org/international/en/campaigns/ toxics/electronics/Guide-to-Greener-Electronics/

27. On the road to cleaner, greener electronics legislation Europe has taken an important step with the passage of the REACH (Registration, Evaluation, Authorisation and Restriction of Chemicals) law. REACH puts the burden on the chemical producers and users to provide and share data about chemical hazards. http://www.chemsec.org/get-informed/eu-chemicals/reach

There was additional progress made with the passage of the Restriction on Hazardous Substances (ROHS) in Europe, which limits the use of six substances in electronic products sold into the EU. But the follow up legislation to expand the list of restricted substances was less successful due to industry opposition. http://www.chemsec.org/images/stories/publications/ChemSec_ publications/100602_ RoHS_vote_Press_Release.pdf

But the US is lagging behind, as there is very inadequate oversight, required testing, or disclosure of toxic chemicals in electronics or most other products in the US. Under our current laws, chemical companies can introduce and sell chemicals in the marketplace, and it's up to the EPA to "prove" when the chemicals are unsafe and shouldn't be sold. This puts all the burden of testing and research on the government, instead of the companies selling the chemicals. It also means that it's hard for manufacturers to find out the hazardous traits of chemicals they use in products.

We need to adopt a more sensible approach to toxic chemical policy, where companies have to prove their chemicals are safe before they put them into products that go into our homes and schools. Some members of Congress are trying to change that by reforming the Toxic Substances Control Act (TSCA)—our primary federal law on toxics. See http://www.nytimes.com/ gwire/2010/04/15/15greenwire-sen-lautenberg-introduces-chemicals-reform-bil-25266.html and http://healthreport.saferchemicals.org/.

Other signs of hope include a new bill to outlaw the export of hazardous e-waste that has been introduced in the US Congress, H.R. 6252, The Responsible

Electronics Recycling Act. For more information, see http://www.electronic stakeback.com/legislation/summary_HR6252.htm

And at the state level, California is establishing Green Chemicals program, http://coeh.berkeley.edu/greenchemistry/

Analyze

1. What does this author mean by the phrase "designed for the dump"? What does she describe as the purpose for "designing for the dump"?
2. What are "takeback laws" and why does Leonard like them?
3. We usually think of Silicon Valley as a place of wealth and happiness. How does Leonard see Silicon Valley?

Explore

1. In a group, discuss whether or not you think the idea of sustainable electronics is realistic. Create a list of electronics that you use and buy that could be designed more sustainably. Imagine and discuss the changes in manufacturing and purchasing that would be required for this to happen. Are there any commonly purchased electronics that you cannot imagine this type of change for?
2. This author talks about serious issues—toxic chemicals, health hazards— and gives disturbing statistics, but she writes throughout the piece in a personal tone. In fact, the author begins the piece by saying, "The other day, I couldn't find my computer charger" and includes phrases like "Augh" in the story. As a class, talk about the effect that this rhetorical choice has on the way the piece comes across to the reader. Does the casual tone take away from the seriousness of the issues? Or, in contrast, does the author's choice in tone make the issues seem more accessible or immediate to the reader? Why or why not?
3. Working in groups, identify a piece of electronics you all use or have and research its life cycle. See how far back towards its origins you can go and how far forward toward its disposal or "afterlife"—the life it has as e-waste. Develop a visual "map" of the life cycle of the electronic device and identify the environmental, ecological, and social "costs" at each stage.

Annie Leonard
"The Story of Stuff: Bottled Water"

The following piece is another text from Annie Leonard's Story of Stuff project. This essay, which documents the life cycle of bottled water, demonstrates that bottled water, contrary to the heavily funded marketing campaigns of several bottled water producers, often is less pure than tap water. Furthermore, the overproduction and overuse of bottled water results in far-reaching environmental problems, particularly in the disposal of the bottles themselves. Leonard points out that the attack on the quality and taste of tap water has largely been spearheaded by those who stand to gain from a decline in the use of tap water. As such, her essay highlights the intersection between environmental considerations and corporate concerns. As you read, think about the questions Leonard raises about recycling plastics and the consequences for what it means to "go green."

One of the problems with trying to use less stuff is that sometimes we feel like we really need it. What if you live in a city like, say, Cleveland and you want a glass of water? Are you going to take your chances and get it from the city tap? Or should you reach for a bottle of water that comes from the pristine rainforests of . . . Fiji?

Well, Fiji brand water thought the answer to this question was obvious. So they built a whole ad campaign around it. It turned out to be one of the dumbest moves in advertising history.[1]

See the city of Cleveland didn't like being the butt of Fiji's joke so they did some tests and guess what? These tests showed a glass of Fiji water is lower quality, it loses taste tests against Cleveland tap and costs thousands of times more.[2]

This story is typical of what happens when you test bottled water against tap water.

5   Is it cleaner? Sometimes, sometimes not: in many ways, bottled water is less regulated than tap.[3]

Is it tastier? In taste tests across the country, people consistently choose tap over bottled water.[4]

These bottled water companies say they're just meeting consumer demand—But who would demand a less sustainable, less tasty, way more expensive product, especially one you can get almost free in your kitchen? Bottled water costs about 2000 times more than tap water.[5] Can you imagine paying 2000 times the price of anything else? How about a $10,000 sandwich?

Yet people in the U.S. buy more than half a billion bottles of water every week. That's enough to circle the globe more than 5 times.[6] How did this come to be? Well it all goes back to how our materials economy works and one of its key drivers which is known as manufactured demand.[7]

If companies want to keep growing, they have to keep selling more and more stuff. In the 1970s giant soft drink companies got worried as their growth projections started to level off.[8] There's only so much soda a person can drink. Plus it wouldn't be long before people began realizing that soda is not that healthy and turned back to—gasp—drinking tap water.

Well, the companies found their next big idea in a silly designer product that most people laughed at as a passing yuppie fad.[9] Water is free, people said back then, what will they sell us next, air?[10]

So how do you get people to buy this fringe product? Simple: You manufacture demand. How do you do that? Well, imagine you're in charge of a bottled water company.

Since people aren't lining up to trade their hard earned money for your unnecessary product, you make them feel scared and insecure if they *don't* have it.[11] And that's exactly what the bottled water industry did. One of their first marketing tactics was to scare people about tap water, with ads like Fiji's Cleveland campaign.

"When we're done," one top water exec said, "tap water will be relegated to showers and washing dishes."[12]

Next, you hide the reality of your product behind images of pure fantasy. Have you ever noticed how bottled water tries to seduce us with pictures of mountains, streams, and pristine nature? But guess where a third of all bottled water in the U.S. actually comes from? The tap! Pepsi's Aquafina and Coke's Dasani are two of the many brands that are really filtered tap water.[13]

But the pristine nature lie goes much deeper. In a recent full page ad, Nestlé said: "bottled water is the most environmentally responsible consumer product in the world."[14] *What?!*

They're trashing the environment all along the product's life cycle. Exactly how is that environmentally responsible?

The problems start here with extraction and production where oil is used to make water bottles.[15] Each year, making the plastic water bottles used in the U.S. takes enough oil and energy to fuel a million cars.[16]

All that energy spent to make the bottle, even more to ship it around the planet, and then we drink it in about 2 minutes?[17] That brings us to the big problem at the other end of the life cycle—disposal.

What happens to all these bottles when we're done? Eighty percent end up in landfills, where they will sit for thousands of years,[18] or in incinerators, where they are burned, releasing toxic pollution.[19] The rest gets collected for recycling.

20   I was curious about where the plastic bottles that I put in recycling bins go. I found out that shiploads were being sent to India.[20] So, I went there. I'll never forget riding over a hill outside Madras where I came face to face with a mountain of plastic bottles from California. Real recycling would turn these bottles back into bottles. But that wasn't what was happening here. Instead, these bottles were slated to be downcycled,[21] which means turning them into lower quality products that would just be chucked later. The parts that couldn't be downcycled were thrown away there; shipped all the way to India just to be dumped in someone else's backyard.

If bottled water companies want to use mountains on their labels, it'd be more accurate to show one of those mountains of plastic waste.

Scaring us, seducing us, and misleading us—these strategies are all core parts of manufacturing demand.

Once they've manufactured all this demand, creating a new multibillion dollar market,[22] they defend it by beating out the competition. But in this case, the competition is our basic human right to clean, safe drinking water.[23]

Pepsi's Vice Chairman publicly said "the biggest enemy is tap water!"[24] They want us to think it's dirty and bottled water is the best alternative.

25   In many places, public water *is* polluted thanks to polluting industries like the plastic bottle industry![25] And these bottled water guys are all too happy to offer their expensive solution[26] which keeps us hooked on their product.

It's time we took back the tap.

That starts with making a personal commitment to not buy or drink bottled water unless the water in your community is truly unhealthy.[27] Yes, it takes a bit of foresight to grab a reusable bottle[28] on the way out, but I think we can handle it.

Then take the next step—join a campaign that's working for real solutions. Like demanding investment in clean tap water for all. In the US, tap water is underfunded by $24 billion[29] partly because people believe drinking water only comes from a bottle! Around the world, a billion people don't have access to clean water right now.[30] Yet cities all over are spending millions of dollars to deal with all the plastic bottles we throw out.[31] What if we spent that money improving our water systems or better yet, preventing pollution to begin with?

There are many more things we can do to solve this problem. Lobby your city officials to bring back drinking fountains.[32] Work to ban the purchase of bottled water by your school, organization or entire city.[33]

This is a huge opportunity for millions of people to wake up and protect our wallets, our health, and the planet. The good news is: it's already started.   30

Bottled water sales have begun to drop[34] while business is booming for safe refillable water bottles.[35] Yay!

Restaurants are proudly serving "tap"[36] and people are choosing to pocket the hundred or thousands of dollars they would otherwise be wasting on bottled water. Carrying bottled water is on its way to being as cool as smoking while pregnant. We know better now.

The bottled water industry is getting worried because the jig is up. We're not buying into their manufactured demand anymore. We'll choose our own demands, thank you very much, and we're demanding clean safe water for all.

NOTES

1. Fiji's ad ran in national magazines with the tagline, "The label says Fiji because it's not bottled in Cleveland," and as you'd expect, the city of Cleveland was not happy. CNNMoney.com ranked it #20 in their 101 Dumbest Moments in Business. To be fair, Fiji president Edward Cochran grew up near Cleveland, and said, "It is only a joke. We had to pick some town." But actually, Fiji, you didn't have to pick on some town. Picking on our public water systems isn't cool. Why don't you go beat up a hospital?

2. After seeing the offensive ad, Cleveland's public utilities director Julius Ciaccia decided to put the two waters to the test; according to the Associated Press, the results found 6.31 micrograms of arsenic per liter in the Fiji bottle. Cleveland tap water, on the other hand, had no measurable arsenic. After safety comes taste: Cleveland's NewsChannel5 held a blind taste test. The result? Testers preferred Cleveland water. "I never had Fiji Water. I thought Cleveland was much more refreshing," one tennis player told reporters. "Just not as good as I thought it would be and not worth the price," one man said.

3. Municipal water in the U.S. is regulated by the Environmental Protection Agency, which does frequent testing, as do local authorities. The federal Safe Drinking Water Act empowers EPA to require water testing by certified laboratories and that violations be reported within a specified time frame. Public water systems must also provide reports to customers about their water, noting its source, evidence of contaminants and compliance with regulations.

The Food and Drug Administration, on the other hand, regulates bottled water as a food and cannot require certified lab testing or violation reporting. FDA monitors the labeling of bottled water, but the bottlers themselves are responsible for testing—kind of like the fox guarding the henhouse. Furthermore, FDA doesn't require bottled water companies to disclose where the water came from, how it was treated or what contaminants it contains. For a good article on the topic, see The New York Times, "Fewer Regulations for Bottled Water Than Tap, GAO Says," at http://www.nytimes.com/gwire/2009/07/09greenwire-fewer-regulations-for-bottled-water-than-tap-g-33331.html

In a survey of 188 brands of bottled water, the Environmental Working Group (EWG) found only two providing such information about its product to consumers. Based on extensive research and testing, EWG developed a "bottled water scorecard" where you can compare brands, and learn more about the process of testing, labeling, and marketing bottled water: http://www.ewg.org/health/report/bottledwater-scorecard-summary

4. In February, 2006, The New York Times submitted six bottled waters (a mix of domestic and imported, natural and purified) and one sample of New York City tap water for chemical analysis. Minerals like magnesium, calcium and even arsenic in trace amounts are expected in water, and nothing out of the ordinary turned up. In a bacteriological examination, six came back with results well within the parameters defined by the EPA. But one bottled spring water showed much higher levels of unspecified bacteria and was labeled "substandard for drinking water." Because only one bottle was tested, the brand was not named.

The Times then brought in its heavy hitters: the Restaurant Reviewers. In a blind tasting, The Times Dining staff sampled nine still waters: New York tap; Biota, a new Colorado spring water in a biodegradable bottle; Poland Spring from Maine; Aquafina, from Pepsi, the country's best seller; Dasani, from Coca-Cola; Saratoga, a natural mineral water from upstate New York; Smartwater, "vapor-distilled and electrolyte-enhanced"; Fiji, artesian water from the South Pacific (artesian water comes from a deep underground source, such as an aquifer, that has no contact with surface air); and Penta, an "ultra-premium" water. None was universally disliked.

"We found that we were able to distinguish among two main types of water," says the New York Times report. Natural spring, mineral and artesian waters, which have "a velvety feel across the tongue and a slightly flatter flavor," and "purified waters, including tap water."

Corporate Accountability International's "Think Outside the Bottle" Campaign has held countless taste tests comparing bottled water to tap water, and the results generally favor the tap. But ultimately, the point isn't whether one tastes better than the other—it's how our taste, and our tastes, are shaped by advertising, rather than by what's good for us.

5. The consumer advocacy group Food & Water Watch offers this assessment, from their Take Back the Tap report (http://www.foodandwaterwatch.org/water/pubs/reports/take-back-the-tap): "A quick calculation comparing the average cost of one gallon of tap water to one gallon of commercial bottled water comes out to: **Tap water:** $0.002 per gallon. **Bottled water:** Ranges from $0.89 to $8.26 per gallon." Here's how they break this out: "Pepsi's Aquafina brand, which is nothing more than tap water further purified, registered $425.7 million in sales in 2005, followed by Coca-Cola's Dasani bottled tap water with a sales tally of $346.1 million. Meanwhile, Nestlé's Poland Spring brand, which does come from spring sources, rang up sales of $199.7 million. That all pencils out to bottled water costing consumers 240 to 10,000 times more per gallon than tap water that is as good, or better, and far more monitored." Fortune magazine writer Marc Gunther paid $1.57 for a 20-ounce bottle of Aquafina, Pepsi's bottled tap water, and spent $3.05 for one gallon (128 ounces) of gas. A bit of math shows that his bottled water bill amounted to $10.05 per gallon: big profits for the bottlers. By comparison, most Americans pay about $2 per 1,000 gallons for municipal water service.

6. In the intro to his book, *Bottled and Sold: The Story Behind Our Obsession with Bottled Water* (2010), Peter Gleick offers the figures like this: ". . . every second of every day in the United States, a thousand people buy and open up a plastic bottle of commercially produced water, and every second of every day in the United States, a thousand plastic bottles are thrown away. Eighty-five million bottles a day. More than thirty billion bottles a year at a cost to consumers of tens of billions of dollars."

To get back to Annie's number, that eighty-five million bottles a day, times seven days a week, gives us 595 million bottles a week. We asked the experts to do a little more math for us, and here's what they came up with: Renee Sharp, Director of the California Office of Environmental Working Group, offered the following calculation: "Assuming each bottle is 8 inches high, which is the height the 20 fl. oz. Aquafina bottle I have on my desk for just this reason, 1 billion bottles would circle the globe 5.4 times, or would span the distance between Los Angeles and Tokyo 23 times." Peter Gleick of the Pacific Institute says, "I also calculated that the bottles would circle the Earth 5 times. But I assumed 600 million bottles (which I think is a more accurate number than a billion) and 12 inches high each (I didn't have a bottle on my desk to measure . . .)." The 600 million 12-inch bottles is more akin to Annie's "more than half a billion bottles every week" being "enough to circle the globe more than 5 times."

You know, when you're talking about numbers this big and planets this fragile, unique, and essential to supporting all life, it's good to consult a variety of sources . . .

7. Manufactured demand is a desire for something that didn't just develop naturally but was stoked by some outside force. Manufacturing demand is a core strategy of today's consumer economy. In order to get people to keep buying stuff, when most of us have plenty of stuff already, companies manufacture demand so we feel like we need ever more and ever newer clothes, cars, toaster, furniture, shoes . . . everything. I mean, it's not like any of us just woke up and said "I need, really need, a new cell phone to replace my perfectly functional one" or " I really need a 15th pair of shoes."

The main tool to promote manufactured demand is advertising. In the past, advertising served to make announcements ("just arrived!") and then to distinguish products from one another, advertising's main role these days is to manufacture demand: to convince us we will be more successful, more happy, more loved if we just had a new (insert any consumer good here).

Now sometimes we really do need something, but a real need is different than manufactured demand. And manufactured demand has become so omnipresent that sometimes we get confused. It's not just bottled water; it's all over the place. Look around. Next time you're about to lay out some hard-earned cash for something, stop for a minute and ask yourself: do I really need this or am I responding to the bombardment of messages convincing me I need this?

Our friends at Polaris Institute tell us, "The real market value of bottled water lies in its perceived social value, a perception companies have worked hard to create. Between 10% to 15% of the price of a bottle of water goes to cover advertising costs." (http://www.bottledwaterfreeday.ca/index2.php?section_id=21) This means *we're actually paying to be manipulated by advertising*.

8. An article in the Financial Times of May 5, 1983, titled *Marketing: Coke plugs market gap*, describes the trend, in part:

"NEVER-A-PLACE for the faint-hearted, the US soft drinks industry is today locked in a competitive battle which could prove to be just too much for some of the weaker contestants. The latest sally comes from the strongest of them all, Coca-Cola. This time last year, Coke had only two cola products on the market: after the launch of three new products this week, it now has six.

The proliferation of brands in this way has become common in the industry, probably because the overall growth in the market place is not what it was. US soft drink consumption, which was rising at an annual 6 percent or more until the late 1970s, has been increasing at less than 3 percent a year since 1980, and, as a result, the manufacturers are hunting for growth at each other's expense.

Coke had a big success with last year's new product, Diet Coke, which it is now launching in the UK with a Pounds 1.5m ad campaign starting this month (see this page April 7). It is now moving into another segment of the market which is being expanded by health conscious Americans—caffeine free colas."

9. Those of you old folks in the audience (that's Generation X and beyond) may recall Orson Welles, circa 1977, gushing on television about "a place in the south of France where there is a spring, and its name is Perrier." That was the first ever television ad for bottled water, and thus began one of the most baffling cons in modern consumerism. The sad fact, though, is that it wasn't a passing Yuppie fad: in the three years following that ad, American sales of Perrier went up more than 3,000 percent. Speaking to the New York Times for an article of February 15, 2006 ("There Must be Something in the Water"), New York resident Johanna Raymond recalled, "I remember thousands of us running in Perrier T-shirts in the 1979 marathon. Perrier was the coolest thing then. It was more than water."

10. Another retro reference: in the 1987 screwball comedy *Spaceballs*, Mel Brooks pops open a can of Perri-Air, brings it to his nose and takes a deep breath of the pure oxygen. Twenty years later, it just goes to show that reality is stranger than science fiction.

11. When Fiji's ad said, "It's not bottled in Cleveland," the underlying message was, "because Cleveland's water is dirty and dangerous." Which is, in fact, not true, but this was the message that the bottled water industry had planted in our collective imaginations.

    Polaris Institute breaks it down: "Wherever there are incidents of contamination or disruption in municipal water systems, companies have been quick to respond with the promise of security, playing on fears about the spread of germs and toxins and a growing lack of faith in governments' ability to provide security through reliable public services." (http://www.bottledwater freeday.ca/index2.php?section_id=21)

    It's curious to note that the marketing of bottled water took off in North America in the 1990s, precisely when cigarette smoking, the fast food industry and the soft drink industry were coming under fire for promoting unhealthy lifestyles. By using images of waterfalls and pristine mountain springs, by associating bottled water with a healthy lifestyle, and by turning it into a status symbol, the bottled water industry has been successful at creating a mass market for their product. A variety of marketing techniques are used to associate bottled water with images of 'activity,' 'health,' 'relaxation,' and 'pureness.'

    In her book *Bottlemania* (2008), Elizabeth Royte refers to ads for Glaceau water "which ask, 'Who Approved *Your* Water?' The copy claims that tap water is 'rejected by Mother Nature'; springwater is approved by nature 'for potty training animals' (accompanied by an ideogram of a fish pooping); and purified water is approved by the FDA, but 'investigated by the FBI' (with an ideogram of a belching factory)." (Royte, *Bottlemania*, 34) In *Bottled and Sold: The Story Behind our Obsession With Bottled Water,* Peter Gleick tells of an ad received in the mail from Royal Spring, a Texas bottled water company, that said "Americans no longer trust their tap water . . . Clearly people are more worried than ever about what comes out of their taps." (Gleick, *Bottled and Sold*, 7). It is these kinds of underhanded marketing techniques that lead us to believe that tap water is dangerous and deadly, often despite any legitimate evidence. As it turns out, from the big picture perspective, if you take into account the real harm from pollution and waste that can be traced directly to the beverage industry, the real danger lies with them . . .

12. The quote is from Susan D. Wellington, president of the Quaker Oats Company's United States beverage division, which makes Gatorade, speaking before industry analysts in 2000. (See Peter Gleick, *Bottled and Sold*, 7.)

13. An article of July 27, 2007 on CNN.Money.com said: "Pepsi-Cola announced Friday that the labels of its Aquafina brand bottled water will be changed to make it clear the product is tap water. The new bottles will say, 'The Aquafina in this bottle is purified water that originates from a public water source,' or something similar, Pepsi- Cola North America spokeswoman Nicole Bradley told CNN. Coca-Cola does not have plans to change the labeling on its Dasani brand bottled water, a company spokesman told CNN, despite the fact the water also comes from a public water supply." Read the article, here: http://money.cnn.com/2007/07/27/news/companies/pepsi_coke/

Now, the companies go to great length to tell you that, while their water originates from a public water source, it is more than "just filtered tap water." They boast proprietary, state-of-the-art, multi-stage filtration processes and esoteric references to mineral additives that make their water more than just water, and certainly better than tap. But, as Tony Clarke of Canada's Polaris Institute points out in his book, *Inside the Bottle* (2005), "unlike other resource production processes, where raw materials like timber, minerals, and oil are transformed into new products, bottled water is different. Bottled water is about 'turning water into water.'" (*Inside the Bottle*, 54.)

14. The ad ran in Canada's *Globe and Mail,* October 20, 2008, page E7; you can see it here: http://www.ecojustice.ca/media-centre/media-release-files/2008.12.01-globe-nestles-complaint.pdf. The ad caused such a stir among environmentalists that it merited an entire article in This Magazine titled "'*Environmentally friendly' Bottled Water? No such thing*" (http://this.org/magazine/2009/05/15/environment-water-bottle/). The article concludes with a sharp observation by Meera Karunananthan, the national water campaigner for the Council of Canadians: "When the carbon footprint of drinking out of your tap is zero, you can't deny that the environmental impact of bottled water is more harmful."

In fact, to say that tap water (or *anything*, for that matter) has no carbon footprint might be an exaggeration, but a recent study commissioned by the Oregon Department of Environmental Quality called "Life Cycle Assessment of Drinking Water Delivery Systems: Bottled Water, Tap Water and Home/Office Delivery Water," (http://www.deq.state.or.us/lq/sw/wasteprevention/drinkingwater.htm) concludes that "consuming water from the tap in an average reusable bottle, even if washed frequently in a highly inefficient dishwasher, reduces energy consumption by 85 percent and greenhouse gases by 79 percent . . . Even the best performing bottled water scenario has global warming effects 46 times greater than the best performing tap water scenario." Which is to say, choosing tap water is not only good for your budget, it's an important way to reduce global warming.

15. Most plastic water bottles are made of PET plastic, or polyethylene terephthalate, which is made from crude oil. The invention of PET in the 1970's made the portable water bottle possible. While plastic is everywhere because it is probably the most convenient material ever made, it comes at a high price. Back in 1993, the Glass Packaging Institute put out a report comparing glass and plastic, in which they noted that, "The production of the organic chemical industry has increased by a factor of ten over the past 40 years, a rate which has far outstripped total industrial production. In the U.S., plastics production has increased from 6 billion pounds in 1960 to 58 billion pounds in 1989. A major consumer of plastic production is the packaging industry, and containers account for nearly half of the total packaging material sales." (And this was before the bottled water boom . . .)

    The report goes on: "The post-war boom in plastic and other petrochemicals has led to an enormous rise in the volume and toxicity of hazardous chemicals and wastes in the environment. The number of chemicals used and released that are known to cause cancer, birth defects and damage to reproductive systems has increased dramatically." (*Advantage Glass! Switching to Plastic is an Environmental Mistake,* by Henry S. Cole, Ph.D. and Kenneth A. Brown, 1993, 60.)

    So much for bottled water being healthy. . . .

16. The Pacific Institute breaks it down like this: "Because bottled water required approximately 1 million tons of PET in 2006, those bottles required roughly 100 billion MJ of energy. A barrel of oil contains around 6,000 MJ, so producing those bottles required the equivalent of around 17 million barrels of oil. This is enough energy to fuel one million American cars for one year." The rest of the details can be found in Pacific Institute's fact sheet on the topic, here: http://www.pacinst.org/topics/integrity_of_science/case_studies/bottled_water_factsheet.pdf

17. Two minutes, three minutes, four minutes, whatever . . . The point is, it takes A LOT of energy and resources to produce a plastic bottle that is meant to be used exactly ONCE. In The Story of Stuff Annie talks about "planned obsolescence": "Planned obsolescence is another word for 'designed for the dump.' It means they actually make stuff that is designed to be useless as quickly as possible so we will chuck it and go buy a new one. It's obvious with stuff like plastic bags and coffee cups, but now it's even big stuff: mops, DVDs, cameras, barbeques even, everything!" A couple of Annie's favorite books on the topic are *The Waste Makers* (1960) by Vance Packard, and *Made to Break* (2006) by Giles Slade.

18. According to the Container Recycling Institute (http://www.container-recycling.org/), in fact, 90 percent of PET bottles end up in landfills, where they take between 450 and 1000 years to break down.

In addition, a 2004 report from the Container Recycling Institute (*The 10¢ Incentive to Recycle*, by Jenny Gitlitz and Pat Franklin, CRI, 2004) tells us that "Beverage containers make up 4.4 percent of the waste stream and 40 to 60 percent of roadside litter," and goes on to say that "While municipal curbside recycling programs rippled nationally during the 1990's, they have been unable to keep up with increasing sales of single-serving beverages and away-from-home consumption of food and drinks. An estimated 118 billion beverage bottles and cans were landfilled, littered, or incinerated in 2002— 83 percent more than were wasted in 1992, and more than twice the amount wasted in 1982."

19. Some good facts on incinerators can be found at http://www. zerowasteamerica .org /Incinerators.htm. To get more in-depth, see *Incineration: A Dying Technology* by Neil Tangri (2003); *Gone Tomorrow* by Heather Rogers (2005) and "Landfills Are Dangerous" in Rachel's Democracy and Health News, September 24, 1998, and *Incineration and Human Health* by Pat Costner, Paul Johnston, Michelle Allsopp (2001).

20. Annie wrote about one such case way back in 1994 in *Multinational Monitor*: "Indian environmentalists, working with investigators from Greenpeace's International Toxic Trade Project, have discovered that Pepsi is involved in both producing and disposing of plastic waste in India. Under Pepsi's two-part scheme, plastic for single-use disposal bottles will be manufactured in India and exported to the United States and Europe, while the toxic by-products of the plastic production process will stay in India. Used plastic bottles will then be returned from these countries to India.

India will bear the burden of environmental and health impacts from plastic production and plastic waste, while consumers in industrialized countries will be able to continue using and disposing of massive quantities of unsustainable and unnecessary beverage packaging without absorbing the true costs—financial, health and environmental. In short, India gets shafted at both ends, while industrialized country consumers receive all the benefits.

Activists first learned of Pepsi's waste exports to India through U.S. Customs Department Data. Greenpeace researchers discovered records listing Pepsi as the exporter of about 4,500 tons of plastic scrap in 23 shipments during 1993.

The U.S. Customs records indicated that all of the waste exports were destined for the Southern Indian City of Madras. All of the shipments left from the U.S. West Coast: eight shipments from San Francisco, two shipments from Long Beach, 10 from Los Angeles, and three from Oakland. The most frequently used shipping lines for these waste shipments were OOCL and Presidential.

Much of the waste was dumped at the site of a factory owned by Futura Industries in Tiruvallur, outside of Madras. 'As we came over the hill in our auto-rickshaw, we saw a mountain of plastic waste,' recounts Madras environmentalist Satish Vangal, one of the researchers who discovered the site. 'Piles and piles of used soda bottles stacked behind a wall. When we got closer to the factory, we found many bottles and plastic scrap along the road and blowing in the wind. Every bottle we saw said 'California Redemption Value.' They were all from California's recycling program and now they are sitting in a pile in India!' explains Vangal . 'We have enough problems dealing with our own plastic wastes; why should we import other peoples's rubbish?'

Pepsi officials in the United States acknowledge the waste is exported to India, but claim it is all recycled. Futura officials also say the waste is imported, but they admit that much of it is not actually recycled. The senior manager of the Futura plant, Dr. L.R. Subbaraman, estimated that 60 to 70 percent of the waste can be processed at his factory, but the rest is either too contaminated with residual materials or other garbage that arrives mixed in with the shipment, or is the wrong type of plastic. Subbaraman refused to disclose the fate of the waste which cannot be reprocessed at the plant.

Subbaraman reports that Futura has imported a total of 10,000 metric tons of plastic waste from Pepsi and other companies since 1992. If only 60 to 70 percent could be processed within the Futura plant, 3,000 to 4,000 metric tons of plastic garbage have been imported which were not recyclable. A visit to the back of the plant revealed a massive pile of plastic discards."

Find Annie's entire article at: http://www.mindfully.org/Pesticide/Dumping-Pepsi-Plastic-India94.htm

21. Most plastic "recycling" is actually "downcycling." In *Cradle to Cradle: Remaking the Way We Make Things* (2002), architect William McDonough and chemist Michael Braungart tell us that when most plastics are recycled, they are mixed with different plastics to produce a hybrid of lower quality, which is then molded into something amorphous and cheap, such as a a park bench or a speed bump. This tells us that even something as "environmentally friendly" as recycling still does not really bring about sustainable use of resources, it just moves our waste around the built environment in ever-more degraded forms. Even worse, McDonough and Braungart say that "Downcycling can actually increase contamination of the biosphere," (*Cradle to Cradle*, 57), because the process releases toxins, and because, "Since downcycled materials of all kinds are materially less rigorous than their predecessors, more chemicals are often added to make the materials useful again."

22. When numbers get this big, they're hard to track, but here are a few: The U.S. Census Bureau (http://www.census.gov/Press-Release/www/releases/archives/miscellaneous/007871.html) reports that Americans drank 23.2 gallons of bottled water per capita in 2004, up from only 2.7 gallons in 1980. Another report says we drink less, but still a lot: "The average American drinks approximately 14 gallons of bottled water a year. Assuming a population of 250 million, this comes to a staggering 13 billion liters (13 Gl = 13 gigaliters)." USEPA quotes the Beverage Marketing Corporation of 2004 (http://www.epa.gov/ogwdw000/faq/pdfs/fs_healthseries_bottlewater.pdf) to tell us that "Bottled water is the fastest growing drink choice in the' United States,

and Americans spend billions of dollars each year to buy it." One report (http://www.fastcompany.com/magazine/117/features-message-in-a-bottle .html) tells us that in 2007, Americans spent more money on bottled water than on ipods or movie tickets: $15 billion.

23. If asked, "Is water a human right?" most of us would say "Of course!" without blinking an eye. And it is . . . sort of. But because "human rights" is a big complicated field of legal and technical concerns, it can get a little . . . sticky. The Universal Declaration of Human Rights, the founding document of modern human rights law, for example, says nothing specifically about water. When it was written in the 1940's it would've been hard to imagine companies buying and selling water in a way that denied it to anyone, so making water a human right would have seemed as silly as making air a human right. The document does say we all have the right to life, to health, to dignity, security, etc. . . . But nothing about water. Of course, without water, there's no life, health, dignity, or security, so. . . . The Universal Declaration protected what are called "political rights." Only later did it become clear that we needed protections also of what are called "economic, social, and cultural rights." In 2002, partly in response to growing concerns that poor people worldwide were being forced to pay for water or go without, the United Nations Committee on Economic, Social, and Cultural Rights wrote General Comment No.15, which is now considered the definitive and official interpretation of human rights laws regarding water. The whole thing can be read here: http://www.righttowater.info/code/No15.asp

For those of you who may not have time to read the whole thing, the gist of General Comment 15 is in its introductory paragraph: *'the human right to water entitles everyone to sufficient, safe, acceptable, physically accessible and affordable water for personal and domestic uses'*. It notes that the right to water has been recognized in a wide range of international documents and reaffirms the fundamental importance of the right stating that: *'the human right to water is indispensable for leading a life in human dignity. It is a prerequisite for the realization of other human rights'*.

24. This quote is from Robert S. Morrison, quoted in 2000, shortly before he was made chairman of Pepsico's North American Beverage and Food division. The full quote is: "The biggest enemy is tap water . . . We're not against water— it just has its place. We think it's good for irrigation and cooking." Both this and the earlier citation, from Susan D. Wellington, are cited in a letter to the New York Times by Peter Gleick of the Pacific Institute, here: http://www .nytimes.com/2001/08/24/opinion/l-tap-water-in-a-bottle-842370. html?scp=2&sq=water%20bottle&st=cse, and in Peter Gleick's book, *Bottled and Sold: The Story Behind Our Obsession With Bottled Water,* page 7.

25. . . . and the oil industry. . . . and the mining industry . . . and big agribusiness . . . That is to say, the manufacturing of demand that we associate with bottled water leads to pollution such as that Annie wrote about back in 1994 (http://www.mindfully.org/Pesticide/Dumping-Pepsi-Plastic-India94.htm) and stunning pollution disasters like the great Pacific garbage patch, a floating

dump the size of Texas, containing shoes, toys, bags, pacifiers, wrappers, toothbrushes, and bottles—approximately 3.5 million tons of trash—out in the ocean midway between Hawaii and San Francisco (http://www.great garbagepatch.org/). The same "manufactured demand" leads to massive over-consumption of fossil fuels and the pollution it causes (http://chevrontoxico .com/), an industrial system of agriculture that leaves toxic pollution in its wake (http://www.greenpeace.org/seasia/en/news/agrochemicals-a-major-source-o), and mining for energy and mineral demand that is way out of control (http://www.earthjustice.org/news/press/2010/scientists-agree-mountaintop-removal-mining-is-destroying-appalachia.html).

That is to say, bottled water is a big problem. . . . But it is also a symptom of a much bigger problem: using too much stuff, and leaving too much waste.

26. We've already covered the "expensive" part; for some critical thinking on the "solution" part, see the next footnote. . .

27. At the heart of the water issues is the fact that literally billions of people around the world—including in parts of the U.S. and other rich countries—do not have access to safe drinking water. The causes are complex, including both man-made political and economic causes, and natural causes; in short, it might be the water, it might be the pipes—or it might be the lack of water or the lack of pipes. In either case, selling bottled water (or even giving it away as some companies and organizations do as part of relief efforts in emergencies) will not fix the problem. The real fix is more public investment in water infrastructure, and community control of that infrastructure to ensure that the poorest and most vulnerable communities have their needs met. Even in places where both tourists and locals are urged to "not drink the water," the long-term solution is not to avoid tap water—but to make the tap water safe to drink. Yes, this solution will cost money, but at least it's an investment in something permanent, and that benefits everyone.

28. . . . or mug . . . or mason jar . . . or sippy cup . . . or . . . With all the empty containers in your kitchen and all the good water flowing from the tap, there's no reason not to carry one.

29. By "underfunded," we mean the difference between what is currently spent and is projected to be spent on water infrastructure investment, and what will actually need to be spent during that same time period to keep service levels roughly comparable to desirable past and current service levels.

The $24 billion projection is based on the rough averaging of two water infrastructure investment gap analyses conducted by the EPA (U.S. Environ-mental Protection Agency, "The Clean Water and Drinking Water Infra-structure Gap Analysis," September 2002, EPA 816-R-02-020, 50, http://www.epa.gov/OGWDW/gapreport.pdf) and by the Water Infrastructure Network, a coalition of labor, environment and water utility officials (see Water Infrastructure Network, Clean & Safe Water for the 21st Century, A Renewed National Commitment to Water and Wastewater Infrastructure, April 2000).

For a more detailed explanation, see the Congressional Research Service's 2008 report, "Water Infrastructure Needs and Investment: Review and Analysis of Key Issues" (http://fas.org/sgp/crs/homesec/RL31116.pdf).

30. More precisely, 1.2 billion people lack access to safe water and 2.6 billion lack access to sanitation, according to the UN Development Program's 2006 Human Development Report (http://hdr.undp.org/en/reports/global/hdr2006/).

31. Bill Sheehan, Director of the Product Policy Institute (http://www.productpolicy.org/), says "Three-quarters of the waste material that local governments are responsible for managing in North America is products and packaging; the costs of collecting PET bottles alone runs about $900 per ton. That amounts to welfare for the makers of products and packaging. Citizens and their governments would be better served if those funds were supporting schools, police and parks, and other services that the market cannot or will not provide, like public water fountains . . . In a time of tight budgets many local governments are asking why taxpayers and ratepayers, and not producers and consumers, are the ones paying to pick up products and associated packaging 'designed for the dump.' The costs of recycling and litter clean up should be the responsibility of producers and included in the purchase price."

32. Anyone remember water fountains? Coincidentally, just before the bottled water craze hit, it was taken for granted that public fountains were part of any public building: schools, offices, sports stadiums, parks. Where did they go? Polaris Institute in Canada has followed the story in that country, here: http://www.insidethebottle.org/bottled-or-tapped-out-where-have-all-water-fountains-gone.

Meanwhile, in the U.S., many state building codes mandate that there be one source of public water for every 1000 people the building has capacity for. This came up in recent news in two cases: In Cleveland (why always Cleveland?), the new sports arena that hosts the Cleveland Cavaliers basketball team removed its drinking water fountains. The only way for thirsty fans to get water was to wait in line at the concessions counter for a free small cup or pay $4 for bottled water—or try to drink water from the bathroom faucets. As Peter Gleick of Pacific Institute wrote, "This wasn't the first time a sports arena ran into trouble over water fountains. In September 2007, the University of Central Florida opened its brand new 45,000 seat football stadium with a sell-out crowd on hand to watch the UCF Knights battle the Texas Longhorns. The loser? The fans. With temperatures near 100 degrees the crowd found out the hard way that the stadium had been built without a single drinking fountain (in apparent violation of building codes). Security concerns kept out personal water bottles. And the only water available (other than the taps in the bathrooms) was $3 bottled water, which quickly sold out. Eighteen people were taken to local hospitals and sixty more were treated by campus medical personnel for heat-related illnesses. After a massive public brouhaha, the University quickly retrofitted the stadium with water fountains." (http://www.sfgate.com/cgi-bin/blogs/gleick/detail??blogid=104&entry_id=56985)

The public fountains were brought back at the Cleveland Cavaliers' stadium, too. The lesson? We like our drinking fountains; in fact, we don't just like them . . . We need them for public health and safety. The other lesson? When people organize to take back our right to public water . . . we win.

33. Bottled water bans are spreading faster than we can count. The Polaris Institute in Canada says that as of December, 2009, 72 municipalities from 8 provinces and 2 territories had implemented restrictions on bottled water. (http://www.wiserearth.org/article/7ccceaf282e8aa3514b2f3e309ed2cb6) In the U.S., San Francisco, Minneapolis, Seattle, and Salt Lake City have all banned bottled water at city functions as a way of reducing budgets while promoting their cities' highly drinkable tap water (and these are just the big cities). At the 75th annual Conference of Mayors the mayors of these three cities introduced a resolution to ban bottled water in city functions nationwide.

34. The Beverage Marketing Corp. documents sales trends of bottled water, soft drinks, fruit juice and many other kinds of drinks. Its data shows that bottled water sales fell 1 percent in 2008 to 8.7 billion gallons, down from 8.8 billion gallons in 2007. In 2009, the company reported, sales remained depressed, on a par with 2008. The biggest hit was taken by Nestle, the Swiss company that is the world's biggest seller of bottled water under such brand names as Perrier, Poland Springs, San Pellegrino and Deer Park. The company reported that the volume of its bottled water sales fell 3.7 percent in the first half of 2009. A report by the World-Watch Institute (http://www.worldwatch.org/node/5878) gives the details.

    Behind the story are some grisly details of what an industry does when its market share is under threat. Richard Girard of Polaris Institute wrote an in-depth article on that topic, here: http://www.stopcorporateabuse.org/alternet-bottled-water-industy-faces-downward-spiral

35. Many companies now sell safe, easy-to-clean, lightweight drinking water bottles; we found a pretty hefty selection available here: http://www.reusable bags.com/store/bottles-accessories-c-19.html. Our partners at Food & Water Watch and Corporate Accountability International offer sleek, stainless steel water bottles to their members.

36. Food & Water Watch, which has been supporting restaurants nationwide in making the switch back to good old tapwater, even offers a handy guide to the topic: http://www.foodandwaterwatch.org/water/bottled/restaurants

Analyze

1. The author says that bottled water companies "manufacture demand" in order to sell water to the public. What does the author mean by "manufactured demand"? And how has this demand been manufactured in this case?

2. Is bottled water better than regular tap water?

3. It costs a lot less in energy to use tap water than bottled water. Where does this difference in energy consumption come from?

Explore

1. Several times, this author follows up statistics with a more concrete analogy. For example, in this article, she says, "Bottled water costs about 2000 times more than tap water.⁵ Can you imagine paying 2000 times the price of anything else? How about a $10,000 sandwich?" In a group, read over the article again and highlight each time the author does this. Then think about and discuss what effect this rhetorical approach has on the way the reader understands and thinks about the information given in the article.

2. Find a current television, newspaper, or magazine advertisement that uses the tactic of manufacturing demand to sell its product or service. Then construct a rhetorical analysis of the ad, describing how it manufactures a demand—does it appeal to health? Fear? Fashion?—and identifying the ad's intended audience.

3. This article has more footnotes than it does actual text, so that when the author says, "In many ways, bottled water is less regulated than tap," she does not have to pause to explain those regulations. Instead, the reader can find out about them by reading the footnote. To get some practice with footnotes, write your own footnoted "Story of" piece on a topic of your choice that you know a lot about. Integrate your knowledge into your writing as you tell your story, but use footnotes to explain how you know about a particular point or to tell readers where they can find more information about an issue.

Chris Caroll
"High Tech Trash"

Chris Carroll is a staff writer for the *National Geographic Magazine*, from which this article is taken. He writes about a wide range of topics, from the decline of fishing in Newfoundland, Canada, to the development of robots and artificial intelligence. The essay "High Tech Trash," which appeared in *National Geographic* in 2008, describes the global trade in "e-waste," the river of discarded electronics that flows from the United States and Europe into the developing world. The essay describes the last, typically unseen, portion of the life cycle of devices such as cell phones, television sets and computers. Like "We Speak for Ourselves" (below), this tells a story of race, poverty, and environmental justice, though not one with a happy ending. As you read about e-waste, think about what it means to "externalize the cost" of waste or any other part of a system.

Will your discarded TV end up in a ditch in Ghana?

June is the wet season in Ghana, but here in Accra, the capital, the morning rain has ceased. As the sun heats the humid air, pillars of black smoke begin to rise above the vast Agbogbloshie Market. I follow one plume toward its source, past lettuce and plantain vendors, past stalls of used tires, and through a clanging scrap market where hunched men bash on old alternators and engine blocks. Soon the muddy track is flanked by piles of old TVs, gutted computer cases, and smashed monitors heaped ten feet (three meters) high. Beyond lies a field of fine ash speckled with glints of amber and green—the sharp broken bits of circuit boards. I can see now that the smoke issues not from one fire, but from many small blazes. Dozens of indistinct figures move among the acrid haze, some stirring flames with sticks, others carrying armfuls of brightly colored computer wire. Most are children.

Choking, I pull my shirt over my nose and approach a boy of about 15, his thin frame wreathed in smoke. Karim says he has been tending such fires for two years. He pokes at one meditatively, and then his top half disappears as he bends into the billowing soot. He hoists a tangle of copper wire off the old tire he's using for fuel and douses the hissing mass in a puddle. With the flame retardant insulation burned away—a process that has released a bouquet of carcinogens and other toxics—the wire may fetch a dollar from a scrap-metal buyer.

Another day in the market, on a similar ash heap above an inlet that flushes to the Atlantic after a downpour, Israel Mensah, an incongruously stylish young man of about 20, adjusts his designer glasses and explains how he makes his living. Each day scrap sellers bring loads of old electronics— from where he doesn't know. Mensah and his partners—friends and family, including two shoeless boys raptly listening to us talk—buy a few computers or TVs. They break copper yokes off picture tubes, littering the ground with shards containing lead, a neurotoxin, and cadmium, a carcinogen that damages lungs and kidneys. They strip resalable parts such as drives and memory chips. Then they rip out wiring and burn the plastic. He sells copper stripped from one scrap load to buy another. The key to making money is speed, not safety. "The gas goes to your nose and you feel something in your head," Mensah says, knocking his fist against the back of his skull for effect. "Then you get sick in your head and your chest." Nearby, hulls of broken monitors float in the lagoon. Tomorrow the rain will wash them into the ocean.

5   People have always been proficient at making trash. Future archaeologists will note that at the tail end of the 20th century, a new, noxious kind of clutter exploded across the landscape: the digital detritus that has come to be called e-waste.

More than 40 years ago, Gordon Moore, co-founder of the computer-chip maker Intel, observed that computer processing power roughly doubles every two years. An unstated corollary to "Moore's law" is that at any given time, all the machines considered state-of-the-art are simultaneously on the verge of obsolescence. At this very moment, heavily caffeinated software engineers are designing programs that will overtax and befuddle your new turbo-powered PC when you try running them a few years from now. The memory and graphics requirements of Microsoft's recent Vista operating system, for instance, spell doom for aging machines that were still able to squeak by a year ago. According to the U.S. Environmental Protection Agency, an estimated 30 to 40 million PCs will be ready for "end-of-life management" in each of the next few years.

Computers are hardly the only electronic hardware hounded by obsolescence. A switchover to digital high-definition television broadcasts is scheduled to be complete by 2009, rendering inoperable TVs that function perfectly today but receive only an analog signal. As viewers prepare for the switch, about 25 million TVs are taken out of service yearly. In the fashion-conscious mobile market, 98 million U.S. cell phones took their last call in 2005. All told, the EPA estimates that in the U.S. that year, between 1.5 and 1.9 million tons of computers, TVs, VCRs, monitors, cell phones, and other equipment were discarded. If all sources of electronic waste are tallied, it could total 50 million tons a year worldwide, according to the UN Environment Programme.

So what happens to all this junk?

In the United States, it is estimated that more than 70 percent of discarded computers and monitors, and well over 80 percent of TVs, eventually end up in landfills, despite a growing number of state laws that prohibit dumping of e-waste, which may leak lead, mercury, arsenic, cadmium, beryllium, and other toxics into the ground. Meanwhile, a staggering volume of unused electronic gear sits in storage—about 180 million TVs, desktop PCs, and other components as of 2005, according to the EPA. Even if this obsolete equipment remains in attics and basements indefinitely, never reaching a landfill, this solution has its own, indirect impact on the environment. In addition to toxics, e-waste contains goodly amounts of silver, gold, and other valuable metals that are highly efficient conductors of electricity. In theory, recycling gold from old computer motherboards is far more efficient and less environmentally destructive than ripping it from the earth, often by surface-mining that imperils pristine rain forests.

Currently, less than 20 percent of e-waste entering the solid waste stream is channeled through companies that advertise themselves as recyclers, though the number is likely to rise as states like California crack down on landfill dumping. Yet recycling, under the current system, is less benign than it sounds. Dropping your old electronic gear off with a recycling company or at a municipal collection point does not guarantee that it will be safely disposed of. While some recyclers process the material with an eye toward minimizing pollution and health risks, many more sell it to brokers who ship it to the developing world, where environmental enforcement is weak. For people in countries on the front end of this arrangement, it's a handy out-of-sight, out-of-mind solution.

Many governments, conscious that electronic waste wrongly handled damages the environment and human health, have tried to weave an international regulatory net. The 1989 Basel Convention, a 170-nation accord, requires that developed nations notify developing nations of incoming hazardous waste shipments. Environmental groups and many undeveloped nations called the terms too weak, and in 1995 protests led to an amendment known as the Basel Ban, which forbids hazardous waste shipments to poor countries. Though the ban has yet to take effect, the European Union has written the requirements into its laws.

The EU also requires manufacturers to shoulder the burden of safe disposal. Recently a new EU directive encourages "green design" of electronics, setting limits for allowable levels of lead, mercury, fire retardants, and other substances. Another directive requires manufacturers to set up infrastructure to collect e-waste and ensure responsible recycling—a strategy called take-back. In spite of these safeguards, untold tons of e-waste still slip out of European ports, on their way to the developing world.

In the United States, electronic waste has been less of a legislative priority. One of only three countries to sign but not ratify the Basel Convention (the other two are Haiti and Afghanistan), it does not require green design or take-back programs of manufacturers, though a few states have stepped in with their own laws. The U.S. approach, says Matthew Hale, EPA solid waste program director, is instead to encourage responsible recycling by working with industry—for instance, with a ratings system that rewards environmentally sound products with a seal of approval. "We're definitely trying to channel market forces, and look for cooperative approaches and consensus standards," Hale says.

The result of the federal hands-off policy is that the greater part of e-waste sent to domestic recyclers is shunted overseas.

15   "We in the developed world get the benefit from these devices," says Jim Puckett, head of Basel Action Network, or BAN, a group that opposes hazardous waste shipments to developing nations. "But when our equipment becomes unusable, we externalize the real environmental costs and liabilities to the developing world."

Asia is the center of much of the world's high-tech manufacturing, and it is here the devices often return when they die. China in particular has long been the world's electronics graveyard. With explosive growth in its manufacturing sector fueling demand, China's ports have become conduits for recyclable scrap of every sort: steel, aluminum, plastic, even paper. By the mid-1980s, electronic waste began freely pouring into China as well, carrying the lucrative promise of the precious metals embedded in circuit boards.

Vandell Norwood, owner of Corona Visions, a recycling company in San Antonio, Texas, remembers when foreign scrap brokers began trolling for electronics to ship to China. Today he opposes the practice, but then it struck him and many other recyclers as a win-win situation. "They said this stuff was all going to get recycled and put back into use," Norwood remembers brokers assuring him. "It seemed environmentally responsible. And it was profitable, because I was getting paid to have it taken off my hands." Huge volumes of scrap electronics were shipped out, and the profits rolled in.

Any illusion of responsibility was shattered in 2002, the year Puckett's group, BAN, released a documentary film that showed the reality of e-waste recycling in China. *Exporting Harm* focused on the town of Guiyu in Guangdong Province, adjacent to Hong Kong. Guiyu had become the dumping ground for massive quantities of electronic junk. BAN documented thousands of people—entire families, from young to old—engaged in dangerous practices like burning computer wire to expose copper, melting circuit boards in pots to extract lead and other metals, or dousing the boards in powerful acid to remove gold.

China had specifically prohibited the import of electronic waste in 2000, but that had not stopped the trade. After the worldwide publicity BAN's film generated, however, the government lengthened the list of forbidden e-wastes and began pushing local governments to enforce the ban in earnest.

On a recent trip to Taizhou, a city in Zhejiang Province south of Shanghai that was another center of e-waste processing, I saw evidence of both the crackdown and its limits. Until a few years ago, the hill country outside Taizhou was the center of a huge but informal electronics disassembly industry that rivaled Guiyu's. But these days, customs officials at the nearby Haimen and Ningbo ports—clearinghouses for massive volumes of metal scrap—are sniffing around incoming shipments for illegal hazardous waste.

High-tech scrap "imports here started in the 1990s and reached a peak in 2003," says a high school teacher whose students tested the environment around Taizhou for toxics from e-waste. He requested anonymity from fear of local recyclers angry about the drop in business. "It has been falling since 2005 and now is hard to find."

Today the salvagers operate in the shadows. Inside the open door of a house in a hillside village, a homeowner uses pliers to rip microchips and metal parts off a computer motherboard. A buyer will burn these pieces to recover copper. The man won't reveal his name. "This business is illegal," he admits, offering a cigarette. In the same village, several men huddle inside a shed, heating circuit boards over a flame to extract metal. Outside the door lies a pile of scorched boards. In another village a few miles away, a woman stacks up bags of circuit boards in her house. She shoos my translator and me away. Continuing through the hills, I see people tearing apart car batteries, alternators, and high-voltage cable for recycling, and others hauling aluminum scrap to an aging smelter. But I find no one else working with electronics. In Taizhou, at least, the e-waste business seems to be waning.

Yet for some people it is likely too late; a cycle of disease or disability is already in motion. In a spate of studies released last year, Chinese scientists documented the environmental plight of Guiyu, the site of the original BAN film. The air near some electronics salvage operations that remain open contains the highest amounts of dioxin measured anywhere in the world. Soils are saturated with the chemical, a probable carcinogen that may disrupt endocrine and immune function. High levels of flame retardants called PBDEs—common in electronics, and potentially damaging to fetal development even at very low levels—turned up in the blood of the electronics workers. The high school teacher in Taizhou says his students found high levels of PBDEs in plants and animals. Humans were also tested, but he was not at liberty to discuss the results.

China may someday succeed in curtailing electronic waste imports. But e-waste flows like water. Shipments that a few years ago might have gone to ports in Guangdong or Zhejiang Provinces can easily be diverted to friendlier environs in Thailand, Pakistan, or elsewhere. "It doesn't help in a global sense for one place like China, or India, to become restrictive," says David N. Pellow, an ethnic studies professor at the University of California, San Diego, who studies electronic waste from a social justice perspective. "The flow simply shifts as it takes the path of least resistance to the bottom."

25   It is next to impossible to gauge how much e-waste is still being smuggled into China, diverted to other parts of Asia, or—increasingly—dumped in West African countries like Ghana, Nigeria, and Ivory Coast. At ground level, however, one can pick out single threads from this global toxic tapestry and follow them back to their source.

In Accra, Mike Anane, a local environmental journalist, takes me down to the seaport. Guards block us at the gate. But some truck drivers at a nearby gas station point us toward a shipment facility just up the street, where they say computers are often unloaded.

There, in a storage yard, locals are opening a shipping container from Germany. Shoes, clothes, and handbags pour out onto the tarmac. Among the clutter: some battered Pentium 2 and 3 computers and monitors with cracked cases and missing knobs, all sitting in the rain. A man hears us asking questions. "You want computers?" he asks. "How many containers?"

Near the port I enter a garage-like building with a sign over the door: "Importers of British Used Goods." Inside: more age-encrusted PCs, TVs, and audio components. According to the manager, the owner of the facility imports a 40-foot (12 meters) container every week. Working items go up for sale. Broken ones are sold for a pittance to scrap collectors.

All around the city, the sidewalks are choked with used electronics shops. In a suburb called Darkuman, a dim stall is stacked front to back with CRT monitors. These are valueless relics in wealthy countries, particularly hard to dispose of because of their high levels of lead and other toxics. Apparently no one wants them here, either. Some are monochrome, with tiny screens. Boys will soon be smashing them up in a scrap market.

30   A price tag on one of the monitors bears the label of a chain of Goodwill stores headquartered in Frederick, Maryland, a 45-minute drive from my

house. A lot of people donate their old computers to charity organizations, believing they're doing the right thing. I might well have done the same. I ask the proprietor of the shop where he got the monitors. He tells me his brother in Alexandria, Virginia, sent them. He sees no reason not to give me his brother's phone number.

When his brother Baah finally returns my calls, he turns out not to be some shady character trying to avoid the press, but a maintenance man in an apartment complex, working 15-hour days fixing toilets and lights. To make ends meet, he tells me, he works nights and weekends exporting used computers to Ghana through his brother. A Pentium 3 brings $150 in Accra, and he can sometimes buy the machines for less than $10 on Internet liquidation websites—he favors private ones, but the U.S. General Services Administration runs one as well. Or he buys bulk loads from charity stores. (Managers of the Goodwill store whose monitor ended up in Ghana denied selling large quantities of computers to dealers.) Whatever the source, the profit margin on a working computer is substantial.

The catch: Nothing is guaranteed to work, and companies always try to unload junk. CRT monitors, though useless, are often part of the deal. Baah has neither time nor space to unpack and test his monthly loads. "You take it over there and half of them don't work," he says disgustedly. All you can do then is sell it to scrap people, he says. "What they do with it from that point, I don't know nothing about it."

Baah's little exporting business is just one trickle in the cataract of e-waste flowing out of the U.S. and the rest of the developed world. In the long run, the only way to prevent it from flooding Accra, Taizhou, or a hundred other places is to carve a new, more responsible direction for it to flow in. A Tampa, Florida, company called Creative Recycling Systems has already begun.

The key to the company's business model rumbles away at one end of a warehouse—a building-size machine operating not unlike an assembly line in reverse. "David" was what company president Jon Yob called the more than three-million-dollar investment in machines and processes when they were installed in 2006; Goliath is the towering stockpile of U.S. e-scrap. Today the machine's steel teeth are chomping up audio and video components. Vacuum pressure and filters capture dust from the process. "The air that comes out is cleaner than the ambient air in the building," vice president Joe Yob (Jon's brother) bellows over the roar.

35   A conveyor belt transports material from the shredder through a series of sorting stations: vibrating screens of varying finenesses, magnets, a device to extract leaded glass, and an eddy current separator—akin to a reverse magnet, Yob says—that propels nonferrous metals like copper and aluminum into a bin, along with precious metals like gold, silver, and palladium. The most valuable product, shredded circuit boards, is shipped to a state-of-the-art smelter in Belgium specializing in precious-metals recycling. According to Yob, a four-foot-square (1.2-meter-square) box of the stuff can be worth as much as $10,000.

In Europe, where the recycling infrastructure is more developed, plant-size recycling machines like David are fairly common. So far, only three other American companies have such equipment. David can handle some 150 million pounds (68 million kilograms) of electronics a year; it wouldn't take many more machines like it to process the entire country's output of high-tech trash. But under current policies, pound for pound it is still more profitable to ship waste abroad than to process it safely at home. "We can't compete economically with people who do it wrong, who ship it overseas," Joe Yob says. Creative Recycling's investment in David thus represents a gamble—one that could pay off if the EPA institutes a certification process for recyclers that would define minimum standards for the industry. Companies that rely mainly on export would have difficulty meeting such standards. The EPA is exploring certification options.

Ultimately, shipping e-waste overseas may be no bargain even for the developed world. In 2006, Jeffrey Weidenhamer, a chemist at Ashland University in Ohio, bought some cheap, Chinese-made jewelry at a local dollar store for his class to analyze. That the jewelry contained high amounts of lead was distressing, but hardly a surprise; Chinese-made leaded jewelry is all too commonly marketed in the U.S. More revealing were the amounts of copper and tin alloyed with the lead. As Weidenhamer and his colleague Michael Clement argued in a scientific paper published this past July, the proportions of these metals in some samples suggest their source was leaded solder used in the manufacture of electronic circuit boards.

"The U.S. right now is shipping large quantities of leaded materials to China, and China is the world's major manufacturing center," Weidenhamer says. "It's not all that surprising things are coming full circle and now we're getting contaminated products back." In a global economy, out of sight will not stay out of mind for long.

Analyze

1. According to this article, what is the impact that electronics have on the environment, and why? What impact do recycled electronics have on people?
2. How do computer monitors from Maryland end up in Ghana?
3. What is the Basel Convention and why did the United States not sign it?

Explore

1. The author says that e-waste recycling changed when the *reality* of e-waste recycling in China was exposed. Get into groups and discuss the term "e-waste recycling." What image and connotations does this term bring to mind? Often, as this article describes, a great deal of complicated reality can be hidden behind a harmless-sounding phrase. In your group, create new, more realistic terms for the reality behind e-waste recycling.

2. Both this article and Annie Leonard's "Story of Stuff: Electronics" use the term "externalizing cost." One now-famous example of externalized cost is that of cigarette smoking; all the health and safety consequences of smoking and the cost to people and the economy are hidden from most consumers and external to the industry, at least until recently. Pick something you use in your everyday life and explore the issue of externalized costs and the hidden consequences of using and disposing of that item.

3. Do some research on how your own community handles its waste. What can you recycle? What can you throw away? What do you do with all the toxic things in your life like dead batteries, used oil, leftover paint, and household chemicals when they are used up? Your community probably has a website that lists the rules and alternatives for handling these things. You can call or even visit the solid waste or hazardous waste disposal division in your community. When you have the information, make a poster, video, or cartoon that lets others know about the problem.

Luke W. Cole and Sheila R. Foster
"We Speak for Ourselves:
The Struggle of Kettleman City"

Luke W. Cole was co-founder of the Center on Race, Poverty and the Environment, a part of the California Rural Legal Assistance Foundation. He represented workers and rural communities across America in their struggles for environmental justice. His work in Kettleman City was part of his commitment to community-based, community-led organizing and action. He died in 2009. The essay below appeared in *From the Ground Up: Environmental Racism and the Rise of the Environmental Justice Movement*, which Cole co-authored with Sheila R. Foster, a professor at Rutgers University School of Law. While the book traces the history of the environmental justice movement and identifies some of the political and legal issues involved, this essay tells the story of Kettleman City and the citizens who live there. Like the article "High Tech Trash," this is a story about race, poverty, and where we dump our toxic wastes. As you read, consider the opportunities and challenges facing citizens who want to participate in decisions about waste or any other environmental impact on their community and about where the power to make change lies.

> *El pueblo unido jamas sera vencido* ("The people united shall never be defeated")
>
> —Chant and slogan from the farm-worker justice movement

Stories are one way we transmit our history, share our successes, and learn from our losses. Stories are also an important part of the movement for environmental justice, which has as one of its central tenets the idea "We speak for ourselves." This book tells the stories of ordinary men and women thrust into extraordinary roles as community leaders, grassroots experts, and national policymakers. We invoke these stories to illustrate the human reality behind the numerous studies that chart the disproportionate distribution of environmental hazards, and the burgeoning grassroots movement for environmental justice that has sprung up around the country.

The first story is about Kettleman City, one of the defining struggles of the early days of the Environmental Justice Movement. The story is a classic David-and-Goliath tale, in which a small farm-worker town took on the largest toxic waste dumping company in the world—and won.

Kettleman City is a tiny farm-worker community of 1,100 residents in Kings County, in California's San Joaquin Valley. Ninety-five percent of Kettleman residents are Latino, 70 percent of the residents speak Spanish at home, and roughly 40 percent are monolingual Spanish speakers. They are primarily farm-workers who work in the fields that spread out in three directions from Kettleman City. Kettleman City is much like many other rural communities in the Southwest, and few people would know about it were it not for the fact that Kettleman City is also host to the largest toxic waste dump west of Alabama, a landfill that is owned and run by Chemical Waste Management, Inc., about three and a half miles from town, hidden behind some low hills. The dump was created in the late 1970s without the community's knowledge or consent.

People marvel that a gigantic toxic waste site can be placed just miles   5 from a community without the community's knowledge. In California, under state environmental laws, government agencies are required to provide public notice in three ways: (1) through notices printed in a newspaper of general circulation, which in Kettleman City means a small box in the classified ads in the Hanford *Sentinel*, published forty miles away; (2) by posting signs on and off the site, which means on a fence post three and a half miles from Kettleman City; and (3) by sending notices through the mail to adjacent landowners. The adjacent landowners to the Chem Waste facility are large agribusiness and oil companies such as Chevron.

Residents of Kettleman City found out about the dump in the early 1980s, after reading in the local paper about multimillion-dollar fines levied against the Chem Waste facility for violations of environmental laws. While residents were unhappy to find out their town was host to a huge toxic waste facility, they saw few ways in which they could challenge the dump.

Things changed in 1988, when Chem Waste proposed to build a toxic waste incinerator at the dump site. Residents in Kettleman City heard about this proposal not from Chem Waste, not from Kings County or state officials, but from a phone call from a Greenpeace organizer in San Francisco. Bradley Angel, Southwest campaigner for Greenpeace's toxics campaign, had received a phone call from the Kings County sheriff one afternoon in January 1988, asking him whether Greenpeace planned to demonstrate at the hearing in Kettleman City that night. After finding out about the hearing, Angel called one of the few people he knew in Kettleman City at the time, Esperanza Maya, and said, "Espy, did you know that there's a hearing tonight in your community about a toxic waste incinerator?" She said, "I haven't heard a thing about it."

Maya grabbed a few of her neighbors and went to the hearing. They were shocked to find out that Chem Waste was proposing to build an incinerator that would burn up to 108,000 tons—216,000,000 pounds—of toxic waste every year. That translates to about 5,000 truckloads of toxic waste that would pass through the Kettleman area each year, in addition to the hundreds of daily truckloads bound for the existing toxic dump.

After the hearing, many Kettleman City residents began to do their homework about the dump, the incinerator, and the company, Chemical Waste Management. They formed a community group, El Pueblo para el Aire y Agua Limpio (People for Clean Air and Water). The group found out that the air in the San Joaquin Valley was already contaminated, that the Valley is considered the second-worst polluted air basin in the United States, ranking behind only Los Angeles. And, whereas Los Angeles has ocean breezes to cleanse it, the San Joaquin Valley, because of its unique bathtub shape, is a closed system, so pollutants stay put and fill the Valley.

10   Members of El Pueblo also found out about a 1984 report done for the California Waste Management Board. That report, known popularly as the Cerrell Report, and paid for by California taxpayers' dollars, [sic] suggested to companies and localities that were seeking to site garbage incinerators that the communities that would offer the least resistance to such incinerators were rural communities, poor communities, communities whose residents had low educational levels, communities that were highly Catholic, communities with fewer than 25,000 residents, and communities whose residents were employed in resource-extractive jobs like mining, timber, or agriculture. When members of El Pueblo looked around Kettleman City, they were startled. "The Cerell report fit us to a T," [sic] says Mary Lou Mares, one of the leaders of El Pueblo. The incinerator proposal suddenly also made sense to Kettleman residents: "If there's a report that specifically tells them what to look for, of course they're going to target us," observes Mares.

El Pueblo also looked at California's other toxic waste dumps. California has three Class I toxic waste dumps—the dumps that can take just about every toxic substance known to science. The group found out that in addition to Kettleman (95 percent Latino), the two other dumps were in Buttonwillow, where 63 percent of the residents are people of color, primarily Latino, and in Westmorland, which is 72 percent Latino. "It seemed like a conspiracy," says Mary Lou Mares, "although it's logical if they are using the Cerrell report." Both Buttonwillow and Westmorland look just like Kettleman: they are small, predominantly Latino, rural farm-worker communities marked by high levels of poverty. People in Kettleman City began to put two and two together.

The Pattern

Then El Pueblo looked at the company, Chemical Waste Management, the largest toxic waste dumping company in the U.S. Chem Waste runs the largest toxic waste dump in the country (and, probably, the world) in Emelle, Alabama, which is in the heart of Alabama's black belt, in a community that is about 95 percent African American. Emelle actually looks a great deal like Kettleman City—small, rural, poverty-stricken—but the residents are black instead of brown.

Even more interesting were the locations of Chem Waste's other incinerators. At the time, Chem Waste owned three other toxic waste incinerators: one on the south side of Chicago in a neighborhood that is 55 percent African American and 24 percent Latino; one in Port Arthur, Texas, in a community that is about 80 percent black and Latino; and one in Sauget, Illinois, which is surrounded by neighborhoods that are 95 percent or more African American, including East St. Louis, an overwhelmingly African American community that has been called "America's Soweto."

The residents of Kettleman City started to see a pattern. "Our initial reaction was outrage," says Maricela Alatorre, a student leader during El Pueblo's struggle who has lived in Kettleman City her entire life. "We felt we were being targeted, that Chem Waste as a corporation was targeting these communities on purpose because their ethnic make-up would make people least likely to protest." Every single community where Chem Waste operated its toxic waste incinerators is a community of color, and substantially so: 79 percent in Chicago and Port Arthur, in the 90s in Sauget, and 95 percent in Kettleman City. They found out later that Chem Waste had planned to build an incinerator in Tijuana, Mexico, thereby hitting the 100 percent mark.

The residents of Kettleman City then turned to Chem Waste's compliance record. At the Kettleman City facility, Chem Waste had been fined $3.2 million for more than 1,500 incidents of dumping too much waste into its evaporation ponds. Chem Waste's incinerator in Chicago had blown up and been shut down by the Illinois EPA. Illinois State Representative Clem Balanoff came to Kettleman City and told residents about Chem Waste's overfilling of the Chicago incinerator, which then spewed black smoke plumes, and about the fine Chem Waste faced for having turning off [sic] the incinerator's air monitoring equipment so that nobody would know what was coming out. And it did so once, not twice, but many times over a period of months [sic]. In Vickery, Ohio, Chem Waste took in

15

PCB-contaminated oil for disposal and then turned around and resold it to a company that used it to repave streets and as fuel oil in nearby communities. The residents took note of Chem Waste's actions in Louisiana, where the company was caught storing toxic waste in one of those store-yourself rental lockers.

El Pueblo also discovered that Chem Waste and its parent company, Waste Management, had paid more than $50,000,000 in fines, settlements, and penalties for price fixing, bribery, and related environmental crimes. "They could get away with all this because they were a multimillion dollar corporation," notes Alatorre. "These fines meant nothing to them." The company, they found out, was such an environmental bad actor that the San Diego District Attorney's Office had told the San Diego Board of Supervisors that "the company's history requires extreme caution by the San Diego County Board of Supervisors or any other governmental entity contemplating any contractual or business relationship with Waste Management" because of a pattern of continuing criminal behavior.

Nor was Chem Waste's behavior ancient history. In the fall of 1992, as the incinerator project was under consideration, Chem Waste was fined a record $11.5 million for a botched Superfund cleanup in Pennsylvania. In Kettleman City, Chem Waste was caught "sample packing." Ten trucks of waste would show up at the gate of the dump; by law Chem Waste was required to sample each truck to determine its contents to ensure that incompatible wastes were not disposed of together. What Chem Waste was doing, however, was taking ten samples from the first truck and then waving all the other trucks through.

Kettleman City residents felt justified in being a little alarmed by the prospect of having this company run yet another facility near their town. The residents figured that if the company can't run a hole in the ground correctly, it shouldn't be given the ability to do something worse.

The Process

As part of the permitting process for the incinerator, Kings County issued an Environmental Impact Report (EIR). The Environmental Impact Report was about 300 pages long, with another 700 pages of appendices, for a total of about 1,000 pages. Kettleman City residents, 40 percent monolingual Spanish speakers, 95 percent Latino, said to Kings County, "Look, to include us in this decision, you need to translate these documents into Spanish." Kings County was unresponsive. The County decision makers likely did not want to set a precedent; if they translated the EIR, they would have to translate documents in other situations, which is something the people of Kettleman City thought would probably be a good idea. Chem Waste, in a generous offer, translated a five-page executive summary and distributed that to every household in Kettleman City. English speakers in Kings County thus had about 1,000 pages of data to pore over, while Spanish speakers had five pages.

Despite being shut out by the lack of environmental review in their own language, Kettleman City residents nevertheless attempted to take part in the process. "We thought if we could get enough people to write and express their opinion, it would be important," says El Pueblo leader Mary Lou Mares. Mares and her allies generated almost 120 letters from the tiny community, and more than two-thirds of all the comments by individuals on the EIR were from the people of Kettleman City—in Spanish. Residents wrote in saying, in effect, "Hey, translate this document. Include us in the process. Let us know what you are proposing to do up on the hill. If you say it's safe, why won't you let us know what you are doing? Why won't you translate this document?"

The public hearing on the incinerator was scheduled not in Kettleman City but forty miles away, in the county seat of Hanford. It was held in the largest venue in Kings County, the County Fairground building, which is about the size of a football field. The hearing room was set up with a raised dais in the front, with a table at which sat the Planning Commission, looking down on the room. Then there was an open space; beyond that, two microphones set up for the public. Behind the microphones were about fifty rows of seats, and there were some bleacher seats at the back of the room. Behind the bleachers was empty concrete floor back to the very rear of the auditorium, about 300 feet from the Planning Commission.

Kettleman City residents showed up at the meeting in force. About 200 people came by bus and carpool from Kettleman City, and, as one of the their leaders [sic] made clear, "We're here, we want to testify on this project, and we brought our own translator." The chair of the Kings County Planning Commission looked down on the crowd and said, "That request has been denied. The translation is taking place in the back of the room and it won't happen up here." Residents looked at where the Planning Commissioner was pointing: they looked from the Planning Commission up on their dais, they looked at the open space and the microphones, they looked at all the rows of chairs, and they looked at the bleachers. And then they looked way

20

back behind the bleachers, nearly at the rear of the room, where there was one forlorn man sitting surrounded by a little circle of about twenty-five empty chairs. The Planning Commission chair said again, "Why don't you go back there? There are monitors back there. We are all in the same room." The 200 people from Kettleman City looked around, and they looked at the back of the room at those twenty-five chairs, and they looked at the empty chairs up front, and they said, "Adelante, adelante" ("forward, forward"), and they moved up to the front of the room. Residents testified in Spanish, from the front of the room, that the last time they had heard about people being sent to the back of the room was when African Americans were sent to the back of the bus—a policy dumped in the dustbin of history a generation ago. They said they weren't going to stand for that. "The incident summed up what the County felt for the people out here in Kettleman City," notes Maricela Alatorre. "Our rights were second to this huge corporation."

The public hearing on the project brought to a close the public's ability to comment on the incinerator. Subsequently, the Planning Commission voted to approve the incinerator, and El Pueblo appealed that decision to the Kings County Board of Supervisors.

The Benefits and Burdens of Waste

California has a compensated siting law. Under the law, local governments can tax hazardous waste facilities up to 10 percent of their gross revenues. What does this have to do with the story? As Kettleman activist Mary Lou Mares sums it up, "When it comes to politics, the ones that have the money win out."

25   Kings County, which is about 65 percent white, has five members on the Board of Supervisors. At the time of El Pueblo's appeal, all the board members were white. Most white residents in Kings County live in one area, while most of the Latinos live in another part of the County. If this page were a map of Kings County, almost all the white people would live up in the upper right corner of the page, in and around the county seat of Hanford. And most of the Latino people would live at the bottom of the page—Kettleman City would be in the lower left of the page, and the Chem Waste dump would be next to it. Every single town in Kings County is majority white except for Kettleman City, which is 95 percent Latino, way down in the lower left of the page. Under the California law that provides for compensated siting, Kings County was receiving about $7 million per year in revenue from

Chem Waste's preexisting dump. That $7 million was about 8 percent of the County's annual budget. Most of the money is spent up near Hanford (in the upper right of the page), in the white community, and very little of it trickles down to the people of Kettleman City (down in the lower left of the page). The incinerator promised to almost double that tax revenue, so the County would be receiving about one-sixth of its annual revenue from this single company. "The County knew people in Hanford didn't give a damn one way or the other," points out Joe Maya, a leader of El Pueblo. Not surprisingly, the white Supervisors voted for the incinerator on a three-to-one vote.

The Lawsuit

Faced with this situation, the residents felt they had no choice but to a lawsuit. The lawsuit was successful when the judge ruled that the Environmental Impact Report had not sufficiently analyzed the toxic waste incinerator's impacts on air quality and on agriculture in the San Joaquin Valley and, most importantly, that the residents of Kettleman City had not been meaningfully included in the permitting process. As the Court eloquently stated: "The residents of Kettleman City, almost 40 percent of whom were monolingual in Spanish, expressed continuous and strong interest in participating in the CEQA [California Environmental Quality Act] review process for the incinerator project at [Chem Waste's] Kettleman Hills Facility, just four miles from their homes. Their meaningful involvement in the CEQA review process was effectively precluded by the absence of Spanish translation."

King's County decided not to appeal the lawsuit, largely because of the political pressure the Kings County Board of Supervisors was receiving from Kings County residents and from their supporters across California. A postcard campaign targeting the Board of Supervisors and the local Farm Bureau, orchestrated by El Pueblo and Greenpeace, generated more than 5,000 postcards to the Board and the Farm Bureau, while a petition campaign in the San Joaquin Valley by Citizen Action generated more than 17,000 signatures in opposition to the incinerator. Chemical Waste Management did not fold as easily, however, and appealed the judgement. Rather than go back and do the environmental study right in order to respond to the judge's (and the residents') concerns, the company was more comfortable staying in court. But Kettleman City's struggle had become a national struggle. The residents of Kettleman City and their representatives were telling Kettleman City's story at meetings, conferences, symposia, and rallies across the country. "I think they thought we would go away," observes Mary Lou Mares, the Kettleman City housewife who appeared on national television to tell the Kettleman story. "But it was too dangerous to let an incinerator come in here—we had to do something about it." The press loved the story, and soon people all around the country knew about the struggles of Kettleman City.

The Community Is Heard

On September 7, 1993, Chem Waste announced that it was withdrawing its application to construct the toxic waste incinerator near Kettleman City. Although Chem Waste cited changing economic conditions and a new public policy turn away from incineration, the General Manager of the Kettleman Hills Facility personally hand-delivered the news to one of the leaders of the community group El Pueblo, acknowledging the group's role in the decision. As the El Pueblo leader Espy Maya said, "I don't care how they word it; we won."

Analyze

1. Explain several reasons why it was difficult for the people of Kettleman City to prevent the construction of a toxic waste incinerator near their town.

2. What are some of the ways Chem Waste got around the few regulations that were imposed by state and federal governments?

3. The author suggests that Chem Waste deliberately attempted to keep Kettleman City's residents unaware of the toxic waste dump in their area. Do you find the author's claims realistic? Can you think of other contemporary situations in which public knowledge of a dangerous event has been minimized?

Explore

1. Do you think that the author of this piece writes about Kettleman City's struggle objectively? Or, in contrast, does the author seem to write from a point of bias? Do you think in this case objectivity helps or hinders the story that the author wants to tell? What is the effect of the author's tone and point of view on the way this story is perceived by the reader?

2. Go into your kitchen, garage, bathroom, or wherever you keep things that might have toxic chemicals in them and read some of the labels. For example, do you have insecticide sprays under the sink to spray for roaches, ants, or wasps? Identify one of those products and the dangerous chemicals in it. Those products usually have health warnings on them. Design an environmental and disposal warning label that you think should be part of the labeling on the product label.

3. The permit to build something like the incinerator in Kettleman City is granted through local, state, or national regulatory agencies. And these regulatory agencies have to go through a process for examining the risks and benefits of proposed changes, whether that be the environmental impact of the Chem Waste incinerator, filling in a local marsh to build houses, or putting a road through a forest or a highway through a neighborhood. Part of most such processes is a "public comment" period or public hearings in which citizens are invited to participate. Identify a proposed change in your community that has environmental or social risks associated with it and research the permitting process. If possible, visit a public hearing and gather written documents in the case. What are the issues on either side of the argument, and was there a fair resolution?

Emily Fontaine
"Where Did Our Clothes Come From?"

Emily Fontaine is a student at Ashford University who studies English and in her spare time hosts a fashion blog on blogspot.com. Her blog, entitled *Le Quaintrelle*, has gathered quite a following over its three-and-a-half-year lifespan and has been featured on a number of websites, including Luckymag.com and Glamour.com, as well as in the book *What I Wore Today*. Fontaine's blog is primarily a fashion and lifestyle blog, and its topics generally do not extend to issues of sustainability. However, in the following post, Fontaine takes a personal inventory of the clothes in her closet to determine where the clothing she owns was made. As you read her post, think about how Fontaine's discoveries of her own closet, and the realizations that she came to as a result, could affect consumers at large to make the fashion industry more sustainable.

As consumers, we have a lot to think about when purchasing clothes, shoes, purses, and accessories. Things like style, color, fit, and price seem to be the most important factors when choosing an item to purchase. But, [something] we all know but seldom think about, is the impact we make when we purchase something. The impact we make on the sales and profits of whatever store or site we're buying from, sure, but also the economic, environmental, and social impact we make as well, things like the material (organic, renewable sources, recycled material, etc.) and the process in which the garment was made (factory environment, child labor, fair trade, etc.) should also be put into consideration when buying a product.

I read this great post last night from 39th and Broadway about the label of origin on garments, and it really got me thinking. The label of origin is the tag that states where the garment was made. If you ever wonder how companies can sell things for so cheap, look at the tag, it was probably made in a developing country where the standard of living is low and there are no laws against child labor or fair wages. Sad to think about, but a reality that we have to acknowledge.

So it got me thinking, how much of my own closet is made in third world, developing countries? And how much of it is domestically made, helping our economy and fellow citizens with jobs? I went through my entire closet (which isn't a small task) and pulled out everything that's label of origin said Made In U.S.A, and this was the result:

To be honest, this is a lot more than I was expecting to pull out. But to put it in perspective, this is only about 1/4 of my closet. I'd say about 85% of the rest of my closet is from China. The rest is everywhere from Turkey to the Philippines, Mexico to India and even places I couldn't point out where they were on a map (and I'm pretty good at geography). Granted, there were numerous pieces that had no tags at all, either because I cut them off or because they were vintage and simply didn't have any. And while I'd like to think all my vintage clothes were made in the good ol' U.S. of A of yesteryear, I didn't want to assume. So if it had no tag, it wasn't included. The sad part is, there just isn't a lot of things still made in the United States. 39th and Broadway makes a good point:

> If we have learned anything from the recent economic collapse, from   5
> the failing auto industry's illumination on the lack of American
> manufacturing and jobs, from the rampant unemployment due to
> out-sourcing, to our abhorrent dependence on foreign oil and more,
> it is that we have gone from a self sufficient country that made things,
> to an indebted country that is dependent on foreign goods.

So let me break it down. I put all the "Made in the U.S." clothes into different piles, to put things in perspective of where the majority of domestically-made clothes come from. The first pile was of clothes that I know 100% were made in the US, that's because it was made by either my or my Mom's own two hands (with addition to a grandma-made and sister-made scarf and Etsy seller skirt). If you ever want to know EXACTLY where an item was made, or how it was made, the only way to be completely sure is to make it yourself.

The second pile was the designer pile.

Granted, I don't own a lot of designer clothes. Aside from another Betsey Johnson shirt (made in China) and a vintage Halston skirt I found at the goodwill (no tag of origin), this is probably all the designer clothes I own. (Does Ralph Lauren count? Even if it does, it was made in India). But what surprised me was that not ONE piece of the Go International for Target for ANY designer that I own was made in the U.S. Actually, these are the only pieces out of ANYTHING I've bought at Target that were:

Two! Two pieces. And you know I love me some Target, my closet is filled with Target things. And these are the only pieces that were made here.

The next pile was the "retail" pile. Meaning places like Forever 21, Alloy, Charlotte Russe, Urban Outfitters.

Surprisingly this is more than I thought would come out of retail. When you think of Forever 21, unfortunately you don't think the highest quality, some might even call it "disposable" fashion. And while being made in America doesn't automatically equal high quality garments, it at least means a better quality of work environment and living standards for those making the garments. I've also noticed that most websites like Forever 21 and Urban Outfitters have whether or not the item is imported or made in the U.S. right in the description.

The next pile was probably the biggest, and it makes sense. It's the "thrifted" pile.

There was a time when out-sourcing wasn't really heard of. Fortunately a lot of the pieces that were made during that time are at your local thrift store or goodwill. I'm sure you will notice the older the garment, the more likely it is to be made in the U.S. (unless it's fancy-schmancy and might have been bought in Europe during a trip abroad).

The last and final pile was things I've bought off Ebay.

Like thrifting, the things you usually buy on Ebay are vintage or second-hand, but sometimes they aren't. It just depends. But notice that the Ebay pile is the only pile that includes shoes and a belt. Those were the ONLY shoes I have made in America and that is the one and only belt. Crazy, right? I've still yet to find a purse that was made in the U.S. 15

I know this is turning out to be a long post, and I'm sorry for rambling, but there are some subjects that I have more to say about than others. This little exercise of going through my closet and actually seeing where all my clothes came from was definitely an eye-opener. Things I *thought* would be made in America like my Levi's were made in Guatemala, and my Tom's Shoes... made in China. The things I *hoped* would be made in America, like my favorite skinny jeans, are from China. Now does this mean that I'm going to throw out all my clothes that aren't American made? No. But it's definitely going to make me think twice about purchasing something from a third world country, and make me think about *who* made it and what conditions it was made in.

I also understand that America isn't the one and only place to buy socially-ethical clothes, either. I'm sure my scarves and shoes made in Germany, Italy and England weren't made in sweatshops, or for less-than-fair wages. And plus, most high-quality clothes come from Europe (Hello Paris!). But being an American during this recession and seeing all the jobs lost in your own country by people in your everyday life makes you want to support your own economy and your fellow citizens.

It all comes down to realizing that each purchase you make is like a vote. Depending on what you buy, that is what you are voting for. By you purchasing something it gives that company the money that says "this is what sells, this is what people want and what they buy" so if you buy imported goods, then companies will continue to out-source their jobs for a cheaper price. But if you vote to buy domestic, or even foreign goods, as long as either are from companies that have fair wages, and acceptable work environments, then you are showing that that is what you want and what you expect from companies.

I know in a perfect world these issues wouldn't even exist, but unfortunately, they do. I'm not saying people are bad if they buy imported things, trust me . . . that's like the pot calling the kettle black. I'm just saying I think we should all think about this the next time we buy something and try to buy domestic when possible.

Analyze

1. What does Emily suggest that consumers do regarding their clothing purchases?
2. Emily says that when you purchase an item, you are casting a vote. But in "The Story of Stuff: Electronics," Annie Leonard says that "we are never going to just shop our way out of this problem because the choices

available to us at the store are limited by choices of designers and policy-makers outside of the store." In a group, discuss this Catch-22. When faced with this conundrum, what is the average person to do?

3. Why are so many of our clothes made overseas?

Explore

1. Take on Emily's challenge, and look at some of the tags of origin of the clothes in your closet. Find out where your clothes came from, keeping in mind that they were likely made somewhere else before they arrived at the store. Using your favorite online search engine, see if you can find out even more information about the origins of your clothes, depending on where and by whom they were made. Then, write a blog post discussing your findings to your friends and describing what those discoveries mean to you and your future clothing purchases.

2. Go to your favorite mall and shop for clothes. Yes. You have a shopping assignment from a textbook! Make a list of where the things you want were made, how much they cost, and whether you can afford them. Then make a map that locates the products in their countries of origin and lists the standard of living and average income in those countries.

3. There is a huge literature on Nike products, mostly in academic journals. Do a little research on Nike and its corporate responsibility record and then defend the company against the criticism that it is unethical or make an argument to your friends for why they should stop buying Nike products.

Lucy Siegle
"Why It's Time to End Our Love Affair With Cheap Fashion"

Lucy Siegle is a British journalist who writes a weekly column for *The Observer* that focuses on the intersection between environmental matters and urban lifestyles. She has also published two books, *Green Living in the Urban Jungle* and *To Die For,* and has worked as a broadcaster on BBC's *The One Show* as an expert on consumer living and waste. The following essay from her column in *The Observer* focuses on the surprisingly potent environmental impacts involved in the crafting and disposing of cheap and non-durable fashion products. Siegle highlights the interrelated environmental and human damages that are produced by the demand for cheap fabrics and materials. She also presents some procedures and efforts being adopted by fashion manufacturers to curb the public interest in ultra-economical clothing. As you read, see if you can identify the unexpected environmental consequences of producing cheap fabrics for "fast fashion."

One can only speculate on the fashion footprint of the wardrobes of Lord Howie of Troon and the Earl of Northesk, both members of the Lords science and technology committee, but you'd have to suspect it is minimal. Given each lord's age, gender and peer-group interests—the highest fashion consumption rates are for women in their early thirties who read glossy magazines—the peers' share will come in well below the average of 35 kg of textiles per person per year (mostly clothing). Much of this will be thrown out within a year; a small part will be recycled or donated to charity, and the rest will be chucked in the bin.

Last week's waste reduction report from the Lords committee read a little in places like an analysis of the woodland defecation procedures of bears. '[The] culture of "fast fashion" encourages consumers to dispose of clothes which have only been worn a few times in favour of new, cheap garments which themselves will also go out of fashion and be discarded within a matter of months,' announced the venerable lords in tones of shock and awe.

Many women are inured to the obscene excesses of fast fashion. One pound in four is now spent on 'value' fashion as provided by the likes of Primark, Asda and Topshop, which has had huge success with model Kate Moss's range of clothes. Between 2003 and 2007 garment prices fell by an average of 10 per cent and over the past five years the rate of frenzied buying has accelerated, while we make room for it by discarding some two million tons every year.

The true weight of this addiction has only really been felt by an unfortunate few such as the Salvation Army which, with around 2,750 of the UK's 9,000 charity clothing banks, has been faced with an ever growing mound of tat to flog to consumers indifferent to pre-worn unless it happens to be vintage. Value fashion retailers will debate forever as to how they can sell clothes so cheaply, usually citing economies of scale, but it has been clear to recyclers for some time that a fall in fibre quality and finishing is part of the equation. This makes the resale of last season's paper thin, slightly shrunken sun dress a distinctly unappetising commercial proposition. Besides, there isn't much incentive for consumers to buy worn when a new dress costs less than a lunchtime panini and coffee.

The bulk of discarded fast fashion is chucked into landfill. Meanwhile, the   5 fashion industry has been particularly adept at avoiding green censure and criticism. While more prosaic sectors—food and drink, electronics, detergents and even car manufacturers—have been forced to own up to environmental shortcomings either to pre-empt legislation or conform to new regulations (such as the EU directive that means your hairdryer or washing machine can no longer be flung into the landfill) fashion appears to have charmed us all in a haze of sequins, air kisses and the seemingly boundless dynamism of fast fashion with its High Street empires and super-rich moguls.

But when Defra, the department for the environment, began to analyse the impact of different materials in the nation's landfills a couple of years ago, fast fashion's get-out-of-jail-free card was unexpectedly revoked. The nation's penchant for 'McFashion'—as one-night-only T-shirts and skinny jeans have been dubbed—was found to translate into more than three million tons of carbon dioxide emissions.

More significant to millions of fashion-lovers than the opinions of a Lords committee or Defra will be the opinion of the style press. And even those who formerly and gleefully proclaimed Primark the new Prada are now suggesting that fast fashion has rather had its day. Apparently it is all about 'investment dressing'—buying one piece and loving it for a long time—now as fashionistas tighten their tiny little belts. 'Gucci or gas?' asks the September issue of *Harper's Bazaar*, advising fashion-lovers feeling the credit crunch to survive on 'one big ticket item, something in between or a little bit of both'.

There's some validity in this argument, as anything that cuts down the rapid turnover begins to reverse the fact that—according to Matilda Lee from the Ecologist—just 2 per cent of the average clothing budget goes on services that repair or lengthen the lifespan of our garments and accessories.

However, to be truly sustainable, the fashion parameters will have to be widened. If fashion is about ingenuity and innovation, this is a good time for the industry to draw on these qualities and return to measuring fashion in terms of something other than quantity. There has already been a shift. Phil Patterson, once textiles manager at Marks and Spencer, has set up ecotextile.com to allow consumers to assess their wardrobe in terms of environmental damage units (EDUs) with the goal that they'll be more fibre-discerning in the future. The London College of Fashion recently launched its Centre for Sustainable Fashion and there has been a renaissance of thrift fashion ideas from reworking existing pieces to sewing classes, kit fashion, clothes swaps and clothes and accessory libraries.

10   There would appear to be some ethical motivation for change too. In the aftermath of the *Observer* and *Panorama* exposé of child labour used in manufacturing a line for Primark, an ICM research poll, commissioned by *Drapers* magazine, found that 42 per cent of people who shop at Primark were less likely or a lot less likely to shop at the retailer because of what they had heard.

In reality, any demise of super-cheap, super-fast fashion probably comes down to market economics. Labour costs have increased 50 per cent in the past four years across provinces in south-eastern China, the sewing room of the world. Meanwhile, fast fashion is scarily dependent on cheap fibres, namely polyester and cotton—which together account for more than 80 per cent of all fibre production worldwide.

Both are dogged by sustainability issues. As petroleum production declines, polyester prices are soaring, while cotton's insatiable need for water (and agrichemicals), coupled with the fact that two-thirds is still rain-grown in areas where rainfall has declined, means there's not enough to go around. Add to this a new, hungry consumer in the form of the Chuppie (the Chinese yuppie) who has developed an appetite for fast fashion herself, meaning that Chinese producers are less eager to export.

It will almost certainly get slower. In order to keep up with the trend for two new lines a week, brought to the high street by Spanish fashion giant Zara, competitors are increasingly reliant on air freight, and that is becoming hugely expensive.

Shipping a standard container from Shanghai to America's east coast costs $8,000 (£4,315) today, as opposed to just $3,000 a few months ago. Container ships are slowing down to cut fuel costs. If fashion stays fast it will need to become more localised, which will increase cost. So it can be slow and cheap, or fast and expensive. It is the combination of cheap and fast that is unsustainable.

15   In any case, we shouldn't overly mourn the passing of cheap fast fashion. We may be short on cheap fibre and oil, but one thing we have an abundance of is creativity. The demise of fast fashion could be as revolutionary as the mini skirt, the Ugg boot and Agyness Deyn all rolled into one.

Analyze

1. What is fast fashion? What are some reasons the author gives to support her claim that "the combination of cheap and fast" fashion is unsustainable?

2. Make a list of all the costs—human, energy and natural resource use— that go into supporting fast fashion.

3. How did Defra "revoke" fast fashion's "get out of jail free" card?

Explore

1. What do you think of this article's suggestion that people move toward "'investment dressing'—buying one piece and loving it for a long time"? In a group, see if you can add to the list of ways that fashion can be slowed down. This article mentions sewing classes and clothes swaps as two examples of extending the lives of our clothes—how else can you imagine clothing being loved for longer and kept out of the trash bin?

2. This article, like other articles in this section, demonstrates the ways terms can make people view a practice or a product in a particular way. For example, using the term "McFashion" turns a seemingly highbrow practice on its head and makes it seem suddenly uncool, and words like "vintage" and "investment dressing" add a positive spin to a term like "old." As a homework assignment, see how you can use new phrases and invented terms to give a fresh sound to buying sustainably. See how many of these slogans you can come up with, and think about how the new term changes the ways that people might think about its associated practice.

3. Siegle says that cotton is a cheap fiber and suggests that it is wrong to buy lots of cheap cotton clothes. But cotton is a natural product— organic and all that. Use the Internet to explore cotton production and identify the problems associated with growing and producing cotton cloth. Then produce a document of some form—a written text, a poster, a video, a vlog (video-blog)—that makes this information accessible to people your age.

Gay Hawkins
"Worm Stories"

Gay Hawkins is Professorial Research Fellow and Deputy Director at the Centre for Critical and Cultural Studies at the University of Queensland in Australia. She studies the ways culture and the environment intersect, especially in the ordinary activities of everyday life. She has published two books on waste, *Culture and Waste: The Creation and Destruction of Value* (2002), and *The Ethics of Waste: How We Relate to Rubbish* (2006), from which the selection below is taken. She is also finishing a book, *Plastic Water,* on the use and consequences of bottled water. In the essay below, Hawkins describes a sustainable house in Sydney and a community composting system in Pennsylvania that use worm farms to transform human and kitchen waste into useable water and fertilizer. This is certainly an imaginative response to a perennial problem, but Hawkins thinks it is more than that. As you read, consider how our normal sense of revulsion to waste, especially human waste, might be transformed into more sustainable practices. How might you pay more attention to the many forms of waste in your life?

I want to tell some worm stories now that show the arts of transience in action. My aim is to think about their ethical significance, to reflect on how they alter ways of living and embodiment. How have worms been deployed in a politics of active experimentation with waste?

In a very old house in Sydney a few miles from the city center sits the now famous sustainable house. It's a typical nineteenth from the outside, narrow and unremarkable. Inside it looks pretty similar to most old houses occupied by a busy family. It's been stylishly renovated with all mod cons, the glass sliding doors at the rear looking onto a lovely landscaped bush garden. But beneath all this inner urban normality is a vastly different infrastructure making the house function: providing power and water and dealing with waste. The house runs on solar power collected from roof panels, with any excess going back into the grid. Potable water is collected from the roof and filtered using sophisticated carbon technology. All waste water from the house flows into a Dowmus waste system, which uses earthworms and microorganisms to break down and filter human effluent, gray water, and food scraps. This waste management system sits outside the back door. It looks like a long garden seat (and that is another function) running along the length of the tiny backyard. Inside worms manage the household waste. At the end of the system, water, which is mostly free of pathogens, is pumped through a compact ultraviolet light disinfector to ensure that it is completely sterile. This water is then used to wash clothes and flush the toilet, with any excess pumped into a reed bed at the bottom of the garden.

While this house is exemplary and pretty unusual in a very dense urban area, it is not exceptional as far as examples of sustainability go. It does all the right things—uses renewable energy, collects rainwater rather than letting it run away down a storm-water system, and manages its waste on-site. This house sits very lightly on the ground; it shows us how we can live far more sustainably without sacrificing "quality of life." It still has a bidet and a dishwasher; being inside it doesn't feel like participating in an alternative lifestyle. Assessments of the house have calculated that it saves over 26,500 gallons of water from Sydney's water supply, keeps more than 21,000 gallons of storm water out of Sydney Harbour, and prevents more than 16,000 gallons of sewage from being pumped into the Pacific Ocean. If environmental ethics are about calculating the impacts of human practices on natural systems, then these figures are impressive. There is no question that the residents of this house should have an easier conscience, but what about the impacts of these different systems on their habits? What does it mean to live with worms eating your shit outside your back door? How does the fact of a different technique for waste management reverberate across the bodies that live there?

When I first visited this house I went on one of its regular public tours. We were shown through the interior and invited to inspect the various systems keeping the house functioning. Then we went into the backyard, and someone asked about waste and whether the house was hooked up to the sewer. The owner showed us the six-foot-long worm farm masquerading as a garden seat. He lifted the lid and let us smell the fecund odor of decay. He poked around and showed us the worms heroically laboring. He collected some water from the end of the system and showed us how clean it was. "You could drink this," he declared. Everyone in the tour shuddered and then laughed with horror. Purity and danger were evoked, the excess of laughter releasing the tension of a taboo transgressed.

Here was a house where it was possible to see the arts of transience in action. Traditional systems of elimination that remove waste fast and invisibly were not in place. There were still underground drains, but they ended up in the backyard. Bodily waste in its most immediate and hazardous form remained hidden, but once it was subject to transformation into compost it was *present*; the worm farm occupied a significant space in the backyard. It was enclosed in an attractive box, it didn't smell, but its reality could not be denied. This household couldn't help but acknowledge waste, not in its brute physicality but as a fact of their daily lives, as something that required attention. You couldn't sustain an ethos of distance and denial in this house because its structural organization presumes a careful and ethical coexistence with waste.

All the quotidian rituals of caring for the worm farm, keeping it functioning efficiently, have impacts on bodies. They require new habits, different corporeal disciplines, and these reverberate across other registers of the self. It is hard for bodily waste to sustain the same level of symbolic force as abject horrifying matter when its management, once it leaves your body, remains your responsibility. Instead, one has to become realistic about it, give it a certain quality of attention. The dynamics of repression are diminished in this new relation with bodily waste. As I've argued elsewhere, different technologies of waste management show how habits and symbolic systems intersect and how these points of intersection can transform affects and micropolitics. Here was a family that had experimented with a different way of living with their waste. This didn't involve messiness or unboundedness, the collapse of all boundaries, or the collapse of a notion of waste. Rather, it involved different technical systems, bodily performances, calculations of value, and the relations between these. Waste in this house wasn't disgusting or abhorrent. It was in transition, in between contaminating and productive. And facilitating that transition involved two crucial things: lots and lots of worms and simple attentiveness. Through these two things a sustainable ethics of waste emerged.

Changes in one house or even hundreds won't save the planet. This is a common criticism of the sustainable house and other strategies that focus on individuals or families taking a stand and radically changing their daily practices. In fact, these strategies have sometimes been interpreted as the privatization of public problems. This is not my position. I would challenge it by arguing that the adoption of strategies at the micropolitical level of the home and the body reverberates across larger political culture in a multiplicity of ways. When the sustainable house is featured on a national lifestyle show, when people who have been on a tour of it talk to friends, when Internet sites showcase it, it impacts on new constituencies. Micropolitics shape an intersubjective ethos of politics. This intersubjective ethos occurs in conversations, in the media, in myriad relations in which practical examples of different ways of managing waste undermine normalized and exploitative practices and nurture receptivity to change.

But what about structural solutions? What about sustainable human waste management on a large scale? In Granville Township in Pennsylvania the Sewer and Water Department decided in 2004 to solve its serious biowaste problem by signing a contract for a full-scale vermicomposting system, the first to be constructed in the United States. The existing sewer system used an aerobic sludge digestion facility that involved intermittent discharge into a river and the transfer of dewatered biosolids, or what was left over, to a landfill. This landfill was rapidly reaching capacity, and so an alternative solution to the problem of biosolid waste was required. Four vermiculture beds six feet wide and ninety-five feet long housing one thousand pounds of worms per bed were the solution. This large-scale use of worms to manage a town's biosolids does not have any impact on householders; it makes no claims on them, and it won't change their habits. But it does show an important shift at the macropolitical level of local systems of governmentality. It shows a willingness to embrace a more sustainable technology, and whether this was done for cost-saving reasons or environmental concerns is irrelevant. The fact is that worms are being productively used to facilitate the arts of transience on a mass scale where once dumping was the solution.

The images used to promote the Granville project show the giant worm 10 farms housed in a shed. There is lots of engineering in evidence: conveyer belts to move and spread the mix, trays and another conveyer system to collect the castings, which are then stabilized and sold as agricultural fertilizer. This is a potent example of how nature is always differentially mixed into culture. All this technology doesn't diminish the great significance of the work being done by those worms as they facilitate transition. In those giant industrial worm farms heightened life and heightened death *go together*, the profound interconnections between destruction and renewal are everywhere evident. Perhaps this system exemplifies what Phillips calls "the ordinary sublime." He uses this term to explain the difficulties Darwin had accounting for experiences of things that overwhelm and overawe us once God drops out of the picture.

It is the immediate (in the literal sense) participation of nature in the experience of men and women that Darwin is promoting. But it is the ordinary sublime of transience that he singles out; there is nothing more ordinary, more natural, than that we should have experiences that no one, not even God, understands: experiences that satisfy us because they overwhelm us, experiences we value because they are strange.

The ordinary sublime of transience is what worms show us. To witness worms at work, whether on a big or small scale, is to encounter the philosophical resonance of biological processes. Worms are the penultimate loss managers, and they give us a powerful example of how quotidian and inevitable change is. And in this very ordinariness we can see how loss and change can be experienced without denial or disgust or despair, and without recourse to grand moral rhetoric. We can see how waste can contribute to renewal, how it can be generative.

I've argued that current waste habits protect us from encountering change. Their predictability and comfort is predicated on technologies of streamlined removal that allow us to avoid the transition that wasted things will inevitably undergo. Most acts of disposal involve relations with technology or containers, not the waste itself. We experience elimination and removal but not decay and change. Managing a worm farm disrupts this. When you live with worms you enter into a different means of engagement with waste: your bodily and kitchen by-products become their food, their waste becomes your garden fertilizer. You have to live with your waste a little more carefully so as to facilitate its effective transition by worms, and in these habits a calmer acceptance of your own transience might be nurtured.

Analyze

1. What is the role of the worms in the sustainable house?
2. What does the author mean when she says that "current waste habits protect us from encountering change"? What kind of change does the author mean here? What happens when we make our waste visible and experience "decay and change?"
3. One of the benefits of the sustainable house, according to the author, is that it shows that sustainable choices do not necessarily mean a sacrifice in quality of life. Do you think that this is an assumption that most people make about sustainable living? Do you agree with Hawkins' assertion that quality of life can be maintained through sustainable living?

Explore

1. Take a waste inventory of your family house, your apartment, or even your dorm room. What comes in? What goes out? How much "stuff" do you consume and what happens to it? Think more broadly than just food and human waste. Energy, water, oil, all sorts of materials come into and flow out of your life. Are there ways to make this more sustainable, friendlier to the environment and to other humans?

2. Using a search engine, investigate other sustainable homes/buildings that utilize alternative energy/waste management strategies. Do you notice any patterns in these structures? What types of sustainable practices are commonly used in these structures? Create a list of some of the most common sustainable practices you found in your search.

3. Do some research on vermiculture and the available technology for this kind of waste management. Then write a guide to backyard vermiculture composting, complete with materials lists, a design, and directions on how to build and maintain the composter.

Forging Connections

1. All of the articles in this section have talked about change in terms of waste—the need for change, the difficulties involved in change occurring, and the circumstances under which change can occur. Using the knowledge you have gained through these readings about our urgent need for a change in waste practices, create a blog page in which you describe three real-life ways the average person can make a significant change in his or her waste habits. Select three of the topics highlighted in this chapter—bottled water, electronics, clothing, human waste—and use the information provided by these readings to support why the change is needed, what impact you suspect the change will have, and how the change can be maintained over a long-term basis. Because this is a blog post, be sure to maintain an appropriate, yet still persuasive, rhetorical approach, style, and tone.

2. The articles in this section have exposed the invisible lives of everyday items, such as electronics and water bottles. Using your new knowledge of the reality of these items' life cycles, select an item and research its origins, sale, disposal, and chemical breakdown. Then write an expository essay that describes its complete life cycle to the average person and the varied and wide-ranging effects that some parts of its life cycle may have.

Looking Further

1. In her essay on worms, Hawkins writes: "There is no question that the residents of this house should have an easier conscience, but what about the impacts of these different systems on their habits? What does it mean to live with worms eating your shit outside your back door? How does the fact of a different technique for waste management reverberate across the bodies that live there?"

   The psychological effects of alternative lifestyles are often not discussed in sustainability advocacy, but they are there. As the readings in the first chapter suggest, part of sustainability is defining our identity and our relations to the human and natural world around us. Construct a list of sustainable waste practices mentioned in this section— drinking tap water, holding onto old clothing, abstaining from quickly replacing old electronics with new ones—and jot down some thoughts on the way that these choices will affect people's perception of themselves and their place in the world. Then broaden your focus and think about the issues of climate change, soil and water use, and food in other chapters. Write a brief essay exploring what it would mean to be an ethical person in these terms. What are the challenges to becoming that person? What benefits, personal and collective, are there to making this change?

2. A great many of the issues you encounter in this book involve small, everyday actions and ordinary practices: throwing away a water bottle, buying tomatoes in the winter, watering your lawn, driving your car more often than you need to. These actions are part of our lives. They are convenient. They are largely unnoticed. And people don't like being told that their behavior is wrong, bad, or destructive. They want to know what they can do. So, think of an action or practice (e.g., riding your bike to class or shopping at the farmers' market) that might change the way a person lives, and make it attractive to readers. Instead of a list of "Thou Shalt Nots," give them reasons to want to change.

3

Food: A Different View of the Food Chain

A formation of large harvesters suggests the scale of industrial agriculture.

Most of us think about food only when we are hungry. We tend to think about what we want, what it costs, how to get it. Many Americans watching their weight think about the number of calories in their food. And whenever there is an outbreak of a food-related illness like *E. coli*, salmonella, or "mad cow disease," we pay attention for a while. And all too many of us have to think about getting enough to eat every day. But food is so ordinary that few of us think about how food production affects natural resources or how agribusiness has altered our relationship to food.

If we look a little more carefully, food sits at the heart of almost every other topic in this book. As Michael Pollan points out in *The Omnivore's Dilemma*, eating connects humans to the ecosystem that produces their food: the fertility of the soil, the abundance of water, and the energy of the sun. As readings in Chapter 6 point out, the use of nitrogen fertilizer to boost corn production in the Midwest contributes to the destruction of the waters off the Mississippi and Texas coasts. And the energy needed to transport food across continents consumes huge amounts of fossil fuels and releases greenhouse gases that contribute to climate change. Overfishing the oceans and overgrazing grasslands to boost food production changes ocean ecosystems, erodes precious soil, and empties underground aquifers faster than they can recharge. If all roads lead to Rome, they also lead to that cheeseburger and French fries I had for lunch.

The importance of food to so many issues has triggered a burst of books, articles, blogs, and documentaries about food. Together these have created the contemporary "food movement." For members of the food movement, bad things happen when food and eating become the for-profit product of large international corporations. Industrial agriculture creates serious social, environmental, economic, and health problems. Concerns about the environmental consequences of food production and distribution include discussions such as Deborah Whitman's essay about genetically modified foods. And writers like Paul Epstein explore the connection between food and climate change. Others in the food movement are concerned about the dietary and health consequences of processed foods that contain a host of additives and are produced using growth hormones, antibiotics, and pesticides.

The environmental, dietary, and health consequences of industrial food are real, but pretty abstract and distant. By contrast, the "slow food" movement is about the pleasures of eating. Snarfing a "to go" meal in the car while you drive to work in the morning or on the way to soccer practice in the evening turns the pleasure of eating into a matter of efficient energy consumption to keep the body running. That seems necessary from time to time, but it misses a lot of the enjoyment we should get from our food. We tend to work so hard to get ahead that we don't have time to enjoy what we earn. As part of this change, people are turning to community-supported agriculture and local cooperatives. Farmers' markets have become popular ways to get fresh local foods but also to meet people, relax, and enjoy music and art. People have started gardening in their backyards, not just to save money, but to get better-tasting food. As the old country-western song says, "money can't buy you love or home-grown tomatoes."

The basic scientific or sustainability principle from Chapter 1 applies here; systems like food production are sustainable when they adapt human behaviors to the capacities of natural systems. The wonderful food production by "grass farmers" described in "The Genius of the Place" (below) actually improves the soil on the farm. By contrast, industrial monoculture—growing huge amounts of the same crop, such as corn—works against ecosystem processes and slowly destroys natural resources. But seeing the many costs of industrial food production is not easy. Soil erosion, water pollution, and overfishing are complicated issues and largely occur "somewhere else." We sit at the top of the food chain and rarely look down or back.

The rhetorical challenges involved in writing about food are unique. Lots of us enjoy reading about good food or about things that can give us pleasure. No one really wants to live off Ramen noodles and fast-food takeout. But food takes time to gather and prepare. You have to have a kitchen and learn how to cook to make wonderful meals, and really "good" food can be expensive. And we have learned to enjoy the taste and convenience of the high-fat, high-sugar processed foods we buy. Unfortunately, true as that is, even saying that last sentence sounds preachy and snobbish. The rhetorical strategies represented in the readings here range from matter-of-fact descriptions of genetically modified foods, to the celebration of grass as a natural wonder, to the plight of seeing "Nemo" on your plate. The question remains: How do you get readers to "go green"? And as the blog post about Starbucks suggests, is "green" really all that green anyway?

Jeff Opperman
"Getting to Know Your Bacon: Hogs, Farms, and Clean Water"

Jeff Opperman is the senior advisor for sustainable hydropower at The Nature Conservancy, a nonprofit conservation organization with more than 550 scientists on its staff. The Conservancy is dedicated to a collaborative approach to preserving natural resources that provide food, clean water, and energy around the world. As a senior staffer at the Conservancy, Mr. Opperman is a regular blogger on the organization's website. In the blog post below, Mr. Opperman uses a personal narrative to introduce readers to the environmental and health problems associated with hog production and eating bacon. His welcoming narrative style in this blog reflects the non-confrontational philosophy of the Conservancy. You might think of it as the language of the open, inviting hand rather than the language of the closed and aggressive fist.

While visiting friends in Toronto I spotted a small poster tacked behind their toaster. It read, "Bacon is like a little hug from God."

So true, I thought, smiling at how much I love those little hugs. But for so many reasons—encompassing cardiac health, the environment and humane farming practices—eating bacon often seems more like making out with the devil.

But I've found one way to wrest bacon away from the dark side and restore it to its rightful place as divine embrace: I mostly eat bacon that comes from pigs that I can visit. Pigs that lounge happily in sun-dappled mud puddles. Pigs that forage for acorns and hickory nuts and stand proudly on the edge of a meadow like some porcine version of Elsa (the lion from *Born Free*).

> "I mostly eat bacon that comes from pigs that I can visit."

I've directly witnessed all of these piggish pursuits during annual visits to "our" farm in Wayne County, Ohio. My family and I are part of a dairy co-op and, along with the milk, we get much of our yogurt, beef, pork, poultry, eggs and various other products (e.g., maple syrup) from this one family farm.

We belong to the co-op for a lot of reasons, including a preference for   5
supporting local family farms, access to fresh, healthy food and, as described
above, the psychic comfort of knowing that our carnivorous tendencies are
sustained by animals that live like, well, animals and not as cogs in some
brutal industrial machine.

There's another reason for supporting farms like our co-op: lower impacts
on lakes and rivers. Agriculture is one of the major sources for water
pollution in the United States. I do not mean to demonize agriculture—we
can't live without it, of course. Global agriculture is what feeds 6 billion
people . . . which means it's the most fundamentally important activity on
the planet. It can also never be free of environmental impacts.

But agriculture can always strive to reduce those impacts.

Take bacon as an example: Most of the bacon consumed in the United
States comes from hog "factory farms" where the animals are raised in
staggeringly crowded conditions. Often more than 10,000 animals are
packed into a single production facility, producing a tremendous amount
of concentrated waste that can pollute rivers, groundwater and drinking
water supplies.

Catastrophic failures of "manure lagoons" have led to massive fish kills
in nearby rivers, such as a spill from a hog-waste lagoon in North Carolina
in 1995 that killed 10 million fish in the New River and halted shellfish
harvests from hundreds of thousands of coastal wetlands.

On the other side of the spectrum is our co-op farm, a diverse patchwork   10
of fields and forests with a small stream running through it that's shaded by
a wide buffer of trees. While not certified organic, the farmer is culturally
predisposed to low-input farm practices. His animals have plenty of room
and, simply due to dramatically different densities, do not produce the
concentrated wastes that can be so harmful to clean water.

I sometimes worry that buying local, low-input farm products is the privilege of the American middle and upper class and that feeding the world's
growing population will require truly intensified agriculture. The grim
business of ensuring that the projected 9 billion people in 2050 have enough
to eat will have no patience for the kumbaya preferences of "locavores."

But wait. This Mark Bittman essay suggests that low-input agriculture
shows great promise—not just in reducing impacts but in actually meeting
global food demands. To explore this further, I did a very simple, back-of-the
envelope calculation* for how many people could be supported in the
Cleveland area with farms similar to our co-op.

The answer was surprising: Nearly 2.8 million people—almost the size of the greater Cleveland metropolitan area—could get much of their meat and dairy from local, low-input farms.

The numbers are approximate but serious. And while small family farms alone likely can't meet all future food demands, this example shows the potential for relatively low-impact agriculture to provide food for many people. Beyond small farms, all forms of agriculture can work to improve their practices and reduce impacts, and The Nature Conservancy is working with a broad range of agricultural interests to find these solutions.

15   So I'll bite into some crisp, local bacon and feel a hug that's not just luxuriously sustainable, but realistically sustainable.

*Calculation:

Our co-op farm is 130 acres of which 70 is pasture and the farmer leases another 100 acres of hayfields for a total of 230 acres. Even though approximately 25% of this total is forest, I'll use it as the total acreage because my overall point is about farms that have this patchwork of natural and agricultural land. Approximately 500 people are supported from this 230 acres (not all their calories, obviously, but a high proportion of their meat and dairy). I estimated the agricultural acres of Wayne and six other predominantly rural counties that form a ring around greater Cleveland (Portage, Erie, Huron, Ashland, Geauga and Lake). Collectively these counties are over 1.8 million acres. To account for towns, cities, parks, etc., I assumed 70% of that acreage could be in farms leaving just under 1.3 million acres. With the ratio provided by my farmer (500 people for 233 acres) this acreage of similarly managed farms could provide meat, dairy and other products to almost 2.8 million people. Green City Blue Lake points out that a surprising amount of production could also come from urban farms, an innovative use for abandoned acres in urban cores that have lost population.

Analyze

1. What does the author mean by "factory farms"?
2. Identify at least five reasons that the author chooses to eat meat from a co-op.
3. What is the difference between "luxuriously sustainable" and "realistically sustainable" according to the author?

Explore

1. Have you ever heard of buying meat from a co-op? Is this something that you think you or your family would be willing to do? As a class, discuss how you think the average American might feel about switching from buying meat at a grocery store to buying meat from a farm he or she can visit. Think about what kinds of changes a person would have to make both practically and mentally to make this switch. Do you think most people would be open to this change?

2. The author of this piece uses a positive, open tone when describing the co-op he visits but also when describing industrial agriculture—and yet his goal is to persuade the reader to support one method of production over another. Go through the piece again, and highlight sentences in which the author makes his major points about both methods of food production. Then, boil down his argument to what you think are the most persuasive five to seven sentences and put them together to make a sort of "Cliff Notes" for the article.

3. Use a search engine to locate a co-op near you where people could go to buy their meat and dairy products. Then, being careful to mimic the positive, inviting tone used by the author, construct a flyer that attempts to persuade the viewer to visit the co-op.

Sarah Lozanova
"Starbucks Coffee: Green or Greenwashed?"

Sara Lozanova is a freelance writer who writes about clean energy and sustainable business practices. She has an M.B.A. in sustainable management from the Presidio School of Management and is a co-founder of Trees Across the Miles, an urban reforestation initiative. The blog post below is a review of Starbucks' business practices and appeared on GreenBiz.com, a website devoted to green and sustainable business practices and investment. Lozanova describes the many ways Starbucks has tried to lessen its environmental footprint, but she also recognizes the basic problems of coffee production and the fast-food industry.

Starbucks is given credit by many for revolutionizing the American coffee drinking experience. The company, however, is both praised and criticized by environmentalists.

Is Starbucks a leader of sustainability or a greenwasher?

The Coffee Industry

The coffee industry itself is inherently unsustainable. Coffee is cultivated in more than 60 tropical countries across tens of millions of acres of land. Tropical soils unfortunately are vulnerable to erosion and loss of topsoil, particularly when the native vegetation is removed. Coffee also has a relatively high water footprint—to produce one cup of coffee requires 140 liters of water.

Historically, much coffee was shade grown under a variety of native trees on small farms. A surge in coffee demand a decade ago significantly increased global production, thus boosting the prevalence of monoculture farming. The land is often cleared of native vegetation and pesticide use became more common.

5   Not all coffee beans are created equal through the eyes of sustainability. Organic shade grown coffee on smaller farms is ideal. The reality is that working conditions, pesticide use and many other factors vary greatly in this industry.

The profits made by farmers became much more volatile when global production of coffee swelled a decade ago. As the markets were flooded with coffee, prices plummeted. This created an economic hardship for those who depended on cultivation for their livelihood.

Starbucks has attempted to avoid the problems that plague the industry by partnering with Conservation International to create Coffee and Farmer Equity Practices (C.A.F.E. Practices). The partnership resulted in a set of environmentally, economically and socially responsible coffee purchasing guidelines. Starbucks purchased 77 percent of its coffee under these guidelines in fiscal year 2008 and has a goal of purchasing 100 percent by 2015. On the global market, Starbucks is a relatively small player with around 1 percent of the global coffee market, yet it has found a way to leverage its might and influence the coffee industry.

Coffee Shops and Natural Resource Use

Coffee shops depend on the consumption of large amounts of fossil fuels and natural resources. Most Starbucks stores are located in areas where coffee is not cultivated, thus coffee must be transported thousands of miles. And with more than 4,500 of Starbucks shops in 47 countries, extensive resources must be used to construct, heat, cool and power these stores.

Starbucks has been under strong criticism recently because of wasteful water practices. Water ran continuously on dipper wells, which are used to wash utensils. This added up to an estimated 6.2 million gallons of water wasted each day. In response, the company is exploring alternatives to the dipper well system, some of which have been put in place this year. Starbucks also said it plans to conduct a comprehensive water footprint audit in 2009 to get a clearer picture of its water use and ways it might be reduced.

On a brighter note, Starbucks recently announced a goal to reduce energy use by 25 percent and purchase enough renewable energy credits for 50 percent of its energy needs by 2010. The company is working with the U.S. Green Building Council to create a prototype for a LEED (Leadership in Energy and Environmental Design) Silver certified store that can be duplicated across its portfolio. A standardized design would allow Starbucks to utilize green building principles for many stores in a more cost-effective manner. It does, however, limit use of location-specific green building practices that might be ideal in one climate or setting but not in another.

10

Disposable Cups and Recycling

While some praise Starbucks for offering coffee grounds for compost piles, others criticize the lack of recycling infrastructure for customers.

Starbucks stores use billions of cups annually by offering disposable paper cups to all customers regardless of where the beverage is consumed. This requires enormous quantities of natural resources and energy before finding their way to landfills. Starbucks does however use cups that contain 10 percent post consumer recycled content.

Although this might sound like a meager quantity, it is estimated to save tens of thousands of trees, half a million gallons of wastewater, and several million pounds of garbage from landfills. Starbucks has also helped shape the industry by using cups with recycled content. This 10 percent achievement required authorization and testing by the Food and Drug Administration and had not been permitted previously.

That authorization, granted in 2004, and Starbucks' efforts prompted comment from David Ford, then-president and CEO of Metafore, a non-profit group that collaborates with leaders in business and society to create innovative, market-based approaches that support forests and communities.

15   "Starbucks should be commended for its groundbreaking efforts of working toward environmentally friendly packaging options that benefit both forests and the businesses that rely on them," Ford had said in a statement. "As a participant in our Paper Working Group project, Starbucks' leadership in responsible purchasing of forest products gives other companies a clear path to follow."

The downside is that Starbucks cups still cannot be processed in many paper recycling systems. This is due to a thin polyethylene plastic coating that stops liquids from leaking out. The company has set a goal to have all cups recyclable by 2012.

Starbucks also plans to reintroduce ceramic "for here" mugs and increase use of reusable commuter mugs tenfold by 2010. They currently offer a $.10 discount to customers who bring in reusable mugs.

Impact on Locally Owned Coffee Shops

It would seem that Starbucks would have a very negative impact on local Ma and Pa coffee shops, but this isn't necessarily the case. Some cafes report soaring sales when a Starbucks moves in because the new shops attract more coffee drinkers to the neighborhood.

Others say they have been the victims of store placement strategy or landlords who hoped to get more rent from an incoming Starbucks. It seems the impacts of Starbucks on local competition must be taken on a case-by-case basis, helping some while hurting others. One thing is certain: A new Starbucks in some neighborhoods is a sign of gentrification.

Employee Relations

20   Starbucks ranked No. 7 in Fortune Magazine's "100 Best Companies to Work For" in 2008. Noteworthy practices by Starbucks include health,

dental and vision insurance to part-time employees and domestic partner benefits for same-sex couples.

Additional perks include tuition reimbursement, adoption assistance and a 401(k) retirement plan for eligible employees.

Does Starbucks Measure Up?

Starbucks is frequently targeted by environmentalists for unsustainable practices, but do they deserve this? The nature of the coffee industry is unsustainable in many ways, but Starbucks has helped lead the industry towards greener practices. I would like to see Dunkin' Donuts ditch Styrofoam and Nestle forgo genetically engineered coffee beans. Although there is certainly room for improvement by Starbucks, other companies have barely even gotten started.

Starbucks' customers, however, are likely to demand more of them than Dunkin' Donuts customers will demand in the area of sustainability, which is warranted partially by higher prices. Chipotle Restaurant, for example, offers only naturally raised chicken, while Taco Bell does not.

In the end, many of the sustainability choices of a company come down to money. Second quarter 2009 net revenue ending March 31 was down 7.6 percent for the Starbucks. While some green initiatives may save money for a business, others do not. The company has closed hundreds of stores in the last year. Although some studies show that consumer demand for sustainable products has remained strong despite economic conditions, it is a challenging time to invest a lot of money in green research and development initiatives.

When looking at the company as a whole, Starbucks has addressed many   25
of the most pressing issues to lessen its impact. Although it deserves to be applauded in some areas, there is still room for growth. Perhaps this is why it is both applauded and criticized by environmentalists.

Analyze

1. What are the steps Starbucks has taken to reduce its negative influence on the environment?
2. What does the article say about Starbucks' impact on locally owned and operated coffeehouses?

3. The author states, "to produce one cup of coffee requires 140 liters of water." How much water is this? In gallons? In quarts? In cups? Why do you think this is? In a group, think about all the processes that go into creating a single cup of coffee—from growing the beans to brewing the cup. What type of machinery is used for the processes involved? How does this translate to 140 liters of water per cup?

Explore

1. What is the purpose of this article? Is the author making an argument? Describing a controversy? How do you know? Construct a brief summary of the article in which you explain what the author is doing—what her purpose is for writing—and what kinds of information or evidence she uses to achieve her goal.

2. This article uses a number of terms that some readers may be unfamiliar with. The terms "greenwash," "monoculture," and "shade grown" are just a few examples. Create a glossary for this piece in which you identify at least six terms discussed and provide a definition or explanation for each.

3. Starbucks locations are found in 47 countries. Select one store location and see if you can find out where its coffee comes from, either by asking a store representative if it is local or by searching on the Internet. Then, calculate the food miles between source and store.

Stephanie Wear
"Finding Nemo on Your Plate"

Stephanie Wear is a marine scientist who directs The Nature Conservancy's coral reef conservation program. In keeping with the Conservancy's collaborative approach to preserving natural resources, Wear works with local fishermen, non-governmental organizations (NGOs), government agencies, community leaders, and stakeholder groups to get them involved in solving their local conservation problems. This is where science, conservation, and communication all come together. In the blog post below, Wear offers her own personal experience in the Virgin Islands to bring home the reality of overfishing and the consequences it can have on coral reefs.

I started my conservation career working in the U.S. Virgin Islands and have a clear memory of my orientation tour of St. Croix. One of our last stops was the Frederiksted pier, where we leapt into the clear blue water to cool off—something that a bunch of local kids were doing that day as well.

After climbing out of the water, I noticed two young boys fishing off the rocks. I went over to see their catch. I was shocked to see that they had a beautiful and tiny reef fish (maybe 4 inches long). Commonly known as the cow fish or box fish, this fish actually doesn't even have much flesh on it, is pretty boney and doesn't get bigger than 18 inches (I've never seen one that big though!).

It is a curious creature and one of my favorite finds when snorkeling— definitely not something I expected to see being fished. I figured that perhaps it was a local delicacy so I inquired further. "What are you going to do with this fish?" I asked. The young boy answered simply "pot fish."

Since I was new to the island, I got some clarification. It turns out that pot fish is a favorite local food—basically a fish stew of sorts, and this little guy was going to be used to give it a fishy flavor. I had always thought of those wild looking critters as a treat to find, but not a treat to eat.

This experience blew me away and was the first of many realizations I had while living there about the state of the fisheries in general, and how much people relied on the sea for their food.

What I learned in my years living and working in the Virgin Islands was that pretty much any fish is fair game, no matter the size, just as long as it was not considered toxic, and even then some folks chose to take their chances.

Long gone are the days of plentiful grouper and snapper that steam on the grill with sweet goodness all around. Today, those fleshy fish are few and far between and now folks rely on fish you would expect to see in your fish tank, not on your dinner plate. Overfishing has become a major problem for coral reefs. For a coral reef ecosystem to function properly, it depends on the presence of the wild diversity that it attracts and is home to.

From the predator to the grazer (herbivore) to the very picky eaters (specialists), each fish plays an important part in the coral reef 'city.' What has happened in the Caribbean and in many other parts of the world is that people have essentially fished down the food chain so that the reef city is out of balance and in some cases, basic functions come to a screeching halt. Think New York City with no garbage pick-up in the summertime—a big stinking mess!

In the case of coral reefs, the fish that are now landing on the dinner plate, the grazers, are extremely important for keeping coral competitors in check (namely, seaweed). If the seaweed doesn't get mowed down by herbivores like queen parrotfish or spiny urchins, they overgrow the corals and the corals disappear. Fish need corals too, so this becomes a vicious cycle if something isn't done to help fish populations recover.

10   There are many ways to address this problem, and we are working locally all over the globe to help communities manage their coral reef and fishery resources so that they benefit long term from the sea's bounty.

In this case, everyone is part of the solution, including you. Make sure that you choose sustainable seafood. There are great guides that help you determine whether the seafood is free of toxic metals, how harmful the fishing method is on ocean habitats and the condition of the particular fish population you are considering for dinner (i.e., in decline, recovering, or healthy).

The latest recommendations change frequently to reflect the latest guidance thanks to proactive programs like Blue Ocean Institute's FishPhone and Monterey Bay Aquarium's Seafood Watch.

These guides are simple, color-coded and have gone from providing wallet cards to smart phone apps, making your decision process easier.

These guides require you to know where your fish comes from because this can make all the difference in terms of how it was farmed or caught. If the menu or market isn't labeling their fish, just ask. These days, most places will be able to tell you where their fish is from. If they don't know, don't buy it.

15   Now with your new tools in hand, and grilling season on the horizon—be sure to take a few extra steps to make sure your seafood isn't harming the reefs and the people that depend on them.

Analyze

1. Why are fish that are herbivores (i.e., "grazers") so important to the maintenance and health of coral reefs?
2. How can you avoid buying endangered species of fish?
3. The author begins with a discussion of how overfishing has affected St. Croix and ends with a plea for readers to eat sustainably from their local markets. Do you believe that there is a connection between the food you eat and the food situations of people in faraway places?

As a class, discuss how your choices in what you buy and eat might have residual impacts that can affect the food available to others.

Explore

1. The author makes the argument that "overfishing has become a major problem for coral reefs." Though this is her claim, she waits until seven paragraphs into the article to state it outright, using the first several paragraphs to talk about her experiences in St. Croix. Construct a version of this article that makes its argument up front and then uses evidence to support that claim. How does this change the tone of the piece? Which version do you think is more effective? Why?

2. The author states:

> Everyone is part of the solution, including you. Make sure that you choose sustainable seafood. There are great guides that help you determine whether the seafood is free of toxic metals, how harmful the fishing method is on ocean habitats and the condition of the particular fish population you are considering for dinner (i.e., in decline, recovering, or healthy).

   Visit your local grocery store and see what kind of seafood they have available. Choose five items, and use a seafood guide (this article recommends Blue Ocean Fishphone and Monterey Bay Aquarium's Seafood Watch) to look up the condition of the different types of seafood. Construct a report in which you detail your findings and make recommendations for consumers based on your research.

3. Using the Internet and the resources in your library, research the health of the oceans' fish populations. What fish populations have dropped severely and how serious is this threat to diversity? Make a poster that displays the health of the fish populations in the world's oceans, provides summary information, and identifies the major causes of the population decline.

Dan Charles
"How Community-Supported Agriculture Sprouted in China"

Dan Charles is a food and agriculture correspondent for National Public Radio (NPR)'s food blog *The Salt*. He has a B.A. from American University in Economics and International Affairs and has published two books, including *Lords of the Harvest: Biotech, Big Money, and the Future of Food*. In this blog Charles introduces the concept of community-supported agriculture and how it has grown in China just as Chinese agriculture has become more like the industrialized model of food production in America. The post is humorous and light, but the links provide access to some of the serious issues concerning sustainable food production in the world's most populous country.

It's a little hard to tell, walking through Little Donkey Farm, in a village northwest of Beijing, whether this is just a charming but ineffectual protest against the tide of Chinese history, or a sign that the tide may be shifting.

Little Donkey is an organic farm. (Yes, there is an actual donkey. More about him later.) Dozens of different vegetables grow here: Eggplant, green beans, Chinese cabbage, corn, and some that I've never seen before. There's also a small barn filled with pigs.

It's also the first Chinese Community-Supported Agriculture (CSA) farm. Four hundred families pay an annual membership and get, in exchange, a share of the harvest. Another 260 families rent small plots of land for their own gardens.

Shi Yan, a soft-spoken but determined young graduate student from Beijing's Renmin University, set up this operation three years ago— inspired, in part, by her experience working for six months with Earthrise Farm, a small CSA in western Minnesota. (There are at least 4,000 CSA farms in the U.S.)

5   "It changed my life," says Shi Yan. She arrived at Earthrise Farm thinking that she would study its business model, "but living with them, I realized that it's not just a model, it's a style of life. Before that, although I cared about rural problems, I never thought about living in a village. After I came back, I moved to this village and started this farm."

It was an audacious move, because it goes against every recent trend in Chinese agriculture—which, it's worth remembering, feeds 20 percent of the people on earth. Young people, especially young men, have been abandoning rural villages for better jobs in cities.

Little Donkey, being organic, uses only manure and compost for fertilizer, but most Chinese farmers abandoned those methods over the past forty years. They're now among the world's biggest users of synthetic fertilizer, and it's helped them boost their food production dramatically.

There's now plenty of food in China, but some people worry about its safety—especially since a nationwide scandal in 2008 involving toxic contamination of milk powder and tests (carried out by the environmental group Greenpeace) that found traces of banned pesticides on supermarket vegetables.

Now, more people are buying food that's labeled "organic." More people are visiting Little Donkey. And at least three dozen other Chinese CSAs are now in business.

But the food is not the only thing that brings people here. In a country   10 that sometimes seems obsessed with making and selling things, Little Donkey Farm is a tiny island of Chinese counterculture. "It's mostly for relaxing," says Gao Xiang, who's there with his family, spending a Sunday tending their part of the community garden.

"Little Donkey Farm isn't just the land, or the food. We can know each other and create new ideas. We make friends here," says Fang Danmin, an editor. "It's small, but it's a trend."

Watching it all, from inside his pen, is an actual donkey named Professor. It's the farm mascot, a symbol of its ideals, but also—unintentionally—the difficulty of realizing those ideals in today's China.

"About this donkey, we have a long story," says Shi Yan. "Five or six years ago, we had a very hot discussion about whether China should keep traditional, small-scale farming. One side said we need to use donkeys to plow the land. The other side said we need tractors. At the end, my advisor Professor Wen said, 'We won't discuss this anymore. But I will buy a donkey, and my wife will name the donkey!'"

"But the embarrassing thing is," Shi Yan continues, "we hoped that we could use this donkey to plow the land. But then we figured out that in the village, there was not even one farmer who knew how to work with the donkey! So right now, she can only stay in the pen."

Analyze

1. What characterizes a CSA farm?
2. Why, according to the author, is it so unusual to see an organic farm in China?
3. How was China able to boost its overall food production?

Explore

1. This article claims that more young Chinese men have recently been leaving rural areas and heading to urban centers. As a homework assignment, locate some figures/statistics that demonstrate this shift and produce a graph or chart depicting this shift. How might such a shift directly, and indirectly, affect the state of agriculture in China?
2. Are there any CSAs or other jointly owned organic farms in your city or state? If so, how many acres are the farming sites? How many separate "owners" are involved? How long have they been operational? After compiling your findings, construct an editorial for your school's newspaper in which you inform readers about the farm's processes and mission.
3. What would it take to start a small community garden in your town or neighborhood? Many cities provide space for community gardens. Explore the possibilities in your community and draw up a plan to start a modest shared garden space.

Michael Pollan
"The Genius of the Place"

Michael Pollan is one of the most prominent food writers in America. A professor of journalism at the University of California at Berkeley, Pollan has written many articles and six books about food, including *The Botany of Desire: A Plant's-Eye View of the World, In Defense of Food: An Eater's Manifesto,* and *The Omnivore's Dilemma.* Like other writers in the "food movement," Pollan is critical of the way agribusiness produces food through industrial farming methods that rely on fossil fuels for fertilizers, pesticides to control bugs, herbicides to control weeds, and huge acreages of one crop to increase efficiency. In his popular book *The Omnivore's Dilemma*, Pollan describes four ways to produce food: the industrial food system, the corporate "organic" system, a self-sufficient small farm, and the ancient hunter-gatherer system. In the excerpt printed below, Pollan describes Polyface Farm, a small farm in Virginia that takes advantage of the natural activity of local plants and animals to produce a wide range of meats, vegetables, grains, and fruits. The farm represents a sustainable system that adapts agriculture to the natural ecosystem rather than the other way around.

Polyface Farm raises chicken, beef, turkeys, eggs, rabbits, and pigs, plus tomatoes, sweet corn, and berries on one hundred acres of pasture patchworked into another 450 acres afforest, but if you ask Joel Salatin what he does for a living (Is he foremost a cattle rancher? A chicken farmer?) he'll tell you in no uncertain terms, "I'm a grass farmer." The first time I heard this designation I didn't get it at all—hay seemed the least (and least edible) of his many crops, and he brought none of it to market. But undergirding the "farm of many faces," as he calls it, is a single plant—or rather that whole community of plants for which the word "grass" is shorthand.

"Grass," so understood, is the foundation of the intricate food chain Salatin has assembled at Polyface, where a half dozen different animal species are raised together in an intensive rotational dance on the theme of symbiosis. Salatin is the choreographer and the grasses are his verdurous stage; the dance has made Polyface one of the most productive and influential alternative farms in America.

Though it was only the third week of June, the pasture beneath me had already seen several rotational turns. Before being cut earlier in the week for the hay that would feed the farm's animals through the winter, it had been grazed twice by beef cattle, which after each day-long stay had been succeeded by several hundred laying hens. They'd arrived by Eggmobile, a ramshackle portable henhouse designed and built by Salatin. Why chickens? "Because that's how it works in nature," Salatin explained. "Birds follow and clean up after herbivores." And so during their turn in the pasture, the hens had performed several ecological services for the cattle as well as the grass: They'd picked the tasty grubs and fly larvae out of the cowpats, in the process spreading the manure and eliminating parasites. (This is what Joel has in mind when he says the animals do the work around here; the hens are his "sanitation crew," the reason his cattle have no need of chemical parasiti- cides.) And while they were at it, nibbling on the short cattle-clipped grasses they like best, the chickens applied a few thousand pounds of nitrogen to the pasture and produced several thousand uncommonly rich and tasty eggs. After a few weeks' rest, the pasture will be grazed again, each steer turning these lush grasses into beef at the rate of two or three pounds a day.

By the end of the season Salatin's grasses will have been transformed by his animals into some 40,000 pounds of beef, 30,000 pounds of pork, 10,000 broilers, 1,200 turkeys, 1,000 rabbits, and 35,000 dozen eggs. This is an astounding cornucopia of food to draw from a hundred acres of pasture, yet what is perhaps still more astonishing is the fact that this pasture will be in no way diminished by the process—in fact, it will be the better for it, lusher, more fertile, even springier underfoot (this thanks to the increased earthworm traffic). Salatin's audacious bet is that feeding our- selves from nature need not be a zero-sum proposition, one in which if there is more for us at the end of the season then there must be less for nature— less topsoil, less fertility, less life. He's betting, in other words, on a very different proposition, one that looks an awful lot like the proverbially unattainable free lunch.

5   And none of it happens without the grass. In fact, the first time I met Salatin he'd insisted that even before I met any of his animals, I get down on my belly in this very pasture to make the acquaintance of the less charis- matic species his farm was nurturing that, in turn, were nurturing his farm. Taking the ant's-eye view, he ticked off the census of a single square foot of pasture: orchard grass, foxtail, a couple of different fescues, bluegrass, and timothy. Then he cataloged the legumes red clover and white, plus lupines— and finally the forbs, broad-leaved species like plantain, dandelion, and Queen Anne's lace. And those were just the plants, the species occupying the surface along with a handful of itinerant insects; below decks and out of sight tunneled earthworms (knowable by their castled mounds of rich castings), woodchucks, moles and burrowing insects, all making their dim way through an unseen wilderness of bacteria, phages, eelish nematodes, shrimpy rotifers, and miles upon miles of mycelium, the underground filaments of fungi. We think of the grasses as the basis of this food chain, yet behind, or beneath, the grassland stands the soil, that inconceivably complex community of the living and the dead. Because a healthy soil digests the dead to nourish the living, Salatin calls it the earth's stomach.

But it is upon the grass, mediator of soil and sun, that the human gaze has always tended to settle, and not just our gaze, either. A great many animals, too, are drawn to grass, which partly accounts for our own deep attraction to it: We come here to eat the animals that ate the grass that we (lacking rumens) can't eat ourselves. "All flesh is grass." The Old Testament's earthy equation reflects a pastoral culture's appreciation of the food chain that sustained it, though the hunter-gatherers living on the African savanna thousands of years earlier would have understood the flesh-grass connection just as well. It's only in our own time, after we began raising our food animals on grain in Concentrated Animal Feeding Operations (following the dubious new equation, All flesh is corn), that our ancient engagement with grass could be overlooked.

Or should I say partly overlooked, for surely our abiding affection for the stuff—reflected in our scrupulously tended lawns and playing fields, as well as in the persistence of so many forms of grassy pastoral, in everything from poetry to supermarket labels—expresses an unconscious recognition of our one-time dependence. Our inclination toward grass, which has the force of a tropism, is frequently cited as a prime example of "biophilia," E. O. Wilson's coinage for what he claims is our inherited genetic attraction for the plants and animals and landscapes with which we coevolved.

Certainly I was feeling the pull of the pastoral that summer afternoon on Joel Salatin's farm; whether or not its wellsprings were in my genes who can really say, but the idea does not strike me as implausible in the least. Our species' co-evolutionary alliance with the grasses has deep roots and has probably done more to ensure our success as a species than any other, with the possible exception of our alliance with the trillion or so bacteria that inhabit the human gut. Working together, grass and man have overspread much of the earth, far more of it than would ever have been possible working alone.

This human-grass alliance has, in fact, had two distinct phases, taking us all the way from our time as hunter-gatherers to agriculturists, or, to date this natural history as the grasses might, from the Age of Perennials, like the fescues and bluegrass in these pastures, to the Age of Annuals, such as the corn George Naylor and I had planted in Iowa. In the first phase, which began when our earliest ancestors came down out of the trees to hunt animals on the savanna, the human relationship with grass was mediated by animals that (unlike us) could digest it, in much the same way it still is on Joel Salatin's postmodern savanna. Like Salatin, hunter-gatherers deliberately promoted the welfare of the grasses in order to attract and fatten the animals they depended upon. Hunters would periodically set fire to the savanna to keep it free of trees and nourish the soil. In a sense, they too were "grass farmers," deliberately nurturing grasses so that they might harvest meat.

10   So at least it appeared to us. Regarded from the grasses' point of view the arrangement appears even cleverer. The existential challenge facing grasses in all but the most arid regions is how to successfully compete against trees for territory and sunlight. The evolutionary strategy they hit upon was to make their leaves nourishing and tasty to animals who in turn are nourishing and tasty to us, the big-brained creature best equipped to vanquish the trees on their behalf. But for this strategy to succeed the grasses needed an anatomy that could withstand the rigors of both grazing and fire. So they developed a deep root system and a ground-hugging crown that in many cases puts out runners, allowing the grasses to recover quickly from fire and to reproduce even when grazers (or lawnmowers) prevent them from ever flowering and going to seed. (I used to think we were dominating the grass whenever we mowed the lawn, but in fact we're playing right into its strategy for world domination, by helping it outcompete the shrubs and trees.)

The second phase of the marriage of grasses and humans is usually called the "invention of agriculture," a self-congratulatory phrase that overlooks the role of the grasses themselves in revising the terms of the relationship. Beginning about ten thousand years ago a handful of particularly opportunistic grass species—the ancestors of wheat, rice, and corn—evolved to produce tremendous, nutritionally dense seeds that could nourish humans directly, thereby cutting out the intermediary animals. The grasses accomplished this feat by becoming annuals, throwing all their energy into making seeds rather than storing some of it underground in roots and rhizomes to get through the winter. These monster annual grasses outcompeted not only the trees, which humans obligingly cut down to expand the annuals' habitats, but bested the perennial grasses, which in most places succumbed to the plow. Their human sponsors ripped up the great perennial-polyculture grasslands to make the earth safe for annuals, which would henceforth be grown in strict monocultures.

· ⋮ ·

Grass farmers grow animals—for meat, eggs, milk, and wool—but regard them as part of a food chain in which grass is the keystone species, the nexus between the solar energy that powers every food chain and the animals we eat. "To be even more accurate," Joel has said, "we should call ourselves sun farmers. The grass is just the way we capture the solar energy." One of the principles of modern grass farming is that to the greatest extent possible farmers should rely on the contemporary energy of the sun, as captured every day by photosynthesis, instead of the fossilized sun energy contained in petroleum.

For Allan Nation, who grew up on a cattle ranch in Mississippi, doing so is as much a matter of sound economics as environmental virtue. "All agriculture is at its heart a business of capturing free solar energy in a food product that can then be turned into high-value human energy," he recently wrote in his column, Al's Obs; here each month he applies the theories of a decidedly eclectic group of thinkers (ranging from business gurus like Peter Drucker and Michael Porter to writers like Arthur Koestler) to the problems of farming. "There are only two efficient ways to do this," he wrote in his column. "One is for you to walk out in your garden, pull a carrot and eat it. This is a direct transfer of solar energy to human energy. The second most efficient way is for you to send an animal out to gather this free solar food and then you eat the animal.

"All other methods of harvest and transfer require higher capital and petroleum energy inputs and these necessarily lower the return to the farmer/rancher. As Florida rancher Bud Adams once told me, 'Ranching is a very simple business. The really hard part is keeping it simple.'"

The simplest way to capture the sun's energy in a form food animals can use is by growing grass: "These blades are our photovoltaic panels," Joel says. And the most efficient—if not the simplest—way to grow vast quantities of solar panels is by management-intensive grazing, a method that as its name implies relies more heavily on the farmer's brain than on capital- or on energy-intensive inputs. All you need, in fact, is some portable electric fencing, a willingness to move your livestock onto fresh pasture every day, and the kind of intimate knowledge of grass that Joel tried to impart to me that early spring afternoon, down on our bellies in his pasture.

"The important thing to know about any grass is that its growth follows a sigmoid, or S, curve," Joel explained. He grabbed my pen and notebook and began drawing a graph, based on one that appears in Voisin's book. "This vertical axis here is the height of our grass plant, okay? And the horizontal axis is time: the number of days since this paddock was last grazed." He started tracing a big S on the page, beginning in the lower left-hand corner where the two axes met. "See, the growth starts out real slow like this, but then after a few days it begins to zoom. That's called 'the blaze of growth,' when the grass has recovered from the first bite, rebuilt its reserves and root mass, and really taken off. But after a while"—the curve leveled out at around day fourteen or so—"it slows down again, as the grass gets ready to flower and seed. It's entering its period of senescence, when the grass begins to lignify [get woody] and becomes less palatable to the cow."

"What you want to do is graze a pasture right at this point here"—he tapped my pad sharply—"at the very top of the blaze of growth. But what you never, ever want to do is violate the law of the second bite. You can't let your cows take a second bite of a grass before it has had a chance to fully recover."

If the law of the second bite were actually on the books, most of the world's ranchers and dairy farmers would be outlaws, since they allow their stock to graze their pastures continuously. By allowing cattle a second or third bite, the most desirable "ice cream" species—clover, orchard grass, sweet grass, bluegrass, timothy—weaken and gradually disappear from the sward, giving way to bald spots and to weedy and brushy species the cows won't touch. Any plant wants to keep its roots and shoots roughly in balance, so grasses kept short by overgrazing lack the deep roots needed to bring water and minerals up from the subsoil. Over time a closely cropped grassland deteriorates, and in a dry or brittle environment, it will eventually turn into a desert. The reason environmentalists in the western United States take such a dim view of grazing is that most ranchers practice continuous grazing, degrading the land by flouting the law of the second bite.

Grass farming done well depends almost entirely on a wealth of nuanced local knowledge at a time when most of the rest of agriculture has come to rely on precisely the opposite: on the off-farm brain, and the one-size-fits-all universal intelligence represented by agrochemicals and machines. Very much on his own in a very particular place, the grass farmer must continually juggle the various elements of his farm in space as well as time, relying on his powers of observation and organization to arrange the appointed daily meeting of animal and grass in such a way as to ensure maximum benefit for both.

20   So is this sort of low-tech pastoralism simply a throwback to preindustrial agriculture? Salatin adamantly begged to differ: "It might not look that way,

but this is all information-age stuff we're doing here. Polyface Farm is a postindustrial enterprise. You'll see."

Analyze

1. What is the "rotational dance" that the owner of Polyface Farm uses? Why does he use it?
2. Why does the owner of Polyface Farm consider himself a "grass farmer"?
3. The author uses the sayings "All flesh is grass" as a metaphor for the system set up on Polyface Farm and "All flesh is corn" as a metaphor for high-production farming. To practice conveying complicated ideas in small sayings, get in a group and construct at least three more "bumper sticker" statements that encapsulate some of the concepts described in this piece.

Explore

1. Construct an informal blog post in which you consider the way that thinking of himself as a "grass farmer" as opposed to a "cattle farmer" reflects not just Salatin's practices but also his values. In your post, discuss what you think is the main difference between the way a farm might be run by these different types of farmers.
2. The owner of Polyface Farm models his farming rotation after the processes of nature; this way, he says, the animals do the work. Along this line, do some research to discover some ways that humans have applied nature's principles to their own practices in other creative ways. For example, a group of researchers designed a house to mimic a snail's shell to reduce the need for air conditioning. As a homework assignment, find an article that details a similar creative use of nature as an inspiration for our own development and share it with the class.
3. In this piece, Pollan describes the rich variety of plant and animal life in the pasture at Polyface Farm. Go out and find an average piece of front yard or park grass and catalog all the plant and animal life you can find in a one-yard-square plot. Try to see what is under the grass as well as on the surface. Then find a piece of uncultivated ground—in a wild space, on the edges of town or in a ditch—and do the same observations. Try writing about the differences in the tone and style Pollan uses.

Deborah Whitman
"Genetically Modified Foods:
Harmful or Helpful?"

Deborah Whitman is a senior editor for life sciences at ProQuest, a digital information company that serves researchers and libraries around the world. She has a B.S. in biology and an M.A. in biotechnology from The Johns Hopkins University. The article from which the excerpt below is taken is heavily researched and provides citations and links to other websites and scientific databases. It is a resource for readers and researchers. Genetically modified organisms (GMOs) are plants and animals whose genes have been altered by researchers in order to give them qualities their "natural" counterparts don't have. For example, some genetically modified plants can resist certain pests, thus reducing the need for pesticides. Others, like genetically modified laboratory rats, have specific traits useful to medical research. While GMOs are highly controversial, the article excerpted here is neutral, providing scientific information in response to commonly asked questions and concerns about GMOs.

What Are Genetically-Modified Foods?

The term "GM foods" or "GMOs" (genetically-modified organisms) is most commonly used to refer to crop plants created for human or animal consumption using the latest molecular biology techniques. These plants have been modified in the laboratory to enhance desired traits such as increased resistance to herbicides or improved nutritional content. The enhancement of desired traits has traditionally been undertaken through breeding, but conventional plant breeding methods can be very time consuming and are often not very accurate. Genetic engineering, on the other hand, can create plants with the exact desired trait very rapidly and with great accuracy. For example, plant geneticists can isolate a gene responsible for drought tolerance and insert that gene into a different plant. The new genetically-modified plant will gain drought tolerance as well. Not only can genes be transferred from one plant to another, but genes from non-plant organisms also can be used. The best known example of this is the use of B.t. genes in corn and other crops. B.t., or *Bacillus thuringiensis*, is a naturally occurring bacterium that produces crystal proteins that are lethal to insect larvae. B.t. crystal protein genes have been transferred into corn, enabling the corn to produce its own pesticides against insects such as the European corn borer. For two informative overviews of some of the techniques involved in creating GM foods, visit "Biotech Basics" (sponsored by Monsanto) http://www.biotechknowledge.monsanto.com/biotech/bbasics.nsf/index or "Techniques of Plant Biotechnology" from the National Center for Biotechnology Education http://www.ncbe.reading.ac.uk/NCBE/GMFOOD/techniques.

What Are Some of the Advantages of GM Foods?

The world population has topped 6 billion people and is predicted to double in the next 50 years. Ensuring an adequate food supply for this booming population is going to be a major challenge in the years to come. GM foods promise to meet this need in a number of ways:

- *Pest resistance*: Crop losses from insect pests can be staggering, resulting in devastating financial loss for farmers and starvation in developing countries. Farmers typically use many tons of chemical pesticides annually. Consumers do not wish to eat food that has been treated with pesticides because of potential health hazards, and run-off of agricultural wastes from excessive use of pesticides and fertilizers can poison the water supply and cause harm to the environment. Growing GM foods such as B.t. corn can help eliminate the application of chemical pesticides and reduce the cost of bringing a crop to market.[1,2]
- *Herbicide tolerance*: For some crops, it is not cost-effective to remove weeds by physical means such as tilling, so farmers will often spray large quantities of different herbicides (weed-killer) to destroy weeds, a time-consuming and expensive process, that requires care so that the herbicide doesn't harm the crop plant or the environment. Crop plants genetically-engineered to be resistant to one very powerful herbicide could help prevent environmental damage by reducing the amount of herbicides needed. For example, Monsanto has created a strain of soybeans genetically modified to be not affected by their herbicide product

Roundup®.[3] A farmer grows these soybeans which then only require one application of weed-killer instead of multiple applications, reducing production cost and limiting the dangers of agricultural waste run-off.[4]

- *Disease resistance*: There are many viruses, fungi and bacteria that cause plant diseases. Plant biologists are working to create plants with genetically-engineered resistance to these diseases.[5,6]
- *Cold tolerance*: Unexpected frost can destroy sensitive seedlings. An antifreeze gene from cold water fish has been introduced into plants such as tobacco and potato. With this antifreeze gene, these plants are able to tolerate cold temperatures that normally would kill unmodified seedlings.[7] (Note: I have not been able to find any journal articles or patents that involve fish antifreeze proteins in strawberries, although I have seen such reports in newspapers. I can only conclude that nothing on this application has yet been published or patented.)
- *Drought tolerance/salinity tolerance*: As the world population grows and more land is utilized for housing instead of food production, farmers will need to grow crops in locations previously unsuited for plant cultivation. Creating plants that can withstand long periods of drought or high salt content in soil and groundwater will help people to grow crops in formerly inhospitable places.[8,9]
- *Nutrition*: Malnutrition is common in third world countries where impoverished peoples rely on a single crop such as rice for the main staple of their diet. However, rice does not contain adequate amounts of all necessary nutrients to prevent malnutrition. If rice could be genetically engineered to contain additional vitamins and minerals, nutrient deficiencies could be alleviated. For example, blindness due to vitamin A deficiency is a common problem in third world countries. Researchers at the Swiss Federal Institute of Technology Institute for Plant Sciences have created a strain of "golden" rice containing an unusually high content of beta-carotene (vitamin A).[10] Since this rice was funded by the Rockefeller Foundation,[11] a non-profit organization, the Institute hopes to offer the golden rice seed free to any third world country that requests it. Plans were underway to develop a golden rice that also has increased iron content. However, the grant that funded the creation of these two rice strains was not renewed, perhaps because of the vigorous anti-GM food protesting in Europe, and so this nutritionally-enhanced rice may not come to market at all.[12]

- *Pharmaceuticals*: Medicines and vaccines often are costly to produce and sometimes require special storage conditions not readily available in third world countries. Researchers are working to develop edible vaccines in tomatoes and potatoes.[13,14] These vaccines will be much easier to ship, store and administer than traditional injectable vaccines.
- *Phytoremediation*: Not all GM plants are grown as crops. Soil and groundwater pollution continues to be a problem in all parts of the world. Plants such as poplar trees have been genetically engineered to clean up heavy metal pollution from contaminated soil.[15]

What Are Some of the Criticisms Against GM Foods?

Environmental activists, religious organizations, public interest groups, professional associations and other scientists and government officials have all raised concerns about GM foods, and criticized agribusiness for pursuing profit without concern for potential hazards, and the government for failing to exercise adequate regulatory oversight. It seems that everyone has a strong opinion about GM foods. Even the Vatican[16] and the Prince of Wales[17] have expressed their opinions. Most concerns about GM foods fall into three categories: environmental hazards, human health risks, and economic concerns.

Environmental hazards

- *Unintended harm to other organisms*: Last year a laboratory study was published in *Nature*[18] showing that pollen from B.t. corn caused high mortality rates in monarch butterfly caterpillars. Monarch caterpillars consume milkweed plants, not corn, but the fear is that if pollen from B.t. corn is blown by the wind onto milkweed plants in neighboring fields, the caterpillars could eat the pollen and perish. Although the *Nature* study was not conducted under natural field conditions, the results seemed to support this viewpoint. Unfortunately, B.t. toxins kill many species of insect larvae indiscriminately; it is not possible to design a B.t. toxin that would only kill crop-damaging pests and remain harmless to all other insects. This study is being reexamined by the USDA, the U.S. Environmental Protection Agency (EPA) and other nongovernment research groups, and preliminary data from new studies suggests that the original study may have been flawed.[19,20] This topic is the subject of acrimonious debate, and both sides of the argument are defending their data vigorously. Currently, there is no agreement about the results of these studies, and the potential risk of harm to non-target organisms will need to be evaluated further.

- *Reduced effectiveness of pesticides*: Just as some populations of mosquitoes developed resistance to the now-banned pesticide DDT, many people are concerned that insects will become resistant to B.t. or other crops that have been genetically modified to produce their own pesticides.

- *Gene transfer to non-target species*: Another concern is that crop plants engineered for herbicide tolerance and weeds will cross-breed, resulting in the transfer of the herbicide resistance genes from the crops into the weeds. These "superweeds" would then be herbicide tolerant as well. Other introduced genes may cross over into nonmodified crops planted next to GM crops. The possibility of interbreeding is shown by the defense of farmers against lawsuits filed by Monsanto. The company has filed patent infringement lawsuits against farmers who may have harvested GM crops. Monsanto claims that the farmers obtained Monsanto-licensed GM seeds from an unknown source and did not pay royalties to Monsanto. The farmers claim that their unmodified crops were cross-pollinated from someone else's GM crops planted a field or two away. More investigation is needed to resolve this issue.

There are several possible solutions to the three problems mentioned above. Genes are exchanged between plants via pollen. Two ways to ensure that non-target species will not receive introduced genes from GM plants are to create GM plants that are male sterile (do not produce pollen) or to modify the GM plant so that the pollen does not contain the introduced gene.[21,22,23] Cross-pollination would not occur, and if harmless insects such as monarch caterpillars were to eat pollen from GM plants, the caterpillars would survive.

5   Another possible solution is to create buffer zones around fields of GM crops.[24,25,26] For example, non-GM corn would be planted to surround a field of B.t. GM corn, and the non-GM corn would not be harvested. Beneficial or harmless insects would have a refuge in the non-GM corn, and insect pests could be allowed to destroy the non-GM corn and would not develop resistance to B.t. pesticides. Gene transfer to weeds and other crops would not occur because the wind-blown pollen would not travel beyond the buffer zone. Estimates of the necessary width of buffer zones range from 6 meters to 30 meters or more.[27] This planting method may not be feasible if too much acreage is required for the buffer zones.

NOTES

1. Insecticidal proteins from Bacillus thuringiensis protect corn from corn rootworms (Nature Biotechnology, Vol 19, No 7, pp. 668–672, Jul 2001).

2. Lepidopteran-resistant transgenic plants (US Patent 6313378, Nov 2001, Monsanto).

3. Roundup Ready ◆ Soybeans.

4. The use of cytochrome P450 genes to introduce herbicide tolerance in crops: a review (Pesticide Science, Vol 55, No 9, pp. 867–874, Sep 1999).

5. Transgenic approaches to combat fusarium head blight in wheat and barley (Crop Science, Vol 41, No 3, pp. 628–627, Jun 2001).

6. Post-transcriptional gene silencing in plum pox virus resistant transgenic European plum containing the plum pox potyvirus coat protein gene (Transgenic Research, Vol 10, No 3, pp. 201–209, Jun 2001).

7. Type II fish antifreeze protein accumulation in transgenic tobacco does not confer frost resistance (Transgenic Research, Vol 8, No 2, pp. 105–117, Apr 1999).

8. Transgenic salt-tolerant tomato plants accumulate salt in foliage but not in fruit (Nature Biotechnology, Vol 19, No 8, pp. 765–768, Aug 2001).

9. Peroxidase activity of desiccation-tolerant loblolly pine somatic embryos (In Vitro Cellular & Developmental Biology Plant, Vol 36, No 6, pp. 488–491, Dec 2000).

10. Genetic engineering towards carotene biosynthesis in endosperm (Swiss Federal Institute of Technology Institute for Plant Sciences).

11. New rices may help address vitamin A- and iron deficiency, major causes of death in the developing world (Rockefeller Foundation).

12. Rice Biotechnology: Rockefeller to end network after 15 years of success (Science, Vol 286, No 5444, pp. 1468–1469, Nov 1999).

13. Medical molecular farming: production of antibodies, biopharmaceuticals and edible vaccines in plants (Trends in Plant Science, Vol 6, No 5, pp. 219–226, May 2001).

14. Oral immunization with hepatitis B surface antigen expressed in transgenic plants (Proceedings of the National Academy of Sciences, USA, Vol 98, No 20, pp. 11539–11544, Sep 2001).

15. Phytodetoxification of hazardous organomercurials by genetically engineered plants (Nature Biotechnology, Vol 18, No 2, pp. 213–217, Feb 2000).

16. GMO Roundup (Nature Biotechnology, Vol 18, p 7, Jan 2000).

17. Questions about genetically modified organisms: an article by The Prince of Wales (http://www.princeofwales.gov.uk/speeches/agriculture_01061999.html) and Seeds of Disaster: An article by The Prince of Wales (http://www.princeofwales.gov.uk/speeches/agriculture_08061998.html).

18. Transgenic pollen harms monarch larvae (Nature, Vol 399, No 6733, p 214, May 1999).

19. GM corn poses little threat to monarch (Nature Biotechnology, Vol 17, p 1154, Dec 1999).

20. Bt and the Monarch Butterfly: Update by Dr. Douglas Powell (AGCare Update Magazine http://www.agcare.org/AGCareUpdate.htm#Monarch).

21. New tools for chloroplast genetic engineering (Nature Biotechnology, Vol 17, No 9, pp. 855–856, Sep 1999).

22. Tandem constructs: preventing the rise of superweeds (Trends in Biotechnology, Vol 17, No 9, pp. 361–366, Sep 1999).

23. Containment of herbicide resistance through genetic engineering of the chloroplast genome (Nature Biotechnology, Vol 16, No 4, pp. 345–348, Apr 1998).

24. Efforts to bioengineer intrinsic resistance to insect pests into crop plants have made use of a natural bacterial toxin, Bt, from Bacillus thuringiensis Berliner (Science, Vol 284, No 5416, p. 873, May 1999).

25. Inheritance of resistance to Bacillus thuringiensis toxin (Dipel ES) in the European corn borer (Science, Vol 284, No 5416, pp. 965–967, May 1999).

26. Buffers urged around Bt corn fields (Environmental News Network: http://www.enn.com/enn-news-archive/1999/07/071499/btbuffer_4342.asp).

27. GM crops: public perception and scientific solutions (Trends in Plant Science, Vol 4, No 12, pp. 467–469, Dec 1999).

Analyze

1. What are some of the problems that GM foods are designed to address?

2. Give two examples of genetic enhancements of plants that come from non-plant organisms.

3. Consider how various groups of people with different interests, values, and problems would feel differently about the growth or consumption of GM foods. For example, how might farmers feel and why? How about mothers? People in the third world? Companies? Scientists? Discuss with your class how these different interest groups might affect the development of GMOs.

Explore

1. Imagine that you work at a large-output farm that produces tomatoes, peppers, and corn. For years the farm has specialized in organic agricultural processes. For this assignment, write a letter to the owner of the farm in which you argue the case for introducing genetic modification

to the farm's agricultural practices. Remember: A good argument also includes potential drawbacks to your plan.

2. In both America and Europe, GM foods have been controversial. Using your library database or an online search engine, research the debate over a specific instance in which GM foods were developed and distributed. If you feel that one side in the debate is right, use the materials in the debate to make your own argument for that side.

3. The debate over GMOs can be very heated; people often take extreme positions and make highly emotional statements in these debates. Find a couple articles in favor of GMOs and a couple that oppose them. Then compare the style and tone to Whitman's. Notice, for example, that when Whitman talks about cold tolerance of GMO strawberries, she includes this qualification: "(Note: I have not been able to find any journal articles or patents that involve fish antifreeze proteins in strawberries, although I have seen such reports in newspapers. I can only conclude that nothing on this application has yet been published or patented.)" Whitman projects a trustworthy persona. Do you trust what you read from the other writers? Why or why not? Write a brief piece of advice telling writers how to write so that readers will listen, believe, and trust them.

Paul Epstein
"Food Security and Climate Change: The True Cost of Carbon"

Paul Epstein was associate director of the Center for Health and the Global Environment at Harvard Medical School and was a medical doctor trained in tropical public health. He co-authored the book *Changing Planet, Changing Health*. He also worked with the Intergovernmental Panel on Climate Change (IPCC), the National Academy of Sciences (NAS), the National Oceanic and Atmospheric Administration (NOAA), and the National Aeronautics and Space Administration (NASA) to assess the health impacts of climate change and to develop health applications of climate forecasting and remote sensing.

Dr. Epstein died shortly after this blog appeared in September 2011. The blog post reproduced below was written by Dr. Epstein and three colleagues, one an undergraduate student at Harvard. The blog post recounts a whole series of climate-related problems that have reduced global food production, increased "food insecurity," and triggered political instability.

With wheat prices surging as major producers are hit by droughts and other extreme weather events, it's costing everyone more to eat.

Writing on page one in the *New York Times* Justin Gillis recently sounded the alarm on what Lester Brown has been warning us for years: Climate change is threatening our food supply.

With fuel prices down (not much) we'd like to think the economy will settle down. But volatility in markets, food baskets, and weather is rattling many. Indeed, food, feed, and fuel prices are contributing to the growing political instability across the globe.

The summer heat engulfed towns felled by fiendish twisters. The Mighty Mississippi breached shores all along its course after being pounded by heavy rains and nourished by melting snow, the hangover from a brutal winter. The hundred-year floods inundated homes, homesteads, and farms, taking a toll on communities and commodities.

5   The wide swings in weather were matched by major outlier events. All of us experienced the shifting weather patterns. This is the new norm. And as the climate changes, the extremes are proving especially costly for global food security.

Grains are taking a particular beating. In the past year, wheat prices increased 75 percent. In 2009, the United Nations estimates, over one billion people were undernourished, and a greater toll is projected. Malnutrition—accounting annually for 2.2 million under-five child deaths (and underlying much of childhood illness)—is increasing, undermining health and well-being.

The U.S. has had more than its share of bad weather (and it doesn't seem to let up). The record-breaking, tornado-packed storm system that hit a dozen states this past spring killed over 300. The Southwest has been in drought and aquifers, already overdrawn and underfed, were further challenged by summer dry spells and heatwaves. In April, 83 wildfires consumed hundreds of square miles of Texas in one week. Extreme weather has reduced grain yields in the Southeast and in the Midwest Corn Belt.

Globally, the trend is more pronounced.

Climate change—warming and altered weather patterns—is contributing to production short-falls and rising grain prices. (Increasing demands for meat and dairy products, higher fuel prices, and displacement of food crops by biofuel-bound crops are compounding factors.)

Warming, itself, is already damaging crops. Writing in *Science* magazine   10
Stanford University's David Lobell and colleagues found that global maize and wheat production declined by 3.8 percent and 5.5 percent, respectively, from 1980 to 2008, due to rising global temperatures. Plants are, as we know, sensitive to warming and water stress, especially when hot days coincide with their reproductive stage (flowering). Warming is now costing consumers, agricultural companies, and livestock producers some $60 billion a year, the authors concluded. But that, unfortunately, is not the worst of it. Extreme weather events were not addressed in the recent study, and they are playing a rapidly escalating role.

Wheat, rice, corn, and soybeans provide the majority of calories for humans and animals, and wheat is the most widely traded grain on the international market. In 2008, 690 million tons of wheat were grown worldwide, with China, the E.U., India, the U.S., and Russia serving as the leading producers.

But prices are rising and the consequences are proliferating. In 2008, prices jumped due to the economic collapse and the growth of biofuels, sparking food riots in Bangladesh, Burkina Faso, Cameroon, Cote D'Ivoire, Egypt, Haiti, India, Somalia, and Yemen. This year, prices have jumped with each extreme weather event.

In July and August of 2010, temperatures exceeded 104 degrees Fahrenheit in a Russian heatwave, far above normal. The extent surpassed that of the 2003 European summer heatwave, and over 50,000 excess deaths were attributed to both. The Russian heatwave and water stress inflamed wildfires that claimed close to 40 percent of the projected wheat crop. The government declared a state of emergency in 27 agricultural regions and wheat prices jumped 45 percent on global markets.

The effects were immediate. Mozambique, one of the world's poorest nations, experienced riots in August due to higher bread (and fuel) prices. Thirteen people died—and food subsidies were reinstated.

Also in July and August of 2010, monster monsoons (an extreme version   15
of a natural event) hit Pakistan. The floods displaced 20 million, killed close to 2,000, sickened thousands more, and inundated grain growing

areas of the Indus. Climate models project additional intensification of Asian monsoons with continued warming.

In November, 2010, an enormous tropical cyclone caused extensive flooding in Queensland, Australia, killing close to 2,000 (indigenous people being disproportionately affected), and costing an estimated $6 billion. Nearly three-quarters of Queensland, including several wheat-growing regions, was declared a disaster zone. Much of the young, winter wheat crop was severely damaged and grain exports were held up in the Brisbane, the state's largest grain terminal.

Protracted drought in central China has cut winter and summer wheat production there, while reduced snowpack in China's Northern Plain has affected 15.8 million acres. Over one-third of China's wheat production has been lost this year. (Minimal rains in January provided some relief.) In June, also in China, historic flooding claimed more homes and farmland. Meanwhile, extreme cold compounded the drought's impact on wheat yields.

China, with $2.85 trillion in foreign exchange reserves, can afford to import grains—and it has recently begun to do so. But internal disparities have surfaced, even in China: In April, truck and taxi drivers protested rising food and fuel prices.

Unfortunately there are biological consequences to altered weather patterns as well. From Morocco to Northern India, wetter winters have ushered in "yellow rust" fungus, destroying some 60 percent of the region's dry climate wheat. More pesticides, fungicides, and herbicides may be called up to control pests, pathogens, and weeds in a warmer world—all with their own health consequences.

20   Suddenly, food security has reached critical proportions for many. With wheat prices surging 83 percent on the Chicago and Paris exchanges, nations where residents spend half of their income on food (Nigerians spend 73 percent and Vietnamese spend 65 percent) are undergoing mounting social strife.

Price hikes and food insecurity are today contributing to political instability. In April, food riots broke out in Uganda and in Burkina Faso, and rising food, feed, and fuel price have helped catapult the cries for democracy in Northern Africa and the Middle East.

While the fossil fuel industry continues its well-funded, well-orchestrated campaign to keep up a drum beat of doubt on climate change, the impacts are becoming self evident, and nowhere are they more pronounced than with the emergence of food insecurity.

Addressing climate change is everyone's business.

The challenges to inertia continue. In the U.S., a new group, Our Children's Trust, filed a suit in May against the U.S. government for its failure to protect the earth for generations unborn. (The brief was written by James Hansen of NASA and other scientists.) The U.K. has just announced accelerated targets to limit greenhouse gas emissions (50 percent by 2025), by reducing fossil fuel combustion and the felling of forests. There are many measures to help our agricultural systems adapt to the changing climate. But this is a critical time to scale up measures to clean up and transform our energy system, to give the climate a chance at restabilization.

Analyze

1. What percentage of the world's population has been deemed undernourished? Is this percentage rising or falling? How do the answers to these questions fit into the larger context of sustainability?

2. Briefly describe how and why climate change and weather events relate to food.

3. How are politics and food linked? Is climate change a national security issue for the United States?

Explore

1. This article claims that weather events have reduced the availability of important agricultural products. One possible result of such a scarcity is an increased need to protect those plants that *do* survive the weather events. As a result, the article suggests that an increased use of pesticides and herbicides may result. In a well-developed paragraph, connect this article's notion that food shortages might result in a higher use of pesticides to Whitman's concerns about the effects of overusing pesticides/herbicides.

2. This article tries to show how climate change affects food availability. Create a web in which you make connections between the two. Include in your web how climate change affects food both directly and indirectly. See how many degrees of separation you can think of as you imagine how climate activities have broader ripple effects that affect food supplies in varied ways.

3. Using any available sources, identify any major agricultural disasters that occurred in your home state in the past decade. Examples might include massive fish death or soil pollution. Then compose a short blog editorial in which you inform the reader about the details of the event and how that event affected people and their food supply.

Forging Connections

1. Using an online search engine, find a series of pictures that visually represent the dangers and problems associated with high-impact agricultural practices, food, and climate change. Think about the impact these images might have on the viewer, and strive to select images that will convey the idea in a way that is not just informative but also emotionally captivating. Then, use ideas from the readings in this chapter to construct short captions for each of the images you selected.

2. The readings in this chapter all discuss the sustainability of food. Using your new knowledge of food sustainability gained from these readings, construct a research paper in which you detail five unsustainable food practices that occur either in this country or foreign nations. Integrate at least three outside sources to support your research. Then, end your report with recommendations for how individuals can make decisions on a local level to increase food sustainability.

Looking Further

1. Readings in many of the chapters in this book refer to the connection between food, food security, and social order. Starving people don't always behave politely. In the first chapter, Diamond connects environmental decline to political unrest. In this chapter, Epstein catalogs the increasing food insecurity around the world due to climate change. In Chapter 6, Montgomery argues that soil and civilization are directly linked through the production of food. Drawing on this idea and examples from other readings, write a worst-case-scenario science-fiction dystopia (the opposite of utopia) story. What is life like when climate change ravages the world and food becomes scarce?

2. Pick your favorite meal at your favorite restaurant and perform a life cycle analysis on the whole meal, its ingredients, preparation, consumption, and waste. This is a complex cradle-to-grave or field-to-flush

analysis that draws on the readings in every chapter of this book. It would be a great group project since it requires a lot of research. What are the ingredients? How were they produced and how does that affect soil and water resources? How much energy was consumed growing, fertilizing, and transporting the food products? What happens to the kitchen waste? To the human waste? You probably can't get precise answers to all these questions, but do your best. When you are done, construct a flow chart that traces the process of producing, delivering, and consuming the meal as well as handling the wastes.

4

Climate Change: What It Is, How It Affects Us, & Why We Argue About It So Much

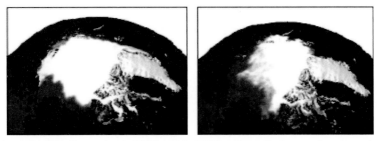

Images of Arctic sea ice in 1979 and in 2003, composite images from remote sensing data from satellite instruments (Comiso et al. 2003); Image credit: Scientific Visualization Studio, NASA Space Flight Center.

Climate change is probably the most dramatic and potentially devastating phenomenon affecting biological, social, and economic sustainability today. And climate change touches almost all the other issues in this book. Energy production and the burning of fossil fuels such as oil and coal are important contributors to climate change. The search for alternative and sustainable energy sources is motivated, to a greater or lesser degree, by concerns about climate change and greenhouse gas emissions. Climate change is causing sea levels to rise because, like everything else, water expands when heated and also because the Arctic, Antarctic, and Greenland ice sheets are slowly melting, adding huge quantities of water to the oceans. The impact of rising sea levels on low-lying coastal areas will be severe. And this is especially true in the third world, where countries have fewer resources to deal with the damage or to adapt to changing conditions. The availability of fresh water in many parts of the world is threatened by the melting of glaciers that supply rivers and by reduced rainfall. The pressure to use water more sustainably is powerfully affected by these emerging changes. Agricultural production, soil erosion, and food security are all affected by climate change. As climate change alters rainfall patterns and as storms become more intense, droughts ruin crops and reduce harvests. Increasingly intense rainfall "events" accelerate soil erosion and cause flooding. As harvests in the third world are reduced and food becomes scarcer and more expensive, social unrest and instability increase. According to the U.S. Centers for Disease Control and Prevention, even human health will suffer from climate change as heat waves increase and as disease-carrying insects such as mosquitoes increase their geographical range and move into areas that had been too cool for them. If Rachel Carson's *Silent Spring* galvanized the early environmental movement in the 1960s, climate change has galvanized the scientific and environmental communities today. For many, climate change is an important part of what the French philosopher Bruno Latour calls "ecocide."

Despite abundant evidence and broad scientific consensus on the basic facts of climate change, many people still have questions and doubt that climate change exists. That is to be expected given how complicated and potentially dangerous climate change is. Beyond the difficulty presented by the complexity of climate science, however, climate change threatens powerful international industries that have spent millions of dollars on public campaigns to undermine confidence in the basic science of climate change. Like the tobacco industry's efforts to deny that smoking can cause cancer, the potential impact of climate change on the oil and gas industry has led to what critics call a "manufactured controversy." The readings in this section address the fundamental questions that arise in contemporary discussions of climate change. Does it really exist? Is it caused by human activity? How bad is it? What will the consequences be? Who has the knowledge and authority to determine the truth about climate change? What can we do about it? These are questions about the *what* of climate change, questions of fact and policy. As you read these essays, you may want to refer back to the book's Appendix for explanations of concepts such as uncertainty, modeling, and scenarios that run through these readings.

As writers you also need to consider *how* to write about climate change. What are the potential rhetorical strategies and appeals that might convince readers and motivate them to take action? These rhetorical issues are discussed at some length in the book's Appendix. As you read the selections in this chapter, think about how you might communicate these ideas to others; how you might convince them if they doubt that climate change exists; how you might motivate them to take some form of action, even if it is as simple as driving less and conserving energy. Simply giving people a lot of facts doesn't always convince them. They might not understand or trust your facts or the science that produced those facts. And facts rarely speak for themselves. Writers need to explain the facts, what they mean, and their significance. Similarly, people don't always act even when they accept the facts, especially if acting involves a significant or inconvenient change in their lives. This is what the Appendix refers to as the "rationalist paradox," people who know the facts still acting as if they didn't. Climate change is too important to ignore or deny, but writing about it can be very difficult.

Ralph Cicerone
"Finding Climate Change and Being Useful"

Ralph Cicerone is past president of the National Academy of Sciences as well as past director of the Atmospheric Chemistry Division at the National Center for Atmospheric Research (NCAR). Over 30 years ago, Cicerone warned of possible dangers to the stratospheric ozone layer, a thin layer of molecules 30 to 50 miles above where you are now sitting that protects all life on Earth from potentially fatal ultraviolet radiation. In addition to teaching at a number of prestigious universities, Dr. Cicerone has received the Bower Award and Prize for Achievement in Science, the 2002 Roger Revelle Medal of the American Geophysical Union, and the World Cultural Council's Albert Einstein World Award in Science. The selection included here is a lecture Dr. Cicerone delivered at the National Council for Science and the Environment in 2006. In this lecture, Cicerone lays out the evidence that climate change is occurring and that it is "anthropogenic" or caused by human activity. As you read, think about how Cicerone constructs his argument by making claims and refuting the arguments of climate change skeptics.

It's a great honor and pleasure for me to be here, as it would be for anyone. Ambassador Richard Benedick sets the standard for all of us with his depth of knowledge, his creativity, and his effectiveness, which I think explains the respect with which all of us hold him in our own minds.

There's a saying in show business that you should never get on a stage after a child performance or a dog act. And at a conference like this, to take the podium after Russell Train has had it, and in the memory of John Chafee, I think it's an analogous situation that no one should try. But nonetheless, whatever the show is, it's going to go on, and I will try to deliver the lecture without being overawed by the memory of John Chafee, the wonderful stories about Senator Stafford, and the lifetime achievement award (for a career that continues) to Russell Train.

Tonight, with the title *Finding Climate Change and Being Useful*, I'm going to talk about detecting climate change, and that it has been done, whether we wanted it or not. And then at the end I will add a few words about being useful.

First of all, as to the very idea of detecting climate change inside of one human lifetime, we shouldn't forget how difficult that is. We know that there have been many climate changes in the Earth's history before now, and there will probably be continuing climate change, with or without human presence. These previous changes are not completely understood, but as one depiction, Figure 4.1 shows a reconstruction of historical ice extent over North America during the last glacial maximum, 18,000 years ago.

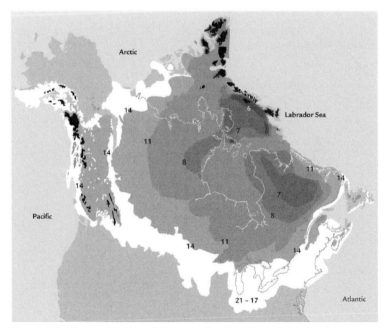

Figure 4.1 Reconstruction of the extent of ice cover during the last ice age (from Ruddiman et al., 2005). Numbered contours indicate the geographical extent of ice cover N thousand years ago.

5   You will see from this figure that the southern extent of the ice went through the Middle Atlantic region of the United States and deep into the Midwest 18,000 and 14,000 years ago. And then as the ice began to recede, 12,000, 10,000, 9,000 years ago, there was still very, very deep ice over parts of Canada and the upper northwestern states. These reconstructions are based on several kinds of evidence from geologists and geographers. This image exemplifies that climate change has occurred often throughout the planet's history and that some epochs of large change continued over thousands of years, so that detecting climate change within one human lifetime is a difficult job.

Figure 4.2 is a photo from a 1979 cover of Science magazine, which I chose for two reasons. It shows an inland glacier, the Quelccaya Glacier in Peru, photographed and explored and measured by Lonnie Thompson, who is a hero in this business because of his intrepid expeditions to high altitudes. If you look closely, you can see the strata, the layers of ice that are essentially annual layers. They are exposed in this photograph, as they

Figure 4.2   A photograph of the Quelccaya ice cap in Peru (from Thompson, 1979). Annual bands of ice are visible in this photograph taken in 1979.

usually are not, because the edges of glaciers don't usually look like this and they are not so accessible. By careful studies of layers like these from ice formations from Greenland and Antarctica, scientists have been able to construct climate histories.

By dating those annual layers and by extracting chemicals from inside such layers, histories of the chemical composition of air have been deduced back to 700,000 years ago; I will show you some data later.

Going back further than 20,000 years ago into paleoclimate, there is evidence of previous cold periods on Earth and, of course, of warmer periods in between. There were apparently times when the polar regions, at least, were much warmer.

Let us now move to contemporary times. Figure 4.3 is a graph of surface temperature measurements (from thermometers) since about 1880. This particular data set is from the NASA center in New York City; there are several similar data sets where a couple of hundred million data points will go into creating a curve like this. There is a five-year running mean in red, and annual mean temperatures are shown with black squares. The data shown are temperature anomalies; that is, temperature differences measured from a reference point. The particular zero reference point is the mean value between the years 1950 and 1980. So, above zero means warmer than the period 1950 to 1980 and below zero means cooler. These data are globally averaged annual or five year averages. The temperatures are taken from the different latitude belts of the Earth, continental regions, and ocean regions and averaged according to the area-weighted latitude belt that they are in—a proper global average, after excluding obvious effects from cities (the urban heat-island effect). There are historical records showing that thermometers measuring temperatures of regions undisturbed by cities that were later overtaken by urban spread produced contaminated temperature records after that point. Those kinds of data have been removed. Figure 4.3 shows global averages, as far away from cities as you can get.

There are several interesting features of Figure 4.3. One striking feature 10 is the record of the last 25 or 30 years, since the late 1970s. This is the fastest temperature rise (or fall) recorded in the instrumental record. The last 25 or 30 years are most notable for two reasons; I will mention one reason now and one later. This rapid rise of temperatures is faster than can be regenerated in any of our climate models, and the total warming from the 1950 to 1980 baseline is larger than can be explained by existing theories—unless

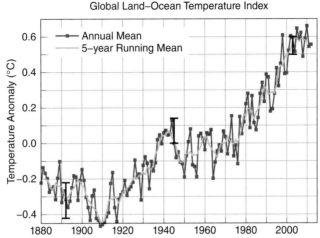

Figure 4.3 Surface temperatures averaged over Earth's surface, graphed as the difference from the global average temperature of 1950 to 1980. Measurement methods, locations, and data handling are described in NASA, 2006, and references therein.

we include the human-enhanced greenhouse effect. The rapid warming since the late 1970's is just as clear in the southern hemisphere (which is mostly ocean and less contaminated in various ways).

This recent warming is statistically very significant (several standard deviations above the noise), and its rate exceeds any natural variability that we can understand mechanistically. And it is faster than any of our computer models can generate from first principles. The total warming since 1880–1890 has been 0.8 to 0.9 degrees C, with more than half of it since the late 1970's. The cooling between 1940 and 1975 was strongest in northern mid- and high latitudes and might have been due to reflection of sunlight from airborne particles due to sulfur pollution (from burning high sulfur-content fossil fuels); see Charlson et. al. (1990) and Santer et. al. (1995).

"This recent warming is statistically very significant."

What happened before 1880? Some very good scientists have worked hard to reconstruct temperatures of the times before the Industrial Revolution, before there were thermometers. Figure 4.4 summarizes several such attempts to reconstruct northern hemisphere temperatures going back 2,000 years.

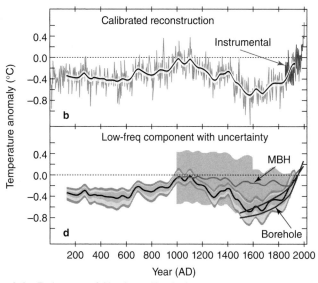

Figure 4.4 Estimates of Northern Hemisphere temperatures over the past 2,000 years, reconstructed from various proxy indicators. The top graph includes temperature records from thermometers, similar to those of Figure 4.3. Ranges of estimates and the meaning of shaded areas are explained in the original reference (Moberg et al., 2005).

These reconstructions are based on tree rings, geological bore holes, coral samples, stable isotopes in various reservoirs, and some historical accounts. The instrumental record (data like those of Figure 4.3) is the green curve on the upper graph on the extreme right. Temperatures of the last 25 or 30 years are higher than those reconstructed for the past 500 years, and probably above those of the past 1,000 years. Reconstructing past temperatures is an active area of research, as is setting confidence limits on the ranges of temperatures in various geographic regions over the past 1,000 or 2,000 years, so the data of (and conclusions from) Figure 4.4, especially those from years prior to 1500 A.D., are less precise than those from Figure 4.3.

Several other notable pieces of evidence have emerged to show us that climate is changing. For example, recent years of ocean data show a similar warming. One such study reported a careful analysis of ocean temperatures and the heat content of the oceans above the thermocline, that is, the top 700 meters or so of the ocean's waters (see Figure 4.5).

The increased heat content of the waters (heat capacity multiplied by 15 temperature increase multiplied by amount of heated water) turns out to

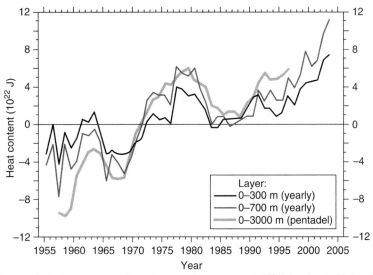

Figure 4.5   Time series of yearly ocean heat content (10^{22} J) for the 0–300 and 0–700 m layers and pentadal (5-year running composites for 1955–1959 through 1994–1998) ocean heat content (10^{22} J) for the 0–3,000 m layer. Each yearly estimate is plotted at the midpoint of the year; each pentadal estimate is plotted at the midpoint of the 5-year period (from Levitus et al., 2005).

equal the extra heat due to the greenhouse gas trapping of heat in the Earth's surface over the same period predicted by climate models (Hansen et al., 2005).

Figure 4.6 presents observed temperature-profile changes (from 1960 through 1999) in various ocean basins and compares them with corresponding profiles calculated through considerations of physical oceanography and heat exchange from the atmosphere. The authors (Barnett et. al. 2005) could reproduce the actual temperature profiles (represented by the red circles on the graphs of Figure 4.6 in all of these different ocean basins) by including the warming from the human-caused greenhouse effect. Similar calculations assuming only a change in strength of the sun's illumination itself could not match the observations, which I will discuss a little more later.

There has been some pronounced warming in the Arctic. Figure 4.7 shows observed temperature increases of the last 50 years, on a two-dimensional representation of the spherical globe. On this kind of projection, the very top of the graphs, going from left to right is 90 degrees north (the North Pole) and the very bottom of each figure going from left to

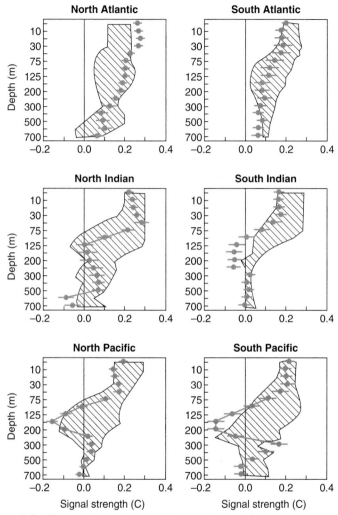

Figure 4.6 Observed and calculated changes in oceanic temperature profiles versus depth for the period 1960–1999 from Barnett et al. (2005). Circles: observed warming signal strength. Hatched area: range of signal strengths in PCM model with anthropogenic forcing included.

right is 90 degrees south. The temperature coding (false color images) is at the bottom; reddish brown indicates a temperature increase (annual average) of almost 3 degrees Centigrade and on the left, light blue indicates an annual average temperature decrease of 0.5 degrees. Contours of

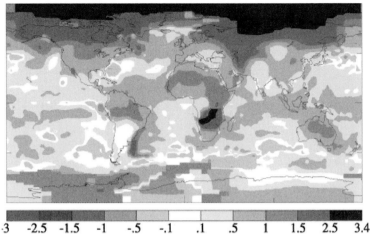

-3   -2.5   -1.5   -1   -.5   -.1   .1   .5   1   1.5   2.5   3.4

Figure 4.7 Annual and seasonal temperature changes observed over the past 50 years, from Hansen et al. (http://data.giss.nasa.gov/gistemp/2005/).

temperature increases have been drawn from actual temperature observations. Largest warmings have occurred in Alaska, Siberia, and the Antarctic Peninsula. Most ocean areas have warmed. The remote location of most warming makes it clear that the warming is not a product of local urban influence.

This very rapid warming of the Arctic region is not fully understood yet, but climate models do predict more warming in the polar regions than anywhere else. Also, although not shown in this figure, the warming is more pronounced in the winter than in the summer. There are, in fact, a couple of small spots that are showing slight cooling in spots here and there around the Arctic. But generally, large warmings, melting of ice, melting of snow pack, and thawing of permafrost have been observed.

Figure 4.8 shows a set of remote sensing images. In the upper depiction, the 1979 summertime sea-ice extent appears as seen from space. You will notice that 24 years later, in 2003, the summertime ice extent observed over the Arctic is less.

20   Now, while these images are very informative, with extensive coverage, we don't need space platforms to tell us that ice is disappearing. People sailing in the Arctic are now finding open water where they couldn't find it before in the summertime. Of course, in winter, ice cover becomes extensive

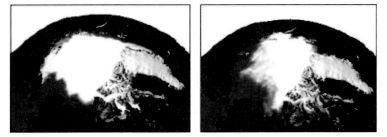

Figure 4.8 Images of Arctic sea ice in 1979 and in 2003, composite images from remote sensing data from satellite instruments (Comiso et al. 2003); Image credit: Scientific Visualization Studio, NASA Space Flight Center.

each year. But the summertime decrease in sea ice in the Arctic is enormous, and this change is happening very rapidly. Future decreases may involve amplifying feedbacks, positive feedbacks that will melt the ice even faster. There are now some predictions that summertime Arctic sea ice could disappear by the end of this century (Northern Hemisphere sea-ice simulations by global climate models (Walsh and Timlin, 2003)).

There is another kind of indication of climate change which is less direct, but very dramatic. Two papers published in 2005 showed a statistically strong correlation between the warming since 1980 and the incidence of very strong hurricanes. Figure 4.9 defines a quantity called the power dissipation index (PDI). It is basically the cube of the speed of the winds rotating inside the storm, integrated over each storm's geographical extent and over time.

Power integrated over time is energy. So PDI is the total energy dissipated in a storm's lifetime. There has been a warming of the sea surface over the last 25 or 30 years; in fact, 40 to 50 years. And that warming has been accompanied by the increased incidence of strong storms. The statistics that hurricanes are more powerful are very clear. In fact, according to Emanuel, there has been something like a 60 percent increase in the incidence of the big category storms in the Atlantic and Pacific Ocean basins in the last 30 years. This graph was created before the enormous hurricanes and the 27 tropical storms of the year 2005, so the correlation will look even stronger when this graph is updated. The statistics about whether there are more hurricanes is not so clear.

Part of the mechanism is understood. It has to do with warmer surface waters evaporating faster, and the latent heat of condensation from the

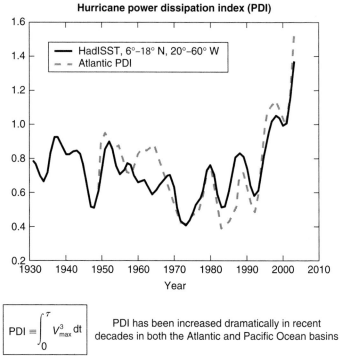

$$PDI \equiv \int_0^\tau V_{max}^3 \, dt$$

PDI has been increased dramatically in recent decades in both the Atlantic and Pacific Ocean basins

Figure 4.9 The dashed curve is a measure of the power dissipated annually by tropical cyclones in the North Atlantic (the power dissipation index, PDI), while the solid curve is sea-surface temperature versus time (from Emanuel, 2005). Data have been smoothed and scaled as described by Emanuel; Atlantic hurricane power dissipation has more than doubled in approximately 30 years.

extra water vapor in the atmosphere then becomes a source of extra energy for storms. But atmospheric conditions must also be conducive, and not all of the data needed to understand this pattern, either statistically or storm by storm, are available. Experts in the field have come to believe that the warming of the sea surface is contributing to the increased frequency of stronger storms (Emanuel, 2005; Curry et al., 2005).

Greenhouse Gases

The greenhouse effect, a natural phenomenon, has operated throughout Earth's history because of the physical properties of certain gases in the air, especially water vapor and carbon dioxide, and there is strong evidence that Earth would be much colder without the greenhouse effect. As humans change the chemical composition of the atmosphere, they also alter the size of the greenhouse effect; increases of the amounts of greenhouse gases were especially clear during the last half of the 20th century.

Figure 4.10 is regarded as a classic graph of data. It is from C. David   25
Keeling and T. P. Whorf. This extensive graph displays their measurements of carbon dioxide from late 1957 through to the year 2005, taken at a very remote place, Mauna Loa, Hawaii, nearly every hour of every day for 47 years. The dots are the monthly averages of the data. You can see the overall increase from 314 parts per million of air to 380 parts per million over this period, along with regular yearly cycles.

The cyclic behavior of the carbon dioxide is similar to the breathing of the planet, if you will. In the wintertime in the northern hemisphere, carbon dioxide is released into the atmosphere by the decaying of vegetation in the previous growing season and by the respiration of soils. Then, in the spring and summer of the following year, the carbon dioxide is drawn down by photosynthesis. So we see these beautiful annual cycles. The cycles enable quantitative study of the carbon cycle.

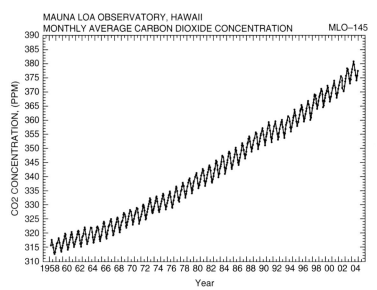

Figure 4.10   Monthly averages of carbon dioxide concentrations in air sampled at Mauna Loa, Hawaii, measured by Professor C. D. Keeling from 1957 through 2004. Graph is available at http://cdiac.ornl.gov/trends/co2/graphics/-mlo145e_ thrudc04.pdf

But the more direct importance of this graph is the large and rapid increase in atmospheric carbon dioxide; many measurements elsewhere verify that the increase has been global, as must be the case for a long-lived gas whose mixing occurs much faster than processes that remove it from air. Carbon dioxide is an effective greenhouse gas, its amounts have increased and we have a very solid theoretical understanding for why climate change, notably a surface warming, should be occurring right now.

The observed increase of CO_2 worldwide can be compared to what is known about CO_2 amounts through geological history. Teams of scientists have obtained and analyzed dated ice cores from Greenland and Antarctica. Some of the dated ice cores have been pulled from two miles deep in particular parts of the Antarctic ice sheets. Figure 4.11 shows some of these data. During four ice ages in the past 450,000 years, CO_2 concentrations (blue curve) were approximately 180 ppm, and in the five warmer periods around the four ice ages, CO_2 concentrations rose to perhaps 280 to 300 ppm. The modern data are shown at the extreme right of Figure 4.11; current concentrations of 380 ppm are unprecedented historically in the sense that they had not appeared at any other time over the previous 450,000 years, during which time Earth had undergone several large climate changes. This set of data has now been extended back to 700,000 years, and the same conclusions hold.

The top graph in Figure 4.11 is a portion of the Keeling curve from the previous Mauna Loa figure with the red curve being the South Pole where the seasonal cycles are not so clear (little photosynthesis and biological respiration and decay occur there).

30   So the planet, in its natural cycles through Ice Ages and the interglacial warm times saw CO_2 amounts between 180 to 280 or 300 parts per million. Now if you hit "fast forward" to the modern times on the top graph, you will see that we have broken out of those natural ranges and the amounts observed are now approaching 385 parts per million in 2005–2006.

There are several kinds of evidence that this extra carbon dioxide is human-produced, through our use of fossil-fuel combustion: isotope evidence, and the geographical patterns of atmospheric CO_2, for example. There is no question in anybody's mind that I know that the modern carbon dioxide amounts are caused by fossil-fuel burning and by some land-use changes (perhaps a 15 to 20 percent effect).

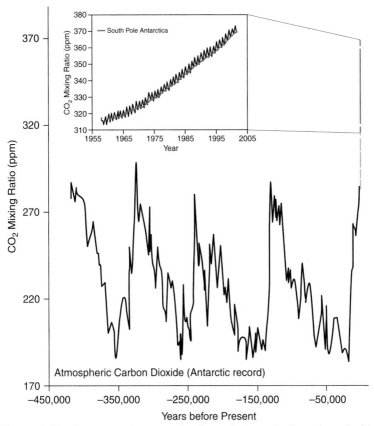

Figure 4.11 Summary of measured values of atmospheric carbon dioxide extracted from dated Antarctic ice cores (Petit et al., 1999) and (inset) from Mauna Loa and South Pole air samples (from Keeling and Whorf, 2005 and earlier Keeling and Whorf CDIAC data sets).

How large are carbon dioxide emissions from human fossil-fuel energy consumption? Figure 4.12 shows that total global CO_2 emissions from burning of coal, oil, natural gas, gasoline, and wood have grown from a few hundred million metric tons of carbon in the form of carbon dioxide 100 years ago to 7 billion metric tons today, or more than one ton per person on Earth. Americans average about six tons of carbon each per year. Amounts emitted prior to 1880 or so are too small to be read from this graph.

Separately colored lines show the individual contributions from the burning of liquid fossil fuels, like oil and gasoline derived from it, from

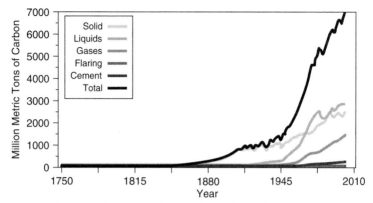

Figure 4.12 Estimated worldwide emissions of annual carbon dioxide due to burning of various carbon-based fuels and from cement manufacture for the period 1750–2002 A.D., from Carbon Dioxide Data Information Center (http://cdiac.ornl.gov/trends/emis/glo.htm).

solids, like coal, and from the burning and the flaring of natural gas. Cement production, which also releases carbon dioxide, is also shown. The annual increase in measured CO_2 amounts in air is approximately 60 percent of the amount that is added annually from these sources. It is estimated that the remainder is absorbed into oceans.

The second-most important greenhouse gas that is growing due to humans is methane. Figure 4.13 represents the sources of atmospheric methane. The yellow part of the pie chart is the portion of methane released to the atmosphere every year that we think is natural. The red part is due to human activities, and it's about twice as big. From direct measurements and from recent ice cores, we know that atmospheric methane has doubled in concentration in the last 100 years, so this ratio of human-driven to natural sources is plausible. The annual total source, 540 million metric tons, is known to within 15 or 20 percent, as is the amount from enteric fermentation (cows). Other individual entries in this figure are not known as precisely. A new report has proposed that there may be another natural source of methane from the exudations of various plants which had not been recognized previously, but various measurements must be replicated before being accepted.

35   The important points are that atmospheric methane has increased by more than a factor of two since the late 19th century, and data from the last few ice ages show that we now have amounts of methane in the global

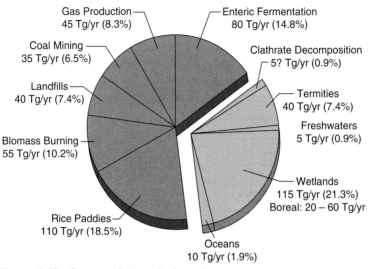

Figure 4.13 Sources of atmospheric methane.

atmosphere that are five times as much as during the glacial periods of the last 700,000 years, and that human-driven sources are the cause.

We are probably seeing the impact of the greenhouse gases on our climate now. Please refer back to Figure 4.3. As noted, there are very interesting features here, the warming from 1900 to 1940 and the cooling from 1940 to 1975. But the dominant feature is this monotonic and rapid rise of the last 25 to 30 years, and I want to reemphasize the importance of this period.

Let me introduce a few more numbers. The impact on the Earth's energy budget due to the increases in greenhouse gases over the last 100 years is about 2.6 watts per square meter (NRC, 2005). Carbon dioxide alone has caused an additional 1.6 watts per square meter of extra power (energy per unit time) to be trapped in the Earth's lower atmosphere regions. Methane (CH_4) is the second most important of the anthropogenic gases (see Figure 4.14).

If the growth of the fluorocarbon industry had continued at the rates of the 1960s and 1970s, it would have resulted in the combined histograms for the CFC's in Figure 4.14 being taller than the carbon dioxide block. In fact, had it not been for the Montreal Protocol, for which we have to thank Ambassador Benedick and some other people, and the creation of substitute

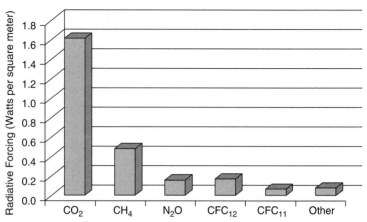

Figure 4.14 Radiative forcing (warming) effect of the increased concentration of several greenhouse gases. Concentration increases, roughly those of the past 100 years, are taken from http://www.cmdl.noaa.gov/climate.html. Radiative forcing (energy trapped per unit time and area in lower atmosphere) is computed by formulas given in IPCC (2001). See also NRC (2005).

chemicals for two refrigerants (CFC-12 and CFC-11), CFC's would have surpassed CO_2 as greenhouse gases by 1990 (Hansen et al. 1990).

So total radiative forcing, that is the impact on the Earth's surface energy budget due to these greenhouse gases now, is about 2.6 watts per square meter. Now let us compare that with what might be happening due to the sun. The last 25 or 30 years is different for another reason. It is the first time in human history that scientists have measured the output of the sun with enough precision to be able to answer the question of whether the sun's output is changing; for example, increasing enough to warm the planet.

40   Figure 4.15 shows solar irradiance data measured between 1979 and 2005. The authors merged the best data possible from different satellite instruments that have been flying since 1978 or 1979 to obtain a record of the observed change in the sun's output over that period. You will see that it is roughly repeatable, with solar cycles like sine waves with eleven-year periods. We knew about 11 year solar cycles, but what we didn't know how the total output of the sun varies every 11 years. The answer is 0.1 percent. When you go through the geometry, that's equivalent to an oscillation of

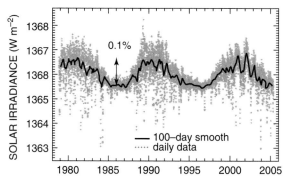

Figure 4.15 Solar irradiance data from Frohlich and Lean (2004) with updates from Frohlich taken from http://www.pmodwrc.ch/. No long-term trend is observed.

0.2 watts per square meter at the surface of the Earth. The greenhouse gases add 2.6 watts per square meter, and the greenhouse effect continues. It is sustained and it grows. It does not go up and down like a sine wave (as does the sun's output).

If someone wants to postulate that the warming of the last 25 years is due to the sun's activity, they have a hard time doing it now that these data are available. It is an untenable argument. Theoretically, if the small changes in the sun's output are causing some climate and weather changes, then we really have to be worried about the greenhouse effect, because it is much larger, it is sustained, and it is growing, so its eventual consequences will be similarly larger.

Energy Efficiency

The theme of this year's NCSE Symposium is energy. As Mr. Train mentioned earlier, we have a polarized situation and many disagreements are going on, especially in the political realm. There remain some things that we can agree on, though. I propose that energy efficiency must be one of them.

What does energy efficiency accomplish for us? Figure 4.16 lists seven benefits. First of all, from a United States point of view, decreasing our dependence on foreign oil has multiple benefits and you can fill in the ones that you put most stock in yourselves, for example, decreased oil imports

Figure 4.16   Immediate action with multiple benefits.

Energy efficiency would:
- Decrease our dependency on foreign oil.
- Improve our national security.
- Decrease our trade deficit.
- Decrease local air pollution.
- Increase our national competitiveness.
- Encourage development of new products for global markets.
- Decrease household energy costs while also slowing the increase of CO_2 and CH_4.

would certainly improve national security. We would be in a stronger negotiating position; we wouldn't have to deploy our military in the case of oil
shortages. We import about 12 million barrels of oil per day, and a typical
oil tanker holds about 800,000 barrels, so there are roughly 15 oil tankers a
day arriving in the United States fully loaded. They are all sitting ducks on
the ocean.

Increasing energy efficiency would also decrease our trade deficit. If you
multiply 12 million barrels a day times 365 days a year by $50 a barrel, you
calculate a number of over $200 billion as a "contribution" to our annual
trade deficit. One might also ask what fraction of this sum of money goes
into the hands of other-than-legitimate interests.

45   We could also decrease local air pollution by improving energy efficiency
and decreasing fossil fuel combustion. Further, we could also increase
national competitiveness. For example, the cost of manufactured goods
includes the cost of energy. In times of low energy prices, people don't pay
much attention. But when energy prices go up, this becomes a significant
part of the cost of manufactured goods. Comparing ourselves to Japan and
Germany—their energy efficiency in manufacturing is probably 40 percent
better than ours.

By committing to a goal of improved energy efficiency, we could
encourage development of new products for global markets, which everyone wants to buy—energy-efficient products. People want to enjoy the
benefits of lower energy costs. There is a growing global demand for energy-
efficient products and devices. If we fail to develop new energy-efficient
products, we will forfeit this growing global market. Another benefit of
energy efficiency would be to decrease household energy costs.

Finally, improved energy efficiency would reduce the emissions of
carbon dioxide and of methane (which comes partly from the handling and

use of fossil fuels—after all, methane is natural gas). With all of these benefits, increased energy efficiency should be a common goal for all of us. There must be ways to get more people to agree that there is some benefit for them to work on energy efficiency.

Being Useful Through Science

As important as it is to have detected contemporary climate change and to develop a theoretical understanding of why it is changing, there is a great deal more that scientists can do to be useful to society. I want to illustrate some of the potential for value, and also express some concern that we not waste that potential. Figure 4.17 lists a few points, the first of which is that our highly polarized discussion is obscuring our priorities.

For example, when environmental groups and anyone who is trying to forward an environmental agenda says that "the science is settled, let's get on with the action," he/she is selling future science short. How often have you heard that phrase that "the science is settled"? I don't like it. While climate change has been detected and the evidence of human-caused climate change is very strong, maybe one question is settled, but there are many more questions that demand answers, and we have a lot more to do.

To say that science is settled is telling people that the scientific challenge is over, that it is not useful anymore, which is an irrational approach to the future. On the other hand, people who say that the science is confused and there is not enough evidence to take any action, are not being at all helpful, even if they are trying to be truthful—which is not always clear. 50

What are the things that we need to do? We have to dedicate more emphasis toward understanding regional precipitation and hydrology. How is

Figure 4.17 Being useful through science.

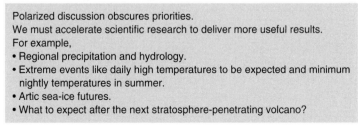

Polarized discussion obscures priorities.
We must accelerate scientific research to deliver more useful results.
For example,
• Regional precipitation and hydrology.
• Extreme events like daily high temperatures to be expected and minimum nightly temperatures in summer.
• Artic sea-ice futures.
• What to expect after the next stratosphere-penetrating volcano?

it changing, how will it change? Water needs are so important in regions where people live, where animals live, where natural biota have adapted to regional climates and to regional precipitation patterns and rivers. We can do a better job of predicting. For example, we must become able to predict the snow pack that accumulates over a winter and how it is going to be changing and what the spring runoff is going to be. These goals are not impossible, but they need much sustained research.

Climate is also very importantly measured by extreme events, not just by average temperatures. In fact, the direct effects of average temperatures don't worry us very much. Instead, it is critical to know how the daily high temperatures will change. What can be expected? And what's happening, and what will happen to the minimum nightly temperatures? Minimum nightly temperatures in the summer drive our demand for water and for air conditioning, and in stressed animals or people, also add more danger. As to electrical power plants, peak power demands determine what generation capacity is needed, while many parameters for electrical transmission networks depend also on minimum nightly temperatures in the summertime. By the way, there is evidence that the daily temperature range is changing. Nighttime temperatures are rising faster than the daytime temperatures are, and this is a signature of the greenhouse effect. While they are both going up, the nighttime temperatures are rising faster.

Arctic sea ice futures demand attention. We have issues of ecology and life in the Arctic, for the organisms that live there, as well as for commercial and strategic issues surrounding the Arctic sea ice. We have great need to be able to predict and understand what's been happening, and progress is feasible if we stay with the task.

And for several reasons, we should research what to expect after the next stratosphere-penetrating volcano, the kind of which Richard Benedick reminded us. It will cool the planet. The last time this happened, in June of 1991, several climate modelers successfully predicted how much the planet would cool, and they predicted the time course of the cooling. Supporting a strong general research program now, we can be ready as soon as the next such volcano goes off to predict how much it should cool and where, and when the cooling will cease and become a warming again.

55   Continued resolve to research the climate system will enable us to deliver a number of other useful results such as those exemplified in Figure 4.18. Certainly we must help policy makers, business leaders, and the general public to figure out the effectiveness of policies to slow down this radiative

Being Useful Through Science - II

- Effectiveness of policies to retard radiative forcing by slowing the CO_2 increase, slowing the N_2O increase, reducing atmospheric CH_4 and tropospheric O_3, reducing emissions of extremely long-lived gases.
- Statistics of storm-driven sea surges for infrastructure and emergency planning and the insurance industry, statistics of hurricane intensities and frequencies.
- Improved predictions of hurricane tracks (sea temperatures (depth), wind measurements by A/C and remote sensing, ships).
- Communications: Climate is more than surface temperatures.
- What is known and not known...

Figure 4.18

forcing, by slowing down the carbon dioxide increase and those of the other greenhouse gases, like nitrous oxide and methane. It is a legitimate and necessary role for scientists to work through those calculations and projections objectively and carefully for everyone who has to make individual choices and governmentally based and commercially based decisions.

We can do a much better job on the statistics of storm-driven sea surges. As sea level rises, sea surges, especially in the presence of severe storms and stronger severe storms, are going to grow. And unfortunately, we keep building more facilities, residences, and installations along coastal domains. Even though we will probably not be able to predict individual storms for the foreseeable future, we can do a much better job on the statistics of these storm events and the sea surges that will come from them, as well as the statistics of hurricane intensities. And I would not be surprised if the hurricane frequencies are there to be predicted, even though trends have not been detected yet because the data are so noisy.

Also, if we get serious about measuring not only the sea temperatures at the surface, but as a function of depth, and by getting better air humidity and wind measurements in individual storms, we should be able to do better predictions of whether or not a specific hurricane is going to make landfall, and where it will dissipate, to gain capability to anticipate and prepare for storms such as those that caused the dramatic tragedies that the Gulf Coast had in 2005. But it is going to take a commitment similar to the kind that Mr. Train mentioned along all environmental lines. It will require a commitment of our government, as well as other people.

Communicating with the general public is ever more important. All of us have much to learn and to discuss about what climate is, and what it means to us. Chris Bernabo made an excellent start on this topic 15 or

20 years ago and showed that those of us on the research side were not doing a very good job of listening and/or communicating with the general public and learning what they need to know about climate change, both to gain support for our research and for making it more useful. And of course, we must always communicate what is known and what is not known.

I want to give an example from 1997–1998, from a field that I did not pay much attention to, research on understanding and predicting El Nino events, historically natural events. The upper graph of Figure 4.19 shows what was predicted in the fall of 1997 in the form of rainfall six to eight months later, in January through May, based on looking at the patterns that were being observed in the eastern tropical Pacific. The 1997 waters were much warmer in the eastern tropical Pacific than normal, and based on the previous eight El Nino southern oscillation events (ENSO), scientists predicted that California would be much wetter than normal in the winter to come.

60   The upper graph is predicted anomalies in January through May precipitation, based on eight El Nino events prior to 1997, and the lower graph is what actually happened at corresponding times and places in 1998.

1997-98 El Nino Precipitation Anamalies

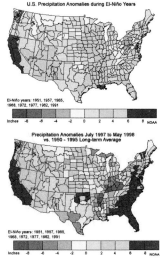

Predicted precipitation anomalies for Jan-May 1998 based on composite of eight previous ENSO events

Actrual precipitation anomalies (realtive to long-term averages for Jan-May 1998)

Figure 4.19   Seasonal precipitation anomalies from National Ocean and Atmospheric Administration (NOAA) Climate Prediction Center (see also Monteverdi and Null, 1997).

As you look at the upper graph on the left, you will see California in blue and violet, indicating predictions for five or more inches of extra winter rain over the coming few months due to this El Nino. The bottom graph shows what actually happened, using the same color code.

For California, these predictions were very good and valuable. For example, on December 7, 1997, in Laguna Beach, there were almost seven inches of rain in six hours in an area that is usually pretty dry. People who had access to, and heeded this prediction three months earlier, who cleaned out their storm drains, cleaned out the brush in ravines, fixed their roofs, repaired leaks on their houses and commercial properties, did very well by themselves. They saved money and they were safer from this very useful prediction.

This is one of the kinds of information that we are going to have to learn to deal with. What is possible for the scientific community to predict may not be exactly what people want. For example, the people of Laguna Beach would have liked to know that there was going to be seven inches of rain in six hours on December 7, 1997. Or that it was going to rain in San Francisco on a particular day, or something similar. That specificity was not in the cards, but still, the coarser prediction was very useful.

There were also some differences between predictions and actual precipitation. For example, the East Coast turned out to be much wetter, Florida and up, than was predicted.

But the prediction, as it was, was still extremely valuable, and as I recall the California patterns were predicted with higher odds than were those for the East Coast.

So we must work together with the general public and the scientific community to understand what can be predicted, what would be useful, and get on with it. Climate change is underway and it will continue, especially because we are not doing very well in slowing down carbon dioxide and our consumption of fossil fuels. Change will probably accelerate, with possible manifestations in severe storms and other extreme events. While we continue to try to suppress human forcing of climate change, we must also gain ability to predict and to make those predictions as useful as possible to the public at large.

It has been an honor to be here with you, in honor of Senator John Chafee. I hope that I have contributed useful thoughts to the day's proceedings. Thank you for the opportunity.

Analyze

1. Why does the author suggest that the elevated levels of modern carbon dioxide emissions are produced by humans? How exactly do human activities produce carbon dioxide?
2. What kind of information does this writer use to make his point? To what kind of audience do you think such appeals would be the most convincing? Do you find his argument compelling? Why or why not?
3. Dr. Cicerone was speaking to a room of scientists and he used many graphs and diagrams. Which of the figures was the most convincing to you? Which one do you want help interpreting?

Explore

1. The author states that "communicating with the general public is ever more important. All of us have much to learn and to discuss about what climate is, and what it means to us." Often, celebrities and songwriters use their status and popularity to share their own opinions on issues like climate change with a wide audience. Locate a song in which the artist expresses his or her opinion on climate change and write a rhetorical analysis of the piece. What message does the artist hope to get across? Who is the target audience? How does the artist try to speak and relate to the audience through word choice and tone?
2. Do some research to determine if there are any local organizations in your community that are working on behalf of climate change initiatives. Where are they? What do they do? Write a profile of this organization for your community or school newspaper detailing the mission and activities of one such organization—be sure to reference any accomplishments they have achieved for the community so far. Alternatively, contact this organization to see if you can collaborate with them on the things they write.
3. Cicerone delivered this talk in 2006 and there has been a great deal of climate research since then. And, unfortunately, the change is even more obvious now. NASA, the National Oceanographic and Atmospheric Administration, and many environmental organizations such as Greenpeace have websites with the most recent information on climate change. Do some research on the most recent discoveries and data on climate change. Then briefly summarize Cicerone's argument about climate change and use the new data to support and extend his argument.

National Research Council
"Advancing the Science of Climate Change"

The National Research Council (NRC) was organized in 1916 by the National Academy of Sciences, the leading interdisciplinary scientific organization in the United States if not the world. The purpose of the NRC is to provide information to the science and engineering community, the government, and the public. The organization is directed by senior scientists and engineers from across America. *Advancing the Science of Climate Change*, from which our selection is taken, is one of four reports on climate change produced by the NRC in 2010. In this report, a panel of scientists summarizes the peer-reviewed research from the national and international community. This report represents a synthesis of the best, most authoritative, and most current research on global climate change. The selections included below offer a brief history of climate science and a clear explanation of "uncertainty" in science; a factual description of the extent of sea-level rise due to climate change and the potential consequences; the effect of climate change on ocean ecosystems such as coral reefs and polar bears; and the consequences for human health. As you read this report, consider how you might explain these complex connections to your friends.

Introduction: Science for Understanding and Responding to Climate Change

Humans have always been influenced by climate. Despite the wealth and technology of modern industrial societies, climate still affects human well-being in fundamental ways. Climate influences, for example, where people live, what they eat, how they earn their livings, how they move around, and what they do for recreation. Climate regulates food production and water resources and influences energy use, disease transmission, and other aspects of human health and well-being. It also influences the health of ecosystems that provide goods and services for humans and for the other species with which we share the planet.

In turn, human activities are influencing climate. As discussed in the following chapters, scientific evidence that the Earth is warming is now overwhelming. There is also a multitude of evidence that this warming results primarily from human activities, especially burning fossil fuels and other activities that release heat-trapping greenhouse gases (GHGs) into the atmosphere. Projections of future climate change indicate that Earth will continue to warm unless significant and sustained actions are taken to limit emissions of GHGs. Increasing temperatures and GHG concentrations are driving a multitude of related and interacting changes in the Earth system, including decreases in the amounts of ice stored in mountain glaciers and polar regions, increases in sea level, changes in ocean chemistry, and changes in the frequency and intensity of heat waves, precipitation events, and droughts. These changes in turn pose significant risks to both human and ecological systems. Although the details of how the future impacts of climate change will unfold are not as well understood as the basic causes and mechanisms of climate change, we can reasonably expect that the consequences of climate change will be more severe if actions are not taken to limit its magnitude and adapt to its impacts.

Scientific research will never completely eliminate uncertainties about climate change and its risks to human health and well-being, but it can provide information that can be helpful to decision makers who must make choices in the face of risks. In 2008, the U.S. Congress asked the National Academy of Sciences to "investigate and study the serious and sweeping issues relating to global climate change and make recommendations regarding what steps must be taken and what strategies must be adopted in response . . . including the science and technology challenges thereof." This report is part of the resulting study, called *America's Climate Choices*. In the chapters that follow, this report reviews what science has learned about climate change and its causes and consequences across a variety of sectors. The report also identifies scientific advances that could improve understanding of climate change and the effectiveness of actions taken to limit the magnitude of future climate change or adapt to its impacts. Finally, the report identifies the activities and tools needed to make these scientific advances and the physical and human assets needed to support these activities (for the detailed statement of task). Companion reports provide information and advice on *Limiting the Magnitude of Future Climate Change* (NRC, 2010c), *Adapting to the Impacts of Climate Change* (NRC, 2010a), and *Informing an Effective Response to Climate Change* (NRC, 2010b).

Scientific Learning About Climate Change

Climate science, like all science, is a process of collective learning that proceeds through the accumulation of data; the formulation, testing, and refinement of hypotheses; the construction of theories and models to synthesize understanding and generate new predictions; and the testing of hypotheses, theories, and models through experiments or other observations. Scientific knowledge builds over time as theories are refined and expanded and as new observations and data confirm or refute the predictions of current theories and models. Confidence in a theory grows if it survives this rigorous testing process, if multiple lines of evidence lead to the same conclusion, or if competing explanations can be ruled out.

In the case of climate science, this process of learning extends back more than 150 years, to mid-19th-century attempts to explain what caused the ice ages, which had only recently been discovered. Several hypotheses were proposed to explain how thick blankets of ice could have once covered much of the Northern Hemisphere, including changes in solar radiation, atmospheric composition, the placement of mountain ranges, and volcanic activity. These and other ideas were tested and debated by the scientific community, eventually leading to an understanding (discussed in detail in Chapter 6) that ice ages are initiated by small recurring variations in Earth's orbit around the Sun. This early scientific interest in climate eventually led scientists working in the late 19th century to recognize that carbon dioxide (CO_2) and other GHGs have a profound effect on the Earth's temperature. A Swedish scientist named Svante Arrhenius was the first to hypothesize that the burning of fossil fuels, which releases CO_2, would eventually lead to global warming. This was the beginning of a more than 100-year history of ever more careful measurements and calculations to pin down exactly how GHG emissions and other factors influence Earth's climate (Weart, 2008).

Progress in scientific understanding, of course, does not proceed in a simple straight line. For example, calculations performed during the first decades of the 20th century, before the behavior of GHGs in the atmosphere was understood in detail, suggested that the amount of warming from elevated CO_2 levels would be small. More precise experiments and observations in the mid-20th century showed that this was not the case, and that increases in CO_2 or other GHGs could indeed cause significant warming. Similarly, a scientific debate in the 1970s briefly considered the possibility that human emissions of aerosols—small particles that reflect sunlight back to space—might lead to a long-term cooling of the Earth's surface. Although prominently reported in a few news magazines at the time, this speculation did not gain widespread scientific acceptance and was soon overtaken by new evidence and refined calculations showing that warming from emissions of CO_2 and other GHGs represented a larger long-term effect on climate.

Thus, scientists have understood for a long time that the basic principles of chemistry and physics predict that burning fossil fuels will lead to increases in the Earth's average surface temperature. Decades of observations and research have tested, refined, and extended that understanding, for example, by identifying other factors that influence climate, such as changes in land use, and by identifying modes of natural variability that modulate the long-term warming trend. Detailed process studies and models of the climate system have also allowed scientists to project future climate changes. These projections are based on scenarios of future GHG emissions from energy use and other human activities, each of which represents a different set of choices that societies around the world might make. Finally, research across a broad range of scientific disciplines has improved our understanding of how the climate system interacts with other environmental systems and with human systems, including water resources, agricultural systems, ecosystems, and built environments.

Uncertainty in Scientific Knowledge

From a philosophical perspective, science never *proves* anything—in the manner that mathematics or other formal logical systems prove things—because science is fundamentally based on observations. Any scientific theory is thus, in principle, subject to being refined or overturned by new observations. In practical terms, however, scientific uncertainties are not all the same. Some scientific conclusions or theories have been so thoroughly examined and tested, and supported by so many independent observations and results, that their likelihood of subsequently being found to be wrong is vanishingly small. Such conclusions and theories are then regarded as settled facts. This is the case for the conclusions that the Earth system is warming and that much of this warming is very likely due to human activities. In other cases, particularly for matters that are at the leading edge of active research, uncertainties may be substantial and important. In these cases, care must be taken not to draw stronger conclusions than warranted by the available evidence.

The characterization of uncertainty is thus an important part of the scientific enterprise. In some areas of inquiry, uncertainties can be quantified through a long sequence of repeated observations, trials, or model runs. For other areas, including many aspects of climate change research, precise quantification of uncertainty is not always possible due to the complexity or uniqueness of the system being studied. In these cases, researchers adopt various approaches to subjectively but rigorously assess their degree of confidence in particular results or theories, given available observations, analyses, and model results. These approaches include estimated uncertainty ranges (or error bars) for measured quantities and the estimated likelihood of a particular result having arisen by chance rather than as a result of the theory or phenomenon being tested. These scientific characterizations of uncertainty can be misunderstood, however, because for many people "uncertainty" means that little or nothing is known, whereas in scientific parlance uncertainty is a way of describing how precisely or how confidently something is known. To reduce such misunderstandings, scientists have developed explicit techniques for conveying the precision in a particular result or the confidence in a particular theory or conclusion to policy makers (see Box 4.1).

A New Era of Climate Change Science: Research for Understanding and Responding to Climate Change

In the process of scientific learning about climate change, it has become   10
evident that climate change holds significant risks for people and the natural resources and ecosystems on which they depend. In some ways, climate change risks are different from many other risks with which people normally deal. For example, as discussed in Chapters 2 and 3, climate change processes have considerable inertia and long time lags. The actions of today, therefore, will be reflected in climate system changes several decades to centuries from now. Future generations will be exposed to risks, some potentially severe, because of today's actions, and in some cases these changes will be irreversible. Likewise, climate changes can be abrupt—they

BOX 4.1 **UNCERTAINTY TERMINOLOGY**

In assessing and reporting the state of knowledge about climate change, scientists have devoted serious debate and discussion to appropriate ways of expressing uncertainty to policy makers (Moss and Schneider, 2000). Recent climate change assessment reports have adopted specific procedures and terminology to describe the degree of confidence in specific conclusions or the estimated likelihood of a certain outcome (see, e.g., Manning et al., 2004). For example, a statement that something is "very likely" in the assessments by the Intergovernmental Panel on Climate Change indicates an estimated 9 out of 10 or better chance that a certain outcome will occur.

In estimating confidence, scientific assessment teams draw on information about "the strength and consistency of the observed evidence, the range and consistency of model projections, the reliability of particular models as tested by various methods, and, most importantly, the body of work addressed in earlier synthesis and assessment reports" (USGCRP, 2009a). Teams are also encouraged to provide "traceable accounts" of how these estimates were constructed, including important lines of evidence used, standards of evidence applied, approaches taken to combining and reconciling multiple lines of evidence, explicit explanations of any statistical or other methods used, and identification of critical uncertainties. In general, statements about the future are more uncertain than statements about observed changes or current trends, and it is easier to employ precise uncertainty language in situations where conclusions are based on extensive quantitative data or models than in areas where data are less extensive, important research is qualitative, or models are in an earlier stage of development.

In this report, *Advancing the Science of Climate Change*, when we draw directly on the statements of the formal national and international assessments, we adopt their terminology to describe uncertainty. However, because of the more concise nature and intent of this report, we do not attempt to quantify confidence and certainty about every statement of the science.

have the potential to cross tipping points or thresholds that result in large changes or impacts. The likelihood of such abrupt changes is not well known, however, which makes it difficult to quantify the risks posed by such changes. Climate change also interacts in complex ways with other ongoing changes in human and environmental systems. Society's decisions about land use and food production, for example, both affect and are affected by climate change.

On the basis of decades of scientific progress in understanding changes in the physical climate system and the growing evidence of the risks posed by climate change, many decision makers—including individuals, businesses, and governments at all levels—are either taking actions to respond to climate change or asking what actions they might take to respond effectively. Many of these questions center on what specific actions might need to be taken to limit climate change by reducing emissions of GHGs: what gases, from what sources, when and where, through what specific technology investments or changes in management practices, motivated and coordinated by what policies, with what co-benefits or unintended consequences, and monitored and verified through what means? Other questions focus on the specific impacts that are expected and the actions that can be taken to prepare for and adapt to them, such as reducing vulnerabilities or improving society's coping and adaptive capacity.

This report explores what these emerging questions and decision needs imply for future scientific learning about climate change and for the scientific research enterprise. As the need for science expands to include both *improving understanding* and *informing and supporting decision making*, the production, synthesis, and translation of scientific knowledge into forms that are useful to decision makers becomes increasingly important. It may also imply a need to change scientific practices, with scientists working more closely with decision makers to improve the scientific decision support that researchers can offer. However, even with this decision focus, scientific knowledge cannot by itself specify or determine any choice. It cannot tell decision makers what they *should* do; their responsibilities, preferences, and values also influence their decisions. Science can inform decisions by describing the potential consequences of different choices, and it can contribute by improving or expanding available options, but it cannot say what actions are required or preferred.

. . .

Sea Level Rise and the Coastal Environment

The coastlines of the United States and the world are major centers of economic and cultural development, where populations and associated structural development continue to grow. The coasts are also home to critical ecological and environmental resources. Coastal areas have always experienced various risks and hazards, such as flooding from coastal storms. However, coastal managers and property owners are concerned about how these risks are being and will be intensified by sea level rise and other climate changes.

Observations of Sea Level Rise

Sea level has been systematically measured by tide gauges for more than 100 years. Other direct and indirect observations have allowed oceanographers to estimate (with lower precision) past sea levels going back many thousands of years. We know that sea level has risen more than 400 feet (120 meters) since the peak of the last ice age 26,000 years ago, with periods of rapid rise predating a relatively steady level over the past 6,000 years. During the past few decades, tide gauge records augmented by satellite

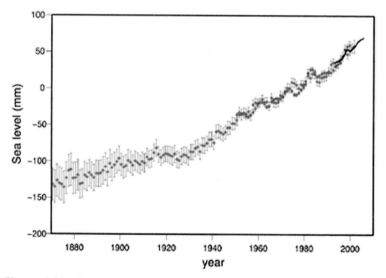

Figure 4.20 Annual, global mean sea level as determined by records of tide gauges and satellite altimetry. Source: Bindoff et al. (2007).

measurements have been used to produce precise sea level maps across the entire globe. These modern records indicate that the rate of sea level rise has accelerated since the mid-19th century, with possibly greater acceleration over the past two decades. The exact amount of sea level change experienced in different locations varies because of different rates of settling or uplift of land and because of differences in ocean circulation.

Causes of Sea Level Rise

Past, present, and future changes in global sea level are mainly caused by   15 two fundamental processes: (1) the thermal expansion of the existing water in the world's ocean basins as it absorbs heat and (2) the addition of water from land-based sources—mainly the shrinking of ice sheets and glaciers.

Because of the huge capacity of the oceans to absorb heat, 80 to 90 percent of the heating associated with human GHG emissions over the past 50 years has gone into raising the temperature of the oceans. The subsequent thermal expansion of the oceans is responsible for an estimated 50 percent of the observed sea level rise since the late 19th century. Even if GHG concentrations are stabilized, ocean warming and the accompanying sea level rise will continue until the oceans reach a new thermal equilibrium with the atmosphere. Ice in the world's glaciers and ice sheets contributes directly to sea level rise through melt or the flow of ice into the sea. The major ice sheets of Greenland and Antarctica contain the equivalent of 23 and 197 feet (7 and 60 meters) of sea level, respectively.

Projections of Sea Level Rise

Projections of future sea level have been the subject of active discussion in the recent literature on climate change impacts. The 2007 Assessment Report by the IPCC estimated that sea level would likely rise by an additional 0.6 to 1.9 feet (0.18 to 0.59 meters) by 2100. This projection was based largely on the observed rates of change in ice sheets and projected future thermal expansion over the past several decades and did not include the possibility of changes in ice sheet dynamics. Scientists are working to improve how ice dynamics can be resolved in models. Recent research, including investigations of how sea level responded to temperature variations during the ice age cycles, suggests that sea levels could potentially rise another 2.5 to 6.5 feet (0.8 to 2 meters) by 2100, which is several times larger than the IPCC estimates. However, sea level rise estimates are rather uncertain, due mainly to limits in scientific understanding of glacier and ice sheet dynamics. For instance, recent findings of a warming ocean around Greenland suggest an explanation for the acceler-ated calving of outlet glaciers into the sea, but the limited data and lack of insight into the mechanisms involved prevent a quantitative estimate of the rate of ice loss at this time. Nevertheless, it is clear that global sea level rise will continue throughout the 21st century due to the GHGs that have already been emitted, that the rate and ultimate amount of sea level rise will be higher if GHG concentrations continue to increase, and that there is a risk of much larger and more rapid increases in sea level. While this risk cannot be quanti-fied at present, the consequences of extreme and rapid sea level rise could be economically and socially devastating for highly built-up and densely populated coastal areas around the world, especially low-lying deltas and estuaries.

Ice Sheet Processes Could Potentially Lead to Abrupt Changes

In addition to rapid accelerations in the rate of sea level rise, a collapse or rapid wastage of major ice sheets could lead to other abrupt changes. For example, if the Greenland ice sheet were to shrink substantially over several decades, a large amount of freshwater would be delivered to key regions of the North Atlantic. This influx of freshwater could alter the ocean structure and influence ocean circulation, with implications for regional and global weather patterns. Compelling evidence has been assembled indicating that rapid freshwater discharges at the end of the last ice age caused abrupt ocean circulation changes, which in turn led to significant impacts on regional climate. The recent ice melting on Greenland and other areas in the Arctic, combined with increased river discharges in the Arctic region (see discus-sion of precipitation and runoff changes below), may have already led to changes in ocean circulation patterns. However, much work remains to develop confident projections of future ocean circulation changes—and the influence of these changes on regional climate patterns—resulting from ongoing freshwater discharges in the North Atlantic.

Sea Level Rise Is Associated with a Range of Impacts on Coastal Environments

Coastal areas are among the most densely populated and fastest-growing regions of the United States, as well as the rest of the world. Such popula-tion concentration and growth are accompanied by a high degree of devel-opment and use of coastal resources for economic purposes, including industrial activities, transportation, trade, resource extraction, fisheries, tourism, and recreation. Sea level rise can potentially affect all of these activities and their accompanying infrastructure, and it could also magnify other climate changes, such as an increase in the frequency or intensity of storms (see below). Even if the frequency or intensity of coastal storms does not change, increases in average sea level will magnify the impacts of extreme events on coastal landscapes.

The economic impacts of climate change and sea level rise on coastal areas in the United States have been an important focus for research. While economic impact assessments have become increasingly sophisticated, they remain incomplete and are subject to the well-recognized challenges of cost-benefit analyses (see Chapter 17). In addition, while studies of economic impacts may be useful at a regional level, general conclusions regarding the total magnitude of economic impacts in the United States cannot be drawn from existing studies; this is because the metrics, modeling approaches, sea level rise projections, inclusions of coastal storms, and assumptions about human responses (e.g., the type and level of protection) vary considerably across the studies.

Coastal ecosystems such as dunes, wetlands, estuaries, seagrass beds, and mangroves provide numerous ecosystem goods and services, ranging from nursery habitat for certain fish and shellfish to habitat for bird, mammal, and reptilian species, including some endangered ones; protective or buffering services for coastal infrastructure against the onslaught of storms; water filtering and flood retention; carbon storage; and the aesthetic, cultural, and economic value of beaches and coastal environments for recreation, tourism, and simple enjoyment. The impact of sea level rise on these and other non-market values is often omitted from economic impact assessments of coastal areas because of difficulties in assigning values.

· · ·

Public Health

Weather and climate influence the distribution and incidence of a variety of public health outcomes. Indeed, any health outcome that is influenced by environmental conditions may be impacted by a changing climate. However, the causal chain linking climate change to shifting patterns of health threats and outcomes is complicated by factors such as wealth, distribution of income, status of public health infrastructure, provision of preventive and acute medical care, and access to and appropriate use of health care information. Additionally, the severity of future health impacts will be strongly influenced by concurrent changes in nonclimatic factors as well as strategies to limit and adapt to climate change.

Extreme Temperatures and Thermal Stress

Heat waves are the leading causes of weather-related morbidity and mortality in the United States, and hot days and hot nights have become more frequent and more intense in recent decades. Their frequency, intensity, and duration are projected to increase, especially under the higher warming scenarios. Warming temperatures may also reduce exposure and health impacts associated with cold temperatures, although the extent of any reduction is highly uncertain, and analyses and projections of the impacts of temperature changes on human health are complicated by other factors. In particular, death rates depend on a range of circumstances other than temperature, including housing characteristics and personal behaviors, and these have not been extensively studied in the context of future climate projections.

Severe Weather

Deaths and physical injuries from hurricanes, tornadoes, floods, and wildfire occur annually across the United States. Direct morbidity and mortality increase with the intensity and duration of such events. As a general trend, climate change will lead to an increase in the intensity of rainfall and the frequency of heat waves, flooding, and wildfire. Uncertainties remain in projections of future storm patterns, including hurricanes. The number of deaths and injuries that result from all of these extreme events can be decreased through advanced warning and preparation. Changes in severe weather events may also lead to increases in diarrheal disease and increased incidence of respiratory symptoms, particularly in developing countries. Mental health impacts are often overlooked in the discussion of climate change and public health. Severe weather often results in increased anxiety, depression, and even posttraumatic stress disorder.

Infectious Diseases

25   The ranges and impacts of a number of important pathogens may change as a result of changing temperatures, precipitation, and extreme events. Increasing temperatures may increase or shift the ranges of disease vectors (and their associated pathogens), including mosquitoes (malaria, dengue

fever, West Nile virus, Saint Louis encephalitis virus), ticks (Rocky Mountain spotted fever, Lyme disease, and encephalitis), and rodents (hantavirus and leptospirosis). Consequently, additional people will be exposed to infectious diseases in many parts of the world. Several pathogens that cause food- and waterborne diseases are sensitive to ambient temperature, with faster replication rates at higher temperatures. Waterborne disease outbreaks are also associated with heavy rainfall and flooding and, therefore, may also increase.

Air Quality

Poor air quality—specifically increased ground-level ozone and/or aerosol concentrations—results in increased incidence of respiratory illness. For example, acute ozone exposure is associated with increased hospital admissions for pneumonia, chronic obstructive pulmonary disease, asthma, and allergic rhinitis, and also with premature mortality. Temperature and ozone concentrations are closely connected; projected increases in temperatures in coming decades may increase the occurrence of high-ozone events and related health effects. Climate change could also affect local to regional air quality through changes in chemical reaction rates, boundary layer heights that affect vertical mixing of pollutants, and changes in airflow patterns that govern pollutant transport. In addition to air quality problems driven by pollution, preliminary evidence suggests that allergen production by species such as ragweed increases with high temperature and/or high CO_2 concentration.

The relationship between climate change, air quality, and public health is further complicated by the fact that policies designed to limit the magnitude of climate change may be at odds with improving public health outcomes. For example, reducing aerosol concentrations would reduce air pollution–related health impacts, but the resulting changes in atmospheric reflectivity could further increase temperatures.

Vulnerable Populations

Vulnerability to the public health challenges discussed above will vary within and between populations. Overall, older adults, infants, children, and those with chronic medical conditions tend to be more sensitive to the health impacts of climate change. Susceptibility varies geographically, with the status of public health infrastructure playing a large role in determining vulnerability differences between populations.

Analyze

1. The author states that progress in scientific understanding "does not proceed in a straight line." What does he mean by this? How so?
2. Can science tell us exactly how much or where seal levels will rise as a result of global climate change? Why or why not?
3. What does the author mean when he says that science never proves anything? If these facts cannot be proven, how do we know they are facts? How do scientists move forward in the face of this uncertainty?

Explore

1. Do some research to determine what, if any, policies are in place or under debate at your local government regarding climate change. Draw up a blog post that captures a snapshot of the political stance on climate policy in your area, as well as the stances on climate initiatives held by your area's representatives.
2. Throughout these readings, you have learned a lot about the tension between scientific findings regarding climate change and public understanding and acceptance of climate science. Can you think of other social situations that arose in the past that have been characterized by similar public tension? What were the circumstances of that situation? What was the public's initial reaction? How did that reaction change? What caused the change? Write a blog post that uses the comparison between public acceptance of climate change and the struggle for the public to accept another issue such as cigarette smoking to convince your peers about the reality of climate change.
3. The NRC is an organization that provides scientific information to the public and to the legislatures that make public policy. Go to their website and to the websites of other similar organizations (NOAA, NASA, NIH, NSF) and read what they say about the connection between science and public policy. When you have read a number of these statements, write your own position paper on whether and how science should be part of our public policy and decision-making processes.

Terry Cannon
"Gender and Climate Hazards in Bangladesh"

The following article appeared in the July 2002 issue of *Gender and Development*, a journal dedicated to supporting development policy and practices that promote gender equality. The author, Terry Cannon, is the director for the Strengthening Climate Resilience program at the Institute of Development Studies. There, he researches rural livelihoods, disaster vulnerability, and climate change adaptation. In 2004, he co-authored *At Risk: Natural Hazards, People's Vulnerability and Disasters*, one of the most widely cited books in the field. In the article below, Cannon says that extreme climate events attributed to climate change are likely to have worse consequences for women than for men because of their different economic situations. Using Bangladesh as a case study, he outlines the unique challenges facing women in climate-related disasters. As you read, consider the connections between this essay and Roman Krznaric's essay on empathy in this chapter and the story of Kettleman City residents in Chapter 2. Is sustainability just about water, soil, food, and energy?

Bangladesh has recently experienced a number of high-profile disasters, including devastating cyclones and annual floods. Poverty is both a cause of vulnerability, and a consequence of hazard impacts. Evidence that the impacts of disasters are worse for women is inconclusive or variable. However, since being female is strongly linked to being poor, unless poverty is reduced, the increase in disasters and extreme climate events linked with climate change is likely to affect women more than men. In addition, there are some specific gender attributes which increase women's vulnerability in some respects. These gendered vulnerabilities may, however, be reduced by social changes.

To many from outside, Bangladesh is almost synonymous with disasters. In a country smaller than Britain, and with more than twice as many people, around one-third of the land is flooded every summer. The monsoon rains cover the low-lying land, and swell the three major river systems that struggle to find outlets to the sea. In some years, such as in 1998, nearly half of the land area of Bangladesh is under water. Tropical cyclones strike the coast at least once a year, bringing rainwater floods, salt-water incursions, and wind damage. Since the 1991 cyclone disaster, effective warning systems, coupled with the use of many more cyclone shelters, have reduced the toll to a fraction of earlier tragedies, and now the number of deaths each year is usually less than a thousand.

The inland rain and riverine floods have attracted considerable foreign attention and aid, as evidenced by the Flood Action Plan (FAP) of the early 1990s. Yet, paradoxically, the deaths caused by these events rarely exceed a few thousand—in contrast to the death toll of cyclones—and never reach tens of thousands. Floods are very visible and may appear to be a disaster, even though they are vital to the livelihoods of almost all of the rural population. Therein lies a second paradox: most of the rural population actually considers it a disaster when there is no flood. Without the annual cycle of inundation and silt, the fertility of fields is diminished, and they produce a much lower yield as a result of lack of water. Moreover, fish breeding is disrupted and output diminished when flooding does not create ponds and interconnections between waterways. This is a severe disadvantage to the poor who depend on fish as their main source of protein (and sometimes income).

This does not mean that floods should always be regarded as beneficial, or that people do not lose lives, assets, or become even poorer as a result of them (for example, those who lose land from erosion by the shifting of river channels in floods). However, while a flood can produce an obvious deepening of poverty, its absence has invisible consequences that may be just as bad. A distinction is made in Bengali between 'good' and 'bad' floods to reflect the difference. In general, the majority of the rural population would lose out rather than benefit from the prevention of flooding, by engineering measures such as embankments and river containment, envisaged in the FAP. The benefits of 'good' floods outweigh the disadvantages of the 'bad' (Blaikie et al. 1994). In a rare sample survey of rural people's attitudes to floods, 86 per cent of households were satisfied with the way that they adjusted to normal inundation, and did not want any change to that situation (Leaf 1997).

Climate Change, Hazards, and Their Gender Dimensions

5   The principal climatic hazards affecting Bangladesh—floods and cyclones—are likely to increase in frequency, intensity, duration, and extent. The summer monsoon rainfall is projected to increase, swelling the main river systems in the wider catchment, and boosting the rainfall impact within the country. More rapid glacial melting in the Himalayan headwaters

will also increase spring and early summer flows, further increasing the flood risk. In winter, problems of drought will increase. The current winter dry season (which already limits agriculture and particularly affects poorer farmers who cannot afford to irrigate) is likely to become significantly worse (World Bank 2000). Cyclones are low-pressure systems, which means that as well as causing rainfall flooding and wind damage, they raise sea levels and bring storm surges that flood the coast with saltwater. With rising sea levels, it is estimated that within a century the coastline will retreat by, on average, about 10 kilometres, causing the loss of 18 per cent of the country's land area. This will mean that the impacts of cyclones will be felt further inland than they have been to date *(op. cit.,* ii).

How these increased hazard impacts will affect women in particular, is extremely difficult to predict. The link between poverty and vulnerability is clearly crucial, and affects women disproportionately. If there is no serious progress in reducing poverty, then it can be assumed that women will become increasingly affected by the impact of intensified hazards, in terms of their ability to resist and recover from them. This outcome may be modified if there are more general reductions in economic inequalities between men and women.

It is also important that non-economic ('cultural') factors which produce gender inequality are also addressed—for instance, so that women can adequately seek shelter without shame and harassment, and are not condemned to poverty and increased vulnerability when widowed or divorced. These are issues that are already on the sustainable development agenda, and so it could be argued that reducing women's vulnerability to hazards will follow from this agenda. However, such an approach does not adequately address the specific gender dimensions of disaster preparedness. Evidence from Schmuck (2002), German Red Cross (1999), Baden *et al.* (1994), Rashid and Michaud (2000), Enarson (2000), Enarson and Morrow (1997), and Khondker (1996), all suggest that there are specific gendered factors which it is essential to take into account in order to reduce the vulnerability of women.

Understanding Disasters and Vulnerability

Disasters happen only when a natural hazard impacts negatively on vulnerable people. The severity of a disaster is therefore a reflection both of the location and intensity of the hazard, and of the number of people of given levels and types of vulnerability. For instance, tropical storms of similar intensity affect the USA and Bangladesh, but with very different outcomes. In 1992, Hurricane Andrew struck Florida, and caused more than 28 billion pounds' worth of damage, but killed fewer than 20 people (Morrow 1997). The year before, the cyclone that struck the southeast coast of Bangladesh killed 140,000 people, and ruined the livelihoods of millions (German Red Cross 1999). This does not mean that the people of Florida were unscathed and that they did not suffer (physically and mentally) from loss of homes, schools, jobs, and possessions. But the illustration shows how the impact of an equivalent hazard on different communities is related to differing levels of social vulnerability. This vulnerability can he considered to have five components, which vary from higher to lower levels according to political and social factors affecting different groups of people: namely, the initial conditions of a person, the resilience of their livelihood, their opportunities for self-protection, and their access to social protection and social capital (Cannon 2000; Blaikie et al. 1994). These differ hugely between the contexts of Bangladesh and the USA.

To understand a disaster, we need to understand the components of vulnerability of different groups of people, and relate these to the hazard risk (Cannon 2000; Blaikie et al. 1994). Vulnerability differs according to the 'initial conditions' of a person—how well-fed they are, what their physical and mental health and mobility are, and their morale and capacity for self-reliance. It is also related to the resilience of their livelihood—how quickly and easily they can resume activities that will earn money or provide food and other basics. The hazard itself must be recognized, and the fact that vulnerability will be lower if people are able to put proper 'self-protection' in place—e.g., the right type of building to resist high winds, or a house site that is raised above flood levels. People also usually need some form of 'social protection' from hazards: forms of preparedness provided by institutions at levels above the household. These supplement what people cannot afford or are unable to do for themselves, and provide opportunities to implement measures that only be provided collectively (e.g. codes to improve building safety, warning systems).

10   Social protection depends on adequate government or non-government systems being in place, while self-protection generally relies on people having an adequate income, knowledge of the hazard, and propensity and capacity to take precautions. In many hazardous places, people's vulnerability is also reduced if they are able to draw on adequate social capital. People may need to rely on each other, on family, and on organizations, at all stages of a disaster—from search and rescue after impact, to coping and sharing in the recovery period. Social capital may not always be neutral and benign:

there are examples of disaster recovery where some people identified in a particular social group received assistance not made available to others, as after the Gujerat earthquake of 2000 (Vidal 2002).

Gender Inequality, Women's Status, and Capacity for Protection

How are these components of vulnerability affected by gender relations, and how different are the vulnerabilities of men and women in relation to disasters in Bangladesh? From an analysis of existing gendered vulnerabilities, can we project what may happen in terms of climate change and the possible increase in frequency and intensity of climate hazards? Vulnerability in Bangladesh correlates strongly with poverty, and it is widely accepted that women make up a disproportionate share of poor people. How much of women's vulnerability to hazards can be apportioned to them being poor, and how much is due to specific 'gendered' characteristics of self-protection, social protection, and livelihood resilience? And how will this be affected by climate change?

In fact, it is difficult to separate these two aspects of female vulnerability, precisely because gender plays a significant role in determining poverty. A recent Asian Development Bank report suggested that over 95 per cent of female-headed households are below the poverty line. The proportion of female-headed households in Bangladesh was officially reported as 10 per cent, but other evidence cited suggests that a more realistic figure is 20–30 per cent (Asian Development Bank 2001). Many of these households consist of women who have been divorced or widowed, and who are culturally discouraged from remarrying. Ninety per cent of those who are single as the result of bereavement or divorce are women *(ibid.)*. As a result, vulnerability to hazards involves a complex interaction between poverty and gender relations, in which women are likely to experience higher levels of vulnerability than men.

Women's Nutritional Status and Coping Capacity

Women's poorer nutritional status is a key aspect of their reduced capacity to cope with the effects of a hazard. In Bangladesh, women of all ages are more calorie-deficient than men, and the prevalence of chronic energy deficiency among women is the highest in the world (del Ninno *et al.* 2001). Although this study of the 1998 flood found no evidence of any increase in discrimination against females, it is clear that the situation is potentially disastrous. "Given the already precarious nutritional state of large numbers of girls and women in Bangladesh . . . any further increase in discrimination against females in food consumption would have serious consequences" *(op. cit., 64)*. Women also receive less and poorer-quality healthcare in comparison with men. Bangladesh is one of the few countries in the world where men live longer than women, and where the male population outnumbers the female (Asian Development Bank 2001).

Women's Domestic Burden and Increased Hardship

There is evidence that floods increase women's domestic burden. The loss of utensils and other household essentials is a great hardship, and floods also undermine women's well-being in general because of their dependence on economic activities linked to the home (Khondker 1996). In their study of gender in Bangladesh, Baden *et al.* found that women are likely to be less successful, and find it more difficult to restore their livelihoods, after a flood. Losses of harvest and livestock have a disproportionate impact on women, many of whom rely on food processing, cattle, and chickens for their cash income (Baden *et al.* 1994). Fetching water becomes much more difficult, and it may be contaminated. Water-borne illness might be expected to be more widespread among women, who are nutritionally disadvantaged. Women are likely to suffer increased mental strain, and bear the brunt of certain social constraints, for instance, they are shamed by using public latrines, or being seen by men when in wet clothing (Rashid and Michaud 2000).

Women's Reduced Ability to Provide Self-Protection

15   Poverty is a key factor affecting people's ability to provide adequate self-protection, and it is likely that in female-headed households, the ability of women to create safe conditions in the face of impending floods or cyclones is reduced. The quality of housing, a location on raised ground, adequate storage for food—all are crucial to self-protection, but are more difficult for poor women to achieve. Both self- and social protection are

also affected by gender issues related to 'culture'. During cyclones, women are handicapped by fear of the shame attached to leaving the house and moving in public. It may be too late when they eventually seek refuge. Societal attitudes restricting interaction between men and women make women more reluctant to congregate in the public cyclone shelters (raised concrete structures that protect from wind and flood) where they are forced to interact with other men. However, NGO activities to increase understanding and make warnings more effective seem to have improved this over the past ten years (German Red Cross 1999). Women's mobility is restricted as a result of their responsibility for their children. Their clothing restricts their mobility in floods and in addition women are less likely than men to know how to swim. It is estimated that 90 per cent of the victims of the 1991 cyclone disasters were women and children (Schmuck 2002).

Social Change: A Glimmer of Hope?

There is evidence that some aspects of social change in Bangladesh are improving women's lives and reducing gender inequalities. The average number of children that a woman bears has declined significantly over the last 20 years, from 6.34 in 1975 to around 3.3 in 2001 (BBC 2001). This has significantly reduced women's child-care burden. It has also made their lives safer: more women die as a result of childbirth in Bangladesh than anywhere else in the world. Whether the significant cultural shifts inherent in this decline in fertility rates can have any impact in other areas of society, including on gender differences in vulnerability to climate hazards, is impossible to predict. If progress continues to be made in improving women's lives and reducing gender inequalities, through other initiatives such as micro-credit schemes for women, and associated empowerment activities by NGOs, then there is potential to reduce women's unequal vulnerability as the hazards increase with climate change.

References

Asian Development Bank (2001) 'Country Briefing Paper: Women in Bangladesh', Manila: Asian Development Bank.

Baden, S., C. Green, A.M. Goetz, and M. Guhathakurta (1994) 'Background report on gender issues in Bangladesh', *BRIDGE Report* 26, Sussex: Institute of Development Studies.

BBC (2001) 'Family planning in Bangladesh', World Service, 1 October, http://www.BBC.co.uk/worldservice/sci_tech/highlights/01100!_bangladesh. shtml [accessed 9 June 2009].

Blaikie, P., T. Cannon, I. Davis, and B. Wisner (1994) *At Risk: Natural Hazards, People's Vulnerability and Disasters,* London: Routledge.

Cannon, T. (2000) 'Vulnerability analysis and disasters', in D.J. Parker (ed.), *Floods,* London: Routledge.

del Ninno, C., P.A. Dorosh, L.C. Smith, and D.K. Roy (2001) 'The 1998 floods in Bangladesh: disaster impacts, household coping strategies, and response', *Research Report* 122, Washington DC: International Food Policy Research Institute.

Enarson, E. (2000) 'Gender and natural disasters', *Working Paper* 1 (Recovery and Reconstruction Department), Geneva: JLO.

Enarson, E. and B.H. Morrow (1997) 'A gendered perspective: the voices of women', in W.G. Peacock *et al.* (eds.), *Hurricane Andrew: Ethnicity, Gender and the Sociology of Disasters,* London: Routledge.

German Red Cross (1999) 'Living with cyclones: disaster preparedness in India and Bangladesh', Bonn: German Red Cross.

Khondker, I-1.I-i. (1996) 'Women and floods in Bangladesh', *International Journal of Mass Emergencies and Disasters,* 14(3): 281–92.

Leaf, M. (1997) 'Local control versus technocracy: the Bangladesh Flood Response Study', *Journal of International Affairs,* S 11: 179–200.

Morrow, B.I-I. (1997) 'Disaster in the first person', in W.G. Peacock *et al. Hurricane Andrew: Ethnicity, Gender and the Sociology of Disasters,* Longman Routledge.

Rashid, S.F. and S. Michaud (2000) 'Female adolescents and their sexuality: notions of honour, shame, purity and pollution during the floods', *Disasters,* 241: 54–70.

Schmuck, I-1. (2002) 'Empowering women in Bangladesh', http://www.reweb.int [accessed 9 June 2009].

Vidal, J. (2002) 'Helping hands', *The Guardian,* 30 January 2002.

World Bank (2000) 'Bangladesh: climate change and sustainable development', Re1 no. 21104 BD, Dhaka: South Asia Rural Development Team.

Analyze

1. In what ways does the article suggest that women, especially in developing countries, will suffer unique consequences from climate disasters?

2. This article looks at the ways in which the effects of climate disasters would be especially destructive to women in Bangladesh, whose social and economic situations position them to respond to disaster situations at a disadvantage. What other groups of people in other parts of the world can you imagine might have similar disadvantages? Why and in what ways?

3. What factors make a group especially vulnerable to disaster and its consequences?

Explore

1. This reading concentrates on natural disasters and the people they affect. How do you think that a focus on disaster and destruction of the lives of people rhetorically affects the way people view climate change? Does giving a human face to the climate issue make it more of an urgent issue in the public mind? Why or why not?

2. Often, in response to tragedy, people resort to forms of art, song, or poetry to express their grief and emotion. Locate a poem, song, or painting that addresses the issues of climate change discussed in this piece. Then write a rhetorical analysis of the piece, describing the ways that it rhetorically affects its audience in a way that is distinctly different from the practice of displaying scientific facts.

3. Natural disasters occur with terrifying frequency. In this country, you might think of Hurricane Katrina or Hurricane Sandy. Use the search engines at your library or the Internet to read about the aftermath of one of these hurricanes. Who bore the worst of the burden and what were the consequences? Why were they especially vulnerable to the disaster? Write a brief letter to your community disaster preparedness organization suggesting specific ways they might minimize the consequences for these vulnerable groups.

Roman Krznaric
"Empathy and Climate Change: A Proposal for a Revolution of Human Relationships"

Roman Krznaric has a doctorate in political sociology from the University of Essex in England and founded the School of Life in London. He is author of *A Guide to the Unknown University* (2006) and the forthcoming book *Empathy*. The selection provided here was originally printed in *Future Ethics: Climate Change and Apocalyptic Imagination*, one of a number of recent books on the ethics of climate change. Krznaric's chapter offers a theory of empathy and argues that we must develop empathy across time and across space in order to motivate people to take action regarding climate change. As you read, consider how well Krznaric's argument about empathy addresses the problem of the rationalist paradox that is explained in the Appendix to this book.

A Passage to India

> *Jenna Meredith can empathise more than most with the 4.5 million people made homeless by flooding in South Asia after her home in Hull, UK, was hit by flooding earlier this year. She travelled to Orissa in eastern India with Oxfam to meet families who have lost their homes.*

This story appeared on the Oxfam website in August 2007. In June that year, the worst flooding in Britain for sixty years had destroyed Jenna's home. Not only had she and her two daughters lost their worldly possessions, but due to financial pressures, she had stopped paying her house insurance six months earlier. Jenna became a spokesperson for local residents on her housing estate who felt that the government was doing too little to help them. When she made a comment in a radio interview about how the people of Hull were living like refugees in the Third World, she was contacted by Oxfam, who invited her to discover what life was like for poor villagers who had recently faced flooding in India.

Figures 4.21 & 4.22

'It was heartbreaking,' she said, after returning from her one-week trip. 'I have been flooded out and lost everything so I know what it is like for the people in India. But in comparison I feel lucky. We can go and buy food from the shops, but the people I've met have lost their crops. They haven't got anything.' One person she spoke to was Annapurna Beheri, whose home and small family shop selling biscuits and tobacco were washed away. 'Annapurna was incredible. Her life has been turned upside down and now she has been reduced to living in a corrugated shack. I cried when the floods hit Hull, but she has nothing left and the family barely have enough food.'

Jenna was overwhelmed by her face-to-face meeting with the villagers in Orissa. 'Until you go to see a country like that for yourself, it's impossible to comprehend what's really happening. I know I can't walk away from this. I am determined to continue the campaign not only to get aid to those in need, but also to try to do whatever we can to reduce the effect of global warming. I have had a life-changing experience. I'll do everything I can to make a difference.'

Empathy and the Climate Gap

How can we close the gap between knowledge and action on climate change? Millions of people in rich countries know about the damaging effects of climate change and their own greenhouse gas (GHG) emissions, yet relatively few are willing to make substantive changes to how they live. They might change a few light bulbs but they do not cut back on flying abroad for their holidays nor do they want to pay higher taxes to confront global warming.

5   One common approach to closing the climate gap is to argue that it is economically beneficial for us to do so: if we don't act now, climate change will become an increasing drain on national income as we try to deal with the damage, and individuals will face a reduction in living standards, for instance due to higher food and energy prices. A second major approach, based on ideas of justice and rights, is to argue that we have a moral obligation not to harm the lives of others through our excessive GHG emissions.

So far economic, moral or other arguments have not been enough to spur sufficient action. I believe that a fundamental approach has been missing: empathy.

Individuals, governments and companies are currently displaying an extraordinary lack of empathy on the issue of climate change, in two different ways. First, we are ignoring the plight of those whose livelihoods are being destroyed today by the consequences of our high emission levels, particularly distant strangers in developing countries who are affected by floods, droughts and other weather events. That is, there is an absence of empathy across space. Second, we are failing to take the perspective of future generations who will have to live with the detrimental effects of our continuing addiction to lifestyles that result in emissions beyond sustainable levels. Thus there is a lack of empathy through time. We would hardly treat our own family members with such callous disregard and continue acting in ways that we knew were harming them.

In this essay I wish to suggest that generating empathy both across space and through time is one of the most powerful ways we have of closing the gap between knowledge and action, and for tackling the climate crisis. The problem is that, until now, empathy has been largely ignored by policymakers, non-governmental organisations and activists. Oxfam's idea of taking a British flood victim to witness the effects of flooding in India is an exception. It is time to recognise that empathy is not only an ethical guide to how we should lead our lives and treat other people, but is also an essential strategic guide to how we can bring about the social action required to confront global warming.

To begin this interdisciplinary journey, I will discuss exactly what empathy means, then show that there is strong historical evidence that it is possible to generate empathy on a large scale and for it to bring about major social change. Following this I will explain in more detail what it would mean to promote greater empathy on climate change across space and through time, and suggest concrete ways of doing so.

Tackling climate change requires nothing less than a revolution of the   10
empathetic imagination.

What Is Empathy?

If you pick up a psychology textbook and look up the meaning of 'empathy' you will usually find that two types are described.

Empathy as Shared Emotional Response

The first form is the idea of empathy as a shared emotional response, sometimes called 'affective' empathy. For instance, if you see a baby crying in anguish, and you too feel anguish, then you are experiencing empathy—you are sharing or mirroring their emotions. This idea is reflected in the original German term from which the English word 'empathy' was translated around a century ago, 'Einfühlung', which literally means 'feeling into'.

However, if you see the same anguished baby and feel a different emotion, such as pity, then you are experiencing sympathy rather than empathy. Sympathy refers to an emotional response which is not shared. One of the reasons people often confuse the two is historical. Up until the nineteenth century, what used to be called 'sympathy' is what we mean today by empathy as a shared emotional response. Thus when Adam Smith begins his book *The Theory of Moral Sentiments* (1759) with a discussion of 'Sympathy', he is actually referring to a concept closer to the modern idea of affective empathy.

Empathy as Perspective-Taking

A second definition of empathy is the idea of empathy as 'perspective-taking', which the psychology literature refers to as 'cognitive' empathy. This concerns our ability to step into the shoes of another person and comprehend the way they look at themselves and the world, their most important beliefs, aspirations, motivations, fears, and hopes. That is, the constituents of their internal frame of reference or 'worldview' (Weltanschaung, as the sociologist Karl Mannheim called it). Perspective-taking empathy allows us to make an imaginative leap into another person's being. This approach to empathy became prominent in the 1960s through the work of humanist psychotherapists such as Carl Rogers.

15   The way we do this quite naturally is evident in common phrases such as 'I can see where you're coming from' and 'Wouldn't you hate to be her?'. Although we can never fully comprehend another person's worldview, we can develop the skill of understanding something of their viewpoint, and may on that basis be able to predict how they will think or act in particular circumstances. Perspective-taking is one of the most important ways for us to overcome our assumptions and prejudices about others. For example, dozens of psychological studies show how perspective-taking exercises can be developed to help challenge racial and other stereotypes, by encouraging people to imagine themselves in the situation of another person, with that person's beliefs and experiences. Hence many empathy researchers, including Daniel Goleman and Martin Hoffman, consider perspective-taking as an essential basis for individual moral development. With perspective-taking, the emphasis is on understanding 'where a person is coming from' rather than on sharing their emotions, as with affective empathy.

While these two kinds of empathy are related, in this essay I will focus on the perspective-taking form, since this is the one that is most susceptible to intentional development and has the greatest potential to bring about social change. But what is the evidence that an apparently 'soft skill' like empathising can not only shape how we treat people on an individual level, but also have a mass social impact and be effective in tackling the hard realities of the climate crisis?

. . .

The Challenge of Distance Through Time

Climate change poses the fundamental problem of motivating us to act, and make sacrifices, on the behalf of future generations—people whose lives are distant from us through time. We need to cut our carbon emissions right now for the benefit of individuals who do not yet exist and whom we shall never meet. While we are aware of some impacts of global warming today, the reports of the Intergovernmental Panel on Climate Change predict with strong certainty that the problems will get worse for future generations. Even if we take concerted action immediately, we are already locked into major and damaging climate impacts, even under the most conservative projections.

But why do we find it so hard to make policies that will benefit future people? A primary reason is because our political systems generally trap us in short-term electoral cycles (of usually four or five years), so politicians are largely unwilling to push for costly reforms that will only have an impact fifty years from now. In Japan in the eighteenth and nineteenth centuries, by contrast, the authoritarian Shogunate system encouraged political rulers to engage in visionary long-term policies such as mass tree planting to deal with extreme deforestation and soil erosion. These were leaders who wanted to preserve the nation for their own descendents, who they believed would inherit their political power. Although I am not an advocate of authoritarian hereditary rule, it is clear that liberal democratic systems have a bias towards the present.

A second important reason for our short-term thinking is that not everybody is our progeny. We tend to care most for the people closest to us, especially those to whom we are biologically related. We worry about the welfare of our children and grandchildren. But the bonds start becoming weaker with respect to our great-grandchildren, and become almost completely absent when we consider the prospects for people a century from now to whom we are not related. This point is illustrated by a remark apparently made in the pub by the evolutionary biologist J.B.S. Heldane, who said that he would happily die for three of his children or six of his grandchildren. Added to this is the fact that we are not even particularly proficient at considering our own future welfare, illustrated by the case of smokers who seem willing to gain the pleasures of a nicotine rush today, even though they know that it may result in lung cancer and death in the future.

Economists have offered an extremely unethical solution to the problem of thinking about future generations in the context of climate change, which is known as discounting. Studies such as the Stern Review propose that we should 'discount' the future costs of climate change impacts, giving greater weight to costs incurred in the present. For instance, using a discount rate of 5%, it would be worth spending only US$9 today to avert an income loss of US$100 caused by climate change in 2057. With no discount, it would be worth spending up to US$100. A high discount rate can consequently generate a strong cost-benefit case for deferring or limiting mitigation efforts. Yet if we believe all human beings are equal, we cannot morally justify deciding not to act today because future generations should be expected to pay more of the costs of climate change. Even Ramsey, the founding father of discounting, observed (in 1928) that it was 'ethically indefensible and arises merely from the weakness of the imagination'.

This suggests a second way of approaching the issue of future generations, which is to argue that we have a moral obligation to act on their behalf to prevent climate change as a matter of social justice and in compliance with the idea of universal human rights. Philosophers have got themselves into knots thinking about this, wondering about how we can ascribe rights to unborn beings, how we can take into account the uncertainties of the future, and how to deal with the ethical dilemmas of allocating scarce resources between those who are in need today and those will be in need in the future. It is certainly true that ethical arguments based on justice and rights can have political force (as they did in the US civil rights movement, for example) and might encourage individuals and governments to take action to cut carbon emissions. But there is little historical evidence that human beings will undertake major efforts for unborn generations on moral grounds.

We need something more than moral or economic arguments to generate social action on climate change. We need to create an empathetic bond between the present and the future. We must become experts at imagining ourselves into the lives and thoughts of our great-grandchildren, and of strangers in distant times. When we fill our car with petrol or fly from London to New York, we need not only to believe that this is morally wrong or that it will have long-run economic costs. We also need to be able to feel that future generations are watching us, to consider what they might think, to put ourselves into their shoes. Such an empathetic connection may stir us into changing how we live and what we do.

The Challenge of Distance Across Space

Climate change is as much a problem across space as it is one through time. Studies by development agencies demonstrate that weather events that are either caused by climate change, or closely resemble those that are likely to become increasingly common due to it, are already devastating the lives of some of the world's poorest people, who usually live in far-away countries about which we know little. From floods in West Bengal to drought in Kenya to rising sea levels in Tuvalu, global warming is already having major human impacts and is forcing people to protect their livelihoods with new flood defences, faster-maturing crops and other emergency measures. Oxfam estimates that the cost of adapting to climate change in developing countries will be at least $50bn each year, every year.

So we need to take action to help alleviate the difficulties faced by people today whose lives are threatened with a severe development reversal caused by excessive GHG emissions in rich countries. Unfortunately rich countries have a poor record of coming to the assistance of those who are distant across space, especially people from developing countries or whose cultures are very different from their own. In 1970 wealthy nations committed to contribute 0.7% of their annual gross national incomes as development aid. Today, the average figure is just 0.28%, with the US providing only 0.16% (Norway and the Netherlands are amongst the few countries to have achieved the target). We occasionally pour money into major emergency situations, as has occurred on multiple occasions since the Biafra crisis of the late 1960s, but our staying power is limited and we are easily distracted by other matters closer to home. By the end of April 2008, rich nations had paid only $92m into a UN fund to help the least developed countries with their most urgent and immediate adaptation needs, which is less than what Americans spend on suntan lotion each month.

Why don't we do more to help? There are major academic industries in politics, sociology and cultural studies that attempt to answer this question. Some people argue that it is due to racial prejudices and the legacies of colonialism. Others, that nationalism prevents us looking beyond borders, or that we maintain ourselves in a state of collective psychological denial about the lives of the poor and our responsibility for their plight. There are those who believe that we have become anesthetised to the images of poverty and destitution we see on television, or who suggest that most people feel that whatever they can give is too little to make any real difference so they do not bother. And there are analysts who claim we are simply too selfish to give a damn.

The most significant explanation, I believe, is simply that these people live far away and we don't know them. They are strangers to us. We cannot really imagine who they are and what their lives are like, let alone how the impacts of our carbon emissions affect them. Jenna Meredith's experience of meeting Annapurna Beheri was an exact counter to this kind of ignorance. If we personally knew people who had been flooded in Bangladesh we would be far more likely to do something about it than if we did not. That is the undeniable power of human relationships and the empathetic bond. When the Asian Tsunami struck at the end of 2004, the unprecedented humanitarian response can be explained not only by the scale of the disaster and its proximity to Christmas, but because there were so many

Western holidaymakers amongst the victims. Tens of thousands of Europeans were sending text messages to check if friends or relatives abroad had been killed or injured. And even if their loved ones were safe, people could easily envision how one of their close friends or children travelling around Asia on a gap year might have lost their lives. The aid that went to countries such as Sri Lanka and Thailand was, to a significant degree, an empathetic reaction. Suddenly Asia was not full of distant strangers but rather friends or people just like us.

I believe that we should be supporting communities in developing countries to adapt to climate change on purely ethical grounds. We must, as a matter of justice, take responsibility for problems caused in poor countries by our own carbon emissions. We must recognise that these emissions are effectively violating human rights, and we need to avoid undermining other people's rights, whether they live around the corner or in a corrugated shack in Orissa. But I know from personal experience that such beliefs are not sufficient to sustain practical action on the behalf of people in distant lands. Something more is needed. And that something is empathy. Whenever we hear of floods in India, we should picture individuals like Annapurna Beheri and try to imagine what she is feeling at that very moment. Whenever we joke about how climate change is giving us a lovely warm summer, we need to imagine that drought-struck farmers in Kenya can hear us chuckling in the sun.

· · ·

A Revolution of Human Relationships

There is no doubt that an empathetic transformation of society to confront climate change faces considerable barriers to its success. Political vision remains excessively short-term, the media can ignore or distort the threats of climate change, advertisers continue to lure us into excessive luxury consumption, and many people remain locked in their personal psychologies of denial about the realities of global warming and its destructiveness. Yet is it worth remembering that all social revolutions have faced obstacles: those who led the movement against slavery and the slave trade in the late eighteenth century had to overcome multiple barriers to achieve their aims.

Moreover, I recognise that, historically, human beings are most likely to take major action and make substantive sacrifices when they fear for their own safety. That is why governments in Britain and the USA were able to introduce strict rationing and price controls during the Second World War. Similar levels of fear around climate change are only likely to arise if rich countries experience multiple climate disasters, for instance a hurricane hitting Manchester, the breaching of the Thames Barrier causing flooding throughout central London, or the shutting down of the Gulf Stream leading to a deep freeze throughout the country. However, the likelihood that such events may not take place until it is far too late to act on climate change, is even more reason to turn to empathy as a way of creating social action now.

Tackling climate change urgently requires an empathetic revolution, a   30 revolution of human relationships where we learn to put ourselves in the shoes of others and see the consequences of global warming from their perspectives. The result will be an expansion of our moral universes so we will take practical measures to help those who are distant through time or distant across space. If we fail to become empathetic revolutionaries, the gap between climate knowledge and action will never be closed. Each of us needs to carve into everything we do, the empathetic credo, 'You are, therefore I am.'

Analyze

1. What is empathy and what does it have to do with climate change?
2. What does the author mean when she says that there is a lack of empathy *across space* and *through time*?
3. The author states that "so far economic, moral or other arguments have not been enough to spur sufficient action" regarding climate change. Why do you think this is? Suspending, for a moment, the manufactured controversy surrounding the validity of climate science, why do you think people who are aware of the reality of climate change act as if they do not?

Explore

1. The introduction to this chapter suggests that complex issues like climate change cannot be reduced to simple "bumper sticker" slogans without obscuring the reality of the situation. Using Google or your other favorite search engine, find bumper stickers that relate to climate

change (e.g., "Global Warming? It's called summer, stupid."). How good of a job do these bumper stickers do at describing the climate change situation? In what ways do the bumper stickers you've found obscure the facts or logic behind climate change?

2. The author states that "we are ignoring the plight of those whose livelihoods are being destroyed today by the consequences of our high emission levels, particularly distant strangers in developing countries who are affected by floods, droughts and other weather events." Many people in the American public in particular seem unaware that there are currently places where climate change is destroying people's lives right now. Find an example, other than in India, or a particular place where climate change has caused devastation to the livelihood of a group of people. Write an editorial for your school's newspaper that raises awareness of the reality of the situation, including specific examples drawn from these readings that describe how you know this is a result of climate change.

3. Empathy is very similar to the concept of "identification." Both concepts involve the ways communication can motivate a person to care about another and even take action on his or her behalf. You have read about empathy. Do some research on "identification" and the ways it can be a useful rhetorical strategy. Then draft a document—written, visual, digital—that uses identification and empathy to motivate change associated with climate change.

New Evangelical Partnership for the Common Good
"Climate Change: An Evangelical Call to Action"

This call to action on climate change is part of the "Evangelical Climate Initiative" and appears on the website of the New Evangelical Partnership for the Common Good. This association of evangelical Christians, founded in 2010 by Richard Cizik, David P. Gushee, and Steve Martin, advocates the religious position known as "creation care." Put simply, creation care holds that all Christians are charged with being good stewards of God's creation, both human and natural. In this statement, the many co-signers make what they call "four simple but urgent claims" about climate change and our moral responsibility to act. This statement reflects the social and intellectual complexity of climate change discussions. The statement mixes scientific evidence with scriptural references to construct an eloquent and compelling case for action on climate change. As you read, listen to the voice of the writers and consider their comment that it took "considerable convincing" to persuade many of them that climate change was real. How do these two elements of the statement affect readers?

Preamble

As American evangelical Christian leaders, we recognize both our opportunity and our responsibility to offer a biblically based moral witness that can help shape public policy in the most powerful nation on earth, and therefore contribute to the well-being of the entire world.[1] *Whether* we will enter the public square and offer our witness there is no longer an open question. We are in that square, and we will not withdraw.

We are proud of the evangelical community's long-standing commitment to the sanctity of human life. But we also offer moral witness in many venues and on many issues. Sometimes the issues that we have taken on, such as sex trafficking, genocide in the Sudan, and the AIDS epidemic in Africa, have surprised outside observers. While individuals and organizations can be called to concentrate on certain issues, we are not a single-issue movement. We seek to be true to our calling as Christian leaders, and above all faithful to Jesus Christ our Lord. Our attention, therefore, goes to whatever issues our faith requires us to address.

Over the last several years many of us have engaged in study, reflection, and prayer related to the issue of climate change (often called "global warming"). For most of us, until recently this has not been treated as a pressing issue or major priority. Indeed, many of us have required considerable convincing before becoming persuaded that climate change is a real problem and that it ought to matter to us as Christians. But now we have seen and heard enough to offer the following moral argument related to the matter of human-induced climate change. We commend the four simple but urgent claims offered in this document to all who will listen, beginning with our brothers and sisters in the Christian community, and urge all to take the appropriate actions that follow from them.

Claim 1: Human-Induced Climate Change Is Real

S ince 1995 there has been general agreement among those in the scientific community most seriously engaged with this issue that climate change is happening and is being caused mainly by human activities, especially the burning of fossil fuels. Evidence gathered since 1995 has only strengthened this conclusion.

5   Because all religious/moral claims about climate change are relevant only if climate change is real and is mainly human-induced, everything hinges on the scientific data. As evangelicals we have hesitated to speak on this issue until we could be more certain of the science of climate change, but the signatories now believe that the evidence demands action:

- The Intergovernmental Panel on Climate Change (IPCC), the world's most authoritative body of scientists and policy experts on the issue of global warming, has been studying this issue since the late 1980s. (From 1988–2002 the IPCC's assessment of the climate science was Chaired by Sir John Houghton, a devout evangelical Christian.) It has documented the steady rise in global temperatures over the last fifty years, projects that the average global temperature will continue to rise in the coming decades, and attributes "most of the warming" to human activities.
- The U.S. National Academy of Sciences, as well as all other G8 country scientific Academies (Great Britain, France, Germany, Japan, Canada, Italy, and Russia), has concurred with these judgments.
- In a 2004 report, and at the 2005 G8 summit, the Bush Administration has also acknowledged the reality of climate change and the likelihood that human activity is the cause of at least some of it.[2]

In the face of the breadth and depth of this scientific and governmental concern, only a small percentage of which is noted here, we are convinced that evangelicals must engage this issue without any further lingering over the basic reality of the problem or humanity's responsibility to address it.

Claim 2: The Consequences of Climate Change Will Be Significant, and Will Hit the Poor the Hardest

The earth's natural systems are resilient but not infinitely so, and human civilizations are remarkably dependent on ecological stability and well-being. It is easy to forget this until that stability and well-being are threatened.

Even small rises in global temperatures will have such likely impacts as: sea level rise; more frequent heat waves, droughts, and extreme weather events such as torrential rains and floods; increased tropical diseases in now-temperate regions; and hurricanes that are more intense. It could lead to significant reduction in agricultural output, especially in poor countries. Low-lying regions, indeed entire islands, could find themselves under water. (This is not to mention the various negative impacts climate change could have on God's other creatures.)

Each of these impacts increases the likelihood of refugees from flooding or famine, violent conflicts, and international instability, which could lead to more security threats to our nation.

Poor nations and poor individuals have fewer resources available to cope with major challenges and threats. The consequences of global warming will therefore hit the poor the hardest, in part because those areas likely to be significantly affected first are in the poorest regions of the world. Millions of people could die in this century because of climate change, most of them our poorest global neighbors.

Claim 3: Christian Moral Convictions Demand Our Response to the Climate Change Problem

While we cannot here review the full range of relevant biblical convictions related to care of the creation, we emphasize the following points: 10

- Christians must care about climate change because we love God the Creator and Jesus our Lord, through whom and for whom the creation was made. This is God's world, and any damage that we do to God's world is an offense against God Himself (Gen. 1; Ps. 24; Col. 1:16).
- Christians must care about climate change because we are called to love our neighbors, to do unto others as we would have them do unto

us, and to protect and care for the least of these as though each was
Jesus Christ himself (Mt. 22:34-40; Mt. 7:12; Mt. 25:31-46).

- Christians, noting the fact that most of the climate change problem is
  human induced, are reminded that when God made humanity he
  commissioned us to exercise stewardship over the earth and its creatures. Climate change is the latest evidence of our failure to exercise
  proper stewardship, and constitutes a critical opportunity for us to do
  better (Gen. 1:26-28).

Love of God, love of neighbor, and the demands of stewardship are more
than enough reason for evangelical Christians to respond to the climate
change problem with moral passion and concrete action.

Claim 4: The Need to Act Now Is Urgent. Governments, Businesses, Churches, and Individuals All Have a Role to Play in Addressing Climate Change—Starting Now

The basic task for all of the world's inhabitants is to find ways now to
begin to reduce the carbon dioxide emissions from the burning of fossil
fuels that are the primary cause of human-induced climate change.

There are several reasons for urgency. First, deadly impacts are being
experienced now. Second, the oceans only warm slowly, creating a lag in
experiencing the consequences. Much of the climate change to which we
are already committed will not be realized for several decades. The consequences of the pollution we create now will be visited upon our children
and grandchildren. Third, as individuals and as a society we are making
long-term decisions today that will determine how much carbon dioxide
we will emit in the future, such as whether to purchase energy efficient
vehicles and appliances that will last for 10–20 years, or whether to build
more coal-burning power plants that last for 50 years rather than investing
more in energy efficiency and renewable energy.

In the United States, the most important immediate step that can be
taken at the federal level is to pass and implement national legislation requiring sufficient economy-wide reductions in carbon dioxide emissions
through cost-effective, market-based mechanisms such as a cap-and-trade
program. On June 22, 2005 the Senate passed the Domenici-Bingaman
resolution affirming this approach, and a number of major energy companies

now acknowledge that this method is best both for the environment and for business.

We commend the Senators who have taken this stand and encourage them to fulfill their pledge. We also applaud the steps taken by such companies as BP, Shell, General Electric, Cinergy, Duke Energy, and DuPont, all of which have moved ahead of the pace of government action through innovative measures implemented within their companies in the U.S. and around the world. In so doing they have offered timely leadership.

Numerous positive actions to prevent and mitigate climate change are being implemented across our society by state and local governments, churches, smaller businesses, and individuals. These commendable efforts focus on such matters as energy efficiency, the use of renewable energy, low CO_2 emitting technologies, and the purchase of hybrid vehicles. These efforts can easily be shown to save money, save energy, reduce global warming pollution as well as air pollution that harm human health, and eventually pay for themselves. There is much more to be done, but these pioneers are already helping to show the way forward.

15

Finally, while we must reduce our global warming pollution to help mitigate the impacts of climate change, as a society and as individuals we must also help the poor adapt to the significant harm that global warming will cause.

Conclusion

We the undersigned pledge to act on the basis of the claims made in this document. We will not only teach the truths communicated here but also seek ways to implement the actions that follow from them. In the name of Jesus Christ our Lord, we urge all who read this declaration to join us in this effort.

Climate Change: An Evangelical Call to Action
SIGNATORIES*

* Institutional affiliation is given for identification purposes only. All signatories do so as individuals expressing their personal opinions and not as representatives of their organizations. **Rev. Dr. Leith Anderson,**

Former President, National Association of Evangelicals (NAE); Senior Pastor, Wooddale Church, Eden Prairie, MN **Robert Andringa, Ph.D.**, President, Council for Christian Colleges and Universities (CCCU), Vienna, VA **Rev. Jim Ball, Ph.D.**, Executive Director, Evangelical Environmental Network; Wynnewood, PA **Commissioner W. Todd Bassett**, National Commander, The Salvation Army; Alexandria, VA **Dr. Jay A. Barber, Jr.**, President, Warner Pacific College, Portland, OR **Gary P. Bergel**, President, Intercessors for America; Purcellville, VA **David Black, Ph.D.**, President, Eastern University, St. Davids, PA **Bishop Charles E. Blake, Sr.**, West Angeles Church of God in Christ, Los Angeles, CA **Rev. Dr. Dan Boone**, President, Trevecca Nazarene University, Nashville, TN **Bishop Wellington Boone**, The Father's House & Wellington Boone Ministries, Norcross, GA **Rev. Dr. Peter Borgdorff**, Executive Director, Christian Reformed Church, Grand Rapids, MI **H. David Brandt, Ph.D.**, President, George Fox University, Newberg, OR **Rev. George K. Brushaber, Ph.D.**, President, Bethel University; Senior Advisor, *Christianity Today*; St. Paul, MN **Rev. Dwight Burchett**, President, Northern California Association of Evangelicals; Sacramento, CA **Gaylen Byker, Ph.D.**, President, Calvin College, Grand Rapids, MI **Rev. Dr. Jerry B. Cain**, President, Judson College, Elgin, IL **Rev. Dr. Clive Calver**, Senior Pastor, Walnut Hill Community Church; Former President, World Relief; Bethel, CT **R. Judson Carlberg, Ph.D.**, President, Gordon College, Wenham, MA **Rev. Dr. Paul Cedar**, Chair, Mission America Coalition; Palm Desert, CA **David Clark, Ph.D.**, President, Palm Beach Atlantic University; Former Chair/CEO, Nat. Rel. Broadcasters; Founding Dean, Regent University; West Palm Beach, FL **Rev. Luis Cortes**, President & CEO, Esperanza USA; Host, National Hispanic Prayer Breakfast; Philadelphia, PA **Andy Crouch**, Columnist, *Christianity Today* magazine; Swarthmore, PA **Rev. Paul de Vries, Ph.D.**, President, New York Divinity School; New York, NY **Rev. David S. Dockery, Ph.D.**, Chairman of the Board, Council for Christian Colleges and Universities; President, Union University, Jackson, TN **Larry R. Donnithorne, Ed.D.**, President, Colorado Christian University, Lakewood, CO **Blair Dowden, Ed.D.**, President, Huntington University, Huntington, IN **Rev. Robert P. Dugan, Jr.**, Former VP of Governmental Affairs, National Association of Evangelicals; Palm Desert, CA **Craig Hilton Dyer**, President, Bright Hope International, Hoffman Estates, IL **D. Merrill Ewert, Ed.D.**, President, Fresno Pacific University, Fresno, CA **Rev. Dr. LeBron Fairbanks**, President, Mount Vernon

Nazarene University, Mount Vernon, OH **Rev. Myles Fish**, President/ CEO, International Aid, Spring Lake, MI **Rev. Dr. Floyd Flake**, Senior Pastor, Greater Allen AME Cathedral; President, Wilberforce University; Jamaica, NY **Rev. Timothy George, Ph.D.**, Founding Dean, Beeson Divinity School, Samford University, Executive Editor, *Christianity Today*; Birmingham, AL **Rev. Michael J. Glodo**, Stated Clerk, Evangelical Presbyterian Church, Livonia, MI **Rev. James M. Grant, Ph.D.**, President, Simpson University, Redding, CA **Rev. Dr. Jeffrey E. Greenway**, President, Asbury Theological Seminary, Wilmore, KY **Rev. David Gushee**, Professor of Moral Philosophy, Union University; columnist, Religion News Service; Jackson, TN **Gregory V. Hall**, President, Warner Southern College, Lake Wales, FL **Brent Hample**, Executive Director, India Partners, Eugene OR **Rev. Dr. Jack Hayford**, President, International Church of the Foursquare Gospel, Los Angeles, CA **Rev. Steve Hayner, Ph.D.**, Former President, InterVarsity; Prof. of Evangelism, Columbia Theological Sem., Decatur, GA **E. Douglas Hodo, Ph.D.**, President, Houston Baptist University, Houston, TX **Ben Homan**, President, Food for the Hungry; President, Association of Evangelical Relief and Development Organizations (AERDO); Phoenix, AZ **Rev. Dr. Joel Hunter**, Senior Pastor, Northland, A Church Distributed; Longwood, FL **Bryce Jessup**, President, William Jessup University, Rocklin, CA **Ronald G. Johnson, Ph.D.**, President, Malone College, Canton, OH **Rev. Dr. Phillip Charles Joubert, Sr.**, Pastor, Community Baptist Church, Bayside, NY **Jennifer Jukanovich**, Founder, The Vine, Seattle, WA **Rev. Brian Kluth**, Senior Pastor, First Evangelical Free Church; Founder, MAXIMUM Generosity; Colorado Springs, CO **Bishop James D. Leggett**, General Superintendent, International Pentecostal Holiness Church; Chair, Pentecostal World Fellowship; Oklahoma City, OK **Duane Litfin, Ph.D.**, President, Wheaton College, Wheaton IL **Rev. Dr. Larry Lloyd**, President, Crichton College, Memphis, TN **Rev. Dr. Jo Anne Lyon**, Executive Director, World Hope; Alexandria, VA **Sammy Mah**, President and CEO, World Relief; Baltimore, MD **Jim Mannoia, Ph.D.**, President, Greenville College, Greenville, IL **Bishop George D. McKinney, Ph.D., D.D.**, St. Stephens Church Of God In Christ, San Diego, CA **Rev. Brian McLaren**, Senior Pastor, Cedar Ridge Community Church; Emergent leader; Spencerville, MD **Rev. Dr. Daniel Mercaldo**, Senior Pastor & Founder, Gateway Cathedral; Staten Island, NY **Rev. Dr. Jesse Miranda**, President, AMEN, Costa Mesa, CA **Royce Money, Ph.D.**, President, Abilene Christian University, Abilene, TX

Dr. Bruce Murphy, President, Northwestern University, Orange City, IA **Rev. George W. Murray, D.Miss.**, President, Columbia International University, Columbia SC **David Neff**, Editor, *Christianity Today*; Carol Stream, IL **Larry Nikkel**, President, Tabor College, Hillsboro, KS **Michael Nyenhuis**, President, MAP International; Brunswick, GA **Brian O'Connell**, President, REACT Services; Founder and Former Executive Director, Religious Liberty Commission, World Evangelical Alliance; Mill Creek, WA **Roger Parrott, Ph.D.**, President, Belhaven College, Jackson, MS **Charles W. Pollard, Ph.D., J.D.**, President, John Brown University, Siloam Springs, AR **Paul A. Rader, D.Miss.**, President, Asbury College, Wilmore, KY **Rev. Edwin H. Robinson, Ph.D.**, President, MidAmerica Nazarene University, Olathe , KS **William P. Robinson, Ph.D.**, President, Whitworth College, Spokane, WA **Lee Royce, Ph.D.**, President, Mississippi College, Clinton, MS **Andy Ryskamp**, Executive Director, Christian Reformed World Relief Committee, Grand Rapids, MI **Rev. Ron Sider, Ph.D.**, President, Evangelicals for Social Action, Philadelphia, PA **Richard Stearns**, President, World Vision, Federal Way, WA **Rev. Jewelle Stewart**, Ex. Dir., Women's Ministries, International Pentecostal Holiness Church; Oklahoma City, OK **Rev. Dr. Loren Swartzendruber**, President, Eastern Mennonite University, Harrisonburg VA **C. Pat Taylor, Ph.D.**, President, Southwest Baptist University, Bolivar, MO **Rev. Berten A. Waggoner**, National Director, Vineyard, USA; Sugar Land, TX **Jon R. Wallace, DBA**, President, Azusa Pacific University, Azusa, CA **Rev. Dr. Thomas Yung-Hsin Wang**, former International Director of Lausanne II, Sunnyvale, CA **Rev. Dr. Rick Warren**, Senior Pastor, Saddleback Church; author of *The Purpose Driven Life*; Lake Forest, CA **John Warton**, President, Business Professional Network, Portland, OR **Robert W. Yarbrough, Ph.D.**, New Testament Dept. Chair, Trinity Evangelical Divinity School, Deerfield, IL **John D. Yordy, Ph.D.**, Interim President, Goshen College, Goshen, IN **Adm. Tim Ziemer**, Director of Programs, World Relief, Baltimore, MD

NOTES

1. Cf. "For the Health of the Nation: An Evangelical Call to Civic Responsibility," approved by National Association of Evangelicals, October 8, 2004.
2. Intergovernmental Panel on Climate Change 2001, Summary for Policymakers; http://www.grida.no/climate/ipcc_tar/wg1/007.htm.

(See also the main IPCC website, www.ipcc.ch.) For the confirmation of the IPCC's findings from the U.S. National Academy of Sciences, see, *Climate Change Science: An Analysis of Some Key Questions* (2001); http://books.nap.edu/html/climatechange/summary.html. For the statement by the G8 Academies (plus those of Brazil, India, and China) see *Joint Science Academies Statement: Global Response to Climate Change* (June 2005): http://nationalacademies.org/onpi/06072005. pdf. Another major international report that confirms the IPCC's conclusions comes from the Arctic Climate Impact Assessment. See their *Impacts of a Warming Climate*, Cambridge University Press, November 2004, p. 2; http://amap.no/acia/. Another important statement is from the American Geophysical Union, "Human Impacts on Climate," December 2003, http://www.agu.org/sci_soc/policy/ climate_change_position.html. For the Bush Administration's perspective, see *Our Changing Planet: The U.S. Climate Change Science Program for Fiscal Years 2004 and 2005*, p.47; http://www.usgcrp.gov/ usgcrp/Library/ocp2004-5/default.htm. For the 2005 G8 statement, see http://www.number-10.gov.uk/output/Page7881.asp.

Analyze

1. Why are the evangelical leaders who signed this statement concerned about climate change?
2. What kind of document is this? A letter? A manifesto? An argument? A sermon? The writers speak directly to you as a reader and talk about themselves and their struggles and their faith. What is the effect of this rhetorical strategy?
3. Notice that the call to action talks about "stewardship" rather than sustainability. Think about the similarity of the religious concept of stewardship and moral responsibility the authors outline and the standard definitions of "sustainability." How could you use these comparisons to help other Christians understand sustainability?

Explore

1. The relations between science and religion are often complex in America. The debates over evolution and creation science are only one example of this tension. The members of the New Evangelical

Partnership for the Common Good cite contemporary science with confidence, but not all religious people believe in climate change. Go explore the New Evangelical Partnership's website and then search for other differing positions among religious groups or associations. How do other groups differ from the Evangelical Climate Initiative? And how does this debate frame the relationship between science and religion?

2. Go back to the Appendix of this book where it discusses arguments and the five actions most arguments include. Then work through this evangelical call to action and identify where and how they make these rhetorical moves as they construct their argument.

3. There are a number of public manifestos denying the reality of climate change. Go find one of them and compare how the authors argue with how the authors of this piece argue. Which kind of argument do you find most compelling and why?

Forging Connections

1. Several of these readings address and refute the argument that climate change is not caused by humans and is instead caused by other factors or is a natural phenomenon. Using several of the chapters from this section, construct an argument that climate change exists and is caused by humans, and offer illustrations about what its consequences are. Your goal is to persuade your audience that anthropogenic climate change exists, and that people ought to do something about it.

2. Many people do not accept the reality of climate change or don't worry about it because they say science is uncertain and doesn't know for sure. Using the readings in this chapter, write a letter to someone you know who thinks this way and try to explain the issue of uncertainty and give him or her good reasons to care about climate change even in the face of some degree of uncertainty.

Looking Further

1. Go online and find a calculator that helps you to calculate your own carbon footprint. Think about your own daily activities and how those activities contribute to your carbon footprint. Then decide what kinds of steps you would have to take to reduce this footprint and what kinds

of changes you have to make in your life to achieve that reduction. How would you make those changes? Would they be difficult? Would they be convenient? Using your own situation as a case in point, write an editorial for your university newspaper that persuades students to actually make changes in their lives to reduce their carbon footprints.

2. In the reading on empathy, Krznaric says that it is difficult to empathize with people distant in time and space. This reflects the book's Preface that says that sustainability is hard to see because of these same distances: time and space. The Appendix also talks about "rhetorical appeals," ways of appealing to readers' beliefs and values, and how they can assist you in persuading readers. Refer back to the Appendix and to the kinds of appeals you see in the readings (e.g., Freidman's essay in Chapter 5 on biodiversity) to write a blog post that tries to get readers to see and care about the distant consequences of our actions.

5 Energy: Supply, Demand, & Invisible Consequences

A wind farm: An ugly intrusion on the landscape? Or a beautiful form of sustainability?

Energy is probably the most obvious and most immediate topic in sustainability for most of us. Unfortunately, it is also one of the most difficult and complex issues as well. Oil, natural gas, and coal are finite resources; they are not being renewed. When we have used them up, they are gone for good. And the renewable alternatives like solar power, wind energy, nuclear energy, and biofuels are all promising and maybe even necessary, but they bring problems and challenges of their own. Almost everything in our industrialized society requires an abundant supply of energy, but supplying that energy at a reasonable price while reducing the environmental and social impact of energy production is difficult at best.

In 1956, Marlon K. Hubbert presented a paper to the annual meeting of the American Petroleum Institute, the oil industry's national trade group. Hubbert predicted that oil production in the United States would peak somewhere between 1965 and 1971. Hubbert's prediction was immediately challenged, but records on U.S. oil production between 1900 and 2010 match his prediction almost perfectly.

But oil is a global commodity, and it is difficult to apply Hubbert's theory of "peak oil" to world oil production and predict when world oil production will start to decline. It is hard to estimate the amount of known reserves worldwide, hard to predict technological innovations and increases in efficiency, hard to predict how many new energy reserves we will discover. So putting an exact date on "peak oil" and when we will reach that point of diminishing supplies is uncertain. Many critics now, however, refer to "peak *cheap* oil." The newly discovered sources of oil such as deep ocean oil fields and tar sands are increasingly difficult and expensive to develop. Almost everyone agrees that "conventional" oil that is relatively easy and cheap to pump and that fueled the economic growth of the 20th century has peaked already.

The theory of peak oil is highly controversial. Environmental groups and the oil industry have widely different estimates and agree on almost nothing. As Liz Barratt-Brown argues in her blog post printed in this chapter, how you "frame" an issue has a lot of influence on what people believe. Competing frames and competing claims can make careful decision making difficult. Despite the controversy, however, it is clear that some form of peak oil is real. The U.S. Department of Energy (DOE) published a report in 2005 titled *Peaking of World Oil Production: Impacts, Mitigation, & Risk Management*. This report doesn't put a date on the peak, but does conclude that "the peaking of world oil production presents the U.S. and the world with an unprecedented risk management problem." Similarly, the U.S. military's Joint Forces Command (USJFC) published a study in 2010 that concludes that "assuming the most optimistic scenario for improved petroleum production through enhanced recovery means, the development of non-conventional oils (such as oil shales, or tar sands and new discoveries) petroleum production will be hard pressed to meet the expected future demand of 118 million barrels per day" (DOE 24). Peak oil or peak *cheap* oil is the reality that makes sustainable energy a pressing issue. If the global supply of oil cannot meet the world's energy demands or if the price of petroleum goes too high, there will be economic and social crisis. And continuing to burn petroleum, especially the dirtier new forms of shale oil and tar sands oil, will increase the rate of global climate change. In their reports, the DOE and USJFC qualify their predictions with terms like "hard pressed" and avoid setting a precise date for peak oil, but both accept the basic theory and urge us to act now before it is too late.

To understand the impact of energy production and use, scientists and economists use many kinds of analysis. Two of the basic principles that shape their analysis are the concepts of *energy balance* and *unintended consequences*. Energy balance can be complicated to calculate, but it is a simple principle. If something takes more energy to produce than we can get from it, we lose. So, ethanol made from corn grain is often a bad option because of all the energy it takes to grow the corn, transport the corn grain to a processing plant, convert the corn into ethanol, and finally transport the ethanol to your local gas station. Similarly, as the essay on fracking points meant below, it takes a lot of energy to drill wells, produce and pump the fracking fluids down the well, transport all that water both to and from the well site, and then transport the gas. It is quite possible that our current boom in cheap natural gas uses more energy than it produces. In the long run, that is a losing proposition. We have to think about the big picture and consider all the parts of a system when we calculate whether an energy source is a "good thing" or not. Any business person makes a similar calculation: if it costs more to produce, market, and sell a product than the income the sale creates, you'll eventually go bankrupt.

Because energy is a global commodity and actions in one place have consequences in other, distant places, we also need to consider the unintended consequences of energy production. As Vandana Shiva points out, the demand for corn to produce biofuels creates an economic incentive for people in countries like Brazil and Indonesia to convert forests, swamps, and grasslands to farms that grow corn or palm oil for biofuel. Forests absorb carbon dioxide from the air and help reduce climate change. And burning forests not only reduces the amount of greenhouse gas they absorb, it also releases huge amounts of carbon dioxide into the atmosphere. The same is true of draining swamps or plowing grasslands. It would take hundreds of years of burning "cleaner" biofuels to make up for the huge pulse of greenhouse gas released by these land-use changes. And these changes also drive up the cost of basic foods for the poor in developing countries and reduce the diversity of plants, animals, and insects upon which the ecosystem depends.

There are many practical challenges facing us as we look for ways to reach a sustainable energy policy or lifestyle. The rhetorical challenges are equally difficult. Even with new technologies and new oilfields, people will have to change their behavior to get to a sustainable form of energy use. The question is: How do we convince people to change, especially when it means altering some of the basic patterns in their lives? The changes in their lives are real and immediate, but the benefits or the reasons for changing are invisible. They are abstract, long-term or distant. They are hard to see and even harder to feel. Similarly, many of the issues in global sustainability are hard for readers to understand and often conflict with their values. Consider Thomas Friedman's attempt to explain biodiversity and persuade readers to care about it. How do you get readers to really care about insects and amphibians in the Brazilian jungle?

National Research Council
"Energy Supply and Use"

The National Research Council (NRC) is an independent research organization associated with the National Academy of Sciences and the National
Academy of Engineering. Along with the Institute of Medicine, the NRC produces independent, expert reports on scientific, technological, and medical
issues. Over 6,000 scientific experts, including over 300 Nobel Laureates,
contribute to NRC reports. Because these reports are produced through a
rigorous process and are independently reviewed, they have an integrity and
authority that is crucial. When policymakers or the public need to make
decisions about what to do concerning scientific or technical issues, NRC
reports provide reliable information. The chapter on "Energy Supply and
Use" excerpted below describes energy use in the United States and reviews
all the possible alternative sources of energy. Notice that it does not make
a recommendation and that it describes the potential benefits as well as the
problems or limitations of each energy source.

Energy is essential for a wide range of human activities, both in the
United States and around the world, yet its use is the dominant source
of emissions of CO_2 and several other important climate forcing agents. In
addition to total demand for energy, the type of fuel used and the end-use
equipment affect CO_2 emissions. The diversity of ways in which energy is
supplied and used provides ample opportunities to reduce energy-related
emissions. However, achieving reductions can be very difficult, especially
because it involves considerations of human behavior and preferences;
economics; multiple time frames for decision making and results; and
myriad stakeholders.

Questions decision makers are asking, or will be asking, about energy
supply and consumption in the context of climate change include the
following:

- What options are currently available for limiting emissions of greenhouse gases (GHGs) and other climate forcing agents in the energy
  sector, and what are the most promising emerging technologies?

- What are the major obstacles to widespread adoption of new energy technologies that reduce GHG emissions?
- What are the best ways to promote or encourage the use of energy-conserving and low-GHG energy options?
- What impacts will climate change have on energy production, distribution, and consumption systems, and how should possible impacts be accounted for when designing and developing new systems and infrastructure?
- What are the possible unintended consequences of new energy sources for human and environmental well-being?

This chapter focuses on what is already known about energy and climate change and about what more needs to be known. Strategies to limit emissions of CO_2 and other GHGs through changes in agriculture practices, transportation, urban planning, and other approaches are addressed in other chapters, and policy approaches that span these strategies are discussed in Chapter 17. Because *America's Energy Future* was the focus of a recent suite of National Research Council reports (NRC, 2009a,b,c,d), and energy-related GHG emissions reductions are a major point of emphasis in the companion volume *Limiting the Magnitude of Future Climate Change* (NRC, 2010c), this chapter provides only a brief summary of critical knowledge and research needs in the energy sector.

Energy Consumption

Globally, total energy consumption grew from 4,675 to 8,286 million tons of oil equivalent between 1973 and 2007 (IEA, 2009). The United States is still the world's largest consumer of energy, responsible for 20 percent of world primary energy consumption. The next largest user, China, currently accounts for about 15 percent. Energy consumption in the United States has increased by about 1 percent per year since 1970, although there is no longer a direct relationship between energy use and economic growth. Between 1973 and 2008, for example, U.S. energy intensity, measured as the amount of energy used per dollar of gross domestic product (GDP), fell by half, or 2.1 percent

"The United States is still the world's largest consumer of energy."

per year (EIA, 2009). Despite this trend, the United States still has higher energy use per unit of GDP and per capita than almost all other developed nations. For example, Denmark's per capita energy use is about half that of the United States (NRC, 2009c).

A nation's energy intensity reflects population and demographic and environmental factors as well as the efficiency with which goods and services are provided, and consumer preference for these goods and services. Comparison of the energy intensity of the United States with that of other countries indicates that about half of the difference is due to differences in energy efficiency (NRC, 2009c). The differences also reflect structural factors such as the mix of industries (e.g., heavy industry versus light manufacturing[1]) and patterns of living, working, and traveling, each of which may have developed over decades or even centuries.

Today, about 40 percent of U.S. energy use is in the myriad private, 5 commercial, and institutional activities associated with residential and commercial buildings, while roughly 30 percent is used in industry and the same amount in the transport of goods and passengers. Most significantly for GHG emissions, 86 percent of the U.S. energy supply now comes from the combustion of fossil fuels—coal, oil, and natural gas (Figure 5.1). The transportation sector is 94 percent reliant on petroleum, 56 percent of which is imported (EIA, 2009).

There are important economic and national security issues related to the availability of fossil fuel resources, as well as significant environmental issues associated with their use—including, but not limited to, climate change. For example, the recent report Hidden Costs of Energy: Unpriced Consequences of Energy Production and Use (NRC, 2009f) estimated that the damages associated with energy production and use in the United States totaled at least $120 billion in 2005, mostly through the health impacts of fossil fuel combustion (and not including damages associated with climate change or national security, which are very difficult to quantify in terms of specific monetary damages). While this is undoubtedly a small fraction of the benefits that energy brings, it reinforces the message that there are significant benefits associated with reducing the use of energy from fossil fuels.

As discussed above and in Chapter 6, limiting the magnitude of future climate change will require significant reductions in climate forcing, and GHGs emitted by the energy sector are the single largest contributor. Hence, many strategies to limit climate change typically focus on reducing

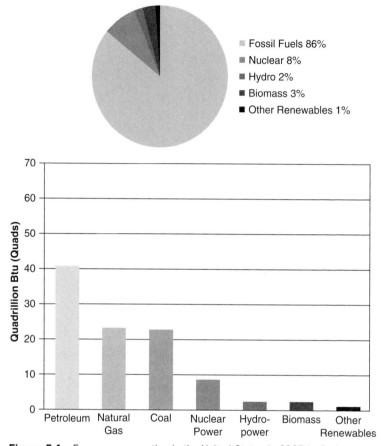

Figure 5.1 Energy consumption in the United States in 2007 by fuel source, in quadrillion Btu (bars) and as a percentage of total energy consumption (pie chart). Fossil fuels serve as the primary source of energy. Source: NRC (2009d).

GHG emissions from the energy sector. These strategies can be grouped into four major categories: (1) *reductions in demand,* typically through changes in behavior that reduce the demand for energy; (2) *efficiency improvements,* or reducing the amount of energy needed per unit of goods and services produced (also called energy intensity) through changes in systems, behaviors, or technologies; (3) development and deployment of *energy systems that emit few GHGs or other climate forcing agents*, or at least emit fewer GHGs per unit energy consumed than traditional fossil fuel-based technologies; and (4) *direct capture* of CO_2 or other GHGs during or after fossil fuel combustion. These general strategies are discussed briefly in subsequent sections.

Reductions in Energy Demand

The price mechanism can be an important part of any policy intended to reduce energy consumption. Prices encourage efficiency, discussed in the next section, but they can also change behavior. For example, if gasoline prices rise, whether from taxes or market forces, people who commute long distances may buy a more efficient vehicle or they may switch to public transportation or move closer to work. Nevertheless, the impact of prices on consumers and the economy is an important area for further research. It should be noted that prices are not the only feature involved in consumer choice, and the response to increased energy prices (the elasticity of demand) is often modest. There are many possible explanations for this: modest changes in price are not noticed, consumers cannot easily change some aspects of their consumption (for example, it is not always feasible to sell a car with low gas mileage to buy one with higher mileage when gas prices rise, at least in the short run), and there are many other factors that influence decisions that affect energy consumption and it may have more influence than prices (Carrico et al., 2010; Stern et al., in press; Wilson and Dowlatabadi, 2007).

Energy Efficiency Improvements

Although energy intensity has declined in the United States over the past 30 years (EIA, 2009; NRC, 2009d), per capita consumption in the United States still exceeds that of almost all other developed countries. In addition, a considerable fraction of the intensity improvements in the United States may be due to the changing nature of demand (e.g., the shift away from manufacturing toward a service- and information-based economy) as well as increased imports of energy-intensive products and materials, which simply shift emissions to other locations. The recent report *Real Prospects for Energy Efficiency in the United States* (NRC, 2009c), part of the *America's Energy Future* suite of activities, carried out a comprehensive review of methods to improve energy efficiency in industry, buildings, and transportation sectors. The report concludes that energy efficient technologies in those sectors exist today that could be implemented without major changes in lifestyles and could reduce energy use in the United States by 30 percent by 2030. The companion report *Limiting the Magnitude of Future Climate Change* (NRC, 2010c) also discusses energy efficiency at length.

10   The building sector offers the greatest potential for energy savings through efficiency; options range from simple approaches like insulation and caulking, to the use of more efficient appliances and lighting, to changing patterns of building use. Investments in these areas could reduce energy use in residences by one-third, although systematic estimates that take account of both technological and behavioral changes have not been made. For example, participation in programs that subsidize weatherization with identical financial incentives can differ by an order of magnitude depending on how the programs are presented to the public (Stern et al., 1986). Efficiency improvements can be made through the development and use of more efficient devices, with more efficient systems for managing devices, and with changing patterns of use—all of which require both technological innovation and a better understanding of human behavior and institutions.

While implementation of current technologies holds immediate opportunities for reducing energy use and GHG emissions, new technological and scientific advances are likely to yield longer-term benefits. For example, the development of new materials for insulation, new kinds of lighting, fundamental changes in heating and cooling systems, computational technologies for energy systems management, and landscape architecture and materials for natural cooling could all contribute to major improvements in energy efficiency. As noted in Chapter 13, energy efficiency advances are also possible in the next decade in the transportation sector due to improved vehicle technologies and behavior changes. However, simply developing and making a new technology available is not sufficient to ensure its adoption; to be effective, research on all energy technologies, including efficiency technologies, needs to include analysis of the barriers to adoption of innovation and of public acceptance of new technology.

Energy Sources That Reduce Emissions of Greenhouse Gases

• Technologies that reduce the amount of GHGs emitted during the production of usable energy include renewable energy sources such as solar, wind, bioenergy, geothermal, hydropower, as well as nuclear power and carbon capture and storage (CCS) applied to fossil fuels or biomass. Even switching among fossil fuels can reduce carbon emissions per unit of energy produced. The *America's Energy Future* study (NRC, 2009d) evaluated the near- and intermediate-term potential of each of these technologies and concluded that fossil fuels are likely to retain their dominant position in energy production over the next several decades; however, the study also identified numerous areas where investments in technologies and policy changes could hasten the transition to a low-GHG energy economy. Some of these areas are briefly summarized below, with an emphasis on the research needed to accelerate technology development and deployment.

Fuel Switching

Natural gas is the cleanest of the fossil fuels, with the lowest GHG emissions per unit of energy, emitting about half of the CO_2 of coal when burned for electricity generation, as well as generally lower emissions of other pollutants. Shifting electric generation from coal to natural gas could significantly reduce emissions. Such a shift would be useful but would not by itself reduce emissions sufficiently for a low-emissions future to minimize climate change. Thus, natural gas is more likely to be a bridge than a final solution. Additionally, the feasibility of natural gas as a bridge fuel will depend on the stringency of any emissions-limiting policies that are adopted.

Until recently, resources of natural gas were thought too small to support a transition. Recent improvements in technology have made economic unconventional gas resources, such as shale, leading to higher resource estimates. If these estimates are confirmed, natural gas could be a long-term option. However, there is some concern that shale gas development may have negative impacts on the local freshwater resources and land resources (DOE, 2009a). Another possible future source is natural gas hydrates found on the ocean floor, which are estimated to contain from one to a hundred times the world resource of conventional natural gas. Methods for recovery of hydrates are under investigation, but it is unlikely that hydrates would contribute significantly to the production of natural gas in the near term without major breakthroughs in the recovery process (NRC, 2010h).

Solar Energy

15   The total solar energy incident on the surface of the earth averages about 86,000 terawatts (TW), which is more than 5,000 times the 15 TW of energy currently used by humans (of which roughly 12 TW now comes from fossil fuels) and more than 100 times larger than the energy potential of the next largest renewable source, wind energy (Hermann, 2006). Hence, the potential resource of solar energy is essentially limitless, which has led many to conclude that it is the best energy resource to rely on in the long run. Currently, this resource is exploited on a limited scale—total installed worldwide solar energy production totaled 15 gigawatts (GW) in 2008,[2] or just 0.1 percent of total energy production, with similar penetration in the United States (EIA, 2009). Solar energy can be used to generate electricity and heat water for domestic use. Passive solar heating can be used in direct heating and cooling of buildings.

There are two main classes of solar energy technology used to generate electricity: concentrating solar power (CSP) and photovoltaics (PVs). CSP technologies use optics (lenses or mirrors) to concentrate beam radiation, which is the portion of the solar radiation not scattered by the atmosphere. The radiation energy is converted to high-temperature heat that can be used to generate electricity or drive chemical reactions to produce fuels (syngas or hydrogen). CSP technologies require high-quality solar resources, and this restricts its application in the United States to the southwest part of the country. However, CSP technologies are commercially available and there are a number of upcoming projects in the United States, particularly in California. The CSP industry estimates 13.4 GW could be deployed for service by 2015 (WGA, 2006). In the short term, incremental design improvements will drive down costs and reduce uncertainty in performance predictions. With more systems installed, there will be increased economies of scale, both for plant sites and for manufacturing. However, new storage technologies, such as molten salt, will be needed in the longer term to make widespread CSP deployment feasible. The global research community is studying the use of concentrated solar energy to produce fuels through high-temperature chemical processing (Fletcher, 2001; Perkins and Weimer, 2004, 2009; Steinfeld, 2005). At the international scale, the SolarPACES organization is working to further the development and deployment of CSP systems.[3] This organization brings experts from member countries together to attempt to address technical issues associated with commercialization of these technologies.

While incremental improvements in CSP performance are anticipated, there is the potential for large improvements in PV electricity generation technologies. Over the past 30 years, the efficiency of PV technologies has steadily improved, though commercial modules achieve, on average, only about 10 to 15 percent efficiency (that is, only 10 to 15 percent of the solar energy incident on the cell is converted into electricity), which is 50 percent or less of the efficiency of the best research cells (NRC, 2009d). Most current PV generation is produced by technologies that rely on silicon wafers to convert photons to electrons (Green, 2003; Lewis, 2007). Recent shortages of polycrystalline silicon have increased prices for PV modules and spurred increases in the use of thin-film solar PV technologies that do not require as much or any silicon. Thin-film solar PV technologies have about a 40 percent market share in the United States (EIA, 2009). In the short term, research is continuing on PV technologies; most of the work on improving these cells has focused on identifying new materials, new device geometries (including thin films), and new manufacturing techniques (Ginley et al., 2008).

The overall costs of a PV system, not just the costs of PV cells, determine its competitiveness with other sources of electricity. For example, approximately 50 percent or more of the total installed cost of a rooftop PV system is not in the module cost but in the costs of installation, and of the inverter, cables, support structures, grid hookups, and other components. These costs must come down through innovative system-integration approaches, or this aspect of a PV system will set a floor on the price of a fully installed PV system. In the medium term, new technologies are being developed to make conventional solar cells by using nanocrystalline inks as well as semi-conducting materials. Thin-film technologies have the potential for substantial cost reduction over current wafer-based crystalline silicon methods because of factors such as lower material use, fewer processing steps, and simpler manufacturing technology for large-area modules. Thin-film technologies have many advantages, such as high throughput and continuous production rate, lower-temperature and nonvacuum processes, and ease of film deposition. Even lower costs are possible with plastic organic solar cells, dye-sensitized solar cells, nanotechnology-based solar cells, and other new PV technologies.

If next-generation solar technologies continue to improve and external costs associated with emissions from fossil fuel-based electricity are incorporated into the cost of electricity, it is possible that solar technologies could produce electricity at costs per kilowatt-hour competitive with fossil fuels. This transition could be accelerated through carefully designed subsidies for solar energy, as several other countries have done, or by placing a price on carbon emissions (Crabtree and Lewis, 2007; Green, 2005). Modifications to the energy distribution network along with energy storage would also improve the ability to exploit solar energy resources. However, it should be noted that a bifurcated market for PV systems exists, depending on whether the system is installed on a customer's premises (behind the meter) or as a utility-scale generation resource. Behind-the-meter systems compete by displacing customer-purchased electricity at retail rates, while utility-scale plants must compete against wholesale electricity prices. Thus, behind-the-meter systems can often absorb a higher overall system cost structure. In the United States, much of the development of solar has occurred in this behind-the-meter market (NRC, 2009d).

20   There are several potential adverse impacts associated with widespread deployment of solar technologies. Utility-scale solar electricity technologies would require considerable land area. When CSP is used with a conventional steam turbine, the water requirements are comparable to fossil fuel-fired plants, making water availability a concern and, in some cases, a limiting factor. For PV technology, there are also concerns associated with the availability of raw materials (particularly a few rare earth elements; NRC, 2008f) and with the potential that some manufacturing processes might produce toxic wastes. Finally, the energy payback time, which is a measure of how much time it takes for an energy technology to generate enough useful energy to offset energy consumed during its lifetime, is fairly long for silicon-based PV.

In addition to electricity generation, nonconcentrating solar thermal technologies can displace fossil fuels at the point of use, particularly in residential and commercial buildings. The most prevalent and well-developed applications are for heating swimming pools and potable water (in homes and laundries). Systems include one or more collectors (which capture the sun's energy and convert it into usable heat), a distribution structure, and a thermal storage unit. The use of nonconcentrating solar thermal systems to provide space heating and cooling in residential and commercial buildings could provide a greater reduction of fossil fuels than do water heaters, but at present it is largely an untapped opportunity. Recently there has been limited deployment of liquid-based solar collectors for radiant floor-heating systems and solar air heaters, but the challenge with these applications is the relatively large collector area required in the absence of storage. Solar cooling can be accomplished via absorption and desiccant cycles, but commercial systems are not widely available for residential use.

Wind Energy

Wind electricity generation is already a mature technology and approximately cost competitive in many areas of the country and the world, especially with electricity generated from natural gas. The installed capacity for electricity generated from wind at the end of 2009 was approximately 159 GW, or about 2 percent of worldwide energy usage (WWEA, 2010). Wind turbine size has been increasing as technology has developed, and offshore wind farms are being constructed and proposed worldwide. As with solar power, wind energy alone could theoretically meet the world's energy needs (Archer and Jacobson, 2005), but a number of barriers prevent it from doing so, including dependence on location, intermittency, and efficiency. Other estimates of the resource base are not as large, but also indicate the United States has significant wind energy resources. Elliott et al. (1991) estimate that the total electrical energy potential for the continental U.S. wind resource in class 3 and higher wind-speed areas is 11 million GWh per year. As noted in NRC (2009d), this resource estimate is uncertain, however, and the actual wind resource could be higher due to the low altitude this estimate was developed at, or lower due to the inaccuracy of point estimates for assessing large-scale wind-power extractions (Roy et al., 2004). Assuming an estimated upper limit of 20 percent extraction from this base, an upper value for the extractable wind electric potential would be about 2.2 million GWh/yr, equal to more than half of the total electricity generated in 2007. This estimate does not incorporate the substantial offshore wind resource base. Development of offshore wind power plants has already begun in Europe, but progress has been slower in the United States. Though offshore wind power poses additional technical challenges, these challenges are being addressed by other countries. However, political, organizational, social, and economic obstacles may continue to inhibit investment in offshore wind power development in the United States, given the higher risk compared to onshore wind energy development (Williams and Zhang, 2008).

The key technological issues for wind power focus on continuing to develop better turbine components and to improve the integration of wind power into the electricity system, including operations and maintenance, evaluation, and forecasting. Goals appear relatively straightforward: taller towers, larger rotors, power electronics, reducing the weight of equipment at the top and cables coming from top to bottom, and ongoing progress through the design and manufacturing learning curve (DOE, 2008a; Thresher et al., 2007). Basic research in materials and composites is expected to lead to improved and more efficient wind energy systems, for example by improving the efficiency of turbines for use in low-windspeed areas (DOE, 2009c). Research on materials reliability and stabilizing control systems could help reduce maintenance requirements and further enable wind machines to survive extreme weather events. Continued research on forecasting techniques, operational and system design, and optimal siting requirements would improve the integration of wind power into the electricity system. As with solar energy technologies, modifications to the electricity transmission and distribution system along with energy storage capacity would also improve the ability to exploit wind energy resources.

Along with technology advances, research on policy and institutional factors affecting the widespread implementation of wind systems is needed, as well as continued assessment of the potential adverse impacts of wind energy systems—for example, past research has shown that adverse impacts on flying animals, especially birds and bats, can be reduced both with advanced turbine technologies and by considering migration corridors when siting wind farms (NRC, 2007e). Siting is also critical in order to reduce potential negative effects on the viewscape, effects on noise, and unintended consequences on local wind and perhaps weather patterns (Keith et al., 2004). Concerns with the adverse effects of wind farms have led to substantial public opposition on some areas (Firestone et al., 2009; Swofford and Slattery, 2010). Further research and analysis of these factors would help decision makers evaluate wind energy plans and weigh alternative land uses—for agriculture, transportation, urbanization, biodiversity conservation, recreation, and other uses—to maximize co-benefits and reduce unintended consequences.

Bioenergy

Bioenergy refers to liquid or solid fuels derived from biological sources and 25
used for heat, electricity generation, or transportation. Electricity generation using biomass is much the same as that from fossil fuels; it generally
involves a steam turbine cycle. The key difference is that typical output for
a wood-based biomass power plant is about 50 MW, while conventional
coal-fired plants generally produce anywhere from 100 to 1,500 MW
(NRC, 2009a).

In the United States, interest in biomass for energy production is usually
in the form of liquid transportation fuels. Such biofuels currently take several forms, including biodiesel, the sugarcane-based ethanol systems used
widely in Brazil, and the corn-based ethanol system that has been encouraged through subsidies in the United States. While the sugarcane system
has an energy output that is more than five times greater than the energy
input, corn ethanol has an energy output that on average is slightly greater
than its input, and thus does not significantly reduce GHG emissions
(Arunachalam and Fleischer, 2008; Farrel et al., 2006). Ongoing research
into cellulosic feedstocks, algae-based fuels, and other next-generation biofuel sources could lead to more favorable bioenergy effects and economics.
Other areas of research include improving the productivity of current
bioenergy crops through genetic engineering (Carroll and Sommerville,
2009), reducing the environmental impact of bioenergy crops by growing
native species on marginal lands (McLaughlin et al., 2002; Schmer et al.,
2008), and developing biofuels that can be used within the current,
petroleum-based fuel infrastructure (NRC, 2009b).

Many different disciplines are contributing to the development of new
bioenergy strategies, including biochemistry, bioenergetics, genomics,
and biomimetics research. For example, research in plant biology,
metabolism, and enzymatic properties will support the development of
new forms of biofuel crops that could potentially have high yields, drought
resistance, improved nutrient use efficiency, and tissue chemistry that en-
hances fuel production and carbon sequestration potential. Significant
research is also being directed toward strategies for cellulose treatment,
sugar transport, and the use of microbes to break down different types of
complex biomass, as well as on advanced biorefineries that can produce
biofuels, biopower, and commercial chemical products. Many developments in biofuels have been recently summarized (see DOE, 2009c;
NRC, 2008a, 2009b).

Widescale development of bioenergy crops could have significant unintended negative consequences if not managed carefully. Conversion of solar energy to chemical energy by ecosystems is typically less than 0.5 percent efficient, yielding less than 1 W/m^2, so relatively large land areas would be required for biomass to be a major source of energy (Larson, 2007; Miyamoto, 1997; NRC, 1980a). If the land required to grow bioenergy crops comes from deforesting or converting natural lands, there could be a net increase in GHG emissions as well as losses of biodiversity and ecosystem services. If grown on marginal lands, increased emissions of N_2O, a potent GHG, may result as a side effect of nitrogen fertilizer use (Wise et al., 2009b). If bioenergy crops are grown on existing agricultural areas, food prices and food security could be compromised (Crutzen et al., 2008; Searchinger et al., 2008). Production of bioenergy crops also has the potential to negatively impact water quality and availability for other uses (NRC, 2008i), and methods are needed to more fully assess their potential impacts on ecosystem services (Daily and Matson, 2008). The recent report *Liquid Transportation Fuels from Coal and Biomass* (NRC, 2009b) contains a more detailed discussion of the potential environmental and ecosystem impacts and provides recommendations for sustainable methods for increased bioenergy use. Focused interdisciplinary research efforts are needed to develop such methods and more fully assess the full spectrum of possible benefits and side effects associated with different bioenergy production strategies.

Geothermal Energy

There are three components to the geothermal resource base: (1) geothermal heating and cooling, or direct heating and cooling by surface or near-surface geothermal energy; (2) hydrothermal systems involving the production of electricity using hot water or steam accessible within approximately 3 km of Earth's surface; and (3) enhanced geothermal systems (EGS) using hydraulic stimulation to mine the heat stored in low-permeability rocks at depths down to 10 km and use it to generate electricity. Currently, geothermal heating provides approximately 28 GW of energy (mainly for heating and industrial applications). For example, municipalities and smaller communities provide district heating by circulating the hot water from aquifers through a distribution pipeline to the points of use. The barriers to increased penetration of direct geothermal heating and cooling systems are not technical, but with the high initial investment costs and the challenges associated with developing appropriate sites. The resource for direct heating is richest in the western states, and geothermal heat pumps have extended the use of geothermal energy into traditionally nongeothermal areas of the United States, mainly the Midwestern and eastern states. A geothermal heat pump draws heat from the ground, groundwater, or surface water and discharges heat back to those media instead of into the air. The electric heat pump is standard off-the-shelf equipment available for installation in residences and commercial establishments. There are no major technical barriers to greater deployment. The United States currently has 700,000 installed units and the rate of installation is estimated to be 10,000 to 50,000 units per year (NRC, 2009d). One barrier to growth is the lack of sufficient infrastructure (i.e., trained designers and installers) and another is the high initial investment cost compared to conventional space-conditioning equipment.

In terms of electricity generation, hydrothermal systems are mature systems relying on conventional power-generating technologies. Technology is not a major barrier to developing conventional hydrothermal resources, but improvements in drilling and power conversion technologies could result in cost reductions and greater reliability. There is some potential for expanding electricity production from hydrothermal resources and thus providing additional regional electricity generation. For example, a study of known hydrothermal resources in the western states found that 13 GW of electric power capacity exists in identified resources within this region (WGA, 2006). However, in general the potential for major expansion of electricity produced from hydrothermal resources in the United States is relatively small and concentrated in the western states.

Enhanced geothermal systems represent the much larger resource base—the theoretical potential EGS resource below the continental United States is over 130,000 times the total 2005 U.S. energy consumption (MIT, 2006). Though this resource is vast, it exists at great depths and low fluxes. Accessing the stored thermal energy would first require stimulating the hot rock by drilling a well to reach the hot rock, and then using high-pressure water to create a fractured rock region. Drilling injection and production wells into the fractured region would follow next, and the stored heat would then be extracted, using water circulating in the injection well. The heat extraction rate would depend on the site. EGS reservoirs can cool significantly during heat-mining operations, reducing extraction efficiency with time and requiring periodic redrilling, fracturing, and hydraulic stimulation. Even so, the MIT report assumes that the individual reservoirs would only last around 20 to 30 years. Other challenges include a general lack of experience in drilling to depths approaching 10 km, concerns with induced seismicity, the need to enhance heat transfer performance for lower-temperature fluids in power production, and improving reservoir-stimulation techniques so that sufficient connectivity within the fractured rock can be achieved. Further research and demonstration projects will thus be needed before EGS is deployed on large scales.

Hydropower

Technologies for converting energy from water to electricity include conventional hydroelectric technologies and emerging hydrokinetic technologies that can convert ocean tidal currents, wave energy, and thermal gradients into electricity. Conventional hydroelectricity or hydropower, the largest source of renewable electricity, comes from capturing the energy from freshwater rivers and converting it to electricity. Hydroelectric power supplies about 715,000 megawatts (MW), or 19 percent, of world electricity. In the United States, conventional hydropower provides approximately 7 percent of the nation's energy (USGS, 2009). Hydropower is regionally important, providing about 70 percent of the energy used in the Pacific Northwest (PNWA, 2009).

Since this resource has been extensively exploited, most prime sites are no longer available. Furthermore, there is increasing recognition of negative ecosystem consequences from hydropower development. Future hydropower technological developments will relate to increasing the efficiency of existing facilities and mitigating the dams' negative consequences, especially on anadromous fish. Existing hydropower capacity could be expanded by increasing capacity at existing sites; installing electricity-generating capabilities at flood-control, irrigation, or water supply reservoirs; and developing new hydropower sites (EPRI, 2007a). Turbines at existing sites also could be upgraded to increase generation. None of these strategies require new technologies.

Because use of the conventional hydroelectric resource is generally accepted to be near the resource base's maximum capacity in the United States, further growth will largely depend on nonconventional hydropower resources such as low-head power[4] and on microhydroelectric generation.[5] A 2004 Department of Energy (DOE) study of total U.S. water-flow-based energy resources, with emphasis on low-head/low-power resources, indicated that the total U.S. domestic hydropower resource capacity was 170 GW of electric power (DOE, 2004). However, these numbers represent only the identified resource base that was undeveloped and was not excluded from development. A subsequent study assessed this identified resource base for feasibility of development (DOE, 2006). After taking into consideration local land use policies, local environmental concerns, site accessibility, and development criteria, this value was reduced to 30 GW of potential hydroelectric capacity (DOE, 2006). A report from the Electric Power Research Institute (EPRI) determined that 10 GW of additional hydroelectric resource capacity could be developed by 2025 (EPRI, 2007). Of the 10 GW of potential capacity, 2.3 GW would result from capacity gains at existing hydroelectric facilities, 2.7 GW would come from small and low-power conventional hydropower facilities, and 5 GW would come from new hydropower generation at existing non-powered dams.

New technologies to generate electricity from ocean water power include those that can harness energy from currents, ocean waves, and salinity and thermal gradients. There are many pilot-scale projects demonstrating technologies tapping these sources, but only a few commercial-scale power operations worldwide at particularly favorable locations. In general, there is no single technological design for converting energy in waves, tides, and currents into electricity. For example, approaches for tapping wave energy include floating and submerged designs that tap the energy in the impacting wave directly or that use the hydraulic gradient between the top and bottom of a wave (MMS, 2006). One such device concentrates waves and allows them to overtop into a reservoir, generating electricity as the water in the reservoir drains out through a turbine. Other approaches include long multi-segmented floating structures that use the differing heights to drive a hydraulic pump that runs a generator or subsurface buoys that generate electricity through their up-down motion. Over the next 10 years, many large-scale demonstration projects will be completed to help assess the capabilities of these technologies, though it will take at least 10 to 25 years to know whether these technologies are viable for the production of significant amounts of electricity (NRC, 2009d). Over the longer term, other significant potential technologies that use ocean thermal and salinity gradients to generate electricity may also be investigated. However, these technologies currently only exist as conceptual designs, laboratory experimentation, and field trials. In general, even though waves, currents, and gradients contain substantive amounts of energy resources, there are significant technological and cost issues to address before such sources can contribute significantly to electricity generation. Storms and other metrological events also pose significant issues for hydrokinetic technologies.

Nuclear Power

35   Nuclear power is an established technology that could meet a significant portion of the world's energy needs. France obtains roughly 78 percent of its electricity from nuclear sources and Japan obtains 27 percent (EIA, 2007). About 20 percent of U.S. electricity comes from nuclear reactors, by far the largest source of GHG-free energy (EIA, 2009).[6] The reliability of U.S. reactors has increased dramatically over the past several decades, but no nuclear power plants had been ordered for over 30 years, largely because of high costs, uncertain markets, and public opposition. Improved availability and upgrades have kept nuclear power's share of generation constant at 20 percent despite the growth of other generation technologies. A nuclear revival has been initiated recently, largely because of concerns over limiting the magnitude of climate change. The U.S. government is providing loan guarantees for the first set of plants now being planned to compensate for uncertainties in costs and regulation. If these plants are successful in coming online at reasonable cost, their numbers could grow rapidly.

While nuclear power does not emit GHGs, there are other serious concerns associated with its production, including radioactive wastes (especially long-term storage of certain isotopes), safety, and security concerns related to the proliferation of nuclear weapons (MIT, 2003). The absence of a policy solution for the disposal of long-lived nuclear wastes, while not technically an impediment to the expansion of nuclear power, is still a concern for decision makers. New reactor construction has been barred in 13 U.S. states as a result, although several of these states are reconsidering their bans. Safety concerns stem from the potential for radioactive releases from the reactor core or spent fuel pool following an accident or terrorist attack. Nuclear reactors include extensive safeguards against such releases, and the probability of one happening appears to be very low. Nevertheless, the possibility cannot be ruled out, and such concerns are important factors in public acceptance of nuclear power. Proliferation of nuclear weapons is a related concern, but after 40 years of debate, there is no consensus as to whether U.S. nuclear power in any way contributes to potential weapons proliferation. A critical question is whether there are multilateral approaches that can successfully decouple nuclear power from nuclear weapons (Socolow and Glaser, 2009). Finally, public opinion is less skeptical of nuclear power in the abstract than it once was, but a majority of Americans oppose the location of nuclear (and coal or natural gas) power plants near them (Ansolabere and Konisky, 2009; Rosa, 2007). Some evidence suggests that the lack of support for nuclear power is based in part on a lack of trust in the nuclear industry and federal regulators (Whitfield et al., 2009).

Current U.S. nuclear power plants were built with technology developed in the 1960s and 1970s. In the intervening decades, ways to make better use of existing plants have been developed, along with new technologies that improve safety and security, decrease costs, and reduce the amount of generated waste—especially high-level waste. These technological innovations include improvements or modification of existing plants, alternative new plant designs (e.g., thermal neutron reactor and fast neutron reactor designs), and the use of alternative (closed) nuclear fuel cycles. The new technologies under development may allay some of the concerns noted above, but it will be necessary to determine the functionality, safety, and economics of those technologies through demonstration and testing.

Finally, research on nuclear fusion has been funded at several hundred million dollars per year since the 1970s. Fusion promises essentially unlimited, non-GHG energy, but harnessing it has proved to be extremely difficult. Most research addresses magnetic confinement (e.g., Tokamak reactors), but laser fusion (inertial confinement) also has promise. While fusion research and development is still worthwhile, it is uncertain whether a workable, cost-effective, power-producing reactor can be developed.

NOTES

1. In accounting for the energy or environmental implications of shifts in the mix of products produced and consumed in the economy, it is important to consider trade flows. For example, if a reduction in domestic production of steel is offset by an increase in steel imports, domestic GHG emissions may appear to decline but there may be no net global reduction in GHG emissions (and emissions may even increase, given the possibility of differences in production-related emissions and the energy expended in transporting the imported product). This concept is an important factor in negotiations over international climate policy.

2. Energy production is generally reported as the "nameplate capacity" or the maximum amount of energy that could be produced from a given source. For energy sources such as solar or wind, which are intermittent in nature, the actual output is often lower than the nameplate capacity.

3. See http://www.solarpaces.org/inicio.php.

4. Vertical difference of 100 feet or less in the upstream surface water elevation (headwater) and the downstream surface water elevation (tailwater) at a dam.

5. Hydroelectric power installations that produce up to 100 kW of power.

6. Total generation of electricity from nuclear power in the United States is greater than in France or Japan.

Analyze

1. According to the article, how does energy relate to climate change?

2. Name at least three problems associated with traditional energy use discussed in the article. What are some of the problems with developing energy sources?

3. The issues concerning energy discussed in this piece affect different people in different ways. In business, affected parties are referred to as stakeholders. Create a chart in which you list as many stakeholders in the energy problem as you can—business owners, drivers, and governmental officials are just a few. List in your chart how or why each stakeholder might have an interest in the issues of energy raised by the article (for example, money might be one interest common to several stakeholders).

Explore

1. In the section "Energy Sources That Reduce Emissions of Greenhouse Gases," the author discusses a number of energy sources at length. Select five energy sources discussed and synthesize the author's explanation into a single sentence for each.

2. In this piece, the terms "energy" and "energy use" refer to a large number of processes and practices. Looking back over the article, write down as many terms as you can find that refer to energy and energy use—for example, agricultural practices and transportation, fossil

fuels, and wind are all relevant terms. Then, create a map using lines and arrows to connect terms that relate to one another in some way. As you make connections, think about how we can categorize "energy" in a number of different ways.

3. This reading suggests that "there is no free lunch" when it comes to energy: every option has advantages and drawbacks. Use this information to construct a reader-friendly blog post that suggests how we might best address the question of sustainable energy use and policy. Is the solution new sources of energy? Is the solution conservation?

Liz Barratt-Brown
"It Is All About the Framing: How Polls and the Media Misrepresent the Keystone XL[Tar Sands] [Oil] Pipeline"

Liz Barratt-Brown is a staff member at the Natural Resources Defense Council (NRDC), a nonprofit, nonpartisan environmental advocacy group. The NRDC was founded in 1970 and has 1.3 million members and employs 400 scientists, lawyers, and other staff. Barratt-Brown, a senior advisor at the NRDC, has an A.B. in Environmental Studies from Brown University and a J.D. from Yale Law School. For the last five years, she has been working to stop tar sands oil production in Canada and the Keystone XL pipeline. The tar sands oil that would flow through the Keystone XL pipeline is an especially "dirty" fuel that creates a great deal of greenhouse gas. Further, mining, processing, and transporting the tar sand oil poses a number of serious environmental risks. As Barratt-Brown's blog post suggests, the Keystone XL pipeline has been a hot-button political topic for the last few years. Her discussion, however, is about how the issue is "framed" in the media. Is it, for example, "the Keystone Energy Project" or the "Keystone Tar Sand Pipeline"?

First of all, you won't find *tar sands* mentioned in any of the polling. And in most polls, you won't even find *oil*. It's just the Keystone XL pipeline, no context, no mention of what it will carry, and certainly no mention of the environmental risks of building a massive pipeline to carry toxic tar sands sludge through the heartland of America to the Gulf of Mexico, where it would be exported out of the U.S.

The question asked by two recent polls, one by Rasmussen and the other by the National Journal, was more or less, "Do you support or oppose building the Keystone XL pipeline?" And the Rasmussen poll also asks if job creation is more important than protecting the environment, posing these two goals as oppositional.

Most Americans don't see it that way. In our opinion research and other opinion research, such as the major new survey in the West, Americans overwhelmingly believe that a strong economy and the environment can go hand in hand. And they show a real concern for protecting resources, such as our water supply, from degradation. But both the Rasmussen and the National Journal polls show a majority of Americans in favor of the Keystone XL pipeline.

But are they really?

5   What if the pollsters changed the question to more accurately represent the actual project and inserted "tar sands oil pipeline"? What if they described to the public that the pipeline would jeopardize one of America's most important freshwater aquifers, the Ogallala? What if they were told that a first pipeline just like the Keystone XL tar sands pipeline and built by the same foreign company, TransCanada, had had over 12 spills in the U.S. (30 if you count Canada) in just its first year of operation? What if they were told that the oil is not really oil but a toxic sludge that is largely strip mined from under the Boreal forest in Canada and has to be diluted with toxic chemicals and pushed through pipelines at high temperature and pressure in pipelines only regulated to carry conventional oil? And what if the public were given the opportunity to choose a tar sands oil pipeline or increasing our reliance on homegrown renewable energy?

No poll has set this tar sands pipeline in any kind of context. Instead most of the questions are preceded or followed by generic questions about jobs and the economy or with questions about whether the country is going in the right direction.

So, without context, what do you think most Americans would first think of when asked about a pipeline?

Jobs and the economy.

And that is just the framing they have also been hearing again and again from the media.

Take jobs as an example. Job creation has been the major argument put   10
forward by pipeline proponents. Even though TransCanada is on record admitting that there would in fact be no more than 6,500 jobs over two years and only hundreds of permanent jobs, that has not stopped the company, the American Petroleum Institute, Republicans on the Hill and the Republican Presidential candidates from saying the pipeline would create hundreds of thousands of jobs and putting it forward as a national jobs plan rather than the single construction project that it is. The jobs estimates have been so wild that Stephen Colbert couldn't resist poking fun at the million jobs pipeline.

Lots of Americans are suffering right now and jobs creation must be a top priority but at what price and who benefits? The one independent study that has been done on the jobs issue, by Cornell Global Labor Institute, found that the Keystone XL tar sands pipeline would be a jobs killer because it would suppress clean energy jobs and because inevitable spills would cost jobs in other sectors of the economy. When all of the risk is being underwritten by American families and the major beneficiaries are the major oil companies, you have to ask is this good for our economy in the long run? Roger Toussaint of the Transit Workers of America said it best when he said, "We want jobs but not as gravediggers for the planet."

So let's dig in a bit regarding what the public has been hearing.

Media Matters, a nonprofit organization that tracks the media, released a survey that analyzed coverage of the Keystone XL tar sands pipeline from August 1 to December 31, 2011. They found that the media overwhelmingly framed the pipeline as a jobs issue. In 33% of the broadcast coverage, the highly inflated jobs numbers were repeated verbatim. In none of this coverage was any criticism of those figures mentioned. It was not much better for cable news. In 45% of the coverage, the figures were repeated verbatim. And only 11% of the coverage mentioned any criticism. Fox News repeated the jobs numbers more than all the other TV networks combined. Print news was not much better, with 29% repeating the jobs figures verbatim and only 5% mentioning any criticism.

It also seems to matter who you interview.

Here is a figure that really made me shake my head—79% of the   15
time, broadcast news reporting on the Keystone XL tar sands pipeline

interviewed a pipeline proponent. Only 7% of the time did they interview a tar sands pipeline opponent. Cable news was not much better: 59% of the coverage featured proponents and only 16% featured opponents. Print news did slightly better with 45% featuring proponents and 31% featuring opponents.

And this was over the period of time when there were 1250 peaceful protesters arrested in front of the White House and then a few months later when nearly 15,000 people gathered and encircled the White House opposing the pipeline. It was during the months when an Inspector General investigation was launched into the State Department mishandling of the environmental review. And it covered the period when the President declared that more environmental studies needed to be conducted to understand the risks of the pipeline to the American public and find a new route that avoided the sensitive Ogallala and Sandhills regions of Nebraska. Media Matters collected data on how jobs and energy security mentions compared to environmental mentions. In broadcast, cable, and print respectively, jobs were mentioned 67%, 77%, and 68% of the time. Energy security was mentioned 22%, 28%, and 54% respectively. And environment was mentioned 17%, 34%, and 65%. Coverage of the State Department mishandling of the review process was scarcely mentioned at all.

What's more is that since Media Matters did their survey, the rhetoric around the pipeline has become even more extreme and even venues like the New York Times, which has been one of the exceptions in providing fair coverage of the pipeline, are running political stories about the pipeline that don't include any environmental perspective.

So it is not surprising that when Americans are polled by Rasmussen and the National Journal, where they throw out a few quick questions or maybe just one question on the pipeline, we're getting higher than expected levels of support. Given the Media Matters survey, I am frankly surprised the numbers aren't worse.

I went to Google Speaker Boehner's statements on Keystone XL and I found that "Keystone" is actually one of the words most frequently associated with the Speaker (after crying, birthday song, and payroll taxes). That's because he and the Republicans in Congress have taken up the pipeline as a holy crucible. The reality is that the "Keystone Energy Project"—as he likes to describe it (notice we lose even the mention of pipeline)—is the top bidding of the oil industry. After defeating the climate legislation on the Hill, there has been no higher priority. And in addition to the lopsided media coverage, Americans have also been deluged with ads about the benefits of the pipeline.

Fortunately, most Americans have a heavy dose of skepticism when it comes to the oil industry. So maybe, just maybe, when people hear the pollsters' question, they hesitate for a moment and wonder what is all this pipeline fuss really about.   20

So what can we conclude? I'd wager that if you ask people if they think building a new pipeline will create jobs, they will inevitably say yes. But if you were to provide context and ask them if they wanted to risk their drinking water, greater energy self-reliance, and providing a future for our kids that does not trade off our climate and drinking water to line the pockets of the multi-national oil companies, I suspect they'd say no.

There desperately needs to be an improvement in both poll taking and in media coverage so that there can be a fair and balanced debate about this tar sands mega pipeline. So far, the debate has been anything but balanced and that does the American public a great disservice.

Addendum: On February 6, Politico reported that a Hart poll showed that once independents better understand the pro and con arguments for the tar sands pipeline, they agree with the President's decision to delay the pipeline by a margin of 47% to 36% (Democrats are already on side in strong margins). They are particularly concerned that risks to water supplies from pipeline spills, especially over the heartland's Ogallala aquifer, be addressed. The poll was conducted in late January in Colorado, Michigan, Iowa, and Ohio.

Analyze

1. According to the article, why did the polls leave the terms "tar sands" and "oil" out of their questionnaires?
2. What does the author mean by the term "framing"?
3. Is the proposed Keystone XL pipeline a jobs project? An energy resource? An environmental hazard? All of the above? How should we "frame" the debate?

Explore

1. The author states that both print and commercial media disproportionately portrayed perspectives in favor of the Keystone pipeline.

Do your own research and find a print article that reports on the pipeline in a critical way. Then construct an abstract of the article that describes how the piece frames the pipeline controversy. What kinds of sources and evidence does it use? Whom does it cite? What is its purpose?

2. The notion of rhetorical choice is important in this article's discussion. Visit a website sponsored by an oil-based company (BP, Mobil, etc.) and look at how they frame their discussion of their jobs, mission statement, or practices. Then, visit a website run by an environmentalist group that strongly opposes infringing on the environment for the purposes of securing more stable oil reserves. Do you notice similarities? Differences? Make a list of the most commonly used buzzwords or terms.

3. When you appeal to readers' values and habits, you are already "framing" an issue in ways that you think readers will understand and with which they will agree. Try reframing the Keystone XL debate in three different ways by appealing to different kinds of beliefs and values.

Climate Guest Blogger
"'Thinking Big' on Efficiency Could Cut U.S. Energy Costs up to $16 Trillion and Create 1.9 Million Net Jobs by 2050"

This news release announcing a major new report on energy efficiency was posted on the *Climate Progress* blog by the American Council for an Energy-Efficient Economy (ACEEE). *Climate Progress* is edited by Joe Romm, a Senior Fellow at American Progress, an independent, nonpartisan education and advocacy organization. Romm has a Ph.D. in physics from MIT and served as Assistant Secretary of Energy for Energy Efficiency in 1997. *Time* magazine named *Climate Progress* one of the 25 "Best Blogs of 2010." While Liz Barratt-Brown criticized the way the Keystone Pipeline project was framed, this *Climate Progress* post takes a very different tack and frames the issue quite differently.

Amerca is thinking too small when it comes to energy efficiency . . . according to a major new report from the American Council for an Energy-Efficient Economy (ACEEE).

The new report outlines three scenarios under which the U.S. could either continue on its current path or cut energy consumption by the year 2050 almost 60 percent, add nearly two million net jobs in 2050, and save energy consumers as much as $400 billion per year (the equivalent of $2600 per household annually).

According to ACEEE, the secret to major economic gains from energy efficiency is a more productive investment pattern of increased investments in energy efficiency, which would allow lower investments in power plants and other supply infrastructure, thereby substantially lowering overall energy expenditures on an economy-wide basis in the residential, commercial, industrial, transportation, and electric power sectors.

"The evidence suggests that without a greater emphasis on the more efficient use of energy resources, there may be as many as three jokers in the deck that will threaten the robustness of our nation's future economy," explains John A. "Skip" Laitner, ACEEE's director of economic and social analysis.

Examples of potential large-scale energy efficiency savings identified by ACEEE include the following:

- Electric Power. Our current system of generating and delivering electricity to U.S. homes and businesses is an anemic 31 percent energy efficient. That is, for every three units of coal or other fuel we use to generate the power, we manage to deliver less than one unit of electricity to our homes and businesses. What the U.S. wastes in the generation of electricity is more than Japan needs to power its entire economy. What is even more astonishing is that our current level of (in)efficiency is essentially unchanged in the half century since 1960, when President Dwight D. Eisenhower spent his last year in the White House.

- Transportation. The fuel economy of conventional petroleum-fueled vehicles continues to grow while hybrid, electric, and fuel cell vehicles gain large shares, totaling nearly three-quarters of all new light-duty vehicles in 2050 in the report's middle scenario. Aviation, rail, and shipping energy use declines substantially in this scenario through a combination of technological and operational improvements.

In the most aggressive scenario, there is a shift toward more compact development patterns, and greater investment in alternative modes of travel and other measures that reduce both passenger and freight vehicle miles traveled. This scenario also phases out conventional light-duty gasoline vehicles entirely, increases hybrid and fuel cell penetration for heavy-duty vehicles, and reduces aviation energy use by 70 percent.

- Buildings. In residential and commercial buildings the evidence suggests potential reductions of space heating and cooling needs as the result of building shell improvements of up to 60 percent in existing buildings, and 70–90 percent in new buildings. The ACEEE scenarios also incorporate advanced heating and cooling systems (e.g., gas and ground-source air conditioners and heat pumps and condensing furnaces and boilers), decreased energy distribution losses, advanced solid-state lighting, and significantly more efficient appliances.

- Industry. In the industrial sector, energy efficiency opportunities reduce 2050 energy use by up to half, coming less from equipment efficiency and more from optimization of complex systems. The ACEEE analysis focuses on process optimization in the middle scenario, but also anticipates even greater optimization of entire supply chains in the most aggressive scenario, allowing for more efficient use of feedstocks and elimination of wasted production.

Are such advances in energy efficiency realistic?

As the ACEEE report points out, the U.S. already has achieved considerable advances in the energy efficiency context and is poised to do more: "The U.S. economy has tripled in size since 1970 and three-quarters of the energy needed to fuel that growth came from an amazing variety of efficiency advances—not new energy supplies. Indeed, the overwhelming emphasis in current policy debates on finding new energy supplies is such that emphasis on new supplies may be crowding out investments and innovations that can help to achieve greater levels of energy productivity. Going forward, the current economic recovery, and our future economic prosperity, will depend more on new energy efficiency behaviors and investments than we've seen in the last 40 years."

Analyze

1. What, according to this article, does it mean to "Think Big" on energy efficiency?

2. The author asks, "Are such advances in energy efficiency realistic?" As a class, discuss the question of feasibility. What kinds of changes would have to be put into place in order for these advancements to be realistic?

3. As a class, discuss the most wasteful energy habits you are guilty of having. Do you never turn off lights? Do you leave your television on all night while you sleep? What do you think it would take to motivate you to develop new "energy-efficient behaviors"?

Explore

1. Using the Internet, locate some statistics regarding the electricity usage of various nations. How does the U.S. electricity consumption rate compare? Make a graph comparing the U.S. consumption rate to that of at least six other countries, and share your findings with your class.

2. When President Bush took office in 2000, his Vice President, Dick Cheney, developed a national energy policy. Find out what the policy said about energy conservation. Is this a good policy? A realistic policy? Write an essay defending or criticizing this policy position.

3. Many people talk about the "green economy" as a potential source of economic growth. What new "green" jobs or industry are possible in the energy sector? Write your dream vision of how America might rise to the challenge of sustainable energy supply and use.

Vandana Shiva
"Food for Cars or People: Biofuels a False Solution to Climate Change and a Threat to Food Security"

Vandana Shiva is a philosopher, activist, and eco-feminist who has written more than 20 books about food, ecology, and globalization. She has a B.A. in physics and an M.A. and Ph.D. in philosophy and has won numerous awards and honors. Shiva is an international activist and works to encourage grassroots movements concerned with food, globalization, and feminist issues. The chapter excerpted below comes from her book *Soil Not Oil*, a response to the often hidden and unintended consequences of biofuel production in the United States and Europe. Her concern is for the effect biofuel production has on the poor in developing countries, a concern shared by the authors of the Evangelical letter on climate change in Chapter 4.

Ecological, Diverse, Decentralized Biofuels vs. Industrial Biofuels

Biofuels, fuels from biomass, continue to be the most important energy source for the poor in the world. The ecological, biodiverse farm is not just a source of food, it is also a source of energy. Energy for cooking the food comes from inedible biomass like the stalks of millets and pulses, farmed trees, and village woodlots. Managed sustainably, village commons have been a source of decentralized energy for centuries. The use of decentralized energy from biomass is a vital part of the transition from fossil fuels to renewable energies. Biomass can be used directly as a cooking and heating fuel. It can be turned into biogas, a decentralized-energy alternative promoted by Gandhi, among others. Biofuels can be used to generate electricity for decentralized use and can be part of a sustainable alternative to fossil fuels and nuclear power. If embedded in a democratic, decentralized framework of management and decision-making, biofuels can rejuvenate biodiversity, recycle carbon, enhance agricultural productivity, increase the resilience of agro-ecosystems in the face of climate change, and increase the food and energy security of the poor.

However, the current euphoria over industrial biofuels is promoting monocultures and destroying biodiversity; promoting continued luxury consumption by the rich at the expense of the basic food and domestic energy needs of the poor; and promoting centralized corporate ownership and control over land and biomass by grabbing them from the poor.

In 1995, there were 34 countries that relied on wood fuels for more than 70 percent of their energy needs; in 13 of these countries wood supplied more than 90 percent. The diverse crop and tree species that have supplied rural energy in biodiverse agro ecosystems do not appear in the new lexicon of "biofuels." Biofuels are no longer an agrarian product meeting the needs of the rural poor. In fact they are not even a complementary product to food. Instead industrial biofuels are in competition with food. They are not part of diversified, decentralized, sustainable, and equitable food and energy systems.

Industrial biofuels are not the fuels of the poor; they are the foods of the poor transformed into heat, electricity, and fuel for the rich. Liquid biofuels, in particular ethanol and biodiesel, are one of the fastest-growing sectors of production, driven by the search for alternatives to fossil fuels. Industrial biofuels have been promoted through legislation and policy. Laws are being enacted to promote and subsidize liquid fuels diverting land from food production. From the richest countries in the North to the poorest countries in the South, food security is being forgotten in order to keep the energy infrastructure of the fossil fuel age "well oiled." The entire structure built on fossil fuels is seeking to be maintained and expanded on the basis of oil from plants.

President Bush is trying to pass legislation to require the use of 35 billion gallons of biofuels by 2017—a massive increase from the estimated 4 billion gallons used in 2005. Alexander Muller of the Sustainable Development Department of the United Nations Food and Agriculture Organization (FAO) has stated: "The gradual move away from oil has begun. Over the next 15 to 20 years we may see biofuels providing a full 25 percent of the world's energy needs." Global production of biofuels has doubled in the past five years and is likely to double again in the next four years. Among the countries that have enacted pro-biofuel policies in recent years are Argentina, Australia, Canada, China, Colombia, Ecuador, India, Indonesia, Malawi, Malaysia, Mexico, Mozambique, the Philippines, Senegal, South Africa, Thailand, and Zambia. Former World Bank president Paul Wolfowitz once said:

> Biofuels are an opportunity to add to the world supply of energy to meet the enormous growing demand and hopefully to mitigate

some of the price effect. It's an opportunity to do so in an environmentally friendly way and in a way that is carbon neutral. It is an opportunity to do so in a way that developing countries like Brazil can provide income and employment for their people.

But are industrial biofuels carbon neutral? Are the poor gaining or losing with the explosive increase in the production of industrial biofuels? What are the soil and ecological implications of the new policy obsession with industrial biofuels? What are the implications for land sovereignty and food sovereignty of the poor?

Industrial Biofuels: Green or Green™

Industrial biofuels are being promoted as a source of renewable energy and as a means to reduce greenhouse gas emissions. However, there are two ecological reasons why converting crops like soy, corn, and palm into liquid fuels can actually aggravate the CO_2 burden and worsen the climate crisis while also contributing to the erosion of biodiversity and the depletion of water resources.

First, deforestation caused by expanding soy and palm oil plantations is leading to increased CO_2 emissions. The FAO estimates that 1.6 billion tons, or 25 to 30 percent of the greenhouse gases released into the atmosphere each year, comes from deforestation. According to Wetlands International, destruction of Southeast Asian forests for palm oil plantations is contributing to 8 percent of global CO_2 emissions. By 2022, biofuel plantations could destroy 98 percent of Indonesia's rainforests. Every ton of palm oil used as biofuel releases 30 tons of CO_2 into the atmosphere, ten times as much as petroleum does. Ironically, this additional burden on the atmosphere is treated as beneficial and as a Clean Development Mechanism (CDM) by the Kyoto Protocol. Biofuels are exacerbating the same global warming that they are supposed to reduce.

Biofuels: A Greenhouse Threat

Two important studies published in February 2008 in the journal *Science* reveal that biofuels cause more greenhouse gas emissions than conventional fuels if the full emissions costs of producing these green fuels are taken into account. The studies follow a series of reports that have linked ethanol and biodiesel production to increased carbon dioxide emissions, destruction of biodiverse forests, and air and water pollution. The destruction of natural ecosystems, whether rainforests in the tropics or grasslands in South America, not only releases greenhouse gases into the atmosphere, but also deprives the planet of natural sponges to absorb carbon emissions. The new cropland, the study reports, also absorbs far less carbon than the rainforests or even scrubland it replaces. Together the two studies offer sweeping conclusions: taken globally, the production of almost all biofuels resulted, directly or indirectly, intentionally or not, in new lands being cleared. Whether that land was rainforest or scrubland, the greenhouse gas contribution is significant.

Joseph Fargione, an author of one of the studies and a scientist at the Nature Conservancy, says, "The clearance of grassland released 93 times the amount of greenhouse gases that would be saved by the fuel made annually on that land." In Indonesia and Malaysia, palm biodiesel, one of the most controversial biofuels currently in use, because of its connection to rainforest deforestation in these countries, has a carbon debt of 423 years. Soybean biodiesel in the Amazonian rainforest has a debt of 319 years. "Until the carbon debt is repaid, biofuels from converted land have greater GHG impacts than the fossil fuels they displace." A "carbon debt" refers to the CO_2 released during the first fifty years from the land conversion. "People don't realize there is three times as much carbon in plants and soil than there is in the air. While we cut down forests, burn them, churn the soil, we release all the carbon that was being stored," says Dr. Fargione.

According to Dr. Fargione, the dedication of so much cropland in the   10 United States to growing corn for ethanol has caused indirect land-use changes far away. Previously, Midwestern farmers had alternated growing corn and soy in their fields, one year to the next. Now many grow only corn, meaning that soy has to be grown elsewhere. The studies show that the purchase of biofuels in Europe and the United States leads indirectly to the destruction of the natural habitats far afield. This has also been proven by the Navdanya study on food versus fuel, which found that the grasslands and common lands are being destroyed in Chhattisgarh and Rajasthan to grow jatropha for biofuel.

David Pimentel and Ted Patzek, professors at Cornell and Berkeley, respectively, have shown that all crops have a negative energy balance when converted to biofuels—it takes more fossil fuel energy input to produce biofuels than the resultant biofuels can generate. It takes 1.5 gallons of gasoline to produce one gallon of ethanol. For each fossil fuel unit of energy spent producing corn ethanol, the return is 0.778 units of energy, 0.688 units for switchgrass ethanol, and 0.534 for soybean diesel. Pimentel and Patzek were criticized by the US government for including the energy used for building new refineries. However, these are new energy investments that do generate emissions, and Pimentel and Patzek are right to include them when calculating the overall energy balance.

In 2006 the US used 20 percent of its corn crop to produce 5 billion gallons of ethanol, which only substituted for 1 percent of its oil use. If 100 percent of the corn crop were used to make ethanol, it would be able to substitute for 7 percent of the total oil used. Even if all US soy and corn were converted to fuel it would only substitute for 12 percent of the gasoline and six percent of the diesel. To satisfy the entire current oil demand of the US with biofuels would take 1.4 million square miles of corn for ethanol or 8.8 million square miles of soy for biodiesel, which is more than all the agricultural land in the US. All the solar energy collected by every green plant in the US in 2006—including agriculture, forests, and lawns—is only half as much as the fossil fuel energy consumed in that year. This is clearly not a solution to either peak oil or climate chaos.

In fact, ethanol is a source of other crises when you look at all the resources it demands. It takes 1,700 gallons of water to produce a gallon of ethanol. Corn uses more nitrogen fertilizer, more insecticides, and more herbicides than any other crop. Ethanol constitutes 99 percent of all biofuel production in the US. In 2004, there were 3.4 billion gallons of ethanol produced and blended into gasoline, amounting to about 2 percent of the nation's gas consumption.

There has been a flood of subsidies in the West for production of biofuels. The cost of support of ethanol varies from $0.29 to $0.36 per liter in the US and $1 per liter in the EU. Support for biodiesel varies between $0.20 per liter in Canada and $1 in Switzerland. In 2007 US taxpayers provided $6 billion to ethanol producers through subsidies.

15   In 2008, the government introduced a tax credit of $0.51 per gallon on ethanol and mandated a doubling of the amount of ethanol to be used in gasoline by 2012, to 7.5 billion gallons. The total cost to the consumer of subsidizing corn ethanol is $8.4 billion per year.

Subsidization of biofuels is creating a deep impact on demand for foodstuffs from the United States. In 2007, for example, the increase in ethanol production will account for more than half of the global increase in demand for corn. Much the same is true in the US and EU for soybeans and rape-seed used in biodiesel. The rising price of food is good for producers. It is dreadful, however, for consumers, particularly for those in poor, food-importing countries. Increased production of biofuels also adds stress on existing land and water supplies.

These subsidies will distort agriculture policy and encourage farmers to divert their crops from food to fuel. They promote monocultures and industrial agriculture, which contribute to climate change. In effect, industrial biofuels will increase climate instability, rather than mitigating it.

According to Patzek, "the United States has already wasted a lot of time, money, and natural resources pursuing a mirage of an energy scheme that cannot possibly replace fossil fuels. The only real solution is to limit the rate of use of these fossil fuels. Everything else will lead to an eventual national disaster."

For Italy to meet the EU requirement to have 5 percent of its gas and diesel be biofuel by 2010 will require 69 percent more land to be farmed than is available in the entire country and require 102 percent more water and 40 percent more chemicals. The UK has set targets of 2.5 percent of fuel to be biofuel by 2008, rising to 5 percent by 2010. Compulsory biofuels are a recipe for disaster. It is a case of the cure being worse than the disease.

The planet and the poor are losing; the rainforests—the lungs, the heart, the liver of the planet—are being bulldozed to plant soy and palm. In Brazil, 22.2 million hectares have been converted to soy plantations, producing in 2004–2005 over 50 million tons. Brazil will clear an additional 60 million hectares of land due to the gold rush for soy. Since 1995 in Brazil, soy cultivation has been increasing at 3.2 percent (320,000 hectares) per year. Twenty-one percent of Brazil's cultivated area is now soy, and 300,000 people have been displaced in Rio Grande do Sul. Since January 2003 nearly 70,000 kilometers of the Amazon rainforest have been cleared for biofuels production. Corporations like Cargill, ADM, and Bunge are at the heart of the destruction of the Amazon, according to Greenpeace. Since 1990, Indonesia has destroyed 28 million hectares of rainforest for palm plantations. The poor are losing because land and water that would have produced food for the hungry is being used to run cars.

Automobile companies and agribusiness are the ones who gain. Using liquid biofuels to run cars allows car manufacturers to keep selling cars despite peak oil and climate crisis. Biofuels gives them another way to avoid doing anything about fuel efficiency. As George Monbiot, the environmental columnist for the *Guardian*, reports:

> The European Commission was faced with a straight choice between fuel efficiency and biofuels. It had intended to tell car companies that the average carbon emission from new cars in 2012 would be 120 grams per kilometer. After heavy lobbying by Angela Merkel on behalf of the car manufacturers, it caved in and raised the limit to 130 grams. It announced that it would make up the shortfall by increasing the contribution from biofuel.

Agribusiness is also benefiting from the expanded market for soy, corn, and palm. Monsanto can sell more herbicide-resistant seeds and collect more royalties from Argentina and Brazil. Cargill can make more profits selling fertilizers, agrochemicals, and agricultural commodities for biofuel, while also increasing its profit margins on the food commodities it sells as prices rise.

. . .

Biofuels a Threat to Food Security

The biofuel sector has been growing rapidly. The United States and Brazil have established ethanol industries and the European Union is fast catching up. Governments all over the world are encouraging biofuel production by mandating that biofuel account for a percentage of their fuel supply. The United States, because of its voracious demand for energy, is promoting industrial biofuels in a big way.

Fidel Castro has strongly criticized the use of biofuels by the US. Lashing out at the 2007 ethanol deal between Brazil and the US, he described it as "the internationalization of genocide."

The deal, coming on the heels of President Bush's widely protested tour of Latin America, aims to encourage the development of biofuels projects in poor countries, particularly in the Caribbean and Central America, and to promote a global biofuels market. Brazil and the US will cooperate more closely on researching and developing biofuel technology.

25   Washington's interest in ethanol accelerated after Bush admitted in January 2006 that the US was "addicted to oil," which posed a "national security problem" because oil is "often imported from unstable parts of the world." In 2006, the US produced 18 billion liters of ethanol from 53 million tons of

corn. Increasing the use of corn for ethanol production has caused corn and other food-crop prices to rise. An internal World Bank report states that biofuels have forced global food prices up by 75 percent.

The increased use of corn and soybean oil for biofuel production has raised world food prices by about 10 percent, according to an IMF report. Biofuel production has pushed up feedstock prices. The clearest example is corn, whose price rose by 23 percent in 2000 and by 50 percent in 2005 and 2006, largely because of the US ethanol program. Spurred by subsidies and the Renewable Fuel Standard issued in 2005, the United States has been diverting more corn to ethanol. Because it is the world's largest corn exporter, biofuel expansion in the United States has contributed to a decline in international grain stocks and has put upward pressure on world cereal prices. Largely because of biodiesel production, similar price increases have occurred for vegetable oils (palm, soybean, and rapeseed). Cereal supply is likely to remain constrained in the near term and prices will be subject to upward pressure from further supply shocks.

Worldwide agricultural commodity price increases were significant between 2004 and 2006: corn prices rose by 54 percent, wheat by 34 percent, soybean oil by 71 percent, and sugar by 75 percent. This trend accelerated in 2007, due to continued demand for biofuels and drought in major producing countries. The World Bank reports that food prices increased by 83 percent from 2006 to 2008. Continued demand and floods in the US Midwest suggest that this trend will continue. Wheat prices have risen more than 35 percent since the 2006 harvest, while corn prices have increased nearly 28 percent. The price of soybean oil has been particularly volatile, due to growing demand in China, the US, and the EU.

The Hamburg-based oilseeds analysts of Oil World have predicted a substantial deficit of 17 to 18 million tons in the output of major oilseeds during 2007 and 2008 and a food crisis unless the use of agricultural products for biofuels is curbed or 2008 proves to be a bumper-crop year.

Inevitably, this massive increase in the demand for grains is going to price poor people out of the food market. The Brazilian Landless Workers Movement declared, "the expansion of the production of biofuels aggravates hunger in the world. We cannot maintain our tanks full while stomachs go empty."

The diversion of food for fuel has already increased the price of corn and soy. There have been riots in Mexico because of the price rise of tortillas. More than 40 countries have had food riots, and this is just the beginning.

The agrarian crisis created by trade liberalization and globalization is being used in India to promote the conversion of food crops to ethanol. The argument is that farmers will get a better price for these crops. In India, the two target crops are sugarcane and sorghum. India grows as much sugarcane as Brazil, but because Brazil uses 55 percent of its sugarcane for ethanol, India is the largest producer of sugar. The sugar industry in India is now promoting the diversion of sugarcane from human nutrition to ethanol for cars. Sorghum, a cereal that grows in the semiarid tropics, is another food crop being promoted for ethanol. The International Crops Research Institute for the Semi-Arid Tropics (ICRISAT), one of the institutes run by the World Bank, is a major promoter of growing sorghum for ethanol production using public funds to promote the conversion of food into fuel. Corporations like Tata and Seagram are jumping onto the ethanol bandwagon, with Tata setting up a 60,000-liter-capacity plant in Nanded.

In 2002, the government of India introduced a policy of supplying gas with 5 percent ethanol. With the automobile explosion in India and high fuel prices, ethanol demand is growing. Projected demand is outpacing supply. Of the 132 million gallons of ethanol required, only 37 percent is in current production.

In Argentina, the pampas, the region's biggest and most diverse ecosystem, is under threat from the expansion of herbicide-resistant soy cultivation. Soy has become Argentina's biggest export. If deforestation continues at the current rate, the forest ranges of the Yungas will disappear by 2010. More than 2.3 million hectares of dry and humid vegetation have been cleared for soy since 1995. Forests are disappearing and people are being displaced. Three out of five people in Chaco province have been driven out of rural areas to Argentina's slums.

. . .

Toward Sustainable, Biodiverse, and Decentralized Bioenergy Alternatives for India

Diverting land and food to produce industrial biofuel undermines the land and food sovereignty of the poor, generating social conflicts and threatening the fragile fabric of democracy. Ethanol production has already contributed to an increase in food prices. With 1 billion people already going hungry, high food prices can only increase hunger around the world. Even when nonfood crops like jatropha are grown on nonagricultural lands, the poor lose. They are losing their commons, which supply them fodder and fuel. This in turn undermines their livelihoods, food security, and energy security.

The climate crisis and the end of cheap oil demand a shift to sustainable 35 energy. However, energy supplied from plants and crops is not necessarily sustainable. Energy can only be considered sustainable if it does not compete with the food supply, does not divert organic matter from the maintenance of the essential ecosystem, is decentralized and based on decisions by local communities, and is based on biodiversity, not monocultures.

Local energy needs decentralized energy systems. Decentralization needs diversity, not monocultures. Biodiversity with multi-functional uses makes for the best local energy supply. It is complementary and not competitive with the local food supply. India has a rich diversity of oilseed trees and crops. Diverse oilseed-bearing tree crops used locally can be an important source of village energy security. A Navdanya report on biodiversity-based organic farming shows that food production can increase with biodiversity intensification and ecological agriculture. And biodiverse organic farming also fixes more carbon in vegetation and the soil.

At the village level, multiple sources of biodiversity provide multiple sources of renewable energy—from animal energy to bio-gas to biomass for electricity. Biogas digesters were first developed in the 1950s in India, using cow dung to produce methane gas and a nitrogen-rich fertilizer. Asia has more than 15 million small digesters in rural areas to provide cooking fuel and fertilizer.

Alternatives to fossil fuel are limitless. Industrial biofuels are not an alternative because

- Their net energy efficiency is negative.
- They restrict themselves to liquid fuels, forgoing the many other forms of bioenergy needed at the village level.
- They promote non-sustainable industrial monocultures that serve to increase greenhouse gas emissions.
- They are becoming a major cause of hunger and landlessness.

Industrial biofuels threaten to impoverish the planet by reducing biodiversity and its benefits. This reductionism is leading to ecological and economic impoverishment. Biodiversity can lead to ecological and economic enrichment. A decentralized, biodiversity-based bioenergy policy can be a major component in rural development.

Democratic decision-making at the village level is the best process for determining the best mix of energy needed to meet local needs. Unfortunately, the current model of industrialized production of ethanol and biodiesel from plants based on monocultures fails the criteria of sustainability, justice, and democracy. It is centralized and driven by corporate greed, not community needs.

40   We need a new model, one that respects people's right to land and food, to their commons and biodiversity. A biodiversity-based, democratically evolved bioenergy program could enhance food security, energy security, and livelihood security of the poor.

Analyze

1. What materials can be used for biofuels?
2. According to the article, how can biofuels be used sustainably at the local level? Why is this a problem when biofuel usage is industrialized? In other words, what is the difference between "ecological, diverse, decentralized biofuels" and "industrial biofuels"?
3. In what ways do industrial biofuels compete with food production? How does the production of industrial biofuels affect soil quality?

Explore

1. According to this article, the production of industrial biofuels actually makes greenhouse gas emissions worse. Following her argument, trace the steps outlined by the author that contribute to this process. Break down the steps into as many parts as you can—for example, take note that before crops can be planted, some land must be cleared. Alongside each step of the process, list how that step might contribute to greenhouse gas emissions.
2. This author clearly argues against industrial biofuels as a carbon-neutral source of fuel. However, she recognizes in her argument that her position is not held by everyone. Using the information given in this article, construct an expository essay that presents both sides of this argument in a neutral way—remember that your goal is to inform, rather than to persuade.

3. Biofuel production in the United States, largely corn-based ethanol production, is a huge growth industry. Using the Internet, do some research on the state of ethanol production in the United States. How much do we produce? And how? And what are the controversies over ethanol production? Write a brief essay that uses this information to follow the title "Corn for Cars: Is This a Wise Idea?"

Thomas L. Friedman
"The Age of Noah: Biodiversity"

Thomas L. Friedman writes about politics, globalization, and the environment for *The New York Times* and has won three Pulitzer Prizes. Friedman has published six books, including *The World Is Flat: A Brief History of the Twentieth Century*, *The Lexus and the Olive Tree: Understanding Globalization*, and *Hot, Flat and Crowded: Why We Need Green Revolution—and How It Can Renew America*, from which the excerpt below is taken. The "hot," "flat," and "crowded" in his book title refer to a world that climate change is making "hot," a society made socially "flat" or homogenous by the growth of the middle class, and a planet more "crowded" because of population growth. "Code Green" is Friedman's term for our emergency need for a "green" revolution.

With more and more species threatened with extinction by the flood that is today's global economy, we may be the first generation in human history that literally has to act like Noah—to save the last pairs of a wide range of species. Or as God commanded Noah in Genesis: "And of every living thing of all flesh, you shall bring two of every sort into the ark, to keep them alive with you; they shall be male and female."

> "Nature is the art of God."
> —Thomas Browne, *Religio Medici*, 1635
> " 'Development' is like Shakespeare's virtue, which grown into a pleurisy, dies of its own too-much."
> —Aldo Leopold, "A Plea for Wilderness Hunting Grounds," 1925

Unlike Noah, though, we—our generation and our civilization—are responsible for the flood, and we have the responsibility to build the ark. We are causing the flood, as more and more coral reefs, forests, fisheries, rivers, and fertile soils are spoiled or overwhelmed by commercial development; and only we can build the ark that is needed to preserve them.

The beginning of wisdom is to understand that it is our challenge and our responsibility to act like Noah—to create arks, not floods. The Energy-Climate Era is about more than just addressing soaring energy demand, drastic climate change, and proliferating petrodictatorships. It is also about dealing with another effect of a world that is hot, flat, and crowded—the threat to the earth's biodiversity, as more and more plant and animal species are endangered or go extinct.

In the past decade, I have traveled throughout the world with Conservation International, which specializes in biodiversity preservation. My wife, Ann, is a member of the CI board, and I frequently call on CI scientists for insight when writing about biodiversity, as I do in this chapter. Species are constantly being discovered and others are going extinct, either due to biological circumstances or to economic development, hunting, or other human activities. But Conservation International currently estimates that one species is now going extinct every twenty minutes, which is a thousand times faster than the norm during most of the earth's history. It is understandably hard to imagine what it means that we humans are causing something in the natural realm to happen a thousand times faster than normal. That is a big number.

5   "Imagine what would happen to us or to our lives and livelihoods and our planet were any other natural rate to be a thousand times higher today than normal," asked Thomas Brooks, a senior director with Conservation International's Center for Applied Biodiversity Science. "What if rainfall were a thousand times more than normal? We would be flooded. What if snowfall were a thousand times more than normal? We would never dig out. What if rates of disease transmission for malaria or HIV/AIDS were a thousand times higher than they are now? Millions would perish. But that is what is happening to plant and animal biodiversity today."

This is not just a problem for zoos. We have no idea how many natural cures, how many industrial materials, how many biological insights, how much sheer natural beauty, and how many parts and pieces of a complex web of life we barely understand are being lost.

"The biodiversity of the planet is a unique and uniquely valuable library that we have been steadily burning down—one wing at a time—before we have even cataloged all the books, let alone read them all," said John Holdren, the Harvard and Woods Hole environmental scientist.

Imagine if the trend toward rapid and widespread extinction continues and accelerates. Imagine a world with little or no biodiversity— a stainless-steel-and-cement world stripped bare of every plant and animal, every tree and hillside. Not only would such a world be barely livable, from a biological point of view—it would be a world we would barely want to live in.

From what landscapes or flowerbeds would future painters draw their inspiration? What would move poets to write their sonnets, composers to craft their symphonies, and religious leaders and philosophers to contemplate the meaning of God by examining his handiwork up close and in miniature? To go through life without being able to smell a flower, swim a river, pluck the apple off a tree, or behold a mountain valley in spring is to be less than fully alive. Yes, one supposes, we would find substitutes, but nothing that could compare with the pristine bounty, beauty, colors, and complexity of nature, without which we are literally less human. Is it any wonder that studies show that hospital patients who have a view of natural scenery from their rooms recover more quickly?

"Destroying a tropical rain forest and other species-rich ecosystems for profit is like burning all the paintings of the Louvre to cook dinner," explained the famed entomologist Edward O. Wilson when I visited him in his lab at Harvard, where the walls are lined with drawers and drawers full of the thousands of different ant species that he and his colleagues have collected from across the world: "That is what we're doing. 'We need this money from our oil palm plantations—sorry about the great forest of Borneo and the orangutans.'"   10

But for those not persuaded by the aesthetic, elegiac, religious, or spiritual values of biodiversity, there are some often overlooked practical benefits to keep in mind. These are known to environmentalists by the rather dry and undescriptive term "ecosystem services." Natural ecosystems provide a wide range of benefits and "services" to people who do not have or cannot afford a local supermarket or plumbing: They supply fresh water, they filter pollutants from streams, they provide breeding grounds for fisheries, they control erosion, they buffer human communities against storms and natural disasters, they harbor insects that pollinate crops or attack crop pests, they naturally take CO_2 out of the atmosphere. These "services" are particularly crucial to poor people in the developing world who depend directly on ecosystems for their livelihoods.

"Critics of environmentalism . . . usually wave aside the small and the unfamiliar, which they tend to classify into two categories, bugs and weeds," Wilson wrote in *The Creation*.

> It is easy for them to overlook the fact that these creatures make up most of the organisms and species on Earth. They forget, if they ever knew, how the voracious caterpillars of an obscure moth from the American tropics saved Australia's pastureland from the overgrowth of cactus; how a Madagascar "weed," the rosy periwinkle, provided the alkaloids that cure most cases of Hodgkin's disease and acute childhood leukemia; how another substance from an obscure Norwegian fungus made possible the organ transplant industry; how a chemical from the saliva of leeches yielded a solvent that prevents blood clots during and after surgery; and so on through the pharmacopoeia that has stretched from the herbal medicines of Stone Age shamans to the magic-bullet cures of present-day biomedical science . . . Wild species [also] enrich the soil, cleanse the water, pollinate most of the flowering plants. They create the very air we breathe. Without these amenities, the remainder of human history would be nasty and brief.

If we destabilize nature by degrading it, Wilson continued, "the organisms most affected are likely to be the largest and most complex, including human beings."

Biodiversity doesn't only help us to live—it helps us to adapt. There is nothing more practical than the role that biodiversity plays in easing adaptation to change for all living things—including us humans. Mark Erdmann, a marine biologist with Conservation International in Indonesia, gave me a mini-lecture about this in March 2008, as we sat on a beachfront overlooking the Lombok Strait, on the island of Nusa Penida in Indonesia. I had gone there to learn about CI's work to save the diversity of marine life in the Indonesian archipelago.

15   "Change is the one constant in life, and without diversity—of species, cultures, crops—adaptation to this change becomes much more difficult," Erdmann explained. "Talk to the farmer who grows just one crop and a disease wipes out his whole farm. Talk to the financial adviser who puts all his money into a single stock... In a nutshell, diversity bequeaths resilience— and we're gonna need all the resilience we can muster to deal with the global

changes rapidly descending upon us." Who knows what catastrophic diseases lie in wait in our future? If we have plowed up our tropical rain forests for palm oil and sugarcane ethanol, it will be like emptying our tool kit of natural medicines. "We need diversity precisely because change is constant, and diversity provides the raw material we need to adapt to change," added Erdmann.

In a world that is hot, flat, and crowded, where all kinds of things are going to be moving and shifting much faster than in ages past, the last thing we want to lose is the tools we need to adapt to change.

When we speak about preserving biodiversity, what exactly does that include? I like the definition offered by the dictionary Biologyreference.com, which defines biodiversity as "the sum total of life on Earth; the entire global complement of terrestrial, marine, and freshwater biomes and ecosystems, and the species—plants, animals, fungi, and microorganisms—that live in them, including their behaviors, interactions, and ecological processes. Biodiversity is [also] linked directly to the nonliving components of the planet—atmosphere, oceans, freshwater systems, geological formations, and soils—forming one great, interdependent system, the biosphere."

In this whole biosphere, scientists today have discovered and described between 1.7 and 1.8 million species of plants, animals, and microorganisms, says Russell A. Mittermeier, president of Conservation International, but some estimates suggest that the total number of species ranges between 5 and 30 million, and some scientists believe there may be as many as another 100 million species that we just have not identified, because they are hidden beneath the earth or seas or in remote locales. Some eighty to ninety new species of primates have been identified in just the last decade and a half, noted Mittermeier, "which means that 15 to 20 percent of all primates have been described by science in just the last fifteen years."

That's why Code Green has to involve both a strategy for the generation of clean energy—in order to mitigate climate change and its effects on weather, temperatures, rainfall, sea levels, and droughts—and a strategy for the preservation of the earth's biodiversity, so we don't also destroy the very plant and animal species that sustain life. Remember: Climate change is a critical issue, but biodiversity loss could also destabilize the systemic and vital carrying capacity of our planet—as much as climate change. In all the very welcome attention to climate change in recent years, the issue of biodiversity loss has gotten lost. That's why Code Green focuses on both generation of a new kind of energy and preservation of the natural world.

20   "Global warming and pollution are just a couple of things that happen when we overtax our natural resources," said Glenn Prickett, senior vice president of Conservation International and an expert on economics and the environment. "What also happens is that oceans get overfished, forests and coral reefs are destroyed, and this has a real impact, not only on the plants and animals who live in these ecosystems, but also on the people who live off them."

We have to consider this problem comprehensively. If the whole world just thinks about halting the emissions of CO_2 into the atmosphere and ignores what is happening within our ecosystems, "much of the world's biodiversity could be wiped out while we're looking the other way," added Prickett. "And don't think for minute that you can have a healthy climate, or a healthy civilization, on a dead planet. Our climate is directly impacted by the health of our tropical forests and other natural systems."

Over the past decade, I have traveled with Glenn to some of the world's biodiversity hot spots and other endangered regions where CI is working—from the Pantanal wetlands in southwestern Brazil to the Atlantic rain forest on Brazil's coast, from the Guyana Shield forest wilderness in southern Venezuela to the Rio Tambopata macaw research station in the heart of the Peruvian jungle, from the exotic-sounding highland of Shangri-La in Chinese-controlled Tibet to the tropical forests of Sumatra and the coral-ringed islands off Bali, in Indonesia. For me, these trips have been master classes in biodiversity, as were my own travels to the Masai Mara in Kenya and the Ngorongoro Crater in Tanzania and the vast Empty Quarter of the Saudi Arabian Desert and—before I had kids—a rappelling trip inside the salt domes of the Dead Sea.

In many ways, though, the first trip Glenn and I ever took taught me everything I needed to know about the biodiversity challenge we are facing. In 1998 we went to Brazil, and the trip began with the most unusual interview—locationwise—that I have ever conducted. It was with Nilson de Barros, then superintendent for the environment for the Brazilian state Mato Grosso do Sul, who insisted that we conduct our talk in the middle of the Rio Negro.

Mato Grosso do Sul is at the heart of the Pantanal region, along the border between Brazil, Bolivia, and Paraguay. The Pantanal is the largest freshwater wetland in the world (the size of Wisconsin), and is home to jaguar and a host of endangered species. Glenn and I flew in on a tiny prop plane, which landed in the front yard of the Fazenda Rio Negro, a ranch and nature lodge on the Rio Negro. We then boarded motorized launches and set off for the meeting point at a shallow bend in the river.

The Pantanal nature reserve is Jurassic Park without the dinosaurs. 25 Moving downriver, we passed scores of caimans lounging on the bank, giant river otters bobbing up and down, with egrets, hyacinth macaws, toucans, ibises, marsh deer, spoonbills, jabiru storks, foxes, ocelots, and rheas (relatives of ostriches) all poking their heads through the forest curtain at different points along our route. It was, quite simply, the most stunning cornucopia of biodiversity—plants and animals—that I have ever encountered at one time. De Barros and his team were waiting for us, standing waist-deep in the middle of the Rio Negro.

"First a beer, then a bath, then we talk," he said, cracking open a can of Skol as the river flowed by.

And I thought I had the best job in the world.

The broad threat to biodiversity and ecosystems worldwide today comes from two directions, de Barros explained. The first is from regions where the poorest of the poor are trying to scrape out a living from the natural ecosystems around them. When too many people try to do that, you lose whatever forests, reefs, and species are within reach. That is a huge problem around the Amazon wetlands and rain forest, but not in the Pantanal. The Pantanal, he explained, is not threatened by poor residents who chop down trees and sell them to timber companies to escape from poverty. The culture in the Pantanal is a rare example of man and nature thriving in harmony—through a mixed economy of ranching, fishing, and, lately, ecotourism.

No, the main biodiversity challenge to the Pantanal came from the outside: from globalization. A global triple threat was converging on the Pantanal: Soy farmers on the plateau above the Pantanal basin, eager to feed a rapidly expanding world soybean market, were widening their fields, and pesticides and silt runoff from their farms were fouling the rivers and wildlife. At the same time, the governments of Brazil, Argentina, Uruguay, Paraguay, and Bolivia had formed a trading block in the hope of making their economies more globally competitive. To better get the Pantanal's soy products to market, these governments wanted to dredge and straighten the rivers in the area in ways that could greatly alter the ecosystem. Finally, a consortium of international energy companies was building a pipeline across the Pantanal, from natural-gas-rich Bolivia to the vast, energy-guzzling Brazilian city of São Paulo.

30   The Pantanal, in fact, is a laboratory of globalization's economic upsides and biodiversity downsides. The biggest upside is that globalization is bringing more people out of poverty faster than ever before in the history of the world. The biggest downside is that in raising standards of living, globalization is making possible much higher levels of production and consumption by many more people. That's flat meeting crowded. And that, in turn, is fueling urban sprawl around the world, an increase in highways and motorized traffic, and bigger homes with more energy guzzling devices for more people. To feed this ravenous global economy, more and more companies are tempted to take over vast native forests in places like Indonesia and Brazil and convert them to oil palm plantations, soybean farms, and other large-scale commercial enterprises at a speed and scope the world has also never seen before.

Over the years, Glenn Prickett explains, NGOs like Conservation International, The Nature Conservancy, and the World Wildlife Fund have developed tools and large-scale education campaigns that can help the rural poor live more sustainably and preserve the very natural systems on which they depend. "But we have not yet developed the tools and scale of operation to meet the globalization threat to biodiversity, which is becoming overwhelming," he explained.

. . .

It starts with connecting the dots. To help cut emissions and boost energy security, the entire European Union has set the target of producing 20 percent of its energy from renewable sources by 2020, including increased use of biofuels—transportation fuels derived either from crops like corn, oil palm, soybeans, algae, or sugarcane or from plant waste, wood chips, or wild grasses, like switchgrass. The EU has declared that the "bio" ingredients of biofuels sold in Europe—palm oil and corn, for example—must not come from tropical forests, nature reserves, wetlands, or grasslands with high biodiversity. But fuels are fungible in a world market and are not always easy to monitor. It is hard to believe the EU mandate about renewable fuels will not accelerate the conversion of rain forests in Southeast Asia to oil palm plantations; some say it already has. Palm oil is the most efficient base for biodiesel fuel, although it is also used for cosmetics and in cooking. The cruel irony is that deforestation will result in more greenhouse gases being released into the atmosphere than the use of biofuels will eliminate. I have flown over an oil palm plantation in north Sumatra, in Indonesia. It looked like someone laid down twenty-five footfall fields in the middle of a tropical forest—just one rectangular block after another.

Michael Grunwald wrote a piece for *Time* (March 27, 2008) in which he described flying over a similar plantation in Brazil with an ecoactivist.

> From his Cessna a mile above the southern Amazon, John Carter looks down on the destruction of the world's greatest ecological jewel. He watches men converting rain forest into cattle pastures and soybean fields with bulldozers and chains. He sees fires wiping out such gigantic swaths of jungle that scientists now debate the "savannization" of the Amazon. Brazil just announced that deforestation is on track to double this year; Carter, a Texas cowboy with all the subtlety of a chainsaw, says it's going to get worse fast. "It gives me goose bumps," says Carter, who founded a nonprofit to promote sustainable ranching on the Amazon frontier. "It's like witnessing a rape." Carter adds, "You can't protect it. There's too much money to be made tearing it down," he says. "Out here on the frontier, you really see the market at work."

The numbers tell the story. Our planet is four billion years old and life has existed on earth for a little more than two billion years. Over those two billion years there has been a very, very slow "normal" pace of extinctions. On average, a species might live for one million years, then go extinct. That very gentle, very slow, background rate of extinctions has been punctuated over the centuries by five massive, catastrophic extinction events that have led to the loss of an extremely high proportion of our planet's life at different periods. The most recent mass extinction, said Thomas Brooks, the Conservation International biodiversity expert, was about sixty-five million years ago—the mass extinction of the dinosaurs, apparently due to an asteroid smashing into the Yucatan Peninsula, in what is now Mexico. That asteroid is believed to have expelled a thick dust cloud into the atmosphere, which apparently triggered global cooling and ended up starving a large proportion of the earth's plants and animals.

. . .

We know that we can restore natural habitats, said Brooks. We know 35 that we can restore populations in order to bring back species whose survival is threatened, like the buffalo. We know that we can clean up pollution, even a river as polluted as the Thames. "It is even within our grasp to reverse climate change," he added. "But extinctions are irreversible. Jurassic Park is a fiction: Once a species is gone, it is lost forever—we have lost that million years of our planetary heritage forever."

Mindlessly degrading the natural world the way we have been is no different than a bird degrading its own nest, a fox degrading its own den, a beaver degrading its own dam. We can't keep doing that and assume that it is just happening "over there." The scale of biodiversity loss happening today is having global impacts. As the team at Conservation International likes to say: "Lost there, felt here." And we can't keep doing that and assume that we will repair it later.

Later is over. That is the psychological biodiversity redline we have passed as we entered the Energy-Climate Era. "Later" was a luxury for previous generations, eras, civilizations, and epochs. It meant that you could paint the same landscape, see the same animals, eat the same fruit, climb the same trees, fish the same rivers, enjoy the same weather or rescue the same endangered species that you did when you were a kid—but just do it later, whenever you got around to it. Nature's bounty seemed infinite and all the threats to it either limited or reversible. In the Energy-Climate Era, given the accelerating rates of extinction and development, "later" is going to be removed from the dictionary. Later is no longer when you get to do all those things in nature you did as a kid—on your time schedule. Later is when they're gone—when you won't get to do any of them ever again. Later is too late, so whatever we are going to save, we'd better start saving now.

Analyze

1. Briefly describe, in a few well-crafted sentences, how the article views globalization as damaging to the stability of ecosystems.
2. What is biodiversity? And why is it so important?
3. Imagine, as a class, that you have been selected to lead the fight against the destruction of the tropical rainforest in the Amazon. Choose three arguments against the destruction of the rainforest that you feel are the most powerful. What types of arguments are these? Are they based in reason? Emotion? Idealism?

Explore

1. In many cases, descriptions of future energy needs frame human actions in a negative light; though this author does argue that humans have caused a "flood" and are responsible for their actions, by making a comparison to Noah, he is ultimately framing people positively, as a savior capable of great things. Along this line, in a small group come up

with as many other metaphors as you can that might appeal to human action in a positive light.

2. A massive number of animals have been placed on endangered watch lists or have become extinct over the past 50 years in the United States. Using the Internet, locate some statistics regarding which region—Northeast, Mid-Atlantic, Pacific Northwest, etc.—of the United States has seen the greatest number of endangered animals or extinctions. Can you connect these results to some generalizations about the region's economic makeup?

3. Use the information in this reading and some of the others in this chapter to persuade your friends that "later is over."

Evan I. Schwartz
"How Not to Make Energy Decisions: Lessons From the Battle Over Cape Wind"

Evan I. Schwartz is an author and journalist who writes about technology and innovation. He is a former editor of *MIT Technology Review*, from which the excerpt below was taken. *MIT Technology Review* was founded in 1899 and is now an independent digital media company dedicated to analysis and review of emerging technology. This excerpt introduces the social and political controversy of Cape Wind, a large wind energy project proposed for Cape Cod Bay off the coast of Massachusetts. It is the topic of the next two selections.

America's first offshore wind farm promises to be a picture of ugliness, with 130 turbines, each as tall as a 40-story skyscraper, marring the scenic Massachusetts waters off Cape Cod, Nantucket, and Martha's Vineyard. Or it promises to be a vision of beauty, each white windmill spinning majestically as it produces an alternative to carbon-spewing fossil fuels. But one thing everyone can agree on is that Cape Wind will be big. The turbines, spread out over an area as large as Manhattan, will be visible from the coastline for miles.

There may be no single power project in the United States that has been contested longer and with more vehemence than Cape Wind, which is meant to generate 450 megawatts of power—about as much as a typical coal plant—from the breeze blowing above Nantucket Sound. Ever since it was proposed in 2001, the privately financed developer, Cape Wind Associates, has been locked in a heated war of words with protest groups and tied up in a string of lawsuits. Arguments have erupted over the environmental benefits of the project and the impact of building the massive turbines in an active fishing zone, an area that also serves as a boating playground for some of the world's richest people. The protracted process, fueled by big bucks on both sides, raises a fundamental question that transcends the project itself: Is this any way to make major energy decisions?

That was the question left hanging in the air after a recent local preview of *Cape Spin*, a new documentary about the project. Above all, the Cape Wind controversy shows that while the problem of climate change is global, it's also true that all energy issues, to paraphrase a famous Massachusetts congressman, are local. And while new power-producing facilities will be most effective if they are sited according to some objective strategy, there's no avoiding the subjective reactions of those who live nearby. In this sense, the showdown over Cape Wind is a microcosm of a much larger debate. "Deciding where to put stuff is never simple," says Lynn Orr, director of the Precourt Institute for Energy at Stanford University. "But this is part of the reason why we've had such a hard time coming up with a national energy policy."

In the film, the camera follows the protests and proclamations of fishermen, sailors, Native Americans, wealthy vacationers, year-round residents, children, business owners, energy executives, lobbyists, and a plethora of politicians, including some from the Kennedy clan, whose family compound in Hyannis Port will have a nearly perfect view of the turbines five miles offshore. Many of these people were in attendance at the packed screening of the documentary, which is coming soon to film festivals and is set to air on the Sundance Channel this spring. "Good Lord," its first-time director, Robbie Gemmel, confessed to the crowd. "I didn't know what I was getting into."

5   Gemmel, who shot 550 hours of footage, says he aimed for an even-handed approach that also entertains. He begins with the frequently heard notion that the opposition stems from super-rich estate owners who simply don't want their views of the water spoiled. "Remember, they paid good

money—or inherited good money—to have these places," says Robert Whitcomb, a newspaper editor who coauthored a 2007 book on the project.

But the demographics of the affected coastal areas are far more diverse than this stereotype suggests. Most of the year-round residents are members of the middle and working classes. To them, the battle is between building a model of a clean-energy future and preserving their way of life. These citizens are portrayed not as victims of the dustup but as active rabble-rousers, planting lawn signs and marching around with banners that shout "Save Our Sound" or "No More Delays" or "Cape Wind Doesn't Float My Boat!"

All along, troops are being massed by the film's two principal characters. Jim Gordon, the president of Cape Wind Associates, is depicted by turns as a tenacious clean-energy champion and a cold-hearted businessman who once tried to construct a diesel power station across from an inner-city school. Before seeing the film, Gordon told me that he hoped it would show how much time and money have already been wasted on the fight. If a small group of local citizens, he says, can hold up a project like Cape Wind, "I want people to see that."

The second main character is Audra Parker, a widowed mother of four who runs the Alliance to Protect Nantucket Sound, the chief opposition group. Her message is crystallized into a sound bite chanted at many protest rallies: "Great idea—but not here!" Parker is able to adapt her main argument to fit the concerns of various audiences: fishermen will be ruined, tourism will suffer, it's about historic preservation, the costs are too high.

These are all valid concerns, and developers who ignore them do so at their peril. "This is a mistake that is made over and over again," says Margot Gerritsen, a colleague of Orr's at Stanford. As an associate professor of energy resources engineering, Gerritsen sometimes attends local meetings and workshops that attempt to hammer out disputes over solar thermal plants in the desert or new transmission lines in rural areas. "People get angry because they feel that they are not listened to," she says. Developers, she adds, need to explain the tangible benefits, such as the prospect of new jobs. She also stresses the need to present hard data from existing energy projects to show the impact on things like real-estate prices and local wildlife.

These local issues are especially tough to sort out because people tend to fear the unknown. "People prefer the evil they know over the evil they don't know," says Gerritsen. Cape Cod, for instance, burns oil to generate electricity. Over the years, tankers delivering oil to the 40-year-old power plant

10

at the Cape Cod Canal have sprung leaks—resulting in spills requiring expensive beach cleanups. What's more, the pollution from its smokestack has contributed to what the American Lung Association calls some of the state's worst air quality. Despite all this, it's still quite common for people to say they'd "rather stick with an old power plant than accept a new one," she says.

Such local debate masks the larger question of whether Cape Wind is a necessary energy alternative. Over the past three years alone, U.S. wind capacity has more than doubled, to more than 35 gigawatts; it now accounts for about 2 percent of America's electricity. But many of the convenient sites suitable for land-based wind farms have already been developed. So even though offshore wind is more expensive (electricity generated by such installations currently costs up to twice as much as electricity from land-based wind farms), developers are now proposing more than 20 plants in U.S. waters—from the Jersey Shore to the Great Lakes to the Gulf Coast of Texas.

No one seems to dispute that many of these spots boast ideal wind resources. In Nantucket Sound, for instance, winds average 20 miles per hour, with little downtime, even in the summer. What's more, the site is protected from large waves by the surrounding land, and it even offers a shallow shoal on which to mount the windmills.

But since the capital costs of building offshore wind farms are high, projected energy prices are steep as well. Under an agreement that must still be ratified by the state utility commission (a decision is expected by the end of the year), Cape Wind has promised to sell half its power to National Grid, a Northeast energy supplier, for 18.7 cents per kilowatt-hour. That's higher than local retail rates for grid energy, which are in the range of 8 to 12 cents per kilowatt-hour. Whether Cape Wind will actually cost or save consumers money in the long run depends in part on what happens with prices for coal, gas, and oil over the next few years and decades, says Stephen Connors, a research engineer with the MIT Energy Initiative. Power produced by Cape Wind will be used by all National Grid's customers, supplying around 4 percent of a typical customer's energy. At current rates, Connors says, the investment in Cape Wind should cost the average National Grid residential customer anywhere from about $1 per month on the low side to "about two Starbucks lattes per month" on the high side.

In the decade that the battle over Cape Wind has been raging, offshore wind farms have been built in the waters of nine European countries, resulting in a capacity of more than 2.4 gigawatts—enough to power more than a million homes. A 10th country, China, recently completed a 102-megawatt turbine cluster off the coast of Shanghai. By 2020, 30 gigawatts of additional offshore wind capacity is expected to be built off the coasts of China. Yet America's effort to tap offshore wind has lagged.

If Cape Wind's Gordon gets his way, the turbines will be spinning by 2013. But that victory will have less to do with the economic and environmental merits of offshore wind power than with which side in the local political standoff has best withstood the epic wrangling. Many of the locals have grown cynical: as one citizen in the film says, "The people with the most money are going to win." 15

In fact, it doesn't have to end that way. The turbines, if they're built, will be in public waters leased by Gordon and his associates. That means the public has a right to decide whether the project makes sense as part of a national effort to increase renewable power. But to make decisions wisely, we need a coherent national energy policy and international agreements that make sense of local energy development. In their absence, each new energy project will be caught in the local crosswinds.

Analyze

1. Why has the Cape Wind project been proposed for the area of the Nantucket Sound?

2. According to this article, why is the Cape Wind project so controversial?

3. The author states that "the showdown over Cape Wind is a microcosm of a much larger debate." Discuss as a class how you think decisions about "where to put stuff," and who should make sacrifices, should be made. How does this reflect similar conversations in issues of sustainability?

Explore

1. In an earlier selection in this chapter, Liz Barratt-Brown argued that "it's all about the framing." One way of framing the issue of Cape Wind, as discussed in this piece, is to describe it as an issue of socioeconomic status—that it's about "super-rich estate owners who simply don't want their views of the water spoiled." But this is not the only

way that this issue could be framed. Construct a series of three different headlines, each which represents the Cape Wind issue in a different way. Choose your wording carefully so that your framing issue is
clear from the caption alone.

2. The Cape Wind debate is an example of NIMBY—Not In My Back
Yard. People rarely want to have things like a wind farm in their view,
their neighborhood, their city. Do some research on development in
your community—new roads, shopping centers, an airport, a landfill—
that drew community controversy. Describe the sides in the controversy and see if you can make each side human, each side a rational
position.

3. Use the Internet to locate the 10 biggest wind farms in the United
States. Where are they? And why are they located where they are? How
much electricity do they produce? And then decide whether they are a
good thing, a bad thing, or a mixed blessing.

Willett Kempton
"The Offshore Power Debate: Views From Cape Cod"

Willett Kempton is a professor of marine policy at the College of Earth,
Ocean and Environment at the University of Delaware. He has a Ph.D. in an-
thropology from the University of Texas and has published many academic
articles on offshore wind power, environmental values, and public perception of environmental issues. The article from which this excerpt is taken is
based on interviews with residents of the Cape Cod area, and it describes
their reasons for supporting or opposing the proposed Cape Wind project.
Taken together, these reasons represent the complex rhetorical context in
which people make arguments about projects such as Cape Wind. Like many
issues in marine policy or sustainability generally, the Cape Wind project is
a "wicked problem" for which there is no simple or best solution, only complex trade-offs.

Abstract

Wind power resources on the eastern U.S. continental shelf are estimated to be over 400 GW, several times the electricity used by U.S. eastern coastal states. The first U.S. developer proposes to build 130 large (40 story tall) wind turbines in Nantucket Sound, just outside Massachusetts state waters. These would provide 420 MW at market prices, enough electricity for most of Cape Cod. The project is opposed by a vigorous and well-financed coalition. Polling shows local public opinion on the project almost equally divided. This article draws on semi-structured interviews with residents of Cape Cod to analyze values, beliefs, and logic of supporters and opponents. For example, one value found to lead to opposition is that the ocean is a special place that should be kept natural and free of human intrusion. One line of argument found to lead to support is: The war in Iraq is problematic, this war is "really" over petroleum, Cape Cod generates electricity from oil, therefore, the wind project would improve U.S. security. Based on analysis of the values and reasoning behind our interview data, we identify four issues that are relevant but not currently part of the debate.

Introduction

Recent assessments of renewable energy show that wind power has, since the turn of the century, become cost-competitive in the sites with the most favorable wind regimes (Herzog et al., 2001). Until very recently, large-scale North American wind resources were believed to exist in the Great Plains of the United States, northern Canada, and central Canada only (Grubb & Meyer, 1993). Although these huge resources are enough to meet the entire continent's electrical needs, they are distant from the large coastal cities where electricity is primarily consumed—imposing a need for costly large-scale transmission lines (Cavallo, 1995). In just the last couple of years, it has been recognized that the Atlantic Ocean also has a large wind resource on the continental shelf, close to East Coast cities. Three or four manufacturers have developed large wind electric turbines designed to be placed offshore, in waters up to 20–30 m in depth. To date these have been placed only in European waters. By late 2003, the resources, the technology, and the economic viability had all come together in the Eastern United States, potentially allowing large-scale deployment to begin by 2005.

The furthest advanced of a handful of proposed U.S. offshore wind developments is in Nantucket Sound, off the Southern coast of Cape Cod, Massachusetts. This proposal has engendered a widespread, well-organized, well-financed, and politically potent opposition. This movement's strength, and the apparent contradiction of such opposition coming from a population thought of as politically liberal and environmentally concerned, have garnered national press coverage (e.g., Burkett, 2003). A second project was proposed by the Long Island Power Authority for the southern edge of Long Island, with an RFP issued in 2003. At least two other developers are exploring additional possible sites but none have concrete proposals under review.

The Nantucket proposal, upon which this article focuses, seems almost a textbook case of environmental policy debates and environmental mobilization. The project would provide clean energy but would intrude on a beautiful, unspoiled natural area. One can see the wind turbines as an ugly intrusion on the seascape or as a beautiful portent of clean energy for the 21st century; as a threat to tourism or an opportunity for year-round local jobs; as a menace to marine and avian species or as pollution reduction; as a government-financed boondoggle or a hedge against foreign oil dependence; as an example of market solutions to environmental problems or as greedy developers spoiling Cape Cod yet further. Because there is an oil-burning electric plant in the same area, the possibility of wind electricity displacing oil electricity makes the air pollution and energy security aspects of wind energy locally immediate and easy to visualize. However, no public commitment has been made to shut down the oil generator if the wind project is built (they are managed by different entities and their generation is governed by fluctuating electricity markets). Another potentially important issue in this locale, one that we will show is not part of the debate, is that parts of Cape Cod are at low elevation, with beaches and salt-water wetlands important environmentally, economically, and culturally; thus climate change caused by burning fossil fuels would have more effect on Cape Cod than most areas. By a quirk of geography and law, the proposed site is surrounded on three sides by lands of the State of Massachusetts, yet the waters are Federal. Only the electrical transmission line would pass through Massachusetts' waters. Thus, the permitting process is led and primarily controlled by the Federal Government, with the state having minimal influence. The Federal law governing the approval or denial of the project is laughably mismatched to the issues under debate, with the lead agency's prime mandate being to determine whether the wind towers would constitute an "obstruction to navigation" (Rivers and Harbors Act, 1899; also see Firestone et al., 2004).

The project, as one informant described it, "has pitted environmentalist against environmentalist" (CP6). It is a revealing and rich case of environmental values, beliefs, and mobilization, operating in the context of environmental policy and law. In this article, we draw on interviews with residents to analyze the reasons for the opposition to, and support for, the proposed offshore wind development. As a prelude to our analysis of the public's views, we describe offshore wind power and the proposed Nantucket Sound development. After analyzing our interview data on the debate, we then lay out issues that seem important but that are not highlighted in the debate so far.

Why Wind Power? Why Offshore?

Wind turbines tap a renewable energy resource. Air motion spins a propeller, which generates electricity. As an electricity source, it competes with coal, natural gas, and petroleum, all of which cause air pollution and give off CO_2, the primary anthropogenic cause of climate change. Why is wind power being pursued now rather than other renewable energy sources like solar energy or tidal power? The answer is a cross between resource size, geophysics, and cost of current technology. For example, solar electricity is abundant and it is cost-effective in remote locations. But for large-scale power, wind is far cheaper (e.g., 4¢/kWh for Class 6 wind versus 28¢/kWh for solar photovoltaic, Hertzog et al., 2001). Hydroelectric power river locations are mostly tapped, and there are concerns about the environmental impact of large dams. There are other niche renewable energy technologies such as geothermal or tidal power, which may be sensible in a few locations but could not provide more than a couple of percent of world electrical power needs, and still others, such as ocean thermal and undersea current generators, which are as yet undeveloped in their technologies, economics, and/or understanding their environmental impacts.

Thus, the short answer to "Why wind?" is: the technology is mature, reliable generators are available, it is already cost-competitive; it produces essentially no pollution or greenhouse gases, and it is a very large resource.

This combination of favorable resources, economics, and recent maturation of technology has led to explosive growth. Figure 5.2 shows the growth in installed capacity, which climbed to 39 GW by the end of 2003.

Wind power also has the economic characteristic of being labor-intensive; it requires more labor per MW generation than any other electric generator (Greenpeace and European Wind Energy Association, 2002). Although modern wind turbines are entirely automated, they are nonetheless large rotating mechanical devices exposed to the elements that require regular inspection, lubrication, and occasional repair. At the local level, wind power creates more long-term employment than other power sources.

10   High labor costs also strongly affect optimum unit size and development size—larger machines and larger clusters are more cost-effective because, for example, mechanics, electricians, ornithologists, and boats or trucks are shared across more output and revenue. It is also important to locate areas of frequent high winds, as the investment in machines and labor only pays back when the wind blows frequently and strongly. Size optimization and favorable wind sites are essential for labor-intensive wind to cost less per MWh than coal.

How much potential power is offshore? Although no thorough assessment of the resources has been made, a preliminary estimate was recently presented by the National Renewable Energy Laboratory (NREL) (Butterfield, Musial, & Laxson, 2004)—in the shallower waters (<30 m) of New England and the Mid-Atlantic States, assuming only 1/3 of that area is available (due to shipping lanes, protected ecosystems, and other coastal uses), summing their estimates yields a 95 GW potential. For comparison, that amount of wind power potential is approximately equal to the entire generating capacity of these coastal states (Maine through Maryland) of 99 GW (Energy Information Administration, 2004). Currently available products use monopile towers that can be placed up to 20 m depth. As deeper-water mountings are developed and become available, there is an additional 386 GW in the deeper waters out to 50 nautical miles from shore. These startling resource numbers, the availability of turbines at competitive market prices to harvest this power, the proximity to load centers, and the now-favorable economics raise the possibility of displacing much of the fossil fuel power on the East Coast of the United States. Whether or not this possibility is realized will depend on public acceptance and the policies for project evaluation and permitting. This article analyzes public acceptance of wind turbines in the ocean; a simultaneous paper by an overlapping set of authors (Firestone et al., 2004) considers permitting and regulatory issues.

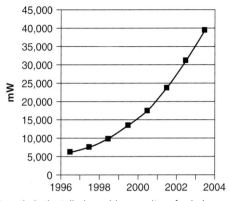

Figure 5.2 Growth in installed world capacity of wind power, 1996–2003 (American Wind Energy Association, 2004).

. . .

The Cape Cod Proposal

A private company, Cape Wind Associates, proposes to install 130 wind turbines in 62 km² (24 square miles) of Nantucket Sound. They plan to use the new General Electric model 3.6s wind generators, designed exclusively for offshore use. These machines are 128 meters from sea level to top blade tip (420 feet, or about 40 stories) and their nameplate electrical output is 3.6 MW. This development is projected to generate a peak power of 420 MW, adding up to 1,491,384 MW hours of electricity per year, which is about 3/4 the electrical needs of Cape Cod, or 1/10 of the demand of the entire state of Massachusetts (Cape Wind, 2004a). Geographically, the developer states that Nantucket Sound is a highly favorable site for wind development, arguably the best on the east coast (strong steady winds, close to power lines on shore, shallow water, protected from high waves, and minimal conflicts with transportation systems). Financially, private investors are supplying about $750M capital; about $12M has been spent to date on environmental impact studies, erecting a wind measuring tower on-site, and an extensive public relations campaign.

The proposal to build what could become the United States' first offshore wind farm, in the waters of Nantucket Sound, has generated a vigorous local opposition movement, focused around the Alliance to Protect Nantucket Sound (an organization specifically created to oppose the development). The Alliance seems to have both popular support and a financially strong core. In 2003 it received $1.7 million from 2,891 individuals, with just 56 of them giving $1.3 million of that; the top four individuals gave over $100,000 each, including a loan that was forgiven (Zindler, 2004). A similar pattern with a small number of large and very large donations was seen in 2002 (Zindler, 2003). Publicly declared opponents of the project include several local environmental and business groups, the Editorial page of the Cape Cod Times, U.S. Sen. Ted Kennedy, U.S. Rep. William Delahunt, several state legislators, and the Massachusetts Governor and Attorney General.

. . .

Conclusion

We analyzed reasons for public support and opposition to a utility-scale wind development off Cape Cod. Apart from differences in beliefs, some of which might be considered based on missing or incorrect information, there are also important value differences.

15   Some beliefs and values led to opposition. For example, many opponents believe that the project is uneconomic and that wind power will not make a significant contribution to electricity supply. Some apparently evaluated the project's environmental effects based on readily accessed factors such as scale, familiarity, and permanence; our quantitative comparison shows that this leads them to vastly overestimate the likely environmental impact of the project in comparison to existing activities such as trawling. On the part of the supporters, there was a facile characterization of the opposition as primarily concerned with aesthetics of their ocean view, and as being wealthy property owners and boaters. These groups appear to be an important financial base for opposition organizations; however, our study and the surveys reviewed earlier show that the opposition sentiment is far broader. Also, our analysis suggests that concern expressed as "the view" is not only visual or aesthetic; it is more importantly a gloss for the value that the ocean is special and humans should not intrude on it, and the value that Cape Cod should be protected from the excessive development that residents feel is destroying its character.

We suggest four areas that, we feel, merit broader or more explicit debate. The first area is the human mortality averted by displacing current fossil fuel use. The second concerns the current Federal decision-making process and the philosophical and justice issues in this versus other decision-making modes. A debate on the decision-making process itself could engage citizens both on the question of the appropriate level of government to make the decision, and the question of licensing and payment for the resource (e.g., should wind developers pay, as do offshore petroleum developers, or should the wind be free, as are fisheries?). Third, are the implications of the scale of development implicit in claims for national-scale benefits—at that scale there appear to be very substantial benefits from offshore wind development, but the impact estimates must be scaled up commensurately. The fourth undebated point is the role of wind power in mitigating global climate change. This can be locally understood as balancing the impact of wind power development in Nantucket Sound now, versus the impact of future damage from climate change and sea level rise.

Underlying the current debate are several basic value questions and tradeoffs. For example, the value of protecting the ocean and keeping it free from human intrusion; the value of cleaner air and less human infirmity and mortality; the value of traditions like sailing and fishing in New England; whether there is a right to a local seascape that residents assumed would be there forever; the tradeoff between proceeding now with an imperfect process to start a clean industry versus first establishing proper procedures, and more globally, whether Cape Cod and the Islands are willing to absorb the negatives of this wind development now, in order to set an example for mitigating climate change, a potentially far larger threat but one they cannot solve alone. We suggest that the debate would have a better chance for true engagement, perhaps even resolution, if these values and missing issues were aired and debated more explicitly.

Analyze

1. According to the selection, what are some of the advantages of wind power over other renewable sources of energy?
2. In what ways does the author suggest that the Cape Wind debate reflects conflict between individual beliefs and values?
3. How do you think the people in your hometown would respond to a proposal like Cape Wind?

Explore

1. You have read a number of different perspectives on the Cape Wind project. Based on your reading, construct a list of the major questions

that have been raised in the debate. Then, using an online search engine, find at least three photos that encapsulate three of those major questions, using only a brief caption to provide context to the visual.

2. This article on Cape Wind has a different function and purpose than the earlier article on the same topic. In a small group, construct a characterization of each of these articles that highlights the differences between each of the approaches to the topic of Cape Wind taken in these pieces. In constructing your snapshots of each piece, think about each author's purpose (was it to explain something? to argue something?), the kinds of topics that appeared in each article, as well as the style of writing exhibited by each.

3. This author complicates the aesthetic controversy over the Cape Wind turbines by stating,

> "our analysis suggests that concern expressed as 'the view' is not only visual or aesthetic; it is more importantly a gloss for the value that the ocean is special and humans should not intrude on it, and the value that Cape Cod should be protected from the excessive development that residents feel is destroying its character."

This distinction made by the author is nuanced; to gain practice recognizing these nuance differences, locate at least four outside articles that discuss "the view" of Cape Cod. For each article, determine what value is being represented. Do you see any values that go beyond the visual?

Christopher Bateman
"A Colossal Fracking Mess"

Christopher Bateman is an associate editor at *Vanity Fair*, a magazine of popular culture, fashion, and current affairs published by Condé Nast. Bateman writes about many topics, but his specialty is politics, business, and economics. The essay excerpted below is about "hydro-fracturing," the new and controversial method of extracting natural gas from deep shale deposits. As Bateman points out, natural gas burns more cleanly than petroleum-based fuels, but fracking creates a host of problems of its own.

Early on a spring morning in the town of Damascus, in northeastern Pennsylvania, the fog on the Delaware River rises to form a mist that hangs above the tree-covered hills on either side. A buzzard swoops in from the northern hills to join a flock ensconced in an evergreen on the river's southern bank.

Stretching some 400 miles, the Delaware is one of the cleanest free-flowing rivers in the United States, home to some of the best fly-fishing in the country. More than 15 million people, including residents of New York City and Philadelphia, get their water from its pristine watershed. To regard its unspoiled beauty on a spring morning, you might be led to believe that the river is safely off limits from the destructive effects of industrialization. Unfortunately, you'd be mistaken. The Delaware is now the most endangered river in the country, according to the conservation group American Rivers.

That's because large swaths of land—private and public—in the watershed have been leased to energy companies eager to drill for natural gas here using a controversial, poorly understood technique called hydraulic fracturing. "Fracking," as it's colloquially known, involves injecting millions of gallons of water, sand, and chemicals, many of them toxic, into the earth at high pressures to break up rock formations and release natural gas trapped inside. Sixty miles west of Damascus, the town of Dimock, population 1,400, makes all too clear the dangers posed by hydraulic fracturing. You don't need to drive around Dimock long to notice how the rolling hills and farmland of this Appalachian town are scarred by barren, square-shaped clearings, jagged, newly constructed roads with 18-wheelers driving up and down them, and colorful freight containers labeled "residual waste." Although there is a moratorium on drilling new wells for the time being, you can still see the occasional active drill site, manned by figures in hazmat suits and surrounded by klieg lights, trailers, and pits of toxic wastewater, the derricks towering over barns, horses, and cows in their shadows.

The real shock that Dimock has undergone, however, is in the aquifer that residents rely on for their fresh water. Dimock is now known as the place where, over the past two years, people's water started turning brown and making them sick, one woman's water well spontaneously combusted, and horses and pets mysteriously began to lose their hair.

Craig and Julie Sautner moved to Dimock from a nearby town in March 5 2008. They were in the process of renovating their modest but beautifully situated home on tree-canopied Carter Road when land men from Houston-based Cabot Oil & Gas, a midsize player in the energy-exploration industry, came knocking on their door to inquire about leasing the mineral rights to their three and a half acres of land. The Sautners say the land men told them that their neighbors had already signed leases and that the drilling would have no impact whatsoever on their land. (Others in Dimock claim they were told that if they refused to sign a lease, gas would be taken out from under their land anyway, since under Pennsylvania law a well drilled on a leased piece of property can capture gas from neighboring, unleased properties.) They signed the lease, for a onetime payout of $2,500 per acre—better than the $250 per acre a neighbor across the street received—plus royalties on each producing well.

Drilling operations near their property commenced in August 2008. Trees were cleared and the ground leveled to make room for a four-acre drilling site less than 1,000 feet away from their land. The Sautners could feel the earth beneath their home shake whenever the well was fracked.

Within a month, their water had turned brown. It was so corrosive that it scarred dishes in their dishwasher and stained their laundry. They complained to Cabot, which eventually installed a water-filtration system in the basement of their home. It seemed to solve the problem, but when the Pennsylvania Department of Environmental Protection came to do further tests, it found that the Sautners' water still contained high levels of methane. More ad hoc pumps and filtration systems were installed. While the Sautners did not drink the water at this point, they continued to use it for other purposes for a full year.

"It was so bad sometimes that my daughter would be in the shower in the morning, and she'd have to get out of the shower and lay on the floor" because of the dizzying effect the chemicals in the water had on her, recalls Craig Sautner, who has worked as a cable splicer for Frontier Communications his whole life. She didn't speak up about it for a while, because she wondered whether she was imagining the problem. But she wasn't the only one in the family suffering. "My son had sores up and down his legs from the water," Craig says. Craig and Julie also experienced frequent headaches and dizziness.

By October 2009, the D.E.P. had taken all the water wells in the Sautners' neighborhood offline. It acknowledged that a major contamination of the aquifer had occurred. In addition to methane, dangerously high levels of iron and aluminum were found in the Sautners' water.

10   The Sautners now rely on water delivered to them every week by Cabot. The value of their land has been decimated. Their children no longer take

showers at home. They desperately want to move but cannot afford to buy a new house on top of their current mortgage.

"Our land is worthless," says Craig. "Who is going to buy this house?"

. . .

Damascus and Dimock are both located above a vast rock formation rich in natural gas known as the Marcellus Shale, which stretches along the Appalachians from West Virginia up to the western half of the state of New York. The gas in the Marcellus Shale has been known about for more than 100 years, but it has become accessible and attractive as a resource only in the past two decades, thanks to technological innovation, the depletion of easier-to-reach, "conventional" gas deposits, and increases in the price of natural gas. Shale-gas deposits are dispersed throughout a thin horizontal layer of loose rock (the shale), generally more than a mile below ground. Conventional vertical drilling cannot retrieve shale gas in an economical way, but when combined with hydraulic fracturing, horizontal drilling—whereby a deeply drilled well is bent at an angle to run parallel to the surface of the Earth—changes the equation.

Developed by oil-field-services provider Halliburton, which first implemented the technology commercially in 1949 (and which was famously run by Dick Cheney before he became vice president of the United States), hydraulic fracturing has been used in conventional oil and gas wells for decades to increase production when a well starts to run dry. But its use in unconventional types of drilling, from coal-bed methane to shale gas, is relatively new. When a well is fracked, a small earthquake is produced by the pressurized injection of fluids, fracturing the rock around the well. The gas trapped inside is released and makes its way to the surface along with about half of the "fracking fluid," plus dirt and rock that are occasionally radioactive. From there, the gas is piped to nearby compressor stations that purify it and prepare it to be piped (and sometimes transported in liquefied form) to power plants, manufacturers, and domestic consumers. Volatile organic compounds (carbon-based gaseous substances with a variety of detrimental health effects) and other dangerous chemicals are burned off directly into the air during this on-site compression process. Meanwhile, the returned fracking fluid, now called wastewater, is either trucked off or stored in large, open-air, tarp-lined pits on site, where it is allowed to evaporate. The other portion of the fluid remains deep underground—no one really knows what happens to it.

Fracking is an energy- and resource-intensive process. Every shale-gas well that is fracked requires between three and eight million gallons of water. Fleets of trucks have to make hundreds of trips to carry the fracking fluid to and from each well site.

15   Due in part to spotty state laws and an absence of federal regulation, the safety record that hydraulic fracturing has amassed to date is deeply disturbing. As use of the technique has spread, it has been followed by incidents of water contamination and environmental degradation, and even devastating health problems. Thousands of complaints have been lodged with state and federal agencies by people all over the country whose lives and communities have been transformed by fracking operations.

In Dimock, where more than 60 gas wells were drilled in a nine-square-mile area, all kinds of ugly things transpired after Cabot came to town. A truck turned over and caused an 800-gallon diesel-fuel spill in April 2009. Up to 8,000 gallons of Halliburton-manufactured fracking fluid leaked from faulty supply pipes, with some seeping into wetlands and a stream, killing fish, in September 2009. Many Dimock residents were having the same problems as the Sautners. A water well belonging to a woman named Norma Fiorentino blew up while she was visiting her daughter. Reports of the havoc appeared in the local press and then gradually trickled into the national media. Reuters and ProPublica were on the story early on; later, everyone from NPR to *The New York Times* was coming to Dimock.

· ❖ ·

With natural gas being heavily promoted in TV ads and by politicians and proponents such as oilman and hedge-fund manager T. Boone Pickens, many Americans have come to see the resource in a positive light. Natural gas burns more cleanly than coal and oil do, we are told, and there's an abundance of it right there, under our soil, making it a logical and patriotic energy source for America. We are told that it can help wean us off our dependence on foreign oil as we make the transition to renewable energy. Yet our supplies of natural gas are ultimately finite, and, increasingly, they must be accessed via hydraulic fracturing. In fact, more than 90 percent of natural-gas wells today use fracking.

Shale gas has become a significant part of our energy mix over the past decade. From 1996 to 2006, shale-gas production went from less than 2 percent to 6 percent of all domestic natural-gas production. Some industry analysts predict shale gas will represent a full half of total domestic gas production within 10 years.

It's not just the oil-and-gas industry that's excited about the possibilities. Last year, even a progressive, Washington, D.C.–based think tank, the

Center for American Progress Action Fund, desperate for solutions to global warming, touted natural gas as "the single biggest game changer for climate action in the next two decades." President Obama has been supportive of shale gas and says he wants to see an increase in domestic natural-gas production.

But shale gas and hydraulic fracturing haven't needed much help from the Obama administration. That's because they already got a huge helping hand from the federal government under the Bush administration. Although fracking was never regulated by the federal government when it was a less prevalently used technique, it was granted explicit exemptions—despite dissent within the E.P.A.—from the Safe Drinking Water Act, the Clean Air Act, and the Clean Water Act by the Energy Policy Act of 2005, the wide-ranging energy bill crafted by Dick Cheney in closed-door meetings with oil-and-gas executives. While the average citizen can receive harsh punishment under federal law for dumping a car battery into a pond, gas companies, thanks to what has become known as the Halliburton Loophole, are allowed to pump millions of gallons of fluid containing toxic chemicals into the ground, right next to our aquifers, without even having to identify them.

Claiming that the information is proprietary, drilling companies have still not come out and fully disclosed what fracking fluid is made of. But activists and researchers have been able to identify some of the chemicals used. They include such substances as benzene, ethylbenzene, toluene, boric acid, monoethanolamine, xylene, diesel-range organics, methanol, formaldehyde, hydrochloric acid, ammonium bisulfite, 2-butoxyethanol, and 5-chloro-2-methyl-4-isothiazotin-3-one. (Recently, in congressional testimony, drilling companies have confirmed the presence of many of these chemicals.) According to Theo Colborn, a noted expert on water issues and endocrine disruptors, at least half of the chemicals known to be present in fracking fluid are toxic; many of them are carcinogens, neurotoxins, endocrine disruptors, and mutagens. But Colborn estimates that a third of the chemicals in fracking fluid remain unknown to the public.

· ❖ ·

Reports of environmental degradation have come out of many places where natural-gas drilling and fracking are going on. The full extent of the problem is difficult to determine because much of the evidence is anecdotal and because drilling companies have been known to buy people off when things go wrong. In Silt, Colorado, a woman named Laura Amos no longer talks about the adrenal-gland tumor and other health complications she developed after her water was contaminated by a gas well drilled less than 1,000 feet from her home. (A state investigation into the matter concluded that a drilling failure had likely led to intermingling between the gas and water strata in the ground.) She signed a non-disclosure agreement as part of a deal to sell her tainted land to EnCana, the large Canadian gas company that drilled the well. But perusing newspapers from towns where fracking is going on reveals how the issue refuses to die, with headlines like "Fears of Tainted Water Well Up in Colorado," "Collateral Damage: Residents Fear Murky Effects of Energy Boom," and "Worker Believes Cancer Caused by Fracking Fluids" appearing regularly.

A macro look at the way oil and gas drilling has transformed entire landscapes out West, carving them up into patterns resembling those of a transistor board, can be seen by typing "San Juan Basin, New Mexico" into Google Maps and clicking on the satellite view. In Colorado, some 206 chemical fluid spills from oil and gas wells, connected to 48 cases of suspected water contamination, happened in 2008 alone. In New Mexico, toxic fluid had seeped into water supplies at more than 800 oil and gas drilling sites as of July 2008. Clusters of unusual health problems have popped up in some of these drilling hot spots. Kendall Gerdes, a physician in Colorado Springs, tells me of how he and other doctors in the area saw a striking number of patients come to them with chronic dizziness, headaches, and neurological problems after drilling began near their homes. One of Dr. Gerdes's patients, 62-year-old Chris Mobaldi, developed idiopathic hemorrhaging, or spontaneous bleeding, as well as neuropathy, a pituitary gland tumor, and a rare neurological speech impediment after alleged frequent exposure to noxious fumes from drilling. Although her health improved after she moved to another part of Colorado, she continues to have trouble speaking and walking to this day.

And with drilling in the Marcellus Shale, the complaints have spread East. Despite making more than a million dollars in royalties from drilling on his 105-acre farm, Wayne Smith, a farmer in Clearville, Pennsylvania, wishes he'd never signed a lease. Some of his livestock mysteriously dropped dead after having motor-skill breakdowns; a veterinarian said the deaths could be attributed to arsenic, high levels of which were found in water on Smith's property. (Smith also worries about health problems he has developed, such as frequent headaches, abscessed teeth, and other mouth problems.) In Avella, Pennsylvania, a wastewater impoundment caught fire and exploded on George Zimmermann's 480-acre property, producing a 200-foot-high conflagration that burned for six hours and produced a cloud of thick, black smoke visible 10 miles away. An E.P.A.-accredited environmental-testing company sampled the soil around the well sites on Zimmerman's property and found arsenic at 6,430 times permissible levels and tetrachloroethene, a carcinogen and central-nervous-system suppressant, at 1,417 times permissible levels. (In January, the state of Pennsylvania fined the company that is drilling on Zimmerman's land, Atlas Energy, $85,000 for environmental violations related to fracking—a drop in the bucket for a corporation that brought in $1.5 billion in revenue last year. As of press time, Atlas had not provided *Vanity Fair* with a comment on the matter.)

These are a number of the ways that fracking can conceivably go wrong. 25 Weston Wilson, a former E.P.A. official who blew the whistle on the agency's flawed report on fracking by writing a letter to Congress, likes to talk about the difference between "bad wells" and "good wells gone bad." "Bad wells" are ones that leak because of poor construction or an accident; "good wells gone bad" refers to the possibility that fracking may pose a more fundamental, generalized risk to water supplies, through seepage of the wastewater that remains in the ground. While shale formations are thousands of feet below groundwater levels, geological studies have shown that the Earth is full of cracks at these depths, and no one has ruled out the possibility that fracking may open up arteries for the toxic fluid to seep into groundwater in a more insidious way.

That's not to mention the risks posed by the above-ground handling of return wastewater and the airborne pollution endemic to natural-gas processing. Leaks and spills have occurred at the on-site pits where wastewater is allowed to fester. And the city of Fort Worth, Texas, which sits atop the country's most productive shale-gas formation, demonstrates the dangers that natural-gas processing poses to "airsheds." Chemical emissions from natural-gas processing in and around Forth Worth now match the city's total emissions from cars and trucks, leading to alarming levels of volatile organic compounds and other pollutants in the air.

Facing increasing lawsuits and scrutiny, the gas industry no longer stands by the position it took for years that there's nothing unsafe in fracking fluid. But it still says that shooting fracking fluid into the ground is a safe and sensible practice. (In a written statement to *Vanity Fair*, American's Natural Gas Alliance, an industry lobbying group, said that the current federal regulation of fracking is adequate.) It continues to hammer home the notion that natural gas is cleaner than its fossil-fuel relatives, coal and oil, and produces lower levels of greenhouse gases.

But a new preliminary assessment by Cornell ecology and environmental-biology professor Robert Howarth of the emissions generated throughout the fracking process suggests that, when the thousands of truck trips required to frack every single well are counted, natural gas obtained by fracking is actually *worse* than drilling for oil and possibly even coal mining in terms of greenhouse-gas production. While Howarth explains that his estimates are subject to uncertainty because of the lack of complete, concrete data about fracking, he concludes, "There is an urgent need for a comprehensive assessment of the full range of emission of greenhouse gases from using natural gas obtained by high-volume, slick water hydraulic fracturing. . . . Society should be wary of claims that natural gas is a desirable fuel in terms of the consequences on global warming."

Yet the shale-gas boom, driven by fracking, continues on a global scale. Shale land is already being leased in Western and Central Europe while foreign companies buy up land in the Marcellus Shale. A May 25 memorandum of economic and strategic dialogue between the U.S. and China prominently lists an initiative to help China assess and extract its own shale gas as an item of agreement. In Australia, where fracking has been sweeping the Queensland countryside and where landowners have little or no control over their mineral rights, a furor has been growing over the water contamination happening around drilling locations.

30   At the same time, the people who have been burned badly by their firsthand experience with what you might call the New Natural Gas, and who have not gone silent, are spreading their message of acute disillusionment, ecological destruction, land-value decimation, and serious health concerns. As I sit and talk with the members of Damascus Citizens for Sustainability, news reports from the tragic *Deepwater Horizon* leak in the Gulf pop up from time to time on their computers. The disaster serves as a grim backdrop to our conversation, reinforcing the hazards of pushing forward with experimental forms of drilling whose risks are not well understood.

At one point, we see a news alert revealing the likely cause of the *Deepwater* explosion: a methane bubble. It's a complication also encountered in land-based gas drilling, and it's just one of the things [local activist] Carullo fears could precipitate a catastrophe in the Delaware watershed. "This is exactly what we're trying to prevent here," Carullo tells me. "This is exactly what we've been talking about."

Analyze

1. What is fracking?
2. What percent of natural gas extraction is achieved by fracking? What dangers, briefly, are associated with the process known as fracking?
3. How does this article's discussion of the dangers posed by contamination caused by fracking relate to Friedman's investigation into the fragility of ecosystems given earlier in this chapter? Does water contamination stand as a true threat to a local ecosystem? Construct a map in which you trace connections you identify.

Explore

1. Natural gas has become an increasingly utilized source of energy across the United States. Locate some statistics that demonstrate the increased use of natural gas as an alternative to fossil fuel. Construct a graph that charts the rise in natural gas usage over the past 50 years. What conclusions can you draw from this graph? Compose an editorial for your school's newspaper in which you argue that your findings are reflective of changing values in America.
2. In the reading about Cape Wind, you saw that local residents sometimes oppose energy projects. Explore the public debates over fracking, especially in states like Pennsylvania and Texas. Write a brief position paper that lays out a plan for managing these sorts of energy policy conflicts.
3. Read some of the reports about natural gas, its cheap, abundant supply and its benefits to our economy. Then watch the movie *Promised Land*. Write an analysis of how the two positions are framed and whether there is another, better frame for the issue.

Forging Connections

1. You have read a number of articles that deal with the energy crisis that is staring the United States—and the world—squarely in the face. A major question that ties all of these readings together is: Is there a will

to change our energy habits? In other words, does the general population feel compelled, by either financial or environmental concerns, to use more efficient or less environmentally damaging sources of energy? In a five-paragraph letter to your fellow global citizens, expand upon the idea of the need for change and the reasons for changing—these reasons can be anything from environmental concerns to financial worries. Remember, this is a letter to your fellow global citizens, so it should combine emotional appeals with hard statistical evidence.

2. One of the repeated mantras of the sustainability movement is the phrase "think globally, act locally." Using the readings from this chapter to inform your ideas, compose an essay in which you sketch the complicated relationship between local and global energy concerns. In your essay, describe how some of these writers (like Evan Schwartz) argue that local energy practices rely on global energy policies, while others (think Vandana Shiva) suggest that global energy policies might be detrimental to local energy needs.

Looking Further

1. Energy is a global commodity; we buy, ship, and sell it around the world—but that also means that getting and using energy has consequences around the world too. Like every topic in this book, energy is part of a closed system: food, soil, water, the bottled water we drink, are all affected by our use of energy. Start with one way you use energy and trace the connections to as many other parts of the political, natural, and social system as you can, and represent these connections in a visual display.

2. Energy use is convenient. We like cheap, easy, ready forms of energy. This is true of food, water, and all the things we consume. But consuming energy, water, food, and commodities is not free. Construct a piece of writing that attempts to persuade readers that convenience is not everything and that we need to think about others, about distant people and consequences. What appeals, what information might change the way your readers think about energy?

6 Soil & Water: Resources We Take for Granted

A healthy coral reef: A beautiful but fragile part of an extended ecosystem.

"Whoever thinks about dirt as a strategic resource?" David Montgomery (below) asks this rhetorical question to make his point that dirt or soil is a crucial resource, but that we usually take it for granted. Like Jared Diamond in Chapter 1, Montgomery argues that maintaining the health of our soil is essential to the civilization itself. And like the thin skin of soil that covers the rocks underneath, water seems so abundant that few people other than hydrologists think about it in long-term strategic ways. We think about water in the middle of a drought, but most of the time we take it for granted and, as Brian Fagan says "we live beyond our hydrological means." For example, as Cynthia Barnett points out (below), Americans use approximately 19 *trillion* gallons of water each year to water their lawns. And this is water that has been pumped, processed, purified for drinking, and piped to everyone's house at considerable expense of money and energy.

One way to measure sustainability is to compare the rate at which a resource can be renewed to the rate at which we are using it. For example, are we pumping water out of aquifers faster than the aquifers can recharge? If you continually spend more money than you make by putting purchases on your credit card and taking out a second mortgage on your house, you are going to run out of money and credit sooner or later. Eventually you will go bankrupt.

Taken together, the readings in this chapter illustrate two concepts from the Appendix that are crucial to understanding sustainability: the concept of "systems analysis" and the concept of "scale." The readings on hypoxia (oxygen-depleted water) in the Gulf of Mexico and on nitrogen fertilizer on Midwestern cornfields provide examples of how seemingly distant and unrelated phenomenon are directly related. The overuse of nitrogen fertilizer for agriculture in the upper Mississippi River basin is killing the aquatic life in the Gulf of Mexico thousands of miles away off the Texas and Louisiana coast. Midwestern agriculture and the fish in the

Gulf of Mexico are part of the same system, connected by the Mississippi River basin.

The second crucial concept here is that of scale. The problem of Gulf hypoxia is a problem of geographic scale. Unless you extend your vision to include the whole system, it is easy to overlook or ignore the physically distant consequences of agriculture. Vandana Shiva's essay "Food for Cars or People" in Chapter 5 is a similar story of the distant consequences in the global agricultural and economic system.

Just as important as geographic scale, but much harder to see, is the issue of time scales. Put most simply, geologic time and most natural or evolutionary processes move at a much slower pace than most human activities. For example, the U.S. Department of Agriculture estimates it takes approximately 500 years to produce an inch of topsoil. Yet widespread agricultural production of corn and soybeans can accelerate the rate at which topsoil is eroded by water runoff or wind so that the rate of soil loss vastly outstrips the rate of soil renewal. The issue of different temporal scales is a fundamental idea in almost all questions of sustainability. The different temporal scales of human and natural activities are central, for example, to Rachel Carson's argument about pesticides in the excerpt from *Silent Spring* in Chapter 1. One of the challenges in writing about sustainability is making the invisible visible. How can you get readers to "see" things that are across the globe, that move at geologic rather than human speeds, or that are off in the distant future?

David Montgomery
"Good Old Dirt"

David R. Montgomery is a professor in the Department of Earth and Space Sciences at the University of Washington. As a geomorphologist, he studies the way the changes in the earth's surface structures affect the evolution of ecological systems and human societies. In addition to *Dirt: The Erosion of Civilization,* from which this chapter is taken, Prof. Montgomery has published two other books, *The Rocks Don't Lie: A Geologist Investigates Noah's Flood* and *King of Fish: The Thousand-Year Run of Salmon,* as well as many articles in academic journals. In this essay, Montgomery argues that "soil is our most underappreciated, least valued, and yet essential natural resource." He worries that the gradual erosion of productive soil will make it harder to produce enough food for the planet's growing population and will lead to political instability. As you read this selection, consider what writers like Diamond and Montgomery mean when they talk about how we "mine" the soil.

O n a sunny August day in the late 1990s, I led an expedition up the flank of Mount Pinatubo in the Philippines to survey a river still filled with steaming sand from the massive 1991 eruption. The riverbed jiggled coyly as we trudged upriver under the blazing tropical sun. Suddenly I sank in to my ankles, then my knees, before settling waist deep in hot sand. While my waders began steaming, my graduate students went for their cameras. After properly documenting my predicament, and then negotiating a bit, they pulled me from the mire.

Few things can make you feel as helpless as when the earth gives way beneath your feet. The more you struggle, the deeper you sink. You're going down and there's nothing you can do about it. Even the loose riverbed felt rock solid after that quick dip in boiling quicksand.

Normally we don't think too much about the ground that supports our feet, houses, cities, and farms. Yet even if we usually take it for granted, we know that good soil is not just dirt. When you dig into rich, fresh earth, you can feel the life in it. Fertile soil crumbles and slides right off a shovel. Look closely and you find a whole world of life eating life, a biological orgy recycling the dead back into new life. Healthy soil has an enticing and wholesome aroma—the smell of life itself.

Yet what is dirt? We try to keep it out of sight, out of mind, and outside. We spit on it, denigrate it, and kick it off of our shoes. But in the end, what's more important? Everything comes from it, and everything returns to it. If that doesn't earn dirt a little respect, consider how profoundly soil fertility and soil erosion shaped the course of history.

5   At the dawn of agricultural civilizations, the 98 percent of people who worked the land supported a small ruling class that oversaw the distribution of food and resources. Today, the less than 1 percent of the U.S. population still working the land feeds the rest of us. Although most people realize how dependent we are on this small cadre of modern farmers, few

recognize the fundamental importance of how we treat our dirt for securing the future of our civilization.

Many ancient civilizations indirectly mined soil to fuel their growth as agricultural practices accelerated soil erosion well beyond the pace of soil production. Some figured out how to reinvest in their land and maintain their soil. All depended on an adequate supply of fertile dirt. Despite recognition of the importance of enhancing soil fertility, soil loss contributed to the demise of societies from the first agricultural civilizations to the ancient Greeks and Romans, and later helped spur the rise of European colonialism and the American push westward across North America.

Such problems are not just ancient history. That soil abuse remains a threat to modern society is clear from the plight of environmental refugees driven from the southern plains' Dust Bowl in the 1930s, the African Sahel in the 1970s, and across the Amazon basin today. While the world's population keeps growing, the amount of productive farmland began declining in the 1970s and the supply of cheap fossil fuels used to make synthetic fertilizers will run out later this century. Unless more immediate disasters do us in, how we address the twin problems of soil degradation and accelerated erosion will eventually determine the fate of modern civilization.

In exploring the fundamental role of soil in human history, the key lesson is as simple as it is clear: modern society risks repeating mistakes that hastened the demise of past civilizations. Mortgaging our grandchildren's future by consuming soil faster than it forms, we face the dilemma that sometimes the slowest changes prove most difficult to stop.

For most of recorded history, soil occupied a central place in human cultures. Some of the earliest books were agricultural manuals that passed on knowledge of soils and farming methods. The first of Aristotle's fundamental elements of earth, air, fire, and water, soil is the root of our existence, essential to life on earth. But we treat it as a cheap industrial commodity. Oil is what most of us think of as a strategic material. Yet soil is every bit as important in a longer time frame. Still, who ever thinks about dirt as a strategic resource? In our accelerated modern lives it is easy to forget that fertile soil still provides the foundation for supporting large concentrations of people on our planet.

Geography controls many of the causes of and the problems created by   10
soil erosion. In some regions farming without regard for soil conservation rapidly leads to crippling soil loss. Other regions have quite a supply of fresh

dirt to plow through. Few places produce soil fast enough to sustain industrial agriculture over human time scales, let alone over geologic time. Considered globally, we are slowly running out of dirt.

Should we be shocked that we are skinning our planet? Perhaps, but the evidence is everywhere. We see it in brown streams bleeding off construction sites and in sediment-choked rivers downstream from clear-cut forests. We see it where farmers' tractors detour around gullies, where mountain bikes jump deep ruts carved into dirt roads, and where new suburbs and strip malls pave fertile valleys. This problem is no secret. Soil is our most underappreciated, least valued, and yet essential natural resource.

> "Fertile soil still provides the foundation for supporting large concentrations of people."

Personally, I'm more interested in asking what it would take to sustain a civilization than in cataloging how various misfortunes can bring down societies. But as a geologist, I know we can read the record previous societies left inscribed in their soils to help determine whether a sustainable society is even possible.

Historians blame many culprits for the demise of once flourishing cultures: disease, deforestation, and climate change to name a few. While each of these factors played varying—and sometimes dominant—roles in different cases, historians and archaeologists rightly tend to dismiss single bullet theories for the collapse of civilizations. Today's explanations invoke the interplay among economic, environmental, and cultural forces specific to particular regions and points in history. But any society's relationship to its land—how people treat the dirt beneath their feet—is fundamental, literally. Time and again, social and political conflicts undermined societies once there were more people to feed than the land could support. The history of dirt suggests that how people treat their soil can impose a life span on civilizations.

Given that the state of the soil determines what can be grown for how long, preserving the basis for the wealth of future generations requires intergenerational land stewardship. So far, however, few human societies have produced cultures founded on sustaining the soil, even though most discovered ways to enhance soil fertility. Many exhausted their land at a rate commensurate with their level of technological sophistication. We now have the capacity to outpace them. But we also know how not to repeat their example.

Despite substantial progress in soil conservation, the United States   15
Department of Agriculture estimates that millions of tons of topsoil are
eroded annually from farmers' fields in the Mississippi River basin. Every
second, North America's largest river carries another dump truck's load of
topsoil to the Caribbean. Each year, America's farms shed enough soil to fill
a pickup truck for every family in the country. This is a phenomenal amount
of dirt. But the United States is not the biggest waster of this critical
resource. An estimated twenty-four billion tons of soil are lost annually
around the world—several tons for each person on the planet. Despite such
global losses, soil erodes slowly enough to go largely unnoticed in anyone's
lifetime.

Even so, the human cost of soil exhaustion is readily apparent in the
history of regions that long ago committed ecological suicide. Legacies of
ancient soil degradation continue to consign whole regions to the crushing
poverty that comes from wasted land. Consider how the televised images
of the sandblasted terrain of modern Iraq just don't square with our
notion of the region as the cradle of civilization. Environmental refugees,
driven from their homes by the need to find food or productive land on
which to grow it, have made headlines for decades. Even when faced with
the mute testimony of ruined land, people typically remain unconvinced
of the urgent need to conserve dirt. Yet the thin veneer of behavior that
defines culture, and even civilization itself, is at risk when people run low
on food.

For those of us in developed countries, a quick trip to the grocery store
will allay fears of any immediate crisis. Two technological innovations—
manipulation of crop genetics and maintenance of soil fertility by chemical
fertilizers—made wheat, rice, maize, and barley the dominant plants on
earth. These four once-rare plants now grow in giant single-species stands
that cover more than half a billion hectares—twice the entire forested area
of the United States, including Alaska. But how secure is the foundation of
modern industrial agriculture?

Farmers, politicians, and environmental historians have used the term
soil exhaustion to describe a wide range of circumstances. Technically, the
concept refers to the end state following progressive reduction of crop yields
when cultivated land no longer supports an adequate harvest. What defines
an adequate harvest could span a wide range of conditions, from the
extreme where land can no longer support subsistence farming to where it
is simply more profitable to clear new fields instead of working old ones.

Consequently, soil exhaustion must be interpreted in the context of social factors, economics, and the availability of new land.

Various social, cultural, and economic forces affect how members of a society treat the land, and how people live on the land, in turn, affects societies. Cultivating a field year after year without effective soil conservation is like running a factory at full tilt without investing in either maintenance or repairs. Good management can improve agricultural soils just as surely as bad management can destroy them. Soil is an intergenerational resource, natural capital that can be used conservatively or squandered. With just a couple feet of soil standing between prosperity and desolation, civilizations that plow through their soil vanish.

20   As a geomorphologist, I study how topography evolves and how landscapes change through geologic time. My training and experience have taught me to see how the interplay among climate, vegetation, geology, and topography influences soil composition and thickness, thereby establishing the productivity of the land. Understanding how human actions affect the soil is fundamental to sustaining agricultural systems, as well as understanding how we influence our environment and the biological productivity of all terrestrial life. As I've traveled the world studying landscapes and how they evolve, I've come to appreciate the role that a healthy respect for dirt might play in shaping humanity's future.

Viewed broadly, civilizations come and go—they rise, thrive for a while, and fall. Some then eventually rise again. Of course, war, politics, deforestation, and climate change contributed to the societal collapses that punctuate human history. Yet why would so many unrelated civilizations like the Greeks, Romans, and Mayans all last about a thousand years?

Clearly, the reasons behind the development and decline of any particular civilization are complex. While environmental degradation alone did not trigger the outright collapse of these civilizations, the history of their dirt set the stage upon which economics, climate extremes, and war influenced their fate. Rome didn't so much collapse as it crumbled, wearing away as erosion sapped the productivity of its homeland.

In a broad sense, the history of many civilizations follows a common story line. Initially, agriculture in fertile valley bottoms allowed populations to grow to the point where they came to rely on farming sloping land. Geologically rapid erosion of hill slope soils followed when vegetation clearing and sustained tilling exposed bare soil to rainfall and runoff. During subsequent centuries, nutrient depletion or soil loss from increasingly intensive farming stressed local populations as crop yields declined and new land was unavailable. Eventually, soil degradation translated into inadequate agricultural capacity to support a burgeoning population, predisposing whole civilizations to failure. That a similar script appears to apply to small, isolated island societies and extensive, transregional empires suggests a phenomenon of fundamental importance. Soil erosion that outpaced soil formation limited the longevity of civilizations that failed to safeguard the foundation of their prosperity—their soil.

Modern society fosters the notion that technology will provide solutions to just about any problem. But no matter how fervently we believe in its power to improve our lives, technology simply cannot solve the problem of consuming a resource faster than we generate it: someday we will run out of it. The increasingly interconnected world economy and growing population make soil stewardship more important now than anytime in history. Whether economic, political, or military in nature, struggles over the most basic of resources will confront our descendants unless we more prudently manage our dirt.

How much soil it takes to support a human society depends on the size   25
of the population, the innate productivity of the soil, and the methods and technology employed to grow food. Despite the capacity of modern farms to feed enormous numbers of people, a certain amount of fertile dirt must still support each person. This blunt fact makes soil conservation central to the longevity of any civilization.

The capacity of a landscape to support people involves both the physical characteristics of the environment—its soils, climate, and vegetation—and farming technology and methods. A society that approaches the limit of its particular coupled human-environmental system becomes vulnerable to perturbations such as invasions or climate change. Unfortunately, societies that approach their ecological limits are also very often under pressure to maximize immediate harvests to feed their populations, and thereby neglect soil conservation.

Soils provide us with a geological rearview mirror that highlights the importance of good old dirt from ancient civilizations right on through to today's digital society. This history makes it clear that sustaining an industrialized civilization will rely as much on soil conservation and stewardship as on technological innovation. Slowly remodeling the planet without a plan, people now move more dirt around Earth's surface than any other biological or geologic process.

Common sense and hindsight can provide useful perspective on past experience. Civilizations don't disappear overnight. They don't choose to fail. More often they falter and then decline as their soil disappears over generations. Although historians are prone to credit the end of civilizations to discrete events like climate changes, wars, or natural disasters, the effects of soil erosion on ancient societies were profound. Go look for yourself; the story is out there in the dirt.

Analyze

1. Why, according to this article, do the dangers of soil degradation remain invisible to a large part of society?

2. Montgomery argues, "Even when faced with the mute testimony of ruined land, people typically remain unconvinced of the urgent need to conserve dirt." Why do you think this is? Do you think there is anything that can be done to change this reality? If not, what might the consequences be?

3. What idea or piece of this reading sticks in your mind the most? Find the page on which that passage appears and read it again. What did Montgomery say or do that made this passage so memorable? If you recall other passages equally clearly, how did Montgomery manage to make them so effective?

Explore

1. Montgomery says, "Good management can improve agricultural soils just as surely as bad management can destroy them." A narrow-minded suggestion might then be that the nation's farmers ought to do a better job of managing their fields. But as our readings have suggested over and over again, these issues are often complicated and involve a number of factors and players that span nations. Keeping this in mind, what are some interrelated factors outside of the farm that you can think of that may contribute to poor soil management? Create a map or a diagram that links stressors outside of a farm to the management of a farm's soil.

2. Montgomery opens this piece with a shocking statistic: the amount of people who grow the food that the rest of us eat has dropped from 98% to 1%. As a homework assignment, go online and do some research on where our food comes from. Start large—what parts of the country

grow and ship the most food? Then dig a bit deeper, and see if you can find out where *you* get your food. If your answer ends at the grocery store, you haven't dug deep enough. Where do they get theirs? How can you find out? Document all of the useful resources and websites you've come across, and come to class the next day to share your resources with your class and see if your findings match those of your classmates. Be sure to document and save the most useful resources for future research.

3. Montgomery opens this essay with an anecdote about climbing Mount Pinatubo in the Philippines. He ends that brief story with these lines: "Few things can make you feel as helpless as when the earth gives way beneath your feet. The more you struggle, the deeper you sink. You're going down and there's nothing you can do about it." Why does he open his essay with this sense of the earth giving way and the sense of going down helplessly? Is this a good way to start an essay about dirt and sustainability?

Monday Creek Restoration Project
"Upstream Rock Run Coal Mine Remediation"

This brief column appeared in *Up The Creek*, the quarterly newsletter of the Monday Creek Restoration Project in southeastern Ohio, while the creek's watershed was being restored. The health of this previously devastated area has improved dramatically as a result of the partnership between the Wayne National Forest and the Monday Creek Restoration Project, Ohio Department of Natural Resources, Ohio University, Ohio Environmental Protection Agency, U.S. Office of Service Mining, and U.S. Army Corps of Engineers. Habitat for aquatic species has been restored, acid mine drainage has been significantly reduced, and recreational opportunities have been enhanced. This award-winning project is an example of the many community-based sustainability and ecological partnerships across the United States, many of which use newsletters such as this to publicize their work. The newsletter's motto, "We All Live Downstream," connects a shared sense of community with an understanding that actions always have consequences "downstream." As you read, consider how this brief document encourages citizens to participate for the benefit of their community.

The Wayne National Forest signed an agreement with Hocking College to work on a portion of the Upstream Rock Run Coal Mine Remediation. This area has been long recognized by the Forest Service, state and private partners, and surrounding communities as an opportunity to create a highly visible recreation area enabling us to explain the need for continued cleanup of old abandoned mine lands, as well as interpreting the natural history of the area. The project site is located just east of State Route 93 between the nearby towns of New Straitsville and Shawnee. The highway gives good access to the project area. Both of the bordering towns are highly interested in cleaning up old mining areas and encouraging more avenues for economic development in the area. The Upstream Rock Run drainage was heavily impacted by underground mining activities in the mid-1800s and by strip mining in the 1900s. The drainages are blocked by piles of old mine waste and soils. Based on average rainfall estimates it is projected that 60 million gallons of water falls here in a typical year. The blockages have created a bowl shaped area which traps the rainfall and prevents it from flowing out of the area as a stream.

In some parts of the drainage the underground mines have collapsed causing fairly deep depressions on the surface of the land called subsidences. The subsidence depicted to the left (Orbiston) is fairly typical of most subsidences on the Forest. However, many are covered over with leaf litter and debris, or have been backfilled with dirt like the ones in the Upstream Rock Run drainage, and they are not readily apparent on the surface. This particular subsidence is located approximately ten miles from Upstream Rock Run.

Water that is captured in these holes seeps into the under-ground mines and is released elsewhere as acid mine drainage. Acid mine drainage is toxic to aquatic life and has a harmful effect on the adjacent riparian vegetation. For nearly a century the aquatic life that once thrived in this watershed has been virtually dead.

The goal of this project is to construct a healthy functioning riparian corridor, restore water quality, create an integrated land management strategy, while increasing species diversity and abundance of fish and other aquatic organisms in the streams by improving overall watershed condition.

Analyze

1. What is a subsidence, and what kinds of problems can they cause for the health of water, aquatic life, and vegetation?
2. Why do you think that the project needed to "explain the need for continued cleanup of old abandoned mine lands"?
3. What is a riparian corridor, and what role does it play in wildlife preservation?

Explore

1. The author makes a clear point that restoration projects like the one described here have an important purpose, but as the introduction to this chapter suggests, it is not always easy to convince people to take action. Go online or search around your campus or your community to find a local environmental project or cleanup near you. Then, create a flyer with both text and visuals that might persuade residents on your campus or in the community to attend the cleanup. Think hard not only about providing accurate information, but also about what would be rhetorically persuasive to that audience.
2. In a group, attend a cleanup or other active environmental project near you. If you cannot find one, then consider making one up as a group. Clearing clutter from local creek beds or even from a campus field is always a good option. Document your event with pictures and videos if you can, then write up a story about your experience for your school's newsletter, attempting to inspire other students to follow your example. Bonus: If you have photos or videos of your cleanup, post them onto a blog, Facebook, or Twitter feed as another means of reaching your intended audience.
3. Go online or ask your friends and find a newsletter from a local environmental or community preservation group like the Monday Creek project. Maybe it might be associated with the Forest Service, or the Parks Department, or even a community garden. Contact the people in charge of the newsletter and ask them if you can write a column for their next issue. Then do the research, perhaps visit the project, and write a short contribution for their next issue.

Sandra Steingraber
"The Case for Gardening as a Means to Curb Climate Change"

Sandra Steingraber is a biologist and writer who studies the effects of environmental toxins on human health, especially cancer. She has a bachelor's degree in biology, a master's degree in English, and a Ph.D. in biology. In addition to *Raising Elijah: Protecting Our Children in an Age of Environmental Crisis* (2011), from which our selection is taken, she has published five other books, including *Living Downstream: An Ecologist Looks at Cancer and the Environment* (1997). She has received numerous awards and in 2010 was named one of the "25 Visionaries Who Are Changing Your World" by the *Utne Reader*. The essay below mixes scientific information with personal narrative to playfully motivate readers to take small personal actions in the face of climate change and environmental threat. As you read, consider how Steingraber presents herself and what voice she develops, and think about why she made that rhetorical decision.

I am quite possibly the world's worst gardener. I would like to blame my yard for this. It's full of shade, and the shade comes from walnut trees, which, as any gardener worth her salt can tell you, exude from their roots a substance called juglone, whose job it is to take out the competition by wilting the neighbors. So, my garden now has raised beds. These are supposed to help keep the tender roots of the garden plants away from the death-peddling juglone below. Of course, the problem of the shade remains. But I am a new gardener, and I am determined to keep at it. So far, I have grown impressive crops of mint, parsley, and lettuce. I once harvested enough peas to feed all four of us. One meal. As a small side dish.

I am upstaged in the gardening department by my own compost pile. All kinds of things take root in it. Two years ago, some member of the squash family—possibly a cross-pollinated wild hybrid of some kind—planted its seedling flag atop the steamy, south-facing slope and began to grow. Soon, its stickle-backed leaves were the size of placemats, and they were attached to a stem as thick as a child's wrist. When it started to climb the sides of the bin and spill over the top, blooming wildly with crepe-y orange flowers and shivering with bees, Elijah became so terrified that he bribed Faith into taking over his every-other-night compost-toting duty.

> *Elijah, you are scared of a squash vine?*
> *It tried to grab me. I am NOT kidding. Please! You can have all my allowance.*

When we came home from a camping trip, Elijah ran into the backyard to check on the compost predator.

> *Mom, come and look! It turned into a balloon tree!*

And so it had. Grabbing hold of a tree trunk next to the bin, the vine had climbed a small maple and entirely covered it. Its flowers had become fruits—deep green globes, each the size of a party balloon. And so we had squashes—or something—dangling above our heads. They tasted good. I sautéed them with garlic and basil, grated them up for soup stock, added them to muffins and pasta sauce, and, in one form or another, we ate them all winter.

If only my garden were half as prolific. To be sure, I'm mostly slumming 5 when I'm working in it. Because our CSA farm is only a half-mile away—and its hoop houses, hen houses, and root cellars provide us eggs and produce year-round—I have the luxury of leaving the serious crop production to the experts and can still carry into my kitchen (via bicycle or sled) locally grown food, burning no carbon to do it.

It's likely that your garden will produce a much bigger fraction of your groceries than mine and thus save fossil fuels twice over—first, in the form of long-distance, refrigerated produce transportation and, second, in local trips to bring the food from market to kitchen. Regardless, the real climate value of the garden lies in three other places. The first is in building skills. If our children are going to grow up in a world of increasing environmental instability and declining oil reserves—and they are—it seems useful for them to know a few things about potatoes.

The second is in preserving the genetic diversity of seeds. In an unpredictable climate, we need as many varieties of as many fruits, grains, and vegetables as possible—the drought-resistant ones, the mildew-resistant ones, the early-blooming and late-blooming kinds. Big commercial seed companies are, for the most part, not interested in the rare, the peculiar, and the untruckable. As a result, many traditional varieties are now on the edge of extinction. But gardens can function as living archives of genetic diversity, especially when backyard gardeners become seed savers. With almost no extra effort on your part, your garden can feed your family while also doubling as a gene bank.

As I think you can see, this is sounding pretty heroic already: *Son, I need your help in the garden today. Our job is to preserve 10,000 years of agrarian heritage.*

The real carbon savings of gardens, however, comes from the compost, and this is the reason I am issuing a universal recommendation for gardening. Together, food waste and yard trimmings make up 26 percent of the municipal solid waste stream in the United States. And, when buried in landfills, they become fuel for the production of methane, a long-lived gas that is 23 times more powerful than carbon dioxide at trapping heat. According to the U.S. Department of Energy, methane is now fully 10 percent of all U.S. greenhouse gas emissions—and its slice of the emissions pie is growing. Furthermore, of the 13 major sources of methane, the largest single one is landfills. (At 184.3 million metric tons per year, landfills add more methane to the atmosphere than "enteric fermentation," which refers to, well, how the nation's 100 million cattle add methane to the atmosphere.)

10   Rerouting one quarter of the waste stream to compost bins would seriously tamp down the number one source of methane gas emissions. And, because it serves as fertilizer for the garden, compost obviates the need to purchase synthetic fertilizers, which are manufactured from fossil fuels, and which, when used as directed, add a second noxious greenhouse gas to the air: nitrous oxide (whose heat-trapping powers are 300 times more potent than carbon dioxide; it is also a precursor of smog).

So, to summarize: By planting a garden, you create the need for compost, and by starting a compost pile, three problems are solved:

1. You direct food scraps away from the methane factories called landfills.
2. You make homemade fertilizer with no fossil fuels.
3. You prevent the formation of a smog-making, heat-retaining gas.

And the best part of all: The compost pile, nature's Crock-Pot, requires almost no work whatsoever. Within months, dead leaves and old food will, all by themselves, transform into rich, black, loamy (non-smelly) humus. Depending on your perspective, this is either a holy blessing or the result of unpaid labor on the part of earthworms, fungi, and other members of the ecosystem service industry.

Depending on how you run your household, you can either send your eight- and five-year-old out to the compost pile on alternate nights, armed with a flashlight and a bucket of food scraps, because come on now, we all have to pitch in around here, or you can pay them.

And depending on your relationship to the various food-providing institutions that surround you—churches, temples, hospitals, schools, nursing homes, restaurants—you can go public with your newfound skills and make monumental changes. Bates College in Maine composts all of its dining hall food scraps and returns them to the farmers' fields that supply the (organic, local) food that is served there. The city of San Francisco has already instituted mandatory, curbside compost pick-up for urban residents. In short, the large-scale diversion of food scraps from methane-generating landfills is a doable project that awaits no technological breakthrough or venture capital investment. So, go do it.

Analyze

1. What, according to Steingraber, is the benefit of running your own garden and compost pile?
2. Why does Steingraber want to avoid using artificial fertilizer on her garden?
3. Why do you think the author begins her story by telling you that she is "quite possibly the world's worst gardener" who "once harvested enough peas to feed all four of us. One meal. As a small side dish"? What effect does this rhetorical choice have on the reader in terms of the author's purpose in writing this article?

Explore

1. Would you ever consider planting your own garden? In a group, create a list of the obstacles that you think prevent most people, including yourself, from planting your own backyard garden. Then, take on the opposite position, and challenge yourselves to address those obstacles and create solutions to them.
2. Many people do not have backyards at all. Might it still be possible for people living in apartments or densely populated areas to grow and compost their own food? Go online and locate some articles, resources, or websites that describe alternative options for gardening when there are space restrictions. Then, based on your knowledge from this reading and from your own research, compose an editorial for your school's newsletter persuading

college students that they can—and should—learn to grow some of
their own food.

3. Steingraber points out that landfills are the biggest single source of
methane in America. Find out how your community deals with its
waste, how it manages its landfills, and what policies it has in place to
deal with the things we throw away. How would you go about getting
your neighbors to care about this?

Bryan Walsh
"Nature: A Major Company Puts a Value on the Environment"

Brian Walsh is a senior writer for *Time* and publishes in what he calls "dead
tree *Time*" as well as writing blog posts for its online space. This blog post
appeared on *Time* magazine's "Science and Space" webpage as one of their
"Ecocentric" entries and reports on an event that occurred the same day.
The blog introduces the scientific concept of "ecosystem services" and describes how this method of assigning a dollar value to the environment
might help businesses develop sustainable business models. As Walsh suggests when he refers to the famous naturalist John Muir and the "romantic"
strain of American environmentalism, corporate economic interests and
environmental interests often compete against each other. In Chapter 1,
Jared Diamond argued that sustainability is not in opposition to economic
growth. As you read, think about Walsh's strategy for making that same
argument.

How much is nature worth? On one hand, the question seems absurd.
Is it possible to put a price on the value of an endangered species?
Or figure out the dollar worth of a clean river, or uncontaminated air.
Environmentalism—at least its more romantic strain—has largely defined
itself in opposition to the naked market, where everything has its price and
everything can be bought. When the naturalist John Muir explored the
Sierra Nevada mountains in the late 19th century—experiences that would

later prompt him to push for national parks and found the Sierra Club—dollar figures weren't first in his mind.

Yet at the same time, even the most hard-headed capitalist can't deny that there's a connection between natural resources and economic growth. Want to build and operate a factory or power plant? You'll need a ready supply of clean water—and it's often a lot cheaper to protect a natural source than build expensive artificial treatment plants. A sustainably logged forest provides a regular supply of timber and fiber, but it can also prevent floods and reduce erosion—protecting economic capital from natural disasters. And there's no denying that in the U.S., at least, things often don't have value until we can put a dollar value on them. "Nature is a source for sustainable business value," says Glenn Prickett, chief external affairs officer for the Nature Conservancy (TNC).

What Prickett is talking about is a concept known as ecosystems services—an economic reckoning of the services provided by the natural world—and it's about to get its biggest test in the real world. This afternoon at a panel in Detroit, TNC and Dow Chemical announced a $10 million, five-year collaboration that aims to make ecosystem services become a major part of Dow's business. TNC's scientists will advise Dow on how the $45 billion company's business decisions impact the environment—and in turn, how the environment affects Dow's business. Ideally, the ecosystem will become a new and major component for Dow's bottom line, putting environmental sustainability on par with business sustainability. "This collaboration is designed to help us innovate new approaches to critical world challenges while demonstrating that environmental conservation is not just good for nature—it is good for business," said Dow CEO Andrew Liveris in a statement. "Companies that value and integrate biodiversity and ecosystem services into their strategic plans are best positioned for the future by operationalizing sustainability."

If it sounds a little technical—"operationalizing sustainability"—that's because it is. Ecosystem services is a relatively recent field, one that is just making its way from scientific journals to business practice. But the concept isn't that tough to grasp. Ask yourself a simple question: if nature weren't available to provide a service that human beings need, how much would it cost to provide that service artificially? In agriculture, for instance, wild bees pollinate a wide variety of crops far more efficiently than human workers ever could. By one estimate, the value of all pollinators for U.S. agriculture alone ranges between $4.1 and $6.7 billion a year—a number that is calculated in part by estimating how much it would cost to replace wild bees with managed bee populations. (A practice that, thanks in part to the baffling drop in bee populations, is becoming more common, adding costs for farmers.)

5   You can run the same calculations for virtually any natural resource: forests, waterways, grasslands, even certain species. According to a 1997 estimate, the total value of the planet's ecosystem services may be as high as $33 trillion a year—nearly twice the total global GNP at the time. That's so big as to be almost meaningless, but once you break it down case by case, it's very often more economical to protect and conserve the natural resources already given rather than replace them with something artificial. New York City, for example, gets its remarkably clean drinking water from the upstate Catskill Mountains—a watershed that the city government supports by purchasing or protecting thousands of acres of upstate land. It would have cost the city far more to build additional treatment plants if the government hadn't protected the natural source of its water. "You're looking at a natural value that just can't really be replaced," says Peter Kareiva, TNC's chief scientist.

That means that businesses—especially large ones like Dow that often own and control significant amounts of land—would be smart to figure out how nature might be impacting their bottom lines, and act accordingly. In a world where human population is growing—and where natural commodities like oil, food and water are becoming more scarce and more expensive—well-run companies will need to manage natural resources for the long run, just as they would any other part of their core business. That means going beyond simply complying with government environmental regulations, and moving to proactively protect nature, if only so they can continue to make use of it. Done right, ecosystem service management can have benefits for all of us. "We want to make this a natural part of business decision-making," says Neil Hawkins, Dow's vice president for sustainability. "This can make a big difference for our core plan of protecting the planet but at the same time growing as a company."

The Dow-TNC partnership is just beginning, so it's still not clear exactly how the collaboration will change the way Dow does business, or where those changes will occur. (As part of the deal, the Dow Chemical Company Foundation will donate $7 million to fund the basic research to help TNC develop an ecosystem services methodology, while the remaining $3 million will go to TNC essentially as payment for consulting services to help Dow carry out that methodology.) But the two organizations have collaborated in the past on similar, if smaller projects, including a $1.5 million deal to help protect forests outside Sao Paulo, Brazil as a way to preserve that city's watershed. Over the next five years Dow and TNC will collaborate on three pilot projects—initially in the U.S. but eventually overseas as well—with the intent of publishing the results from their work as case studies. Ideally, Dow will be able to use ecosystem services to guide its management and expansion of its chemical plants—nearly all of which depend on reliable water supplies. "We're approaching this with a lot of excitement," says Hawkins.

So are the experts over at TNC, who see the partnership as a chance to make ecosystem services work on just about the biggest corporate stage possible. Nonetheless, this is still more theory than practice, and I wonder how Dow will make it work. Air, water and forests have usually been seen as public goods, even though they've always been a part of business—and companies have been able to make money in part by privatizing the value of those public goods while leaving the costs to the rest of us to clean up. Government environmental regulations came into being because private companies, left to their own devices, didn't exactly prove themselves as reliable stewards of the natural world. There may be times when the short-term values of the shareholders of Dow conflict with longer-term ecosystem needs—and if that happens, can we trust that nature will really win out?

Of course, given the new Congress's generally hostile attitude towards environmental regulations, greens might be better off putting their trust in smart companies than in the power of the federal government—at least for now. "We won't have unlimited streams of state and federal dollars for this," says Prickett. "Having the business community at the table is important." It may be tough to put a dollar figure on nature, but now is not the time to sell the planet short.

Analyze

1. Explain what ecosystem services are in everyday language.
2. What are the benefits of ecosystem services for businesses?
3. Why should we care about honey bees?

Explore

1. According to the author, "there may be times when the short-term values of the shareholders of Dow conflict with longer-term ecosystem needs—and if that happens, can we trust that nature will really win out?" What do you think about this? In the form of a personal

response, write out your own ideas of the benefits, potential downfalls, and complications of natural resources being owned and operated by large businesses.

2. Using just the information found in this article, draft a letter to a large business or organization, hypothetical or real, that persuades the business to adopt ecosystem services into its business practices. Be detailed, and provide as many persuasive arguments from the article that you can, but extrapolate from there, including additional benefits to the company that you can imagine as well.

3. Lots of companies are "going green" like Dow Chemical, and they often use this in their advertising and marketing. Go to The Nature Conservancy's website and see how they talk about the collaboration between conservation and business. Is this a good model for managing threats to our environment?

Dan Charles
"Putting Farmland on a Fertilizer Diet"

Dan Charles is the food and agriculture correspondent for National Public Radio (NPR). Charles graduated magna cum laude from American University with a degree in economics and international affairs. In addition to writing for NPR, Charles has taught journalism and published two books: *Master Mind: The Rise and Fall of Fritz Haber, The Nobel Laureate Who Launched the Age of Chemical Warfare* (2005) and *Lords of the Harvest: Biotech, Big Money, and the Future of Food* (2001). This blog post appeared in the NPR food blog *The Salt* on December 14, 2011. While *The Salt* is a food blog, this post helps readers see the connection between the food they eat, the farming practices that produce that food, and the distant environmental consequences of those farming practices. As you read, consider how and why Charles' blogging style differs from that of the LUMCON piece below.

The U.S. Department of Agriculture released a document yesterday that got no attention on the nightly news, or almost anywhere, really. Its title, I'm sure you'll agree, is a snooze: National Nutrient Management Standard.

Yet this document represents the agency's best attempt to solve one of the country's—and the world's—really huge environmental problems: The nitrogen and phosphorus that pollute waterways.

There's a simple reason why this problem is so big, and so hard to solve. Farmers have to feed their fields before those fields can feed us. Without fertilizer, harvests would dwindle. But lakes, estuaries, and coastal waters lie downstream from highly fertilized farmland, and now they are choking to death on too much nutrition.

Those nutrients typically come from commercial fertilizer, but they don't have to. Organic growers need to feed their fields, too. Farmers can also use animal manure (which is really recycled fertilizer from the fields that fed those animals) and legumes—crops like alfalfa or chickpeas, which add nitrogen to the soil.

The problem is, those nutrients don't stay where they're needed. They 5 migrate into groundwater, streams, or the air, and everywhere, they cause problems. They feed the growth of microbes and algae, turning clear water cloudy and depriving fish and other creatures of essential oxygen. (There are other important sources of nutrient pollution as well, including urban sewage and the burning of fossil fuels, but fertilizer is the biggest.)

In the United States, the best-known casualties of nutrient pollution include the Chesapeake Bay and a portion of the Gulf of Mexico called the "dead zone." But similar problems exist in many other places as well, including lakes and coastal areas of China and Europe.

So around the world, environmentalists and scientists are mobilizing to fight the plague of over-nutrition. That's where the new USDA document comes in. It lays out a host of steps that farmers can take—and will have to take, if they get funding from certain USDA programs—to minimize the spread of nutrients outside farm fields.

Essentially, it involves putting farmland on a sensible diet. Only feed the land as much as it really needs. And don't apply fertilizer, including manure, when the crops don't need it. Also, try to capture and store any excess nutrients. For instance, grow wintertime "cover crops" that can trap free nitrogen before it leaches into groundwater.

Dave White, the head of USDA's Natural Resources Conservation Service, told reporters that the new guidelines "could have a tremendous, continental impact." The guidelines do not have the force of actual regulations, but state governments can make them mandatory. Maryland, which is fighting a desperate battle to clean up the Chesapeake Bay, already requires its farmers to come up with detailed "nutrient management plans" that are supposed to minimize, and hopefully prevent, nutrient runoff.

10   At yesterday's briefing, White suggested that farmers will follow these guidelines voluntarily, simply out of economic self-interest. Fertilizer is expensive, and wasting it costs money. "If you're looking for someone who wants to regulate agriculture, you're talking to the wrong guy," he said.

Yet a long-running experiment at Michigan State University's Kellogg Biological Research Station suggests that economic self-interest alone can actually work against a solution. The experiment, which has been studying the environmental impact of different farming practices for the past 20 years, shows that it is possible to dramatically reduce nutrient releases from farmland—but it seems to require farmers to scale back their expectations modestly, rather than pursuing the highest yields of the most profitable crop, which is corn.

Ken Staver, a research scientist for the University of Maryland, says getting the flood of nutrients truly under control will take many years. "It's incrementalism," he says. "We went in a wrong direction incrementally, and we're working our way back incrementally. It's not going to give us the water quality that we would wish for. But it's all moving in the right direction."

Analyze

1. What is the secret to using fertilizer wisely?
2. What is the relationship outlined in this article between watersheds and the nutrients in fertilizer?
3. Is there a solution to the problem of fertilizer polluting our coastal waters?

Explore

1. The author comments that "economic self-interest alone can actually work against a solution. The experiment, which has been studying the environmental impact of different farming practices for the past 20 years, shows that it is possible to dramatically reduce nutrient releases from farmland—but it seems to require farmers to scale back their expectations modestly, rather than pursuing the highest yields of the most profitable crop, which is corn." Discuss as a class what this means for the fertilizer diet solution. How do you think a farmer

might respond to the idea of a fertilizer diet? And, if "economic self-interest alone" is not enough, what more may be needed to make solutions like this a reality?

2. Combining what you learned in this article and in "Good Old Dirt," write a newspaper article that describes the delicate relationship between the problems of nutrient runoff and soil degradation. Be sure to include the ways that the solutions to each of these problems might affect the other. Conclude with a suggestion of how these issues may be addressed simultaneously.

3. Use the concept of ecosystem services from the previous reading to construct an argument for putting farmland on a fertilizer diet.

Louisiana Universities Marine Consortium "About Hypoxia"

This introductory overview of hypoxia appears on the website of the Louisiana Universities Marine Consortium (LUMCON), directed by Dr. Nancy Rabalais. The hypoxia research team at LUMCON has 4 researchers and 10 collaborators at university research centers across Louisiana. LUMCON researchers have published 45 papers or book chapters, 3 books, and 6 reports concerning hypoxia in the Gulf of Mexico. This website offers a clear and accurate definition of hypoxia and a careful explanation of its causes and describes the history of hypoxia research. While this is not a research publication in a scientific journal, the language and style are carefully qualified and the document does not make strong, unsupported claims. As you read, think about whether you trust these writers or not, and how they explain difficult concepts in ways that you can understand.

Hypoxia, or oxygen depletion, is an environmental phenomenon where the concentration of dissolved oxygen in the water column decreases to a level that can no longer support living aquatic organisms.

Hypoxia in the northern Gulf of Mexico is defined as a concentration of dissolved oxygen less than 2 mg/L (2 ppm). This figure is based on observational data that fish and shrimp species normally present on the sea floor are not captured in bottom-dragging trawls at oxygen levels <2 mg/L. In other oceans of the world, the upper limit for hypoxia may be as high as 3–5 mg/L.

Hypoxia occurs naturally in many of the world's marine environments, such as fjords, deep basins, open ocean oxygen minimum zones, and oxygen minimum zones associated with western boundary upwelling systems. Hypoxic and anoxic (no oxygen) waters have existed throughout geologic time, but their occurrence in shallow coastal and estuarine areas appears to be increasing as a result of human activities (Diaz and Rosenberg, 1995). The largest hypoxic zone currently affecting the United States, and the second largest hypoxic zone worldwide, occurs in the northern Gulf of Mexico adjacent to the Mississippi River on the Louisiana/Texas continental shelf. The maximum areal extent of this hypoxic zone was measured at 22,000 km^2 during the summer of 2002; this is approximately the same size as the state of Massachusetts.

The average size of the hypoxic zone in the northern Gulf of Mexico over the past five years (2004–2008) is about 17,000 km^2, the size of Lake Ontario. For comparison, the entire surface area of the Chesapeake Bay and its major tributaries measures about 11,000 km^2.

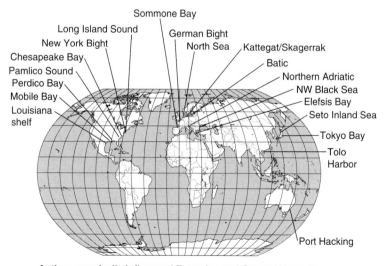

Anthropogenically Influenced Estuarine and Coastal Hypoxia

Figure 6.1   Hypoxia, a worldwide problem: areas of anthropogenically-influenced estuarine and coastal hypoxia worldwide.

What Causes Hypoxia?

Major events leading to the formation of hypoxia in the Gulf of Mexico   5
include:

- Freshwater discharge and nutrient loading of the Mississippi River
- Nutrient-enhanced primary production, or eutrophication
- Decomposition of biomass by bacteria on the ocean floor
- Depletion of oxygen due to stratification

The Mississippi River basin drains approximately 41% of the land area of
the conterminous United States, ranging as far west as Idaho, north to
Canada, and east to Massachusetts.

The Mississippi River system is the dominant source of freshwater and
nutrients to the northern Gulf of Mexico. The discharge of the Mississippi
River system is controlled so that 30% flows seaward through the
Atchafalaya River delta and 70% flows through the Mississippi River bird-
foot delta. About 53% of the Mississippi River delta discharge flows westward onto the Louisiana shelf.

Mississippi River nutrient concentrations and loading to the adjacent
continental shelf have greatly changed in the last half of the 20th century.

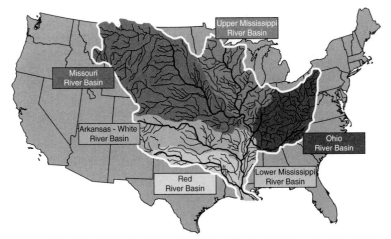

Figure 6.2 The Mississippi River Basin: The Mississippi River Basin is divided
into six sub-basins.

During this time there has been a marked increase in the concentration of nitrogen and phosphorous in the Lower Mississippi River. This increase has been attributed to the increased use of nitrogen and phosphorous fertilizers, nitrogen fixation by leguminous crops, and atmospheric deposition of oxidized nitrogen from the combustion of fossil fuels. Nitrogen and phosphorous occur in four inorganic forms in the river: nitrate (NO_3^-), nitrite (NO_2^-), ammonium (NH_4^+), and orthophosphate (PO_4^{-3}). Many of these nutrients enter the river from non-point sources like runoff, which are much more difficult and complex to control and monitor than point sources of pollution.

Eutrophication follows when ocean systems are over enriched with nutrients beyond natural levels, causing significant increases in primary production, or growth of algae in marine systems. In the same way that nitrogen and phosphorous fertilize human crops, they also fertilize plants in the ocean. The spring delivery of nutrients initiates a seasonal progression of biological processes that ultimately leads to the depletion of oxygen in the bottom water.

10   In the northern Gulf of Mexico, eutrophication initiates a massive growth of phytoplankton on the water's surface. The size of this plankton population is well beyond the natural capacity of predators or consumers to graze it down to a balanced level. Phytoplankton have a relatively short life span, and after dying sink down to the bottom waters where they await decomposition by bacteria.

During this time of year, the water column is also stratified, meaning that environmental factors like temperature and salinity are not uniform from top to bottom. Freshwater flowing from the river, and seasonally warmed surface water, has low density and forms a layer above the saltier, cooler and more dense water masses near the bottom. This stratification leaves the bottom layer isolated from the surface layer and cut off from a normal resupply of oxygen from the atmosphere.

As bacteria on the ocean floor decompose the abundant carbon in the phytoplankton that sinks down, oxygen is consumed. Because of water column stratification, oxygen consumption rates at the bottom of the ocean easily exceed those of resupply and the result is hypoxia, or low dissolved oxygen. Organisms capable of swimming (i.e., fish, shrimp, and crabs) evacuate the area, but less motile fauna experience stress or die as a result of low oxygen. Hypoxia has the potential to damage important commercial fisheries in the Gulf of Mexico over the long term as food webs become disrupted and organisms at all trophic levels are impacted.

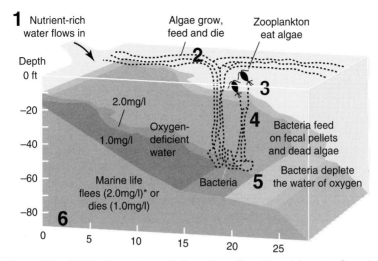

Figure 6.3 Nutrient-based hypoxia formation: 1) nutrient-rich water flows in; 2) algae grow, feed, and die; 3) zooplankton eat the algae; 4) bacteria feed on fecal pellets and dead algae; 5) bacteria deplete the water of oxygen; 6) marine life flees or dies.

Hypoxia can persist several months until there is strong mixing of the ocean waters, which can come from a hurricane or cold fronts in the fall and winter.

History of Hypoxia Research in the Northern Gulf of Mexico

Hypoxia was first documented in the northern Gulf of Mexico off the Louisiana coast in 1972. Sporadic occurrences were observed in subsequent years. In 1975 and 1976, two cruises were conducted specifically to map a suspected area of low oxygen along the Louisiana coast. These maps indicated small, disjunct areas of hypoxia. With an increase in oceanographic research in the Gulf of Mexico, more reports of hypoxia emerged. The first concerted, continuous, and consistent documentation of the temporal and spatial extent of hypoxia on the Louisiana and Texas continental shelf began in 1985 with funding from the National Oceanic and Atmospheric Administration, National Ocean Service. Dr. Don Boesch, then Director of Louisiana Universities Marine Consortium (LUMCON), initiated the study, which was led by Dr. Nancy N. Rabalais of LUMCON and Drs. R. Eugene Turner and William J. Wiseman, Jr. of Louisiana State University.

15   Over the next 25 years, the research team expanded their studies, included more components and collaborators, and began unraveling the dynamics of hypoxia in this river-dominated coastal ecosystem. For more information, and to read about current research efforts, please visit the Research and Resources sections of our website.

Analyze

1. Nitrogen and phosphorus are nutrients. Farmers put nitrogen and phosphorus on their fields to make them more productive. So, why is nitrogen a problem in the Gulf of Mexico?
2. This article suggests that hypoxia is both a natural phenomenon as well as a human-induced phenomenon. Succinctly describe why that is. Why, if hypoxia occurs naturally, does this article suggest it is a problem?
3. Pick a paragraph you understand but had trouble reading and rewrite it so that it is easier to understand.

Explore

1. Who do you think is affected by hypoxia? An immediate and correct answer might be "fishermen," but as this book suggests over and over again, consequences can be complicated and far-ranging. In a group, thinking on as wide a scale as you can, make a list of all of the people or groups that you can imagine might be affected by hypoxia and why. Bonus: Who affects hypoxia? Is it just farmers? Or can you think of any other groups of people whose actions or choices may have an indirect effect on hypoxic conditions as well?
2. Hypoxia is a major problem, but not the only significant problem with water and ecosystems we face in America. Do some research to identify the critical water sources and issues in your state, county, or town. You might begin with the notion of the watershed, the area that drains into a single river, lake, or estuary. Create a poster or digital map that represents the whole system and explains how the pieces of the problem are connected to each other.
3. Using the third visual, "Nutrient-based Hypoxia Formation," create a larger visual or map that integrates additional systems in play that contribute to or result from hypoxia, based on your knowledge from

the readings in this chapter. For example, the current visual begins with "Nutrient-rich water flows in." But what causes that? Extend the map both from the beginning of the cycle and the end, also incorporating some ideas about what might occur after "Marine life flees or dies."

Cynthia Barnett
"The Illusion of Water Abundance"

Cynthia Barnett in a journalist who has written about the issues of water supply, use, and scarcity in America for 25 years. She has a bachelor's degree in journalism and a master's degree in environmental history from the University of Florida. Her writing has won many awards, including the 2007 Florida nonfiction book award for *Mirage: Florida and the Vanishing Water of the Eastern U.S.* The essay reprinted here comes from her newest book, *Blue Revolution: Unmaking America's Water Crisis,* in which she argues that our false sense of a never-ending supply of water is leading to a water crisis in America. Echoing Aldo Leopold's earlier call for a "land ethic," Barnett calls for a "water ethic" to inspire a "blue revolution" in which we pay careful attention to our cheapest necessity—water. As you read, consider why Barnett includes stories of how citizens and local governments have changed their water management practices.

During America's retreat to the suburbs in the 1950s, large home lots, disposable incomes, and a nifty concrete spray called gunite gave families a new marker of success: the backyard swimming pool. For the rest of the twentieth century, residential pools symbolized upward mobility and offered a sense of seclusion not possible at city pools or even private clubs. The following decades redefined our relationship with water itself—from essence of life to emblem of luxury. By the time of the twenty-first-century housing run-up, even the plain blue pool had lost its luster. Adornments were needed. Aquatic affluence meant floating fire pits, glass portholes, and vanishing edges, which create the illusion of never-ending water.

The amenity to envy was no longer the diving board. The must-have, now, was the waterfall.

No community glorified the trend like Granite Bay, California.

Granite Bay is nestled on the north shores of Folsom Lake, commuting distance east of Sacramento. The upscale suburb is named for the Cretaceous age rock that underlies this region in the foothills of the Sierra Nevada. But during the housing boom, Granite Bay's developers were determined to upstage the area's natural geologic outcroppings.

5   In Granite Bay's best backyards, rocky waterfalls cascade artfully into boulder-lined swimming pools, set off with grottoes, swim-up bars, and built-in hot tubs. Thick bushes and trees bearing flowers and fruit adorn the watery wonders, making a place naturally dominated by needlegrass and sedge look more like Fiji. Precisely groomed lawns, a quarter acre and larger, complete the sublimely unnatural tableau.

On Waterford Drive, a beige ranch home with a trim green carpet out front only hints at the tropical excess out back: a pair of waterfalls flow into a clear-blue lagoon, with large rocks positioned for sunning and for diving. This is one of the more subdued motifs. Sacramento landscape architect Ronald Allison tells of a two-and-a-half-acre residential design in Granite Bay with a waterfall, a grotto, a cave, six fountains, a pool with a bridge and an island, *and* a ninety-foot water slide: "It's fun for the grandkids."

Such fun has helped push average water use in Granite Bay to among the highest on Earth. Its residents use nearly five hundred gallons of water a person every day—more than three times the national average. Even when drought conditions cut federal water deliveries to California farmers and closed the state's salmon fisheries, Granite Bay residents continued to consume water as if it were as plentiful as air. After three consecutive years of California drought, Folsom Lake—actually a reservoir created by a dam on the American River—was so dry, it looked like a moonscape. As water levels plummeted in summer 2009, officials from the U.S. Bureau of Reclamation, which manages the lake, ordered all boats removed from the Folsom Marina. Yet the San Juan Water District, which supplies Granite Bay from the reservoir, informed its customers that summer they would have to endure no mandatory water restrictions.

Spectacular squander in the middle of a water crisis is not much of a shock in the United States, where we use about half our daily household water bounty outdoors. The dryer the conditions, the more we tend to pour. What is surprising, however, is to find some of the world's worst waste in the Sacramento metropolitan area. That's because Greater Sacramento has become a national leader in finding solutions to America's energy and climate challenges—and in working to solve other problems brought about by suburban growth. Sacramento glitters with all things green. But when it comes to water, the city represents a national blind spot.

Somehow, America's green craze has missed the blue.

California's capital likes to call itself "Sustainable Sacramento." The 10 progressive municipal government is spending heavily on light rail and constructing only green city buildings. The utility generates solar, wind, biomass, and hydro power for customers willing to pay more for renewable energy. Sacramento's citizens choose to do so at some of the highest rates in the nation.

The city is so green, it provides organic food to public school children, bike racks to businesses, and free trees to residents who want to cool their homes with natural shade.

But with water, Sacramento isn't so enlightened. The metropolitan area, which lands regularly on lists of top green cities, smart cities, and livable cities, also has earned this startling ranking: it squanders more water than anywhere else in California. That distinction makes it one of the most water-wasting places in the United States. And that makes it one of the most water-wasting places on the planet.

Residents of the metro region use nearly 300 gallons of water per person every day—double the national average. By comparison, the equally affluent residents of Perth, Australia, use about 75 gallons per day. Londoners tap about 42 gallons per day. The water-rich Dutch use about 33 gallons daily.

. . .

"As a society, from a water standpoint, we're fat, dumb, and happy," says Tom Gohring, executive director of the Sacramento Water Forum, a coalition of business, environmental, and other competing water interests that work together to find solutions to the region's water woes. "In the history of our country, we've had some serious water shortages, but very, very seldom have people been told that they cannot turn on the taps but for an hour in the afternoon, or that they must boil water. "Water is just too easy to take for granted," Gohring says. "It's always there."

This is true in Sustainable Sacramento, and it's true in the scorched 15 Southwest. The most conspicuous water consumption in America is often found in those parts of the country where water shortages are most serious. Nationwide, we use an average of 147 gallons each day. In wet Florida, the average hits 158 gallons. In Las Vegas, it's 227 gallons per person—in one of the most water-scarce metro areas of the United States, where water managers lose sleep at night thinking about what will happen when the level in Lake Mead drops below the intake pipes that carry water to the city.

. . .

Profligate water use today will imperil future generations, the same as profligate use of oil, destruction of forests, and other environmental tipping points will. But water is much more important to our future than oil. That's because there are no alternatives to it, no new substitute for life's essential ingredient being cooked from corn, french fry grease, or algae.

Like our other great, national illusions—say, the unending bull market, or upward-only housing prices—the illusion of water abundance is a beautiful bubble doomed to pop. With petroleum, those $4 gas prices sparked a collective "Aha!" moment for Americans. But there's been no "Aha!" in the case of water, even though the largest of our waterworks are beginning to show a few cracks.

Let's put it this way: It will not be fun for the grandkids.

Rising 726 feet above the Colorado River between Arizona and Nevada, Hoover Dam stands as a breathtaking marvel of U.S. engineering. Its mammoth hydraulic turbines generate energy for hundreds of thousands of homes. Its reservoir, Lake Mead, supplies water to millions of Americans and another million acres of farmland. The dam's iconic symbolism makes a study by the University of California's Scripps Institution of Oceanography that much more unsettling. In a grim paper titled "When Will Lake Mead Go Dry?" marine physicist Tim Barnett (no relation to this book's author) and climate scientist David Pierce say there's a fifty-fifty chance it will happen by 2021. By 2017, they say, there's an equally good chance water levels in the reservoir will drop so low that Hoover Dam will be incapable of producing hydroelectric power.

20   Most Americans, including the millions who visit this popular tourist spot each year, don't yet seem to fathom that the largest reservoir in the United States is in danger of drying up, that the famous dam's turbines could cease to hum. Even the Scripps scientists say they were "stunned at the magnitude of the problem and how fast it was coming at us."

A dried-up Lake Mead is only the most dramatically visible of the collapses that scientists say could play out in the seven states—Arizona, California, Colorado, Nevada, New Mexico, Utah, and Wyoming—that rely on the Colorado River and its tributaries as ever-increasing water use, ever-growing population, and a changing climate shrink its flow. Scientists who study tree rings to learn about long-ago climate now say that the twentieth century, when America built its grand waterworks and divvied up its rivers, was the wettest in a thousand years. Now, the wet period is over; the National Academy of Sciences reports it unlikely that the Southwest will see its return. Instead, the region is expected to become dryer, and to experience more severe droughts, than in the twentieth century. Trees in the West are already showing the strain, dying off and burning at unprecedented rates. Now, people must adjust, too, conclude Barnett and Pierce, to forestall "a major societal and economic disruption in the desert southwest."

This dry, dusty American future is not confined to the desert. In the Great Plains, farmers are depleting the enormous High Plains Aquifer, which underlies 225,000 square miles of Colorado, Kansas, Nebraska, New Mexico, Oklahoma, South Dakota, Texas, and Wyoming, far faster than it can recharge. We pump an average of one million acre-feet from the High Plains every day. (That's the equivalent of one million acres covered to a depth of one foot.) If that rate continues, scientists say, this ancient aquifer responsible for nearly one-third of all agricultural irrigation water in the United States will dry up within the century. We've even managed to tap out some of the wettest parts of the United States. Florida has so overpumped its once abundant groundwater that the hundred-thousand-square-mile sponge known as the Floridan Aquifer, one of the most productive aquifers in the world, can no longer supply the state's drinking-water needs. The Atlanta region has come within ninety days of seeing the reservoir Lake Sidney Lanier, primary water source for five million people, dry up.

But here's the confounding thing: practically every scientific study that describes these catastrophes and the gloomy future they portend also concludes that it doesn't *have* to be this way. In the Southeast and in the Great Plains, and even in the arid states supplied by the Colorado River, it's possible to reverse the parched path we've set out for our grandchildren and their grandchildren, not to mention ourselves. Conserving water and changing the way we manage water would "play a big part in reducing our risk," says Kenneth Nowak of the University of Colorado at Boulder, coauthor of a recent study that shows the likelihood of depleting the Colorado River's massive reservoirs depends on human actions.

America needs nothing less than a revolution in how we use water. We must change not only the wasteful ways we consume water in our homes, businesses, farms, and energy plants but also the inefficient ways we move water to and away from them. This revolution will bring about the ethical use of water in every sector. Such an ethic is as essential—and as possible— as past awakenings to threats against our environment and ourselves: on the large scale, the way we halted use of DDT and other deadly chemicals; in our communities, the way we stopped tossing litter out car windows and trashing public parks; and at the family level, the way we got used to setting out recycling bins alongside the garbage.

25   Using water ethically isn't difficult. It's revolutionary only because it's so different from the way modern America relates to water. But this revolution isn't big, costly, or bloody. It's a revolution of small technologies over mega-waterworks. It's a savings of billions of dollars in infrastructure and energy costs. It's as painless as floating on your back in an azure spring. Call it a blue revolution.

America's Big Gulp

In all, America guzzles about 410 billion gallons of water per day. That's more than the daily flow of the entire Mississippi River. Power plants drink up more than any other sector of the economy, and while much of what they use is returned, it is often at higher temperatures that can change the ecology of the source. Agricultural irrigation, which accounts for about 40 percent of all freshwater sucked up in the United States each day, is by far the largest drain on our aquifers and rivers.

. . .

Many Americans seem resigned to the notion that agriculture and big industries require a ton of water, and there's not much we can do to change that. This is an especially common refrain in California, where agricultural irrigation accounts for three-fourths of water use. Farmers pump so much, what impacts could citizens possibly have on the water crisis? But this is like throwing up our hands and concluding that because coal plants are the nation's top emitters of greenhouse gases, there's nothing we can do about climate change. It is time, now, to turn our attention to water. Since the turn of the century, Americans have not been involved in the workings of water; we haven't had to be. The conveyance of clean water to homes was one of the most successful feats of technology and engineering in modern times. But occasionally, we've gotten fed up with the nation's direction on water—when pollution-plagued rivers led to the Clean Water Act, for example, and when fed-up ordinary citizens joined environmentalists more than thirty years ago to help bring an end to the era of mega-dams.

. . .

The blue revolution will require deliberately different choices and the political backbone to make them: No wasted water in agriculture. No subsidies for crops that are irreparably harming aquifers. Water-efficient power plants. Restoring floodplains rather than building taller and taller levees. Planting trees and installing green roofs on the grand scale, rather than expanding sewers and costly new wastewater-treatment plants. Reusing water and harvesting rain to irrigate our lawns and to cool commercial air conditioners. Replacing wasteful, outdated fixtures in our homes and businesses rather than building expensive new reservoirs.

Though the driest coastal cities will still build desalination plants and the largest ones, like New York City and Los Angeles, will still import water from outside their regions, the blue revolution is a turn from the vast waterworks of the twentieth century toward solutions. It's an appreciation for local water in much the same way we're embracing local produce.

In that spirit, the blue revolution begins in our own backyards. Just 30 as it's no longer possible to give all large water users as much as they want, any time they want, it's no longer possible for every one of us to use 150 gallons a day from our ailing aquifers and rivers. It's a lot like America's bank accounts: we are seriously overdrawn for luxuries we didn't even need.

So, how much of that daily 410 billion-gallon Big Gulp is just *us* watering our lawns, flushing our toilets, and washing our dishes? Coming in third after power plants and agriculture, about 43 billion gallons a day, or 10.5 percent of the total, goes to public and private utilities. That's where the majority of us get our household water. For the most part, this water comes from aquifers (groundwater) or from surface waters (rivers and lakes). Water managers like to accentuate the difference between groundwater and surface water, but those terms simply refer to the location of water at a given moment. Water is often moving between the two. After falling as rain, water percolates into the soil, then flows underground to river channels. Evaporation and transpiration from plants pick it up again to cycle back into the atmosphere.

To satisfy the Big Gulp, we pump this freshwater from underground, or from a reservoir or river, filtering and treating it at great cost so it meets state and federal drinking-water standards. Then, we move water through a network of millions of miles of pipes under our cities and highways—some the diameter of a small pizza, some wide enough to drive a Volkswagen Beetle through. All of this takes a remarkable amount of energy. About 13 percent of all electricity generated in the United States is spent pumping and treating water and moving it around. That's nearly double the most generous estimate of U.S. electricity spent powering computers and the Internet. (This means a good way to save energy is to save water, and vice versa.)

And then, the vast majority of this painstakingly purified drinking water is never drunk. Some of it goes down our toilets. But the lion's share is soaked, sprayed, or sprinkled on grass. Waterfalls and grottoes aside, the distance between Americans and their global neighbors who use less than 50 gallons of water per person each day is about one-third of an acre. That's the average size of the American lawn.

The Fifty-First State

California State University research scientist Cristina Milesi grew up in northeast Italy and moved to the United States to pursue a PhD in ecosystem modeling. When she arrived, she was struck by the size of lawns compared with those in Italy and wondered how much they contributed to Americans' super-sized water consumption.

35   In the early 2000s, Milesi, a remote-sensing expert, wanted to design computer systems that use weather and climate information to help homeowners make better decisions about when and how much to water their lawns. But no one had ever figured out how much lawn actually carpeted the United States. There were no Google Maps for lawns to overlay with rainfall, soil moisture, and other data. So Milesi, who works at the NASA Ames Research Center at California State University, Monterey Bay, began to create her own using satellite imagery.

The findings so surprised her that she repeated her calculations over and over to make sure they were accurate. Her satellite analysis showed that, between our homes and our highway medians, our golf greens and our grassy sports fields, lawns are America's largest crop. We're growing far more grass than corn—with 63,240 square miles in turfgrass nationwide. That's larger than most individual American states.

To irrigate this "fifty-first state," Milesi estimates that we use as much as nineteen trillion gallons of water per year. That's more than it takes to irrigate all the feed grain in the nation. "People don't believe their water use makes a difference, especially because agricultural consumption is so high," Milesi says. "But water is probably the most important issue facing urban areas in the future—and the primary pressure point on urban water use is the lawn."

It's not that we don't have enough water. It's that we don't have enough water to waste. And we definitely don't have enough to pour off nineteen trillion gallons a year, most of it drinking water created at high cost to both wallets and wetlands. Sure, some of our lawn water, now spiked with pesticides and fertilizers, percolates back underground. But much of it becomes so-called stormwater, which local governments then have to handle through an entirely different network of drains, storm sewers, pipes, and treatment to make it safe enough to flow back to streams and rivers. Sometimes, the stormwater never makes its way back to its source; in the coastal United States, hundreds of millions of gallons of freshwater shoot out to sea every day.

. . .

Landscaping and sod soak up about half of all household water drawn in the United States. Scientists report that Americans who live in cooler climates use up to 38 percent of their water outside, and those who live in hotter, drier climates use up to 67 percent of theirs outdoors. Water managers say this pattern persists despite multimillion-dollar public-education programs to convince Americans that they need not water their grass every day—or even every other day—to keep it green.

In recent years, environmentalists have drawn a bead on high-maintenance turfgrasses, not only for their intense water use but also for the pesticides and fertilizers that run off and pollute rivers and estuaries. Lawn lovers—and the $60 billion dollar turfgrass industry—are arming up to defend their turf. But it doesn't have to be all grass, or no grass. There's nothing wrong with a little, especially if it's of a native variety able to thrive in local conditions. We've simply gone way over the top.

Moms and dads with small kids will tell you it's better to play and picnic on grass than, say, gravel or smelly recycled tire treads—the lawn substitutes showing up on urban playgrounds. Life is good with a patch of grass to spread a picnic blanket and let your kids run. But should it really be America's No. 1 crop? Irrigated at more than double the rate needed?

Grass is not the root of our country's water problems; it's a symptom. A 63,240 square mile indicator of the real ailment—our lack of an ethic for water in America. The illusion of abundance gives us a false sense of security, a deep-down belief that really, there's enough water for anything, anytime. Grottoed new subdivision in the desert? We'll find the water. Sprinklers leaking down the sidewalk? We'll get to it.

Analyze

1. What does the author refer to when she uses the term "America's Big Gulp"? For what is most of the water consumed in America used, according to this article?

2. Scientific models suggest that Lake Mead may well go dry in the next 50 years. What are the causes of this threat?

3. This reading discusses water use in Granite Bay, California, as a means of achieving luxury and beauty. Do you think that water conservation necessarily equates to a sacrifice in aesthetics? Why or why not? As a class, discuss what you think makes a community beautiful, and whether or not that type of aesthetic beauty can be achieved sustainably.

Explore

1. The author points out the irony that the luxurious water usage in Granite Bay that is intended "for the grandkids" today will leave behind much greater problems with water availability for that generation in the future. Create a rhetorical image that gets this point across visually. How does your visual tell the same story in a different way? Which story do you think is more effective in what situations?

2. Barnett notes that while the citizens of Sacramento use about 300 gallons of water per person per day, the "residents of Perth, Australia, use about 75 gallons per day" and the people of London "tap about 42 gallons per day." Do some research to find out about more about the water practices of your own city or town. Check the city website for policies, regulations, and facts. You might interview the city water manager or the people who run the water works. Depending on what you learn, write an opinion piece for your local paper that acknowledges the work of your city officials or argues that they need to do better. Or both.

3. For one day, track your own water usage habits. How many times do you turn on a faucet? For how many minutes do you leave it on? Keep a running tab of your habits, and type up an overview of your findings at the end of the day. The goal of this assignment is to make your own water usage more visible—to teach yourself to see it. Bring your findings to class the next day, and discuss together what it might take to make water usage less invisible for the public at large. What do you come up with?

Michael Specter
"Why Sewers Should EXCITE Us"

Michael Specter is a staff writer at the *New Yorker* magazine and writes about science, technology, and public health. In 2009 he published *Denialism: How Irrational Thinking Hinders Scientific Progress, Harms the Planet, and Threatens Our Lives*, an exploration of the ways people reject scientific facts in favor of more comfortable fictions. This excerpt is taken from his essay "We're All Downstream," which appeared in *Blue Planet Run: The Race to Provide Safe Drinking Water to the World*. This collection of photographs and essays was published by the Blue Planet Network and the profits go toward providing clean water in developing countries. Specter opens this essay with a bold statement: "When used properly, nothing drives growth and eliminates poverty more effectively than water." And he connects the dots between water, public health, economic development, and the ethical issues of equity and justice. As you read, consider the effect on readers of Specter's flamboyant tone and his rhetorical questions.

When used properly, nothing drives growth and eliminates poverty more effectively than water. Clean water has done more for the health of humanity than any medicine of scientific achievement. In developed countries, diseases that were responsible for the great majority of deaths in human history—cholera, typhoid and malaria, for example—have been washed away by clean water. Often, all it took was a working sewer system.

Figure 6.4

Good water has not only prevented illness, it has also produced the healthy crops that improve our nutrition. Irrigation for agriculture accounts for more than two-thirds of all water use. Sophisticated systems and giant water projects have helped produce an ever-increasing yield of food to satisfy the surging population of the Earth. Nearly a quarter of all electricity is powered by hydroelectric turbines. Our products and services, the building blocks of our cities and towns, our ability to forge steel and build spaceships, water plays a role in everything we do.

Sadly, in most countries water is not used effectively or governed well or intelligently controlled. Nearly half of the people on Earth fail to receive the level of water services available 2,000 years ago to the citizens of ancient Rome.

The result is both predictable and staggering. Half the hospital beds on Earth are occupied by people with easily preventable waterborne diseases. In just this past decade, more children have died from diarrhea than all the people who have been killed in armed conflicts since World War II. If we did nothing other than provide access to clean water, without any other medical intervention, we could save 2 MILLION lives each YEAR.

5   The tragedy is not just one of illness, it's also the devastating loss of human productivity. Across vast stretches of the developing world, there is

Figure 6.5

a daily routine that has hardly changed throughout the course of human history. Every day, for millions of women, the first duty is to forage for water. And as rivers run dry, sometimes along with the aquifers beneath them, the women have to keep going farther to find that water. In parts of India and Africa, these women walk an average of 3.7 miles simply to collect potable water and bring it back to their families—a long march home with 44 pounds of water balanced precariously on their heads (more than most airlines allow for luggage).

Heavy as the burden may be, though, it is almost never enough. Back in the slums and huts that half the planet's population considers home, each person will need 1.3 gallons just to make it through the day, roughly the amount of water used in a single flush of a standard American toilet.

Without enough water, no country can achieve even modest economic goals. Irrigation helps communities overcome poverty. When water is plentiful more children go to school, they are healthier, and their parents work more. Yet, throughout the Middle East and south Asia and much of Africa, water is growing scarcer by the month. Since reservoirs aren't sufficient, and many rivers have turned into junkyards or fetid swamps, millions have turned to digging wells to suck the groundwater from their land. But dig

Figure 6.6

too deep and you'll eventually hit arsenic, a deadly poison that pollutes all the water above it. In Delhi there are fewer than 30 days of rain each year, so people simply force tubes into deeper and deeper holes and take what they can get away with. But when that water is gone, it is gone forever. The city and its 15 million residents already suffer. When the water disappears from the wells it will get infinitely worse.

. . .

The number of illnesses caused by lack of water is hard to fathom. More than 3 million people—most of them under age 5—die each year of malaria and diarrhea alone. To put that another way, according to the World Health Organization, nearly 10,000 people die every day from easily preventable water-related diseases. Simply providing access to clean water, without any other medical intervention, could save 2 million of those lives each year. And THE SOLUTION IS DEVASTATINGLY SIMPLE: Studies show that access to piped water and sewers can, in many places, nearly eliminate waterborne disease at a cost of less than $1,000 per death averted.

A THOUSAND DOLLARS. What is a life worth? It's not a small sum, but we live in an era when it is possible to participate in video conferences that link New York with China, or Tokyo with Tibet. There are people who earn millions of dollars of interest income every day. What would it take to convince the rich world to spend enough so that African children no longer die of illnesses that some of us don't even realize still exist?

Figure 6.7

In 2000, the United Nations established a series of urgent targets, called 10 the Millennium Development Goals, aimed at eliminating the world's most desperate poverty. One of the goals seeks, over the next decade, to cut by half the proportion of people without access to clean drinking water. Another sets a similar target for improving sanitation services. The United Nations, which has designated this the "Decade of Water for Life," estimates that if both goals are met, "only" 30 million to 70 million people would die in the next 15 years from preventable water-related diseases. Yes, you read that right: "ONLY" 30 million to 70 million.

Peter Gleick, president of the Pacific Institute for Studies in Development, Environment and Security, argues that management failures and political myopia are at least as responsible for water problems as shortages and population growth. "Providing enough water to grow food for the planet is and will continue to be a challenge," he said. "So is limiting the damage pollution has caused. Still, how can any government that cares for its people let them die of something so simple as a lack of clean water? But they do, in numbers that are staggering. The problem is so fundamental and so widespread, yet it's not like curing AIDS or eradicating malaria. It is not scientifically challenging. It's just a matter or whether or not we care about the most vulnerable people on our planet."

While Gleick can cite dreary statistics, evidence of governmental inaction, and worrisome trends with great rhetorical force, his central message,

Figure 6.8

which is often ignored by both planners and environmentalists, is surprisingly hopeful. "It is a little-known fact that the United States today uses far less water per person, and less water in total, than we did 25 years ago," he said. "It's a shocker. People don't believe it, but it's true. We have changed the nature of our economy, and we have become more efficient at doing what we want to do."

. . . "I would argue that almost everything we do on Earth we could do with less water," Gleick told me. "This is really good news, you know. Because it means we can do better. We don't need to run out of water. We just need to think more seriously about how we can avoid using it."

Try to think about the next time you water the lawn with federally funded filtered water, which is safe enough to drink. Or brush your teeth. Or when we leave the shower running for a few minutes to answer the phone. Every drop of water we casually waste is literally a drop of life taken from the mouth of someone else we will likely never meet, but whose fate we will most certainly determine.

Analyze

1. How big is the problem of inadequate access to clean drinking water worldwide, and what are the effects of inadequate water and sanitation?
2. In what sense is water a woman's issue?
3. In countries where there is a shortage of drinkable water, why can't they just dig more wells or dig them deeper?

Explore

1. At one point in his essay, Specter asks a hard question: "What would it take to convince the rich world to spend enough so that African children no longer die of illnesses that some of us don't even realize still exist?" It is not very realistic to try to convince the whole world of something, but you might convince a smaller audience. As a group, identify a specific audience who might be made to care about this problem and develop a rhetorical strategy that has a good chance of convincing and motivating them.

2. There are many organizations concerned with the crisis in water and sanitation in the developing world; Water.org, the Blue Planet Network, and UNESCO are only a few of them. After doing research on the problem and existing efforts to improve the situation, write a group blog post, complete with pictures and links to other sites, that helps students at your university understand this issue and motivates them to take some small form of action.

3. Find out where your own water comes from and how it gets to the tap in your house or apartment and then draw a detailed map, complete with written inserts, that traces the process.

Lisa Stiffler
"All You Need to Know About Storm Water Runoff"

The blog post below was written by Lisa Stiffler, a former newspaper reporter, and appeared in April 2011 in *Sightline Daily*, the online publication of the Sightline Institute. The Sightline Institute is an independent, nonprofit research and communications center—a think tank—whose mission is to make the Pacific Northwest a global model of sustainability. *Sightline Daily* is designed to provide timely and dependable information to citizens and policymakers. This excerpt from a longer blog post introduces a major environmental and economic problem facing many cities in the United States and around the globe. Stormwater that runs off houses, roads, parking lots, even front yards delivers massive amounts of pollutants to our rivers, lakes, and bays every time it rains. As you read, consider how Stiffler tries to get average readers in Seattle to care about this issue, and maybe even change the way they manage water.

A woman drowns when the basement of her Seattle home suddenly fills with a torrent of filthy water.

An overflow of 15 million gallons of sewage and stormwater fouls the shoreline of picturesque Port Angeles, putting the waterfront off limits to the residents and visitors of the Olympic Peninsula town due to health concerns.

Portlanders are socked with some of the nation's highest water utility rates in order to pay for the city's $1.4 billion "Big Pipe" projects.

Northwest scientists document coho salmon dying in urban streams with their bellies full of eggs, perishing before they can spawn.

5   The culprit in each of these stories is the most mundane of villains: the rain. As rainwater streams off roofs and over roadways and landscaped yards, it mixes a massive toxic cocktail. It scoops up oil, grease, antifreeze, and heavy metals from cars; pesticides that poison aquatic insects and fish; fertilizers that stoke algal blooms; and bacteria from pet and farm-animal waste. A heavy rainfall delivers this potent shot of pollutants straight into streams, lakes, and bays—threatening everything from tiny herring to the region's beloved orcas to our families' health.

Stormwater doesn't match the traditional image of pollution. There are no factory smokestacks belching waste, no pipes with a steady trickle of noxious industrial effluent. Despite appearances, stormwater packs a wallop. Polluted runoff long ago surpassed industry as the number one source for petroleum and other toxic chemicals that wash into the Northwest's water bodies.

Each year, the Puget Sound is sullied by 14 million pounds of toxic chemicals and oil and grease—and that's a conservative estimate. The amount of petroleum waste is so vast, it's as if more than 70,000 cars pulled up to the beach and emptied their tanks straight into the Sound each year.*

The polluted runoff threatens to make water from Lake Whatcom—the sole source of drinking water for the city of Bellingham—undrinkable, and has helped put shellfish harvesting off limits for beachgoers from north of Everett to south of Tacoma. Some residents of BC's Salt Spring Island had to temporarily switch to bottled water this winter when toxic algae contaminated their water supply. Where did the nasty plants come from? The algal bloom was triggered as "a result of excess phosphorous . . . from surrounding properties," according to news reports.

How has the Northwest's iconic rain been transformed into such a menace? A century of building pipes, gutters, and impervious surfaces is to blame—along with pollution from cars, lawns, farming and more. Our goal has been to shunt water away from buildings and pavement as quickly as possible. So when the rain hits hard surfaces, it grabs dirt and pollutants and flushes them into drains that often lead directly into sensitive waterways without any kind of treatment.

In some cases, the runoff merges with sewer waste, resulting in overflows   10
of raw sewage during heavy storms. And that stuff can make you sick. Over the past three years, sewage-tainted runoff has forced the closure of 32 Washington beaches, some for a couple of days, others for weeks.

Stormwater runoff mixed with sewage can carry salmonella bacteria, parasitic giardia, and Norwalk-like viruses. Ailments caused by exposure to sewage-tinged water include: diarrhea, vomiting, stomach cramps, fever, hepatitis, bronchitis, pneumonia, and swimmers itch.

But there's a solution for Cascadia's flood waves of runoff. It's an affordable fix that curbs the environmental damage while making our neighborhoods and communities more walkable, sustainable, and inviting. It's called low-impact development, or LID. The approach uses a suite of conservation and engineering tools to make developed areas behave more like natural ecosystems.

Low-impact development is starting to catch on across the Northwest, but before exploring these green-building strategies, let's dig a little deeper into the challenges posed by polluted runoff.

Rivers of Costly Runoff

Ten bathtubs full of water. That's how much rain pours off one average-size house during a good-sized drenching. In a typical year in Portland or Seattle, approximately 26,600 gallons of stormwater rush into the gutters and streams from that single home. And there are more than 2.6 million houses in Oregon and Washington, as well as countless more apartments, condos, warehouses, offices, stores, and other buildings.

15   When the rain runs off that home's roof—and its driveway, sidewalk, and lawn—it flows into a labyrinth of stormwater infrastructure. Even relatively arid cities such as Spokane must maintain more than 300 miles of stormwater sewers. Traditional approaches to handling stormwater have been costly to governments as well as to home and business owners. Cities and counties in Washington spend more than a quarter billion dollars a year trying to control and clean contaminated runoff.

For nearly two decades, Portland has been working on its "Big Pipe" projects to stop billions of gallons of raw sewage and stormwater from fouling the Columbia Slough and Willamette River. The $1.4 billion projects should be completed this year. The seaside town of Port Angeles is trying to finalize plans for a project that will cost at least $40 million to control its storm sewer waste. Last year, the city's combined sewer system spewed nearly 24 million gallons of sewage-contaminated stormwater into Port Angeles Harbor.

Victoria and Vancouver in British Columbia, Spokane, and Coquille near the Oregon Coast are still other Northwest cities and towns facing expensive upgrades to stop overflows of sewage and polluted runoff that are triggered after a downpour.

And there are the untold millions spent repairing stormwater-related damage from flooding, landslides, and sinkholes. Over the course of one particularly wet weekend this past December, Seattle Public Utilities reported more than 700 calls about flooding and sent crews to 332 locations. The city has paid millions of dollars to settle flood claims over the past decade, spending more than $6 million for the damage caused in the December 2006 storm that drowned a woman.

Putting a LID on Polluted Stormwater

A stroll down a stretch of 2nd Avenue Northwest in Seattle is almost a walk in the park. The slightly meandering residential street is lined with wide strips of native grasses, small shrubs, and trees. Along the shoulder, interspersed among parking spots, are swales—or gentle depressions—that fill with water during a downpour. You won't find sludgy gutters brimming with muddy water and trash, or deserts of black asphalt that foster shoe-soaking puddles.

The street was one of the Northwest's first experiments in natural drain- 20 age systems, or low-impact development. A decade ago, workers jackhammered up the block and rebuilt it to catch and clean stormwater the way it's done in nature. In a forest, rainwater falls on branches and leaves and slowly evaporates, or it soaks into the ground and gets sucked up by plants. The soil and organisms living in the soil help clean and filter the polluted stormwater. The Seattle project—called SEA Street—has been wildly successful, nearly eliminating polluted runoff, even during heavy rains. The slightly narrowed street is safer for kids and pedestrians, and creates natural spaces that are inviting to wildlife and people.

"LID systems really do have the ability to filter water naturally and create much nicer, softer, greener stormwater facilities that really engage the public a lot more," said Tim Bailey, a geotechnical engineer and experienced practitioner of low-impact development with GeoEngineers, Inc., in Seattle.

The philosophy of low-impact development is to try to replicate nature's way of managing rainfall. It means taking surfaces that normally repel water—roofs and pavement—and making them spongy.

Low-impact development can mean building green roofs covered in water-trapping soil and plants. It can mean hooking downspouts to rain barrels or cisterns to store the water that does run off, or having downspouts flow into "rain gardens" featuring swales. It can mean building driveways from a lattice of pavers that leave some of the soil exposed, or using a permeable concrete that lets water pass through to the soil below. It also means protecting, preserving, and restoring native vegetation.

"There is no reason not to make every single residential-scale property do something (to reduce stormwater)," said Peg Staeheli, a principal with Seattle's SvR Design Co., a local leader in low-impact development. "There are a lot of tools out there now that can be used."

Shifting From Gray to Green

Seattle is far from alone in realizing that there are alternatives to traditional 25 gutter-and-storm-drain systems—also called "gray" infrastructure—that cost too much and don't work well. In recent years, low-impact development projects have cropped up as smart investments across the region. Here are some noteworthy examples:

BREMERTON: A blue-collar city on the shores of Puget Sound, Bremerton is being permeated with green stormwater infrastructure. A new 1,600-foot-long bridge and an industrial roadway project will both use low-impact development to treat much of its polluted runoff. In each case, state and local partners pushed for conventional stormwater treatment for the projects, but Bremerton officials successfully made the case for using low-impact development because it was cheaper.

PORTLAND: The City of Roses has so many natural drainages that it has published a walking tour for visitors interested in viewing its attractive rain gardens and swales. Portland has grown its green infrastructure in part through policy incentives. It pays residents to unhook their home downspouts from the city's storm sewer system and redirect the water into rain gardens, and its green roof program offers rebates to residents and businesses installing ecoroofs. There are at least 350 ecoroofs in Portland, topping condos, the central library, government offices, and a university building, covering about 26 acres in all.

LACEY: One of the first cities in the state to approve regulations back in 1999 to encourage low-impact development, Lacey has continued pursuing green stormwater solutions. The city requires a developer to use low-impact development to soak up all the rain that falls on a site rather than pipe it into a storm sewer system, provided the ground is sufficiently absorbent. Lacey's Regional Athletic Complex completed in 2009 features pervious concrete to reduce runoff.

Lacey also has strict tree-protection provisions that call on developers to protect or replant trees, and homeowners must get permission to fell even sick and hazardous trees.

30   **VICTORIA:** There are a number of high profile green roof projects in British Columbia (Vancouver's Convention Center and Olympic Village to name two), but the province has surprisingly fewer examples of rain gardens and swales. One exception is Victoria's Trent Street rain gardens. The 2009 pilot project includes two roadside rain gardens that help soak up street runoff that would otherwise pollute nearby Bowker Creek.

PRINGLE CREEK COMMUNITY: Called "the nation's first full-scale porous pavement project" by the Asphalt Pavement Association of Oregon, the 32-acre sustainable community near Salem boasts 7,000 feet of porous asphalt roadways and 2,000 feet of porous alleys. Pringle Creek also features swales and narrower roads to create fewer hard surfaces. And it's a leader in tree conservation: 80 percent of the development's trees were protected and one-third of the community is green or open space.

SPOKANE: In 2007, Washington State University Spokane County Extension and Spokane County Stormwater Utility planted a dozen swales in front yards around the city in order to test which plants worked best in that climate, to monitor for pollutants, and to raise awareness about rain gardens. A recent study shows that many of the swales are performing better over time.

In these examples and others, low-impact development has been shown to be less expensive and more effective at cleaning stormwater than the traditional gutter-and-storm-drain systems. A study by the US Environmental Protection Agency compared the cost of stormwater projects that were built using green techniques to what they would have cost using conventional strategies. In 11 of 12 cases examined across North America, the low-impact development option was cheaper by anywhere from 15 to 80 percent.

A study by ECONorthwest, an economic consulting firm, also found that low-impact development cost less for both residential and commercial projects in Cascadia and beyond. The researchers concluded that low-impact development would fare even better in comparisons that considered more than just construction costs. In many instances, low-impact development treats larger volumes of water than traditional approaches, is cheaper to maintain, boosts property values, creates wildlife habitat, and reduces air pollution and greenhouse gases by planting and protecting trees and other vegetation.

Death by a Thousand Rainstorms

Ailing Northwest rivers and lakes face death not so much by a thousand cuts as by a thousand rainstorms, each flushing filthy stormwater into environmentally and economically important waterways. 35

While low-impact development is gaining popularity, it's far from being standard practice. Developers, planners, and government agencies often are more comfortable sticking with the conventional systems that they know. In many cases, regulations require traditional infrastructure, whether mandating wider roads to accommodate parking plus emergency vehicles, or prescribing stormwater pipes when a swale would work better and cost less.

But work is underway to change this. In recent years, the Puget Sound Partnership helped 36 Washington municipalities upgrade their codes to encourage the use of low-impact development. Now the Partnership is writing a local-code guidebook for governments that want to incorporate low-impact development requirements into their codes and regulations. It should be done in July.

There are stormwater training programs for landscapers and other contractors as well as city and county planners and permit writers. Local universities, utilities, and nonprofit organizations are teaming up to offer seminars and workshops. Washington State University and the Puget Sound Partnership are offering a series of two-day workshops on low-impact development technologies; Oregon Environmental Council, the Central Oregon Intergovernmental Council, and Oregon State University Extension/Oregon Sea Grant are partnering to hold Stormwater Solutions workshops in Central Oregon.

It's important to improve the level of expertise of those doing low-impact development. Because while green infrastructure offers a great stormwater fix, trained practitioners are needed—particularly for large projects.

40   Seattle recently had a painful reminder that green solutions still require careful planning. A rain garden pilot project in the Ballard neighborhood hasn't worked as expected, resulting in swales that fill with water and don't drain well. The city has formed a task force to solve the problem.

"LID is something you have to look at with the willingness to be flexible and use the most appropriate systems for a given site," Bailey said." It takes a lot more creativity.

"For small scale (projects) you can come up with something that works most of the time, most of the places."

There are additional opportunities for making low-impact development more widespread. In 2010, Washington legislators pledged $50 million for stormwater improvements. This year, a coalition of Washington's city and county leaders, labor representatives, and environmental advocates are working with the Legislature to establish a long-term funding source to pay for more low-impact development. The Clean Water Jobs Act would put a 1 percent fee on petroleum products, pesticides, herbicides, and fertilizers.

Oregon lawmakers are considering a ban on copper in vehicle brake pads in an effort to remove one of the prime sources of a pollutant that's harmful to fish and other aquatic life. Washington approved a similar measure last year, becoming the first state to do so.

There is an urgency to act. The Washington Department of Ecology is 45 working on rules that will require more use of low-impact development, and final regulations should be completed by summer 2012. The US Environmental Protection Agency is strengthening national stormwater regulations that should take effect in less than two years and will encompass more towns and cities than ever before. And the stormwater problem is only likely to worsen if the population of Washington, Oregon, and Idaho swells to an expected 14.5 million residents by 2030, a roughly 20 percent increase from today.

"Time is not on our side," said Tom Holz, a stormwater and low-impact development expert from Olympia. "We may lose the battle just simply through dallying."

Analyze

1. What, succinctly, is LID? What are its main goals? How does LID differ from traditional drainage systems?
2. What are the destructive consequences of rainwater runoff?
3. How do you think rainwater runoff affects things in your area? Are you in a region that experiences high precipitation rates? Can you think of other measures or procedures by which to minimize the amount of rainwater runoff that occurs in your area?

Explore

1. According to this article, the city of Portland "has so many natural drainages that it has published a walking tour for visitors interested in viewing its attractive rain gardens and swales." Apparently, Portland's sustainability initiative is not only sustainable, it's also attractive. Based on this, create an advertisement for your town with both visuals and text persuading it to adopt LID strategies based on their aesthetic value—not based on their green value. How do you think an appeal to beauty rather than to sustainability will affect your argument?

2. Do some research to determine how interested citizens could influence the development decisions made in their communities. Write up a short "Did you know?" column for a local periodical based on your findings, guiding readers to the information and opportunities they need to express their own opinions to their local governments.

3. Take a short walk around your house, apartment, or dorm building and look at the surfaces that make up your surroundings with new, stormwater-aware eyes. What types of surfaces do you see around you that will help to filter rainwater? What types of surfaces may contribute to stormwater contamination? Are there simple but practical things that you or others can do to manage rainwater more sustainably?

Elizabeth Kolbert
"The Darkening Sea"

Elizabeth Kolbert writes about the environment for the *New Yorker* magazine. Her three-part series on global warming, "The Climate of Man," won the 2006 National Magazine Award for Public Interest, the 2005 American Association for the Advancement of Science Journalism Award, and the 2006 National Academies Communication Award. In 2010 she received the annual Heinz award that focused on global change as well as the 2010 Sierra Club's David R. Brower Award for outstanding environmental reporting. She has published two books: *The Prophet of Love: And Other Tales of Power and Deceit* (2004) and *Field Notes from a Catastrophe* (2006). The selection excerpted below, which appeared in the *New Yorker* magazine in 2006, describes the causes, mechanisms, and possible consequences of "ocean acidification," the decrease in ocean pH (the measure of how acidic or alkaline water is) caused by the ocean's absorbing CO_2 from the atmosphere. As you read, think about the difference between providing facts and telling a compelling story.

Pteropods are tiny marine organisms that belong to the very broad class known as zooplankton. Related to snails, they swim by means of a pair of winglike gelatinous flaps and feed by entrapping even tinier marine creatures in a bubble of mucus. Many pteropod species—there are nearly a hundred in all—produce shells, apparently for protection; some of their predators, meanwhile, have evolved specialized tentacles that they employ much as diners use forks to spear escargot. Pteropods are first male, but as they grow older they become female.

Victoria Fabry, an oceanographer at California State University at San Marcos, is one of the world's leading experts on pteropods. She is slight and soft-spoken, with wavy black hair and blue-green eyes. Fabry fell in love with the ocean as a teenager after visiting the Outer Banks, off North Carolina, and took up pteropods when she was in graduate school, in the early nineteen-eighties. At that point, most basic questions about the animals had yet to be answered, and, for her dissertation, Fabry decided to study their shell growth. Her plan was to raise pteropods in tanks, but she ran into trouble immediately. When disturbed, pteropods tend not to produce the mucus bubbles, and slowly starve. Fabry tried using bigger tanks for her pteropods, but the only correlation, she recalled recently, was that the more time she spent improving the tanks "the quicker they died." After a while, she resigned herself to constantly collecting new specimens. This, in turn, meant going out on just about any research ship that would have her.

Fabry developed a simple, if brutal, protocol that could be completed at sea. She would catch some pteropods, either by trawling with a net or by scuba diving, and place them in one-litre bottles filled with seawater, to which she had added a small amount of radioactive calcium 45. Forty-eight hours later, she would remove the pteropods from the bottles, dunk them in warm ethanol, and pull their bodies out with a pair of tweezers. Back on land, she would measure how much calcium 45 their shells had taken up during their two days of captivity.

In the summer of 1985, Fabry got a berth on a research vessel sailing from Honolulu to Kodiak Island. Late in the trip, near a spot in the Gulf of Alaska known as Station Papa, she came upon a profusion of *Clio pyramidata*, a half-inch-long pteropod with a shell the shape of an unfurled umbrella. In her enthusiasm, Fabry collected too many specimens; instead of putting two or three in a bottle, she had to cram in a dozen. The next day, she noticed that something had gone wrong. "Normally, their shells are transparent," she said. "They look like little gems, little jewels. They're just beautiful. But I could see that, along the edge, they were becoming opaque, chalky."

5   Like other animals, pteropods take in oxygen and give off carbon dioxide as a waste product. In the open sea, the CO_2 they produce has no effect. Seal them in a small container, however, and the CO_2 starts to build up, changing the water's chemistry. By overcrowding her *Clio pyramidata*, Fabry had demonstrated that the organisms were highly sensitive to such changes. Instead of growing, their shells were dissolving. It stood to reason that other kinds of pteropods—and, indeed, perhaps any number of shell-building species—were similarly vulnerable. This should have represented a major discovery, and a cause for alarm. But, as is so often the case with inadvertent breakthroughs, it went unremarked upon. No one on the boat, including Fabry, appreciated what the pteropods were telling them, because no one, at that point, could imagine the chemistry of an entire ocean changing.

Since the start of the industrial revolution, humans have burned enough coal, oil, and natural gas to produce some two hundred and fifty billion metric tons of carbon. The result, as is well known, has been a transformation of the earth's atmosphere. The concentration of CO_2 in the air today—three hundred and eighty parts per million—is higher than it has been at any point in the past six hundred and fifty thousand years, and probably much longer. At the current rate of emissions growth, CO_2 concentration will top five hundred parts per million—roughly double pre-industrial levels—by the middle of this century. It is expected that such an increase will produce an eventual global temperature rise of between three and a half and seven degrees Fahrenheit, and that this, in turn, will prompt a string of disasters, including fiercer hurricanes, more deadly droughts, the disappearance of most remaining glaciers, the melting of the Arctic ice cap, and the inundation of many of the world's major coastal cities. But this is only half the story.

Ocean covers seventy percent of the earth's surface, and everywhere that water and air come into contact there is an exchange. Gases from the atmosphere get absorbed by the ocean and gases dissolved in the water are released into the atmosphere. When the two are in equilibrium, roughly the same quantities are being dissolved as are getting released. But change the composition of the atmosphere, as we have done, and the exchange becomes lopsided: more CO_2 from the air enters the water than comes back out. In the nineteen-nineties, researchers from seven countries conducted nearly a hundred cruises, and collected more than seventy thousand seawater samples from different depths and locations. The analysis of these samples, which was completed in 2004, showed that nearly half of all the carbon dioxide that humans have emitted since the start of the nineteenth century has been absorbed by the sea.

When CO_2 dissolves, it produces carbonic acid, which has the chemical formula H_2CO_3. As acids go, H_2CO_3 is relatively innocuous—we drink it all the time in Coke and other carbonated beverages—but in sufficient quantities it can change the water's pH. Already, humans have pumped enough carbon into the oceans—some hundred and twenty billion tons— to produce a .1 decline in surface pH. Since pH, like the Richter scale, is a logarithmic measure, a .1 drop represents a rise in acidity of about thirty per cent. The process is generally referred to as "ocean acidification," though it might more accurately be described as a decline in ocean alkalinity. This year alone, the seas will absorb an additional two billion tons of carbon, and next year it is expected that they will absorb another two billion tons. Every day, every American, in effect, adds forty pounds of carbon dioxide to the oceans.

Because of the slow pace of deep-ocean circulation and the long life of carbon dioxide in the atmosphere, it is impossible to reverse the acidification that has already taken place. Nor is it possible to prevent still more from occurring. Even if there were some way to halt the emission of CO_2 tomorrow, the oceans would continue to take up carbon until they reached a new equilibrium with the air. As Britain's Royal Society noted in a recent report, it will take "tens of thousands of years for ocean chemistry to return to a condition similar to that occurring at pre-industrial times."

Humans have, in this way, set in motion change on a geologic scale. The question that remains is how marine life will respond. Though oceanographers are just beginning to address the question, their discoveries, at this early stage, are disturbing. A few years ago, Fabry finally pulled her cloudy shells out of storage to examine them with a scanning electron microscope. She found that their surfaces were riddled with pits. In some cases, the pits had grown into gashes, and the upper layer had started to pull away, exposing the layer underneath.

The term "ocean acidification" was coined in 2003 by two climate scientists, Ken Caldeira and Michael Wickett, who were working at the Lawrence Livermore National Laboratory, in Northern California. Caldeira has since moved to the Carnegie Institution, on the campus of Stanford University, and during the summer I went to visit him at his office, which is housed in a "green" building that looks like a barn that has been taken apart and reassembled at odd angles. The building has no air-conditioning; temperature control is provided by a shower of mist that rains down into a tiled chamber in the lobby. At the time of my visit, California was in the midst of a record-breaking heat wave; the system worked well enough that Caldeira's office, if not exactly cool, was at least moderately comfortable.

Caldeira is a trim man with wiry brown hair and a boyish sort of smile. In the nineteen-eighties, he worked as a software developer on Wall Street, and one of his clients was the New York Stock Exchange, for whom he designed computer programs to help detect insider trading. The programs functioned as they were supposed to, but after a while Caldeira came to the conclusion that the N.Y.S.E. wasn't actually interested in catching insider traders, and he decided to switch professions. He went back to school, at N.Y.U., and ended up becoming a climate modeler.

Unlike most modelers, who focus on one particular aspect of the climate system, Caldeira is, at any given moment, working on four or five disparate projects. He particularly likes computations of a provocative or surprising nature; for example, not long ago he calculated that cutting down all the world's forests and replacing them with grasslands would have a slight cooling effect. (Grasslands, which are lighter in color than forests, absorb less sunlight.) Other recent calculations that Caldeira has made show that to keep pace with the present rate of temperature change plants and animals would have to migrate poleward by thirty feet a day, and that a molecule of CO_2 generated by burning fossil fuels will, in the course of its lifetime in the atmosphere, trap a hundred thousand times more heat than was released in producing it.

Caldeira began to model the effects of carbon dioxide on the oceans in 1999, when he did some work for the Department of Energy. The department wanted to know what the environmental consequences would be of capturing CO_2 from smokestacks and injecting it deep into the sea. Caldeira set about calculating how the ocean's pH would change as a result of deep-sea injection, and then compared that result with the current practice of pouring carbon dioxide into the atmosphere and allowing it to be taken up by surface waters. In 2003, he submitted his work to *Nature*. The journal's editors advised him to drop the discussion of deep-ocean injection, he recalled, because the calculations concerning the effects of ordinary atmospheric release were so startling. Caldeira published the first part of his paper under the subheading "The coming centuries may see more ocean acidification than the past 300 million years."

Caldeira told me that he had chosen the term "ocean acidification" quite 15
deliberately, for its shock value. Seawater is naturally alkaline, with a pH
ranging from 7.8 to 8.5—a pH of 7 is neutral—which means that, for now,
at least, the oceans are still a long way from actually turning acidic. Meanwhile, from the perspective of marine life, the drop in pH matters less than
the string of chemical reactions that follow.

The main building block of shells is calcium carbonate—$CaCO_3$. (The
White Cliffs of Dover are a huge $CaCO_3$ deposit, the remains of countless
tiny sea creatures that piled up during the Cretaceous—or "chalky"—
period.) Calcium carbonate produced by marine organisms comes in two
principal forms, aragonite and calcite, which have slightly different crystal
structures. How, exactly, different organisms form calcium carbonate remains something of a mystery. Ordinarily in seawater, $CaCO_3$ does not
precipitate out as a solid. To build their shells, calcifying organisms must, in
effect, assemble it. Adding carbonic acid to the water complicates their efforts, because it reduces the number of carbonate ions in circulation. In
scientific terms, this is referred to as "lowering the water's saturation state
with respect to calcium carbonate." Practically, it means shrinking the
supply of material available for shell formation. (Imagine trying to build
a house when someone keeps stealing your bricks.) Once the carbonate
concentration gets pushed low enough, even existing shells, like those of
Fabry's pteropods, begin to dissolve.

To illustrate, in mathematical terms, what the seas of the future will
look like, Caldeira pulled out a set of graphs. Plotted on one axis was aragonite saturation levels; on the other, latitude. (Ocean latitude is significant
because saturation levels tend naturally to decline toward the poles.) Different colors of lines represented different emissions scenarios. Some scenarios project that the world's economy will continue to grow rapidly and
that this growth will be fuelled mostly by oil and coal. Others assume that
the economy will grow more slowly, and still others that the energy mix will
shift away from fossil fuels. Caldeira considered four much studied scenarios, ranging from one of the most optimistic, known by the shorthand B1,
to one of the most pessimistic, A2. The original point of the graphs was to
show that each scenario would produce a different ocean. But they turned
out to be more similar than Caldeira had expected.

Under all four scenarios, by the end of this century the waters around
Antarctica will become undersaturated with respect to aragonite—the
form of calcium carbonate produced by pteropods and corals. (When water

becomes undersaturated, it is corrosive to shells.) Meanwhile, surface pH will drop by another .2, bringing acidity to roughly double what it was in pre-industrial times. To look still further out into the future, Caldeira modelled what would happen if humans burned through all the world's remaining fossil-fuel resources, a process that would release some eighteen thousand gigatons of carbon dioxide. He found that by 2300 the oceans would become undersaturated from the poles to the equator. Then he modelled what would happen if we pushed still further and burned through unconventional fuels, like low-grade shales. In that case, we would drive the pH down so low that the seas would come very close to being acidic.

"I used to think of B1 as a good scenario, and I used to think of A2 as a terrible scenario," Caldeira told me. "Now I look at them as different flavors of bad scenarios."

20   He went on, "I think there's a whole category of organisms that have been around for hundreds of millions of years which are at risk of extinction—namely, things that build calcium-carbonate shells or skeletons. To a first approximation, if we cut our emissions in half it will take us twice as long to create the damage. But we'll get to more or less the same place. We really need an order-of-magnitude reduction in order to avoid it."

Caldeira said that he had recently gone to Washington to brief some members of Congress. "I was asked, 'What is the appropriate stabilization target for atmospheric CO_2?' " he recalled. "And I said, 'Well, I think it's inappropriate to think in terms of stabilization targets. I think we should think in terms of emissions targets.' And they said, 'O.K., what's the appropriate emissions target?' And I said, 'Zero.'

"If you're talking about mugging little old ladies, you don't say, 'What's our target for the rate of mugging little old ladies?' You say, 'Mugging little old ladies is bad, and we're going to try to eliminate it.' You recognize you might not be a hundred per cent successful, but your goal is to eliminate the mugging of little old ladies. And I think we need to eventually come around to looking at carbon-dioxide emissions the same way."

Coral reefs grow in a great swath that stretches like a belt around the belly of the earth, from thirty degrees north to thirty degrees south latitude. The world's largest reef is the Great Barrier, off the coast of northeastern Australia, and the second largest is off the coast of Belize. There are extensive coral reefs in the tropical Pacific, in the Indian Ocean, and in the Red Sea, and many smaller ones in the Caribbean. These reefs, home to an estimated twenty-five per cent of all marine fish species, represent some of the most diverse ecosystems on the planet.

Much of what is known about coral reefs and ocean acidification was originally discovered, improbably enough, in Arizona, in the self-enclosed, supposedly self-sufficient world known as Biosphere 2. A three-acre glassed-in structure shaped like a ziggurat, Biosphere 2 was built in the late nineteen-eighties by a private group—a majority of the funding came from the billionaire Edward Bass—and was intended to demonstrate how life on earth (Biosphere 1) could be recreated on, say, Mars. The building contained an artificial "ocean," a "rain forest," a "desert," and an "agricultural zone." The first group of Biosphereans—four men and four women—managed to remain, sealed inside, for two years. They produced all their own food and, for a long stretch, breathed only recycled air, but the project was widely considered a failure. The Biosphereans spent much of the time hungry, and, even more ominously, they lost control of their artificial atmosphere. In the various "ecosystems," decomposition, which takes up oxygen and gives off CO_2, was supposed to be balanced by photosynthesis, which does the reverse. But, for reasons mainly having to do with the richness of the soil that had been used in the "agricultural zone," decomposition won out. Oxygen levels inside the building kept falling, and the Biosphereans developed what amounted to altitude sickness. Carbon-dioxide levels soared, at one point reaching three thousand parts per million, or roughly eight times the levels outside.

When Biosphere 2 officially collapsed, in 1995, Columbia University 25 took over the management of the building. The university's plan was to transform it into a teaching and research facility, and it fell to a scientist named Chris Langdon to figure out something pedagogically useful to do with the "ocean," a tank the size of an Olympic swimming pool. Langdon's specialty was measuring photosynthesis, and he had recently finished a project, financed by the Navy, that involved trying to figure out whether blooms of bioluminescent algae could be used to track enemy submarines. (The answer was no.) Langdon was looking for a new project, but he wasn't sure what the "ocean" was good for. He began by testing various properties of the water. As would be expected in such a high-CO_2 environment, he found that the pH was low.

"The very first thing I did was try to establish normal chemistry," he recalled recently. "So I added chemicals—essentially baking soda and baking powder—to the water to bring the pH back up." Within a week, the alkalinity had dropped again, and he had to add more chemicals. The same thing happened. "Every single time I did it, it went back down, and the rate at which it went down was proportional to the concentration. So, if I added more, it went down faster. So I started thinking, What's going on here? And then it dawned on me."

Langdon left Columbia in 2004 and now works at the Rosenstiel School of Marine and Atmospheric Science, at the University of Miami. He is fifty-two, with a high forehead, deep-set blue eyes, and a square chin. When I went to visit him, not long ago, he took me to see his coral samples, which were growing in a sort of aquatic nursery across the street from his office. On the way, we had to pass through a room filled with tanks of purple sea slugs, which were being raised for medical research. In the front row, the youngest sea slugs, about half an inch long, were floating gracefully, as if suspended in gelatine. Toward the back were slugs that had been fed for several months on a lavish experimental diet. These were the size of my forearm and seemed barely able to lift their knobby, purplish heads.

Langdon's corals were attached to tiles arranged at the bottom of long, sinklike tanks. There were hundreds of them, grouped by species: *Acropora cervicornis*, a type of staghorn coral that grows in a classic antler shape; *Montastrea cavernosa*, a coral that looks like a seafaring cactus; and *Porites divaricata*, a branching coral made up of lumpy, putty-colored protuberances. Water was streaming into the tanks, but when Langdon put his hand in front of the faucet to stop the flow, I could see that every lobe of *Porites divaricata* was covered with tiny pink arms and that every arm ended in soft, fingerlike tentacles. The arms were waving in what looked to be a frenzy either of joy or of supplication.

Langdon explained that the arms belonged to separate coral polyps, and that a reef consisted of thousands upon thousands of polyps spread, like a coating of plaster, over a dead calcareous skeleton. Each coral polyp is a distinct individual, with its own tentacles and its own digestive system, and houses its own collection of symbiotic algae, known as zooxanthellae, which provide it with most of its nutrition. At the same time, each polyp is joined to its neighbors through a thin layer of connecting tissue, and all are attached to the colony's collective skeleton. Individual polyps constantly add to the group skeleton by combining calcium and carbonate ions in a medium known as the extracytoplasmic calcifying fluid. Meanwhile, other organisms, like parrot fish and sponges, are constantly eating away at the reef in search of food or protection. If a reef were ever to stop calcifying, it would start to shrink and eventually would disappear.

"It's just like a tree with bugs," Langdon explained. "It needs to grow   30 pretty quickly just to stay even."

As Langdon struggled, unsuccessfully, to control the pH in the Biosphere "ocean," he started to wonder whether the corals in the tank might be to blame. The Biosphereans had raised twenty different species of coral, and while many of the other creatures, including nearly all the vertebrates selected for the project, had died out, the corals had survived. Langdon wondered whether the chemicals he was adding to raise the pH were, by increasing the saturation state, stimulating their growth. At the time, it seemed an unlikely hypothesis, because the prevailing view among marine biologists was that corals weren't sensitive to changes in saturation. (In many textbooks, the formula for coral calcification is still given incorrectly, which helps explain the prevalence of this view.) Just about everyone, including Langdon's own postdoc, a young woman named Francesca Marubini, thought that his theory was wrong. "It was a total pain in the ass," Langdon recalled.

To test his hypothesis, Langdon employed a straightforward but time-consuming procedure. Conditions in the "ocean" would be systematically varied, and the growth of the coral monitored. The experiment took more than three years to complete, produced more than a thousand measurements, and, in the end, confirmed Langdon's hypothesis. It revealed a more or less linear relationship between how fast the coral grew and how highly saturated the water was. By proving that increased saturation spurs coral growth, Langdon also, of course, demonstrated the reverse: when saturation drops, coral growth slows. In the artificial world of Biosphere 2, the implications of this discovery were interesting; in the real world they were rather more grim. Any drop in the ocean's saturation levels, it seemed, would make coral more vulnerable.

Langdon and Marubini published their findings in the journal *Global Biogeochemical Cycles* in the summer of 2000. Still, many marine biologists remained skeptical, in no small part, it seems, because of the study's association with the discredited Biosphere project. In 2001, Langdon sold his house in New York and moved to Arizona. He spent another two years redoing the experiments, with even stricter controls. The results were essentially identical. In the meantime, other researchers launched similar experiments on different coral species. Their findings were also the same, which, as Langdon put it to me, "is the best way to make believers out of people."

Coral reefs are under threat for a host of reasons: bottom trawling, dynamite fishing, coastal erosion, agricultural runoff, and, nowadays, global warming. When water temperatures rise too high, corals lose—or perhaps expel, no one is quite sure—the algae that nourish them. (The process is called "bleaching," because without their zooxanthellae corals appear white.) For a particular reef, any one of these threats could potentially be fatal. Ocean acidification poses a different kind of threat, one that could preclude the very possibility of a reef.

35   Saturation levels are determined using a complicated formula that involves multiplying the calcium and carbonate ion concentrations, and then dividing the result by a figure called the stoichiometric solubility product. Prior to the industrial revolution, the world's major reefs were all growing in water whose aragonite saturation level stood between 4 and 5. Today, there is not a single remaining region in the oceans where the saturation level is above 4.5, and there are only a handful of spots—off the northeastern coast of Australia, in the Philippine Sea, and near the Maldives—where it is above 4. Since the takeup of CO_2 by the oceans is a highly predictable physical process, it is possible to map the saturation levels of the future with great precision. Assuming that current emissions trends continue, by 2060 there will be no regions left with a level above 3.5. By 2100, none will remain above 3.

As saturation levels decline, the rate at which reefs add aragonite through calcification and the rate at which they lose it through bioerosion will start to approach each other. At a certain point, the two will cross, and reefs will begin to disappear. Precisely where that point lies is difficult to say, because erosion may well accelerate as ocean pH declines. Langdon estimates that the crossing point will be reached when atmospheric CO_2 levels exceed six hundred and fifty parts per million, which, under a "business as usual" emissions scenario, will occur sometime around 2075.

"I think that this is just an absolute limit, something they can't cope with," he told me. Other researchers put the limit somewhat higher, and others somewhat lower.

Meanwhile, as global temperatures climb, bleaching events are likely to become more common. A major worldwide bleaching event occurred in 1998, and many Caribbean reefs suffered from bleaching again during the summer of 2005. Current conditions in the equatorial Pacific suggest that

2007 is apt to be another bleaching year. Taken together, acidification and rising ocean temperatures represent a kind of double bind for reefs: regions that remain hospitable in terms of temperature are becoming increasingly inhospitable in terms of saturation, and vice versa.

"While one, bleaching, is an acute stress that's killing them off, the other, acidification, is a chronic stress that's preventing them from recovering," Joanie Kleypas, a reef scientist at the National Center for Atmospheric Research, in Boulder, Colorado, told me. Kleypas said she thought that some corals would be able to migrate to higher latitudes as the oceans warm, but that, because of the lower saturation levels, as well as the difference in light regimes, the size of these migrants would be severely limited. "There's a point where you're going to have coral but no reefs," she said.

. . .

Calcifying organisms come in a fantastic array of shapes, sizes, and taxonomic groups. Echinoderms like starfish are calcifiers. So are mollusks like clams and oysters, and crustaceans like barnacles, and many species of bryozoans, or sea mats, and tiny protists known as foraminifera—the list goes on and on. Without experimental data, it's impossible to know which species will prove to be particularly vulnerable to declining pH and which will not. In the natural world, the pH of the water changes by season, and even time of day, and many species may be able to adapt to new conditions, at least within certain bounds. Obviously, though, it's impractical to run experiments on tens of thousands of different species. (Only a few dozen have been tested so far.) Meanwhile, as the example of coral reefs makes clear, what's more important than how acidification will affect any particular organism is how it will affect entire marine ecosystems—a question that can't be answered by even the most ambitious experimental protocol. The recent report on acidification by Britain's Royal Society noted that it was "not possible to predict" how whole communities would respond, but went on to observe that "without significant action to reduce CO_2 emissions" there may be "no place in the future oceans for many of the species and ecosystems we know today."

Carol Turley is a senior scientist at Plymouth Marine Laboratory, in Plymouth, England, and one of the authors of the Royal Society report. She observed that pH is a critical variable not just in calcification but in other vital marine processes, like the cycling of nutrients.

"It looks like we'll be changing lots of levels in the food chain," Turley told me. "So we may be affecting the primary producers. We may be affecting larvae of zooplankton and so on. What I think might happen,

40

and it's pure speculation, is that you may get a shortening of the food chain so that only one or two species comes out on top—for instance, we may see massive blooms of jellyfish and things like that, and that's a very short food chain."

Thomas Lovejoy, who coined the term "biological diversity" in 1980, compared the effects of ocean acidification to "running the course of evolution in reverse."

"For an organism that lives on land, the two most important factors are temperature and moisture," Lovejoy, who is now the president of the Heinz Center for Science, Economics, and the Environment, in Washington, D.C., told me. "And for an organism that lives in the water the two most important factors are temperature and acidity. So this is just a profound, profound change. It is going to send all kinds of ripples through marine ecosystems, because of the importance of calcium carbonate for so many organisms in the oceans, including those at the base of the food chain. If you back off and look at it, it's as if you or I went to our annual physical and the body chemistry came back and the doctor looked really, really worried. It's a systemic change. You could have food chains collapse, and fisheries ultimately with them, because most of the fish we get from the ocean are at the end of long food chains. You probably will see shifts in favor of invertebrates, or the reign of jellyfish."

45   Riebesell put it this way: "The risk is that at the end we will have the rise of slime."

Analyze

1. How does the release of CO_2 from the burning of fossil fuels affect the world's oceans, and what impact will that have on coral reefs?

2. How do the models the scientists built help us understand the problem of "ocean acidification"?

3. What do you think Kolbert's main point is in this reading? Is she writing to inform, to persuade, to argue? How do you know?

Explore

1. Why does Kolbert spend so much time telling us about the researchers she talked with? Why doesn't she just give us the facts? Why does she use the conventions of the detective story genre to organize her essay?

2. Using your computer, identify the major coral reefs in the world and find out what is happening to them. Then see if you can identify the major consequences of these changes. Write a blog post that summarizes what you have learned about coral reef health and its consequences in a way that you think will get readers to care about the problem.

3. As the Appendix to this book points out, the complicated information regarding issues of sustainability needs to be explained thoroughly, but writers still need to maintain a reader's attention. This rhetorical problem—the problem of how to accurately and succinctly yet effectively explain complex problems—is a central problem of the sustainability movement. This article in particular struggles to convey a great deal of complicated information relatively succinctly. To test your own skills of conveying important points efficiently, choose one of the author's main points and describe it first in a blog post, then in a Facebook post, and then in a Twitter post. The challenge of each is to convey your point as effectively as possible as succinctly as possible. Then, consider which medium you feel will most effectively reach your goal and why.

Forging Connections

1. These writers struggle to get readers to take notice of the everyday elements of life that have become invisible to us—food, water, and soil. Take a moment to reflect on the societal constructs and cultural habits that have helped to make these elements of life invisible, and how things would be different if those constructs were no longer in place. For example, perhaps we don't notice the dirt beneath our feet as much because everyone travels by car. Or perhaps we don't notice the water we use because it flows freely from a faucet. So imagine a world without cars or without faucets—how would that change the way we think about the ground and the water? How would that change the way we think about everything? In a narrative essay, create a world in which we are forced to see these invisible elements more clearly, and tell the story about what that would mean and look like for the everyday person.

2. In "The Illusion of Water Abundance," Cynthia Barnett says that "America needs nothing less than a revolution in how we use water.

We must change not only the wasteful ways we consume water in our homes, businesses, farms, and energy plants but also the inefficient ways we move water to and away from them." This statement stands in contrast to many green initiatives that advocate for small changes made by individual people, such as taking shorter showers or turning off the faucet while we brush our teeth. Using your knowledge of the big-picture connections between water use, soil, the ocean, and other essential resources, construct a well-defended proposal that describes what this kind of revolution would look like, how it might be put into effect, and why such a revolution is needed.

Looking Further

1. In the reading "Nature: A Major Company Puts a Value on the Environment," Bryan Walsh introduces the concept of "ecosystem services" and suggests that the economic incentive for business is a better solution to environmental problems than government action. In the "Tragedy of the Commons" in Chapter 1, Garrett Hardin makes exactly the opposite argument. The issue of how we might motivate necessary change on a large scale is a recurring theme throughout this book. Using examples from more than one chapter, make an argument about the relative roles of individual action, business or corporate self-regulation, and government regulation and policy in addressing core problems in sustainability.

2. In "The Illusion of Water Abundance," Cynthia Barnett says that educating people about the problem of water supply is not enough to change their water use habits. This is a version of what the Appendix calls the rationalist paradox; people just aren't often motivated to change by facts alone. Using words, images, sound, and any other media you want, construct a document, film, or website that appeals to readers in ways that you think might be successful in getting them to actually change what they do so that they live more sustainably.

appendix

Carl Herndl with Barbara Rockenbach and Aaron Ritzenberg[1]

This Appendix has three major sections, each of which can be used independently of the others. The first two sections, "Understanding the Scientific Principles Behind Sustainability" and "Rhetorical Strategies and Writing for Change," are specific to the material in this book. The first section explains five concepts that lie at the heart of the science associated with sustainability and that explain the science behind many of the readings. The second section describes many of the challenges involved in getting readers to understand and care about sustainability enough to consider changing their behavior. This section uses the readings in the book as examples of these rhetorical strategies. This section also contains a guide to doing research so that whatever you are writing, you have something to say. The final section of the Appendix is a brief guide to writing research papers. It treats the research paper as an important genre of academic writing but one that uses the research practices required for the other genres represented in the book.

---

1. Barbara Rockenbach, Director of Humanities & History Libraries, Columbia University; Aaron Ritzenberg, Associate Director of First-Year Writing, Columbia University.

UNDERSTANDING THE SCIENTIFIC PRINCIPLES BEHIND SUSTAINABILITY

Whether you are writing a blog post, a piece for a community newsletter, a proposal for installing solar panels at your church, or an academic research paper that concerns sustainability, you need to understand some of the central concepts in the science of sustainability. Much about sustainability is not intuitive. The definition of the concept in the Preface is not common knowledge. Similarly, there are a handful of concepts that are crucial to the science concerning sustainability, and they are not widely understood. This section of the Appendix explains five of these important concepts: systems analysis, scale, uncertainty, modeling, and scenarios.

The first of these core concepts is the notion of **systems analysis**. There are many technical definitions of systems analysis, and they differ depending on what kind of thing you want to study: an economy, a political system, a biological community. In sustainability, systems analysis might begin with the basic insight from ecology that all parts of an ecosystem are related to each other in some way. For example, no plant, animal, or insect in an ecosystem exists all alone; it interacts with other living things, but also with the soil, water, and weather in the ecosystem. The basic idea that everything in a system is connected in some way to other elements in the system explains the conservationist's motto "lost there, felt here." This is the ecological idea behind Aldo Leopold's essay "Thinking Like a Mountain" in Chapter 1. A mountain is an interconnected system.

To analyze a system, you need to identify all the parts of the system and discover how they interact. That puts each part of a system and what happens to it in an appropriate context and helps you see the possible consequences of actions. But identifying all the parts of a system and understanding how they affect one another is extremely complicated. The readings on soil and water in Chapter 6 provide an example of one kind of system: an "agroecosystem." That awkward word refers to the way agriculture interacts with the surrounding land, soil, water, and all the plants and animals living in the system. The readings on "hypoxia" (oxygen-depleted water) in the Gulf of Mexico and on nitrogen fertilizer used on Midwestern corn fields outline one kind of system. The basic idea is that what we do to raise corn in the Midwest has serious consequences for the health of the Gulf of Mexico. As the readings from National Public Radio's food blog *The Salt* and the website of the Louisiana Universities Marine Consortium say, a major cause of the hypoxic zone in the Gulf of Mexico is the overuse of nitrogen fertilizer in the upper Mississippi River basin that drains into the Gulf of Mexico.

The hypoxic zone in the Gulf is an area bigger than the state of Connecticut where there is almost no oxygen in the water and all the plants, fish, and shellfish have either died or moved away. People call it the "dead zone." There are lots of parts to this system and they all interact, but Midwestern agricultural practices and their economic incentives are contributing to the death of the aquatic life in the Gulf of Mexico off Texas and Louisiana thousands of miles away. To understand the sustainability of agriculture in the Midwest, you need to consider the effects on other parts of the system.

The concept of an interconnected system explains the popular phrase "think globally, act locally." If you see the whole system, you can make better decisions about how to act in your local context. There are a series of important ideas that fall under the general category of systems analysis. As Vandana Shiva argues in Chapter 5, our production of biofuel in the United States is part of a global economic system. If we use a lot of corn to make ethanol for our cars, it raises the price of corn around the world, and that, in turn, encourages people in Brazil and Indonesia to turn forests and grasslands into farms for growing biofuel materials. Ethanol production causes "unintended land use change" in other parts of the world. A different application of systems analysis might consider the production of natural gas by fracking. If you include all the energy it takes to produce natural gas through fracking, do you get more energy out in the end than you put into the process? That's called "energy balance." It is like measuring a financial investment. On balance or in the end, do you get more out than you put in?

Complicated as all this analysis can be, one of the hardest tasks in systems analysis is deciding where the system begins and ends. How you determine the boundaries of the system sets the rules of the game. People argue a lot about the boundaries and what is and is not part of the system. Is the Gulf of Mexico part of the same system as a cornfield in Iowa? Or does the system end at the edge of the cornfield?

The concept of a system in which local actions have distant consequences suggests a second crucial concept in sustainability: **scale**. The problem of Gulf hypoxia is a problem of geographic scale. Unless you extend your vision to include the whole system in which a practice like Midwestern industrial agriculture exists, it is easy to overlook or ignore the physically distant consequences of that way of farming. Lots of the essays in this book deal with problems of geographic scale, especially in a globalized world.

Just as important as geographic scale, but much harder to see, is the issue of time scales. Put simply, geologic time and most natural or evolutionary processes move at a much slower pace than most human activities. For example, the U.S. Department of Agriculture estimates it takes approximately

500 years to produce an inch of topsoil. Yet widespread agricultural production of corn and soybeans can accelerate the rate at which topsoil is eroded by water runoff or wind so that the rate of soil loss vastly outstrips the rate at which soil is renewed. Similarly, the rate at which we are drawing water from deep underground aquifers such as the Oglala aquifer in the West and the Florida aquifer is much faster than these underground storage systems can recharge. The level of these aquifers, like that of many surface reservoirs such as Lake Mead, are dropping steadily as a result. One basic measure of sustainability is whether you are using a resource faster than it can be renewed. Finally, as Rachel Carson points out in her essay in Chapter 1, our chemical industry produces hundreds of new pesticides and herbicides every year that we then use on fields and lawns. But it takes much longer for the organisms in the ecosystem to adapt to these new chemicals. Evolution moves slowly. The production of new chemicals moves at light speed. That is like dancing a slow stately waltz to a hot pop dance tune. It doesn't work, and it destroys the balance of the ecosystem.

Three final concepts in sustainability science are uncertainty, modeling, and scenarios. And like the notion of systems and where they begin and end, these concepts prompt a lot of debate.

In everyday conversation, saying you are *uncertain* usually means that you don't know or have no real opinion. In science, **uncertainty** means something different. As the authors of the National Research Council selection in Chapter 4 say, "in scientific parlance uncertainty is a way of describing how precisely or how confidently something is known" (22). The more complex and dynamic a system is and the fewer observational data scientists have about it, the higher the uncertainty and the less confident we can be in predicting the future behavior of something like global climate. But that does not mean that scientists have no facts, or that they do not know a great deal. It simply means that they know that there are things they don't know.

Climate change is probably the best-known case where uncertainty has become a huge issue. Some people, often called "climate change skeptics," seize on uncertainty as a reason to deny that climate change exists or to argue against taking any action to prevent it. Climate scientists work hard to reduce uncertainty and explain what they know. The clearest discussion of uncertainty in climate change science appears in the Intergovernmental Panel on Climate Change fourth report (IPCC 4). In that report the Nobel Prize–winning authors explain that there are at least three different kinds of uncertainty: unpredictability, structural uncertainty, and value uncertainty.

Human behavior or chaotic systems are just *unpredictable*. For example, whether countries in the world cooperate on climate change policy and how they do so makes a great difference to our future. Unfortunately, it is very difficult to predict how citizens and governments around the world will act and what international relations will look like in 20 years. Incomplete or inadequate models or systems whose exact boundaries we don't know produce *structural uncertainty*. It would be hard, for example, to predict the behavior of something in your neighborhood if you don't know exactly where your neighborhood begins and ends. Much scientific work goes into trying to resolve these uncertainties. Finally, *value uncertainty* generally means that scientists don't have enough data to determine something like the rate at which a glacier is melting with absolute precision. If they haven't measured the melting or have measured it only for a short time and in a few places, they can't be very confident in their information. Again, scientists work hard to gather more data to reduce this uncertainty (IPCC 4).

In writing about climate change the IPCC developed a set of terms to indicate levels of uncertainty, and most climate science has adopted this terminology. Something is "virtually certain" if there is a 99% probability of it happening. Something is "unlikely" if there is less than a 33% chance of it happening. So, admitting different degrees and kinds of uncertainty doesn't mean science does not know things or can't predict the future behavior of climate systems, it just means that scientific reports are very careful to be honest and accurate about just how certain or confident they are about things. Table 1 describes the degrees of uncertainty and the terms science uses to describe them.

Table 1   **Likelihood Scale**

Terminology	Likelihood of the occurrence/outcome
Virtually certain	>99% probability of occurrence
Very likely	>90% probability
Likely	>66% probability
About as likely as not	33% to 66% probability
Unlikely	<33% probability
Very unlikely	<10% probability
Exceptionally unlikely	<1% probability

Source: IPCC 4.

A good way to see what uncertainty means is to think of the hurricane tracking reports you see on the television news during hurricane season. Weather maps usually indicate where a hurricane is at the present and predict where it will go over the next few days. The projected path of the storm is drawn as a shaded cone or a funnel that gets wider as you get farther away from the storm's current location marked by that familiar counterclockwise swirl on the map. There is usually a solid line drawn down the middle of the "cone of probability" that is the predicted path of the storm. But the storm could also strike land anywhere in the shaded area in the cone. Scientists know how certain they are about the storm's path in the next 12 hours, and they know how uncertainty increases as we go farther into the future. Weather is notoriously complex and dynamic: things change and one change leads to other changes. The width of the cone of probability is the degree of scientific uncertainty about where the storm will land. The wider the cone of probability, the less confidence forecasters have in the accuracy of the path drawn down the middle of the cone. But that uncertainty does not mean that forecasters can't tell us with confidence the general area where the storm will hit.

To predict how things might change in the future, science uses **models** to understand the behavior of complex systems that they can't simply control and manipulate. In an extremely simplified version of experimental science, a scientist could identify all the variables or factors in a situation and keep all of them the same except for one and see what happens. For example, you might plant two different kinds of corn in two adjacent fields that are exactly the same and then plow, fertilize, and irrigate them in exactly the same way. If one field produces more or better corn, you know that seed is better than the other seed for producing corn. Unfortunately, you can't do that with most things in the real world. Weather forecasters can't control a hurricane and test individual variables, so they use models. Traffic engineers use models to predict how drivers will react to different road conditions. Economists use models to predict how consumers will respond to price increases or interest rates. In the same way, climate science uses immensely sophisticated models to simulate the future change in climate.

The technique of modeling is similar in many ways to the virtual worlds produced by computer games like Civilization (aka Civ). These programs model how a city or a civilization might develop under different situations or **scenarios**. The software in the game includes a set of rules, basic principles, relationships, and interactions that guide how the civilization develops. What you do in early stages of the game determines the situation you have to deal with later in the game. A scenario is a storyline that plays itself out throughout the game. In weather modeling, climate modeling, or soil erosion modeling, the scenario is a set of "inputs." Change the scenario or inputs, and you change the outcome in the future. In climate modeling, for example, the outcome changes a great deal if you assume that we will continue burning coal for electricity and driving big inefficient cars. That is an input to the model. If we shift from coal-generated electricity to wind, solar, and geothermal and put energy-saving technology in place, the outcome of the model changes. If we drive smaller, more fuel-efficient cars and take more mass transit, the scenario changes and the future looks very different.

The models used in climate science operate on similar principles but are infinitely more sophisticated, which can lead to doubt about their accuracy. Fortunately, climate models can be checked against measurements in the real world. Typically, scientists test their models by simulating past conditions and seeing how well or poorly the model "predicts" what actually happened. Dr. Cicerone uses this idea in his argument about climate change in the selection in Chapter 4. The great benefit of climate models is that once they are built and tested, they allow scientists to simulate what will happen around the world under different conditions. No one can know the future with certainty, but carefully built models can give us predictions in which we can have very high levels of confidence. Like the polls politicians take to determine who is leading in the approach to an election, models are not absolutely precise. They have "margins of error." But those margins of error and the uncertainty can be reduced to quite low levels.

Even with a known degree of uncertainty associated with them, models can provide very useful information to guide our decisions and actions. The model or the politician's poll is a neutral tool. Scientists are continually improving their models by increasing the number and accuracy of their real-world measurements and by incorporating more sophisticated understanding of the systems they study. (This reduces the "structural uncertainty" and "value uncertainty" described above.) But at any given time, the model is static; like the rules in Civ, how the model works doesn't change. But we can change the scenario we test. We can ask the model what the change in global temperature will be in 100 years if we keep burning petroleum at the rate we are now, or we can ask the model what the temperature change will be if we reduce our petroleum consumption by, say, 1% a year for the next 100 years. This is a very simplified example; models have to calculate the interaction of many, many elements, not just how much petroleum we use. But the basic principle holds. A good model will take our scenario of inputs and tell us pretty reliably what the average global temperature change will be in 100 years.

RHETORICAL STRATEGIES AND WRITING FOR CHANGE

How to get readers to see, understand, care and then act is the rhetorical challenge of sustainability. Indeed, the rhetorical scholar Kenneth Burke calls rhetoric "an inducement to action." But motivating people to change is very difficult. Alas, there is no simple solution to this problem. We always face the **rationalist paradox**: people who "know" the facts often continue to act as if they didn't. Knowing the facts about sustainability and changing the way you live are two different things. There are lots of reasons that people continue doing what they have always done despite what they have learned about sustainability. We are not purely rational animals, and facts alone are rarely enough to get us to change how we live. People can be persuaded by facts and logical arguments, but they are more often motivated to act or change by what is immediate and concrete and what feels good. Pleasure is a big motivator. In her essay on gardening and climate change, Steingraber appeals to both our parental commitment to our children and to the pleasure of eating fresh, tasty food we grow ourselves to encourage us to take up gardening. Most of us will make sacrifices for our children or our families. It is an emotional matter. And all of us are willing to do things that give us pleasure. **Affective** appeals to sources of emotion or pleasure can be a great rhetorical strategy to induce or encourage people to act.

One of the most common ways to make an affective appeal is to put a human face on a problem. Politicians do it all the time. How many times have you heard a politician open a speech with the story of an individual who is suffering or who is an illustration of the argument? They are smart speakers. They know people like concrete examples and will **identify** with the individuals in the story. Similarly, putting a human face on climate change or the problem of electronic waste can be as powerful as all the facts combined. As Roman Krznaric argues in his essay on empathy (in Chapter 4), getting people to change their behavior is very difficult, and creating empathy for others who are distant in space or in time can be a powerful strategy. Krznaric's theory of empathy and its role in ethics not only explains a great deal about ethics, it also suggests a way to motivate readers to care enough to change. Similarly, Terry Cannon's essay about the effect of climate change on women and the very poor in Bangladesh (in Chapter 4) helps put a human face on the potential consequences of climate change. These are not only important aspects of climate change, they offer possibilities for making readers care about the issue. If readers identify with the people who experience the consequences of unsustainable actions, they are more likely to feel the importance of the issue and act accordingly.

So how do you begin to make these distant or overlooked things visible and compelling? It can be difficult to explain scientific and technical concepts or complicated ecological systems. New terms and complex relationships are hard for readers to grasp. In "The Darkening Sea" in Chapter 6, for example, Elizabeth Kolbert has to explain the chemical process of ocean acidification and its effect on coral reefs. She has to be clear enough to be understood but brief enough to keep readers' attention. Rhetorical scholars refer to this as the **accommodation** of technical information to non-expert audiences. In the readings throughout this book, writers like Jared Diamond use metaphors like "the world is a polder" (a low-lying area in the Netherlands that is surrounded by dikes that keep out the sea) and analogies to help explain difficult concepts. Maps, diagrams, and charts are very helpful if they are not too complicated and if the writer explains what they mean carefully. Visual rhetoric is the field that studies when and how to present information graphically.

Even in the excerpted version of "The Darkening Sea," the story Kolbert tells is long and complicated. That much technical information, no matter how important, can easily begin to bore or overwhelm readers, especially those unfamiliar with the topic. Notice that Kolbert tells readers a great deal about the researchers involved in her story and about how they did their work. Why doesn't she just lay out the technical facts of carbon dioxide absorption, the effect on water acidity, and the chemistry of coral shell secretion?

Kolbert isn't just communicating facts; if she were, few people would bother to read her essay. She is telling a detective story that she presents as a mystery to be solved. So besides straightforward explanations of ocean chemistry, Kolbert uses an interesting **narrative** about the process of discovery to keep her reader's attention. The twists and turns in the narrative make the technical information less of a burden on the reader.

The detective story Kolbert uses to explain why coral reefs are dying is a familiar kind of story. We already know what to expect in a mystery narrative. There is usually a smart and intuitive detective, a mystery to be solved, lots of challenges and breakthroughs along the way—and, if things work out, an answer at the end. A detective mystery is a standard type of narrative, and all detective mysteries have a lot in common no matter what the particular mystery is. The detective story is an example of a **genre**, a flexible but stable pattern or form that writers use all the time and with which readers are generally familiar. In movies, genres are everywhere. The Western movie is a genre that we all recognize when we see it. So is the horror movie, or the romantic comedy. No matter how different they are, members of a genre have a lot in common, and we know what to expect when we read or watch them.

A genre is a common solution to a problem writers have run into frequently. There is no need to reinvent the wheel, so writers follow the conventions of common and successful genres to do what they need to do in writing. A genre helps a writer know what to say and how to organize the material, but it also places a lot of constraints or expectations on the writer as well. In "Thinking Like a Mountain," for example, Aldo Leopold writes a story about self-discovery and coming to insight. It is a kind of parable, and we know it has an importance or meaning that is implied or indirect. What could it mean to "think like a mountain"? But parables are short and usually poetic, and they don't allow for long explanations. Leopold is so successful because he found the right genre for his situation and purpose, and he fulfilled the expectations so beautifully.

Other genres useful in writing about sustainability have different forms but common moves and expectations. Ralph Cicerone's lecture "Finding Climate Change and Being Useful" in Chapter 4 is an academic **argument** that climate change is real and that it is caused by human activity. Cicerone has a case to prove the same way a lawyer does in a criminal trial. The classical tradition of making these sorts of arguments says that in making an argument that climate change is real and caused by humans (or that your client is innocent of the charge) you need to do five types of things: 1) open with an "exhortation" that tells readers what is at stake or gets them to care about the topic; 2) narrate the background or information readers need to understand and trust your argument; 3) make your case by stating what you claim to be true and offering evidence to support it; 4) refute the common or most likely objections to your position; and 5) close in a way that provides a powerful insight or conclusion. And it is important to recognize that you are "doing" something; every time you say or write something, you are also doing something with words. The academic research paper that the next section discusses is a special genre with its own form of argument. Scholarly arguments are a very specific kind of writing in a very specific context—the university. But they share most of the same elements and purposes as the arguments that are everywhere in our daily lives. Knowing how to make a persuasive argument is useful in almost any context.

Many of the works included in this book start with a **compelling story or example** of the problem the author is writing about to illustrate what is at stake. Somehow you have to engage a reader's attention and make him or her care enough about the topic to continue reading. Cicerone doesn't do this since he was giving a talk to a group of scientists and policymakers who came to hear him because they were already convinced that climate change was a global problem. And very few academic research papers begin with a compelling story or illustration. But in Chapter 6 Cynthia Barnett uses the example of a suburb full of swimming pools in the desert to open her essay on "The Illusion of Water Abundance" as an exhortation.

Once you show a reader that you have something interesting and important to say, you have to do at least four more things, not necessarily in this order. You have to give readers enough **background information** that they can understand what you are saying and trust you. You have to **make your case**: present what you claim to be true and provide enough evidence to support your claims. It is also a good idea to **counter or refute objections** from skeptics or opponents. If you already know what they are likely to say against your case, provide evidence to discount their objections before they make them. And, finally, you need to close with a sense that you and the readers both **know more now** than you did in the beginning and that your argument makes a difference. Cicerone does all these things in his lecture, and in one form or another so do the other writers in this book who are writing in the genre of the argument. As you read their essays, you should watch how they do these things.

Leopold's parable and Cicerone's academic argument are two genres, but there are many others in this book. Recently we have seen new genres emerge online or in social media; many of the readings below are blog posts of different kinds. Online writing is different from traditional printed text in many ways. The style, the embedded links, the visual elements of blogs and other online forms offer a whole new repertoire of strategies for writers.

Whether you are writing online or in print form, when you are trying to persuade someone you are always making different kinds of **appeals**. When lawyers want to persuade juries that their clients have been wrongly accused, they say, "I appeal to your sense of justice." If you know what your readers value and what is important to them, you should appeal to that value or that standard if you want to convince them. In his argument to scientists, Cicerone appeals to their logic and belief in science. He offers facts, diagrams, and data. That strategy usually works with scientific audiences. By contrast, in his essay on biodiversity, Thomas Friedman makes a whole range of appeals to his readers. When he talks about the natural beauty of the world and the amazing sounds of a jungle full of a myriad of animals, he appeals to our sense of beauty, to our aesthetic sensibility. But he recognizes that not all readers will be moved by that kind of argument, so he offers other appeals. He points out that the diverse plants and animals in the world have provided a host of life-saving cures for disease. When he does that, he is appealing to our sense of self-interest. Who knows what disease they'll come down with someday and what cure they might need in the future? Friedman also makes an economic appeal: diversity saves money by providing all sorts of "ecosystem services" that we would have to pay for ourselves if it weren't done for free by a diverse ecosystem. By opening with an allusion to Noah and God's command to Noah, he implies a religious appeal; for religious people, we too are commanded by God to be good stewards of his creation. No single appeal always works, and none works for every reader. Friedman opts for a range of appeals so he might connect with a broader range of readers.

Another important strategy available to writers trying to persuade readers to live sustainably is the persona, personality, or **ethos** they create for themselves. If a writer appears credible, honest, and authoritative, readers are more likely to believe him or her. And writers often try to identify themselves with their readers in what they believe or in their past actions. In the beautiful letter on creation care in Chapter 4, the authors rely on their commitment to Christ and their own past skepticism about climate change to identify with their readers and persuade them to believe and change. They appeal to a spiritual sense of responsibility.

Doing Research and Having Something to Say

Whether you are writing a blog post, a long Facebook post, a request for funding for a project in your church, or a paper for one of your classes, you need to know what you are talking about. You need to have done enough research to have evidence for your argument and to be able to persuade your readers. And research helps you understand the context for writing, the conversation between people of which your writing will be a part. In one way or another, all good writing is a response to what other people have said. When you write, you join an ongoing conversation. A professional basketball player can write about physical training or game strategy without doing research: his or her whole life has been a process of learning and talking about training and game strategy. If I were to write about these things, I'd have to do a lot of research: reading books and articles, interviewing basketball players, watching games with experienced players, and asking questions. I would have to learn a great deal about game strategy, but I'd also have to learn what people have already said so I would know what readers might want to hear, what is worth talking about. Doing research can be exciting if you enjoy the topic, and it is essential to having something to say that is worth reading.

When you begin investigating a topic, your first instinct might be to go to Google or Wikipedia, or even to a social media site. This is not a bad instinct: in fact, Google, Wikipedia, and social media can be great places to start because they can help you discover a topic. However, most writing, especially academic research and writing, requires you to go beyond these sites to find resources that will make the work of researching and writing both easier and more authoritative.

Let's start with **Google**. You use Google because you know you are going to find a simple search interface and that your search will produce many results. These results may not be completely relevant to your topic, but Google helps get you started. For instance, if you are writing about sustainability, a Google search will give you a whole range of topics, each of which will give a different set of citations.

Similarly, a **Wikipedia** search on sustainability will give you a brief overview and lead you to several articles about the topic. The great thing about Wikipedia is that it is an easy way to gain access to a wealth of information about thousands of topics. However, it is crucial to realize that Wikipedia itself is not an authoritative source in a scholarly context. Even though you may see Wikipedia cited in mainstream newspapers and

sustainability - Google Search

+You   Search   Images   Maps   Play   YouTube   News   Gmail   Drive   Calendar   More -

SIGN IN

sustainability
sustainability
sustainability **jobs**
sustainability **definition**
sustainability **accounting standards board**

Safe Search

Ads

Sustainability - Wikipedia, the free encyclopedia
en.wikipedia.org/wiki/Sustainability ▼
Sustainability is the capacity to endure. In ecology the word describes how biological
systems remain diverse and productive over time. Long-lived and healthy ...

SustainAbility | Independent think tank and strategy consultancy
www.sustainability.com/ ▼
Established in 1987, **SustainAbility** delivers illuminating foresight and actionable insight
on **sustainable** development trends and issues.

News for **sustainability**

Artists have unique knowledge and must claim **sustainability** power
The Guardian - 7 hours ago
The artist and renewable energy entrepreneur, Olafur Eliasson, discusses
his solar lamp project, and the link between art and **sustainability**.

Gap Inc. Expands **Sustainability** Reporting with GRI's G4
Triple Pundit - 4 hours ago

The scoop on **sustainability**: You sir, are a hippie
UNH The New Hampshire - 4 hours ago

Sustainability at the EPA | US EPA
www.epa.gov/**sustainability**/ ▼
US Environmental Protection Agency programs, research and activities related to Urban
Sustainability, Water and Ecosystem Services; Energy, Biofuels and ...

Sustainability Basic Information - US Environmental Protection Agency
www.epa.gov/**sustainability**/basicinfo.htm ▼
Sustainability You are here: EPA Home · **Sustainability**, Basic Information. What is
sustainability? | What is EPA doing? | How can I help? What is **sustainability**?

UC Berkeley **Sustainability**
sustainability berkeley.edu/ ▼
Welcome to UC Berkeley **Sustainability**. UC Berkeley's renowned dedication to
excellence does not stop at academics - it also translates into efforts to be an ...

UC Berkeley Office of **Sustainability** - UC Berkeley **Sustainability**
sustainability.berkeley.edu/os/ ▼
University of California, Berkeley - Office of **Sustainability**.

Engineering and Business for **Sustainability** - University of California ...
sustainable-engineering.berkeley.edu/ ▼
About. The Engineering and Business for **Sustainability** (EBS) Certificate Program is a
new initiative to train UC Berkeley graduate students to understand the ...

UC Berkeley Office of **Sustainability** - **Sustainability** Newsletter
sustainability.berkeley.edu/os/pages/newsletter/ ▼
University of California, Berkeley Office of **Sustainability** · **Sustainability** Newsletter.

Home Page: Office of Energy and **Sustainable** Development - City of ...
www.cityofberkeley.info/energy_and_**sustainable**_development/ ▼
Welcome to the Office of Energy and **Sustainable** Development at the City of Berkeley,
CA. We are part of the Department of Planning & Development. The Office ...

https://www.google.com/webhp?source=search_app#q=sustainability&safe=off

A simple Google search on "sustainability" yields a variety of results.

popular magazines, academic researchers do not consider Wikipedia a
reliable source. They may consult it in the early stages of research on
a completely new topic, but they do not cite it in their own research.
Wikipedia itself says that "Wikipedia is not considered a credible
source . . . This is especially true considering that anyone can edit the
information given at any time." So, think about the genre you are writing

sustainability - Google Search

Images for **sustainability** - Report images

In-depth articles

Is **Sustainable**-Labeled Seafood Really **Sustainable**?

Industry demand for the "**sustainable** seafood" label, issued by the Marine Stewardship Council, is increasing. But some environmentalists fear fisheries are being certified ...

npr NPR - Feb, 2013

A Manifesto for **Sustainable** Capitalism

In The Wall Street Journal, Al Gore and David Blood write about how businesses can embrace environmental, social and governance metrics.

WSJ The Wall Street Journal - Dec, 2011

Creating **Sustainable** Performance

What makes for **sustainable** individual and organizational performance? ... and remain energized at work is valiant on its own merits—but it can also boost performance in a **sustainable** way.

HBR Harvard Business Review

Searches related to **sustainability**

environmental sustainability	**food** sustainability
sustainability **definition**	**corporate** sustainability
sustainability **topics**	sustainability **jobs**
business sustainability	sustainability **defined**

1 2 3 4 5 6 7 8 9 10   **Next**

A Wikipedia search on "sustainability" yields basic information.

and the audience to whom you are speaking. For research papers in college, you should use Wikipedia only to find basic information about your topic and to point you toward scholarly sources. Use the References section at the bottom of the Wikipedia article to find other, more substantive and authoritative resources about your topic.

References

1. ^ *a* *b* Al-Rodhan, Nayef R.F. and Gérard Stoudmann. (2006, 19 June). "Definitions of Globalization: A Comprehensive Overview and a Proposed Definition." 📄

2. ^ *a* *b* Albrow, Martin and Elizabeth King (eds.) (1990). *Globalization, Knowledge and Society* London: Sage. ISBN 978-0803983243 p. 8. "...all those processes by which the peoples of the world are incorporated into a single world society."

3. ^ Carpenter, John B., 1999, "Puritan Missions as Globalization," *Fides et Historia*, 31:2, p. 103.

4. ^ Stever, H. Guyford (1972). "Science, Systems, and Society." *Journal of Cybernetics*, 2(3):1-3. doi:10.1080/01969727208542909 🔗

5. ^ *a* *b* Frank, Andre Gunder. (1998). *ReOrient: Global economy in the Asian age.* Berkeley: University of California Press. ISBN 978-0520214743

6. ^ "*Globalization and Global History* (p.127)" 📄. Retrieved 3 July 2012.

7. ^ Ritzer, George (2011). *Globalization: The Essentials.* NY: John Wiley & Sons.

8. ^ Google Books Ngram Viewer: Globalization 🔗

Use the References section at the bottom of the Wikipedia article to find other, more substantive and authoritative resources about your topic.

Social media such as Facebook and Twitter can be useful as you brainstorm about your topic, but you will have to use these tools in new ways. You may have a Facebook or Twitter account and use it to keep in touch with friends, family, and colleagues. These social networks are valuable, and you may already use them to gather information to help you make decisions in your personal life and your workplace. But both Facebook and Twitter have powerful search functions that can lead you to resources and help you refine your ideas even when you are doing academic research.

After you log in to Facebook, use the "Search for people, places, and things" bar at the top of the page. When you type search terms into this bar, Facebook will first search your own social network. To extend beyond your own network, try adding the word "research" after your search terms. For instance, a search on Facebook for "sustainability" will lead you to a Facebook page for sustainability (the "interest"), as well as Katerva, a nonprofit organization. The posts on the page link to current news stories on sustainability, links to other similar research centers, and topics of interest in the field of sustainability research. You can use these search results as a way to see part of the conversation about a particular topic. This is not necessarily the scholarly conversation, but it is a social conversation that can still be useful in helping you determine what you want to focus on in the research process.

Twitter is an information network where users can post short messages (or "tweets"). While many people use Twitter simply to update their friends ("I'm going to the mall" or "Can't believe it's snowing!"), more and more individuals and organizations use Twitter to comment on noteworthy events or link to interesting articles. You can use Twitter as a tool because it aggregates links to sites, people in a field of research, and noteworthy sources. Communities, sometimes even scholarly communities, form around topics on Twitter. Users group posts together by using hashtags—words or phrases that follow the "#" sign. Users can respond to other users by using the @ sign followed by a user's Twitter name. When searching for specific individuals or organizations on Twitter, you search using their handle (such as @ barackobama or @whitehouse). You will retrieve tweets that were created either by the person or organization, or tweets that mention the person or organization. When searching for a topic to find discussions, you search using the hashtag symbol, #. For instance, a search on #sustainability will take you to tweets and threaded discussions on the topic of sustainability.

There are two ways to search twitter. You can use the search book in the upper right hand corner and enter either a @ or # search as described above. Once you retrieve results, you can search again by clicking on any of words that are hyperlinked within your results, such as #ecology or #resilience.

If you consider a hashtag (the # sign) as an entry point into a community, you will begin to discover the conversations around a topic. For instance, a search on Twitter for #sustainability leads you to US EPA Research (@EPAResearch). News agencies such as Reuters are also active in

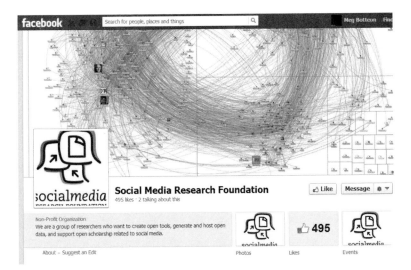

Facebook page for the Social Media Research Foundation.

Twitter searches can connect you to articles on and organizations involved in your topic area.

Twitter, so an article from a Reuters publication will be retrieved in a search. Evaluating information and sources found in social media is similar to how you evaluate any information you encounter during the research process. And, as with Wikipedia and Google searches, this is just a starting point to help you get a sense of the spectrum of topics. This is no substitute for using library resources. Whether you should cite Facebook, Twitter, or Wikipedia in a piece of writing depends on the context and medium of the writing and the degree of authority you need to establish in your writing. You would not usually cite these social media in an academic research paper, but you can use them to find more credible, authoritative sources.

Keyword searches are another useful strategy to explore the general topic in which you are interested. They generally produce the most results and can help you determine how much has been written on your topic. You want to use keyword searches to help you achieve a manageable number of results. What is manageable? This is a key question when beginning research. A keyword search in Google on sustainability will produce thousands of results. The same search in JSTOR.org (an online archive of academic journals) produces fewer results, but still way too many to manage. You can narrow your search using AND, OR, NOT between keywords to find areas of overlap that target your interest much more closely.

1. Use AND when you are combining multiple keywords. For example, you can use AND to look for information about sustainable resource use:

sustainability AND resources

The AND ensures that all your results will contain both the terms "sustainability" and "resources." Many search engines and databases will assume an AND search, meaning if you type

sustainability resources

the search will automatically look for both terms. However, in some cases the AND will not be assumed and sustainability resources will be treated as a phrase. This means that "sustainability" will have to be next to the word "resources" to return results. Worse yet, sometimes the search automatically assumes an OR. That would mean that all your results would come back with either sustainability or resources. This will produce a large and mostly irrelevant set of results. Therefore, use AND whenever you want two or more words to appear in a result.

2. Using OR can be very effective when you want to use several terms to describe a concept such as:

sustainability OR water

A search on sustainability OR water can be broadened to include water supply, waterborne diseases, or even the sustainability of the ocean and its ecosystem. The following search casts a broader net because results will come back with sustainability and either water supply, disease, or ocean:

Sustainability AND (water supply OR disease OR ocean)

Not all of these words will appear in each record. Note also that the parentheses set off the OR search, indicating that sustainability must appear in each record and then either water supply, disease, or ocean needs to appear along with sustainability.

3. Use quotation marks when looking for a phrase. For instance, if you are looking for information on water and sustainability in developing nations, you can ensure that the search results will include all of these concepts and increase the relevance by using the following search construction:

sustainability AND water AND "developing world"

This phrasing will return results that contain both the word "sustainability" and the phrase "developing world."

4. Use NOT to exclude terms that will make your search less relevant. You may find that a term keeps appearing in your search that is not useful. Try this:

sustainability NOT politics

If you are interested in the technical side of this debate, getting a lot of results that discuss the politics of sustainability may be distracting. By excluding the keyword "politics," you will retrieve far fewer sources and (we hope) more relevant results.

Finding Books

Locating useful books in the library is probably the most common research strategy. You can search your library's online catalog by subject, title, or author's name. You can search for books using a subject like "climate" or "climate change." If you know the name of a prominent scholar in sustainability, say Bill McKibben, you can search using his name and you'll get a list of all his books.

If you find one book on your topic, use it as a jumping-off point for finding more books or articles on that topic. Most books will have bibliographies either at the end of each chapter or the end of the book in which the author or authors have compiled all the sources they used.

Consult these bibliographies to find other materials on your topic that will help support your claim.

Another efficient way to find more sources once you've identified a particularly authoritative book is to go back to the book's listing in your library's online catalog. Once you find the book, look carefully at the record for links to subjects. By clicking on a subject link you are finding other items in your library on the same subject.

Using Databases

Books are great sources if you can find them on your topic, but often your research question will be something that is either too new or too specific for a book to cover. Books are very good for historical questions and overviews of large topics, but for current topics or more specialized topics, you will want to explore articles from magazines, academic journals, and newspapers. The best way to find this information is by using a database, an online resource that organizes research material of a particular type or content area. For example, *Environmental Sciences and Pollution Management* is a multidisciplinary database that provides comprehensive coverage of the environmental sciences. Abstracts and citations are drawn from over 4,000 scientific journals and thousands of other sources, including conference proceedings, reports, monographs, books, and government publications. Your library's website will list all the databases available to you, organize them by area, and provide a way to search relevant databases. Database searches are an incredibly powerful way to refine your search and locate useful information and ideas. Libraries differ in how well developed their websites are and how much guidance they can offer. My own library, for example, has a special research guide dedicated to sustainability and a librarian who specializes in research on sustainability. In most instances, your best bet is to ask a librarian which database or databases are most relevant to your research. And librarians will show you how to use these databases if you need help. Asking a librarian for help will make your life much easier and improve your research process.

Evaluating Sources

A common problem in research isn't a lack of sources, but an overload of information. Information is more accessible than ever. This presents an interesting challenge, however. If you rely on the sources you read for information and incorporate that material into your own writing, you need to know whether a source is reliable and trustworthy. Evaluating online sources is more challenging than traditional sources because it is harder to make distinctions between good and bad online information than with print sources. It is easy to tell that *Newsweek* magazine is not as scholarly as an academic journal, or that material in *Sport Fishing Magazine* will not be as authoritative as information in the *Handbook of Fish Biology and Fisheries*. But online everything may look the same. There are markers of credibility and authoritativeness when it comes to online information, and you can start to recognize them. We'll provide a few tips here, but be sure to ask a librarian or your professor for more guidance whenever you're uncertain about the reliability of a source.

1. **Domain** – The "domain" of a site is the last part of its URL. The domain indicates the type of website. Noting the web address can tell you a lot. A .edu site indicates that an educational organization created that content. This is no guarantee that the information is accurate, but it does suggest less bias than a .com site, which will be commercial in nature with a motive to sell you something, including ideas.

2. **Date** – Most websites include a date somewhere on the page. This date may indicate a copyright date, the date something was posted, or the date the site was last updated. These dates tell you when the content on the site was last changed or reviewed. Older sites might be outdated or contain information that is no longer relevant.

3. **Author or editor** – Does the online content indicate an author or editor? Like print materials, authority comes from the creator of the content. It is now easier than ever to investigate an author's credentials. A general Google search may lead you to a Wikipedia entry on the author, a LinkedIn page, or even an online résumé. If an author is affiliated with an educational institution, try visiting the institution's website for more information.

No matter what you are writing, you need to be careful about the credibility and trustworthiness of the sources you use.

WRITING RESEARCH PAPERS

The academic research paper is a specialized genre with its own conventions, requirements, purpose, and expectations, and it is a very important genre for students who want to do well in college. It requires most of the skills required for any kind of writing, but it exists in a different context (the classroom) with a unique audience (the instructor) and a relatively narrow purpose (to articulate and defend a thesis that answers an academically interesting question or provides new information and insight). Like all writing, research papers are part of a conversation, but it is a conversation between experts who have a great deal of knowledge about a topic and an interest in increasing the scope of that knowledge. Again, like all interesting writing, research papers require considerable research, but they typically use sources that are themselves part of the academic conversation; research papers rely mostly on articles published in academic journals or books written by scholars. And the argument in a research paper is a special case of everyday argumentation. Research papers perform all the actions of everyday argument, but they tend to be much more focused on creating knowledge or answering questions than changing the ways people act in the world. This is not an absolute distinction, but it generally holds for most academic research papers.

To write a successful research paper, you have to do five things:

- develop a good research question that is worth asking;
- articulate a thesis or claim that proposes an answer to the question;
- make an argument to defend your claim that provides enough credible evidence to be convincing;
- integrate your evidence into your argument; and
- organize the material so that it is easy to follow and easy to understand.

The material that follows explains what these five tasks are and suggests ways to accomplish them.

Developing a Research Question

You need to read enough about a topic to form a question that is worth asking. People do research and write research papers because they want to answer a question that is important in one way or another. So, you need to formulate a question that is not so broad as to be uninteresting or impossible (e.g., "How can we feed the world sustainably?") but that can be answered with some reasonable argument (e.g., "Can we raise fish on farms without harming the surrounding natural ecosystem?"). A general topic like "sustainability" is too broad. It is a general topic but not a question, and if you write about this, you will end up merely reporting a lot of information but not answering an interesting question. Asking whether a sustainable water supply and effective wastewater management is good for developing cities is not a useful research question; the answer is obvious. But asking whether having many local supplies of water spread across an urban area (a "distributed system") and reusing treated waste water for things like gardening, washing cars, and watering lawns is cost effective and saves money is a great research question. In the case of research papers, the cliché that "knowing the right question is half the battle" turns out to be true. Every minute you spend developing a question that is worth asking will pay huge dividends later. And the only way to develop that question is to use the research strategies discussed in the previous section to learn more about the general topic.

Stating a Thesis

Simply put, your thesis is the answer to the research question you asked. Your thesis is the central claim of your paper—the main point that you'd like to defend. In the case of the question about "distributed water systems," you might claim that having many small water supplies distributed around a city and reusing waste water for things other than drinking, cooking, and washing is more efficient, saves money, and is less vulnerable to a single catastrophic failure than a big centralized system where everything depends on a single water treatment plant. Your thesis is your governing claim, the central argument of the whole paper, but you may make a number of smaller claims throughout the paper that use a piece of evidence you've found. In the example of a distributed water system, you might provide evidence gathered through research that demonstrates that it is cheaper to pipe water a short distance instead of a long distance across hilly ground, pumping it uphill using expensive pumping stations. You might provide evidence that in the case of an earthquake or hurricane, having many small, local systems allows you to lose a few systems without putting the whole city out of water. And remember to connect these smaller "sub-claims" to your central thesis so that readers can see how each piece fits into the general argument.

Make sure, too, that your thesis is a point of persuasion rather than one of belief or taste. "Bottled water tastes better than tap water" is certainly an argument you could make to your friend, but it is not an adequate thesis for an academic paper because there is no evidence that you could provide that might persuade a reader who doesn't already agree with you. But you could make an argument that your university should install water fountains that fill personal water bottles because bottled water wastes energy, produces waste plastic, and costs much more than municipal drinking water. The first is a matter of opinion; the second can be defended by an argument using evidence gathered through research from reliable sources.

Making an Argument

A great deal of writing and talk in everyday life makes an argument. When your minister, priest, rabbi, or imam offers you a sermon about charity, for example, he or she is making an argument that you should behave charitably and is trying to persuade you to believe and act in a specific way. Not all writing makes an argument, at least not explicitly. Research papers, however, always make an argument. A research paper states a thesis or a claim about an important question and then argues that the thesis is correct or true. The previous section of this Appendix discussed the five tasks involved in making an argument. This section interprets those in terms of the research paper.

The core of making an argument defending a thesis or claim is providing evidence that the claim is true. And the evidence has to be trustworthy, adequate, and appropriate to the claim.

The question of whether your evidence is trustworthy or credible is really an issue of the sources you have used and whether you have ignored evidence that contradicts your thesis. The previous section discussed evaluating sources. This is crucial to having trustworthy or credible evidence for your claims. The question of cherry-picking evidence or ignoring evidence that conflicts with your argument is more difficult. The best arguments take into account a wide array of evidence, carefully considering all sides of a topic. As you probably know, often the most fruitful conversations occur not just when you are talking to people who already agree with you, but when you are fully engaging with the people who might disagree with you. Coming across unexpected, surprising, and contradictory evidence, then, is a good thing! It will force you to make a complex, nuanced argument and will ultimately allow you to write a more persuasive paper. As you do your research you may find that you have to modify your initial thesis in light of contradictory evidence or that you have to spend some time refuting that evidence if you think it is not accurate. This is what the previous section described as refuting counter-arguments. Think of a defense lawyer in court who defends his client by undermining the prosecutor's evidence. In a research paper, however, it is always both easier and better to modify your thesis to fit the evidence than to select, modify, or ignore evidence to protect a thesis that has holes in it. Your goal is truth and accuracy, not winning a trial.

The question of whether your evidence is adequate is a matter of context. Writers often wonder whether they have offered enough evidence. And they sometimes struggle with knowing when to stop providing more and more evidence for a claim. There is no hard-and-fast rule to apply here, but there are a few reasonable principles you can follow. The more controversial your claim is, the more evidence you need to support it. It takes a lot of compelling evidence to change someone's mind when your claim goes against what he or she already thinks. Also, the more that is at stake in the claim or the greater the consequences of your argument, the more evidence you will need. In the case of the distributed water system discussed above, you would need a great deal of powerful evidence because you are asking a city or a planner to consider renovating the city water system, and that is expensive and troublesome. As a rule of thumb, any time your thesis goes against the status quo or the accepted belief, you need more rather than less evidence.

Finally, the issue of whether your evidence is appropriate asks whether the evidence really relates to the claim you made or is about some other issue. For example, if you are trying to support the claim that greenhouse gases are destroying coral reefs, offering evidence that coral reefs are important to ocean fisheries may be true, but it doesn't support your claim. Talking about the importance of reefs to ocean fisheries makes a claim about the *consequences* of destroying the reef, not the *causes* of the destruction.

There are lots of forms of evidence that you might use in a research paper. We've talked about finding evidence in books, magazines, journals, and newspapers. Here are a few other kinds of evidence you may want to use.

Interviews can be a powerful form of evidence, especially if the person you are interviewing is an expert in the field that you're investigating. Interviewing can be intimidating, but it might help to know that many people (even experts!) will feel flattered when you ask them for an interview. Most scholars are deeply interested in spreading knowledge, so you should feel comfortable asking a scholar for his or her ideas. Even if the scholar doesn't know the specific answer to your question, he or she may be able to point you in the right direction.

Remember, of course, to be as courteous as possible when you are planning to interview someone. This means sending a polite email that fully introduces yourself and your project before you begin asking questions. Email interviews may be convenient, but an in-person interview is best, since this allows for you and the interviewee to engage in a conversation that may take surprising and helpful turns.

It's a good idea to write down a number of questions before the interview. Make sure not just to get facts (which you can likely get somewhere else). Ask the interviewee to speculate about your topic. Remember that "why" and "how" questions often yield more interesting answers than "what" questions.

If you do conduct an in-person interview, act professionally. Be on time, dress respectfully, and show sincere interest and gratitude. Bring something to record the interview. Many reporters still use pens and a pad, since these feel unobtrusive and are very portable.

Write down the interviewee's name, the date, and the location of the interview, and have your list of questions ready. Don't be afraid, of course, to veer from your questions. The best questions might be the follow-up questions that couldn't have occurred to you before the conversation began. You're likely to get the interviewee to talk freely and openly if you show real intellectual curiosity. If you're not a fast writer, it's certainly OK to ask the interviewee to pause for a moment while you take notes. Some people like to record their interviews. Just make sure that you ask permission if you choose to do this. It's always nice to send a brief thank-you note or email after the interview. This would be a good time to ask any brief follow-up questions.

Because we live in a visual age, we tend to take **images** for granted. We see them in magazines, on TV, and on the Internet. We don't often think about them as critically as we think about words on a page. Yet, a critical look at an image can uncover helpful evidence for a claim. For example, if you are writing about the impact of greenhouse gases on coral reefs, you could easily find an image of a damaged reef with a Google search and place it in your paper.

Images can add depth and variety to your argument and they are generally easy to find on the Internet. The previous section described the first move in an argument as an "exhortation" or a compelling story that helps a reader see what is at stake. An image of a dead coral reef is a great exhortation; it is a compelling story in visual form. Use Google Image search or flickr.com to find images using the same keywords you used to find books and articles. Ask your instructor for guidance on how to properly cite and acknowledge the source of any images you wish to use. If you want to present your research outside of a classroom project (for example, publish it on a blog or share it at a community event), ask a research librarian for guidance on avoiding any potential copyright violations.

Like images, **multimedia** such as video, audio, and animations are increasingly easy to find on the Internet and can strengthen your claim. For instance, if you are working on climate change you could find audio or video news clips illustrating the effects of climate change on Arctic ice sheets or rainfall patterns in the American Midwest. There are several audio and video search engines available such as Vimeo (vimeo.com) or Blinkx (blinkx.com), a search engine featuring audio and video from the BBC, Reuters, and the Associated Press, among others. As with images, ask your instructor for guidance on how to properly cite and acknowledge the source of any multimedia you wish to use. As with images, if you want to present your research outside of a classroom project (for example, publish it on a blog or share it at a community event), ask a research librarian for guidance on avoiding any potential copyright violations.

Integrating Your Evidence Into Your Argument

There are three basic ways to incorporate evidence into your argument: summarize, paraphrase, or quote.

Summaries are an efficient way to capture the main ideas of a source. You should summarize a source when the source is large, like a book or a chapter in a book, and you want to present its main idea in one or two sentences. Because they leave out all the detail of a longer source, summaries are best used to provide background information or set the context for more detailed material. The trick to summarizing is to capture the main idea in a short space and to be accurate. You do not need to cite the source for a summary, but you should mention it in the summary itself.

Paraphrasing involves putting a source's ideas into your own words. It's a good idea to paraphrase if you think you can state the idea more clearly or more directly than the original source does. Typically a good paraphrase is almost as long as the original passage, but it is phrased in terms that fit into your paper and represent your interpretation of the original source. With a paraphrase, you do need a citation to the source at the end of the paraphrase, and you need to include the whole citation in the Works Cited or References.

Quoting a source can be a very powerful form of evidence, but it takes a great deal of space. You should quote something word for word only when the precise words themselves are important, when the quotation is especially eloquent and striking, or when it conveys specific information that is essential to your argument. You should choose things to quote very carefully and avoid using too many quotations. A paper that just strings together other writers' words is usually incoherent and never makes a strong argument.

When you use a quotation in your argument, you need to quote it exactly and place it in quotation marks. You also need to cite the source and the page on which the quoted passage appears and then include the full citation in the Works Cited or References. And when you do use a quotation, you need to introduce the quotation by identifying who wrote the passage and providing some context for the reader. Finally, because readers might misunderstand the quotation or fail to see its relation to your argument, you need to interpret the quotation so readers see the connection you are making.

Organizing Your Paper

The organization of a research paper begins with an introduction that lays out the major elements of your argument. The introduction can be more than one paragraph and it should:

introduce your research question and explain why it is important;

offer a precise statement of your thesis or central claim;

indicate what kind of evidence you'll offer to support that claim.

Some readers describe well-organized papers as having a sense of flow, by which they mean that the argument moves easily from one sentence to the next and from one paragraph to the next. This allows your reader to follow your thoughts easily. When you begin writing a sentence, try using an idea, keyword, or phrase from the end of the previous sentence. The next sentence, then, will appear to have emerged smoothly from the previous sentence. This tip is especially important when you move between paragraphs. The best transition from one paragraph to the next starts with a brief reference to the topic of the previous paragraph and then adds the new information to the end of that sentence.

Making and Managing Notes

Taking careful notes as you read and managing them using a good piece of software can save you huge amounts of time. And it can also help you avoid unintentional plagiarism (discussed in the next section). Researchers used to have to depend on paper note cards, but computer software has made managing notes immensely easier and more efficient.

Chances are your college library provides software, such as **EndNote** or **RefWorks**, to help you manage citations. These are two commercially available citation management software packages that are not freely available to you unless your library has paid for a license. EndNote or RefWorks enables you to organize your sources in personal libraries. These libraries help you manage your sources and create bibliographies. Both EndNote and RefWorks also enable you to insert endnotes and footnotes directly into a Microsoft Word document.

If your library does not provide EndNote or RefWorks, a freely available software called **Zotero** (Zotero.org) will help you manage your sources. Zotero helps you collect, organize, cite, and share your sources, and it lives right in your web browser where you do your research. As you are searching

Google, your library catalog, or library database, Zotero enables you to add a book, article, or website to a personal library with one click. As you add items to your library, Zotero collects both the information you need for you bibliography and any full-text content. This mean that the content of journal articles and ebooks will be available to you right from your Zotero library. To create a bibliography, simply select the items from your Zotero library you want to include, right-click and select "Create Bibliography from Selected Items . . . ," and choose the citation style your instructor asked you to use for the paper. To get started, go to Zotero.org and download Zotero for the browser of your choice.

Avoiding Plagiarism

Writers constantly build their arguments using ideas and material from other writers, but it is crucial that you never claim someone else's ideas, or especially their exact words, as your own. If you use a diagram or a graph on the change in CO_2 levels in the atmosphere, for example, you need to identify the source of the graph in your text where you insert the graph. The best way to avoid plagiarism is to plan ahead and keep careful notes as you read your sources. Remember the advice (above) on Zotero and taking notes: find the way that works best for you to keep track of what ideas are your own and what ideas come directly from the sources you are reading. Most acts of plagiarism are accidental. It is easy when you are drafting a paper to lose track of where a quote or idea came from; plan ahead and this won't happen. Here are a few tips for making sure that confusion doesn't happen to you.

- Know what needs to be cited. You do not need to cite what is considered common knowledge such as facts (the day Lincoln was born), concepts (the Earth orbits the sun), or events (the day Martin Luther King was shot). You do need to cite the ideas and words of others from the sources you are using in your paper.
- Be conservative. If you are not sure if you should cite something, either ask your instructor or a librarian, or cite it. It is better to cite something you don't have to than not cite something you should.
- Direct quotations from your sources need to be cited as well as anytime you paraphrase the ideas or words from your sources.
- Finally, extensive citation not only helps you avoid plagiarism, but it also boosts your credibility and enables your reader to trace your scholarship.

Citation Styles

It is crucial that you adhere to the standards of a single citation style when you write your paper. The most common styles are MLA (Modern Language Association, generally used in the humanities) and APA (American Psychological Association, generally used in the social sciences). If you're not sure which style you should use, ask your instructor.

There are a number of helpful guidebooks that will tell you all the rules you need to know in order to follow the standards for various citation styles. If your instructor hasn't pointed you to a specific guidebook, try the following online resources:

Purdue Online Writing Lab: owl.english.purdue.edu/

Internet Public Library: www.ipl.org/div/farq/netciteFARQ.html

Modern Language Association (for MLA style): www.mla.org/style

American Psychological Association (for APA style): www.apastyle.org/

Sample Student Research Paper

Climate Change and Sea Level Rise

Global climate change is a reality in the twentieth century, and it will have huge consequences for the future. It is important to understand that even if climate change seems unbelievable, it is inevitable. We have already altered the Earth's atmosphere enough to begin changing the global climate. This change will bring extreme heat, extreme cold, droughts, and more powerful hurricanes, and it will raise the costs of many everyday things such as the cost to heat and air condition homes.

Climate change has been happening for a long time, and many scientists have studied its causes and its effects. Unfortunately, many people often confuse climate change with weather and global warming. Weather is the condition of the atmosphere over a short period of time, while climate is a measure of the behavior of the atmosphere over a long period of time (Dictionary.com). Global warming suggests a steady and even increase in the temperature of the Earth's atmosphere, whereas climate change refers to an average increase in temperature but predicts uneven changes that increase or decrease heat in specific areas but over time.

The primary cause of climate change is the rapid increase in carbon dioxide in the atmosphere and the resulting increase in the Greenhouse Effect. The Greenhouse Effect is a property of the Earth's atmosphere that helps the Earth remain warm enough for people to live in. "Because of the physical properties of certain gases in the air, especially water vapor and carbon dioxide, there is strong evidence that Earth would be much colder without the greenhouse effect" (Cicerone 12). The water vapor and CO_2 in the air allow the atmosphere to retain solar energy and warm the planet. But changing the concentration of these gases changes the balance in the atmosphere and the amount of solar energy the planet retains. This is an example of why the temperature and weather of the earth need balance.

Unfortunately, the amount of CO_2 in the atmosphere has increased steadily in recent years and disrupted the natural balance. This is occurring globally and has been measured, showing that the increase of CO_2 occurs a lot faster than the process that removes it from the air, causing an imbalance in the chemical composition of the atmosphere. The graph below (Figure 1) is a record of the CO_2 concentration in the atmosphere on Mount Mauna Loa, Hawaii, from 1957 to 2005.

As this graph suggests, the concentration of CO_2 in the atmosphere has been rising steadily since these measurements began in 1957.

In order to put this increase in CO_2 in perspective, scientists have analyzed dated ice cores from the Arctic to measure the amount of CO_2 in the atmosphere for the last 450,000 years. Figure 2 presents the concentration of CO_2 in the atmosphere going back 450,000 years.

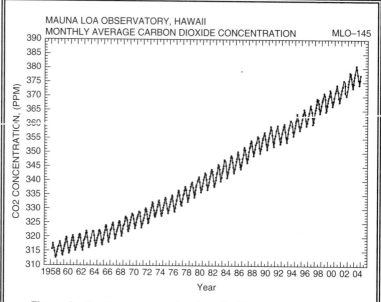

MAUNA LOA OBSERVATORY, HAWAII
MONTHLY AVERAGE CARBON DIOXIDE CONCENTRATION   MLO–145

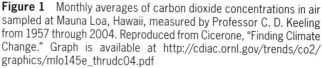

Figure 1 Monthly averages of carbon dioxide concentrations in air sampled at Mauna Loa, Hawaii, measured by Professor C. D. Keeling from 1957 through 2004. Reproduced from Cicerone, "Finding Climate Change." Graph is available at http://cdiac.ornl.gov/trends/co2/graphics/mlo145e_thrudc04.pdf

The concentration of CO_2 varies over time, but the highest concentration over the last 450,000 years is about 280 ppm. The far right of the graph, however, shows the current concentration in red at about 370 ppm. As the graph suggests, CO_2 concentration has increased dramatically in the last 150 years since the Industrial Revolution. Furthermore, according to the IPCC report, "The annual carbon dioxide concentration growth rate was larger during the last 10 years (1995–2005 average: 1.9 ppm per year)" (IPCC 2). And research reports show that this increase has been driven by human activities in everyday life, primarily fossil fuel use, land use change, and agriculture.

This steady increase in greenhouse gas concentration and climate change will have many consequences, but sea level rise is one of the most apparent and dangerous. Currently, 33 countries in the world have areas that are below sea level. In the past

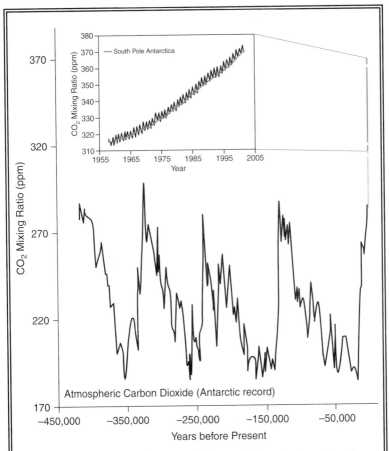

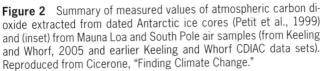

Figure 2 Summary of measured values of atmospheric carbon dioxide extracted from dated Antarctic ice cores (Petit et al., 1999) and (inset) from Mauna Loa and South Pole air samples (from Keeling and Whorf, 2005 and earlier Keeling and Whorf CDIAC data sets). Reproduced from Cicerone, "Finding Climate Change."

100 years, the Earth's climate has warmed about 1.8 degrees F and the sea level has risen about 15–20 centimeters. Recently, however, "the rate of increase has jumped to about 3.1 mm/year" (Climate Change and Sea Level Rise). Although 3.1 millimeters may seem like very little, over time this number is projected to grow, which will in turn have terrible consequences on the human, animal, and plant life in those low-lying areas.

Climate change will raise the sea level in three ways. First, as the world gets warmer, the ocean also gets warmer. And as the ocean gets warmer, it slowly begins to expand. This thermal expansion is responsible for the gradual rise in sea level in the 20th century. The second cause of sea level rise is the melting of glaciers and ice caps, which will contribute roughly 10–12 centimeters to sea level rise (Climate Change and Sea Level Rise). The third and most dangerous cause is the loss of ice mass in Greenland and Antarctica. The Antarctic ice sheet is the largest body of ice in the world, covering almost 14 million square kilometers, and the Greenland Ice Sheet is the second largest body of ice in the world. It covers roughly 80% of Greenland's surface and is almost 2,400 kilometers long (Science Daily). If these two ice sheets melted significantly, the rise in sea level would be insurmountable. "Complete melting of these ice sheets could lead to a sea level rise of about 80 meters, whereas melting of all the other glaciers could lead to a sea-level rise of only half a meter" (Sea Level and Climate).

Although this kind of side effect of global climate change would not happen immediately, over time the melting effects of these ice sheets may become apparent to those all over the world, not just those who live by them. Even locally, the rise in sea level without inclusion of the ice sheets is still terrible.

Florida is a state that is largely near sea level. Because of this, if even a small amount of sea level rise were to occur, large areas would be affected. Figure 3 gives a projected image of what Florida may look like with 3 meters of sea level rise. The area in red is underwater when sea level rises three meters.

It is clear that much of Florida's outer land mass would be completely covered with water and that the water seems to slowly make its way to more land. The millions of people who reside in those areas would not be able to stop the water from reaching their homes, so they would be forced to relocate.

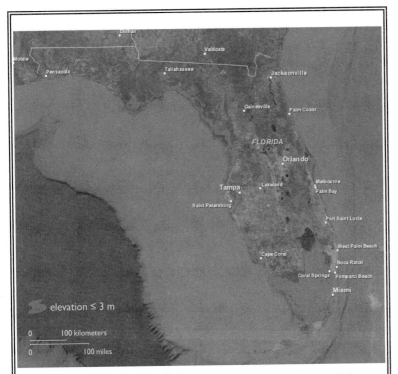

Figure 3 The projected depiction of the state of Florida if the sea level rose 3 meters. Map is also available at http://www.geo .arizona.edu/dgesl/research/other/climate_change_and_sea_level/ mapping_slr/.

If the Antarctic and Greenland ice sheets were to melt, then all of Florida would likely be gone and many lives would be lost.

Sea level rise is one of the many consequences of global climate change. There are only three options that people are left with when dealing with climate change. J.P. Holdren says that "Our options in this domain are three. They are mitigation, adaptation and suffering" (5). Mitigation means to take action to moderate the situation; adaptation means that we have to adjust to the worsening situation; and suffering needs no explanation. The most wide-scale way of mitigating climate change would be through governmental policies. Unfortunately, according to the Intergovernmental Panel on Climate Change, one of the biggest issues with mitigation is the financial cost to each country. Conversely, adaptation requires change on a more personal level than mitigation. Adaptation requires adjustments that reduce vulnerability or enhance resilience in response to changes in climate and weather. As the effects of climate change worsen, one must realize that the options are becoming more limited.

Although the idea of global climate change is terrifying, humans need to understand that it is happening and getting worse as time progresses. The many facts are in place and it is obvious that things need to change drastically to give future generations a fighting chance at survival on this planet. If we choose to neither mitigate nor adapt, the planet and its inhabitants will surely suffer. The charts are available. The graphs are as accurate as possible. And the research is endless. It is now time to realize that we are slowly shortening our own time on this planet.

Works Cited

"Chapter 17: Assessment of Adaptation Practices, Options, Constraints and Capacity - 17.1 Concepts and Methods." *www.ipcc.ch*. IPCC - Intergovernmental Panel on Climate Change. Web. 11 Apr. 2011. http://www.ipcc.ch/publications_and_data/ar4/wg2/en/ch17s17-1.html.

Cicerone, Ralph J. *Finding Climate Change and Being Useful*. Washington, D.C.: National Council for Science and the Environment, 2006. Print.

"Climate Change and Sea Level Rise." *Climate.org*. Climate Institute. Web. 11 Apr. 2011.http://www.climate.org/topics/sea-level/index.html.

"Coastal Zones and Sea Level Rise." *EPA.gov.* US
Environmental Protection Agency, 19 Aug. 2010.
Web. 11 Apr. 2011. http://www.epa.gov/climate-
change/effects/coastal/index.html.

"Greenland Ice Sheet." *Sciencedaily.com.* Science
Daily: News & Articles in Science, Health,
Environment & Technology. Web. 11 Apr. 2011.
http://www.sciencedaily.com/articles/g/
greenland_ice_sheet.htm.

Holdren, John P. *Meeting the Climate-change
Challenge.* Vol. 8. Washington, D.C.: National
Council for Science and the Environment, 2008.
Print.

"Sea Level and Climate." *Pubs.usgs.gov.* USGS
Publications Warehouse, 31 Jan. 2000.
Web. 11 Apr. 2011. http://pubs.usgs.gov/fs/fs2-00/.

Chapter 1:
Page 4 from "The Obligation to Endure" from SILENT SPRING by Rachel Carson. Copyright © 1962 by Rachel L. Carson, renewed 1990 by Roger Christie. Reprinted by permission of Houghton Mifflin Harcourt Publishing Company. All rights reserved.

Page 12 from A SAND COUNTY ALMANAC by Leopold (1949) "Thinking Like a Mountain" pp. 129–133 © 1949, 1977 by Oxford University Press, Inc. by Permission of Oxford University Press, USA.

Page 15 from "The World as a Polder", From COLLAPSE: HOW SOCIETIES CHOOSE TO FAIL OR SUCCEED by Jared Diamond, copyright © 2005 by Jared Diamond. Used by permission of Viking Penguin, a division of Penguin Group (USA) Inc.

Page 28 from Science Magazine, December 13, 1968. Reprinted with permission from AAAS.

Chapter 2:
Page 50 from www.storyofstuff.org.

Page 62 from www.storyofstuff.org.

Page 78 from Chris Carroll/National Geographic Stock.

Page 88 from Luke W. Cole and Sheila R. Foster. "From the Ground Up: Environmental Racism and the Rise of the Environmental Justice Movement." *NYU Press.*

Page 97 from "Where did our clothes come from?" By Emily Fontaine.

Page 103 Copyright Guardian News & Media Ltd 2012.

Page 108 from Gay Hawkins. "Worm Stories" pp. 124–128 from THE ETHICS OF WASTE. *Rowman & Littlefield Publishing Group.*

Chapter 3:
Page 118 from "Getting to Know Your Bacon: Hogs, Farms, and Clean Water" by Jeff Opperman, posted on The Nature Conservancy, March 21, 2011.

Page 121 reprinted by permission of Sarah Lozanova.

Page 126 from "Finding Nemo on Your Plate" by Stephanie Wear, posted on The Nature Conservancy, March 21, 2011.

Page 130 ©2011 National Public Radio, Inc. NPR news report titled "How Community Supported Agriculture Sprouted In China" was originally published online on NPR's *The Salt* blog on September 24, 2011 and is used with the permission of NPR. Any unauthorized duplication is strictly prohibited.

Page 132 from THE OMNIVORE'S DILEMMA by Michael Pollan, copyright © 2006 by Michael Pollan. Used by permission of The Penguin Press, a division of Penguin Group (USA) LLC.

Page 140 excerpts from "Genetically Modifed Foods: Harmful or Helpful?" by Deborah Whitman, *CSA Discovery Guide,* released April 2000. Reproduced with permission of ProQuest LLC. Further reproduction is prohibited. www.proquest.com.

Page 147 from Paul Epstein. "Climate Change and Food Security: The True Cost of Carbon." *The Atlantic,* September 27, 2011.

Chapter 4:
Page 158 from Ralph Cicerone. "Finding Climate Change and Being Useful. *National Council for Science and the Environment,* January 26, 2006.

Page 183 from Advancing the Science of Climate Change by America's Climate Choices: Panel on Advancing the Science of Climate Change ; National Research Council Reproduced with permission of National Academies Press in the format post on a secure intranet/extranet via Copyright Clearance Center.

Page 197 from "Gender and Climate Hazards in Bangladesh." Terry Cannon. *Gender and Development,* Copyright © Oxfam

GB reprinted by permission of (Taylor & Francis Ltd, http://www.tandfonline.com) on behalf of Oxfam GB.

Page 206 © Stefan Skrimshire, 210, Future Ethics: Climate Change and Apocalyptic Imagination, Continuum, an imprint of Bloomsbury Publishing Plc.

Page 216 from Richard Cizek. "Climate Change: An Evangelical Call to Action." *The Evangelical Climate Initiative,* January 2006.

Chapter 5:
Page 233 from Advancing the Science of Climate Change by America's Climate Choices: Panel on Advancing the Science of Climate Change; National Research Council Reproduced with permission of National Academies Press in the format post on a secure intranet/extranet via Copyright Clearance Center.

Page 253 from NRDC/nrdc.com.

Page 258 from © American Council for an Energy-Efficient Economy.

Page 262 from Vandana Shiva. "Soil Not Oil." *South End Press.*

Page 273 excerpts from "The Age of Noah" from HOT, FLAT AND CROWDED: WHY WE NEED A GREEN REVOLUTION- AND HOW IT CAN RENEW AMERICA by Thomas Friedman. Copyright © 2008 by Thomas Friedman. Reprinted by permission of Farrar, Straus and Giroux, LLC.

Page 283 from Evan Schwartz. "How Not to Make Energy Decisions: Lessons from the Battle over Cape Wind." *Technology Review MIT.* Nov./Dec. 2010.

Page 288 from Coastal management: an international journal of marine environment, resources, law, and society by TAYLOR & FRANCIS INC. Reproduced with permission of TAYLOR & FRANCIS INC. in the format republish in a book/textbook via Copyright Clearance Center.

Page 296 Copyright © 2010 Condé Nast. Vanity Fair. All rights reserved. By Christopher Bateman.

Chapter 6:
Page 309 from Dirt: the Erosion of Civilizations by Montgomery, David R. Reproduced with permission of University of California Press in the format Republish in a book via Copyright Clearance Center.

Page 317 from Pam Stachler. "Upstream Rock Run Coal Mine Remediation" *Monday Creek Restoration Project,* Fall 2010.

Page 320 from *Raising Elijah* by Sandra Steingraber. Reprinted by permission of Da Capo Press, a member of the Perseus Books Group.

Page 324 from Bryan Walsh. "Nature: A Major Company Puts a Value on the Environment." *Time.com.* © 2011 Time Inc. All rights reserved. Reprinted/Translated from **Time.com** and published with permission of Time, Inc. Reproduction in any manner in any language in whole or in part without written permission is prohibited.

Page 328 ©2011 National Public Radio, Inc. NPR news report titled "Putting Farmland On A Fertilizer Diet" was originally published online on NPR's *The Salt* blog on September 24, 2011 and is used with the permission of NPR. Any unauthorized duplication is strictly prohibited.

Page 331 from http://www.gulfhypoxia.net/Overview/.

Page 337 from "Blue Revolution" by Cynthia Barnett. Copyright © 2011 by Cynthia Barnett. Reprinted by permission of Beacon Press, Boston.

Page 347 reprinted by permission of International Creative Management, Inc. Copyright © **2007 by Michael Specter.**

Page 353 by Lisa Stiffler, Copyright 2011, Sightline Institute.

Page 362 from Elizabeth Kolbert/The New Yorker.

index

"About Hypoxia" (Louisiana Universities Marine Consortium), 331–37

"Advancing the Science of Climate Change" (National Research Council), 183–96

"The Age of Noah: Biodiversity" (Friedman), 273–83

"All You Need to Know About Storm Water Runoff" (Stiffler), 353–62

Barnett, Cynthia, 308
    "The Illusion of Water Abundance," 337–47

Barratt-Brown, Liz, 230–31
    "It Is All About the Framing: How Polls and the Media Misrepresent the Keystone XL [Tar Sands] [Oil] Pipeline," 253–58

Bateman, Christopher, "A Colossal Fracking Mess," 296–306

Cannon, Terry, "Gender and Climate Hazards in Bangladesh," 197–205

Caroll, Chris, "High Tech Trash," 78–87

Carson, Rachel, 3, 157, 309
    "The Obligation to Endure," 4–11

"The Case for Gardening as a Means to Curb Climate Change" (Steingraber), 320–24

Charles, Dan
    "How Community-Supported Agriculture Sprouted in China," 130–32

    "Putting Farmland on a Fertilizer Diet," 328–31

Cicerone, Ralph, "Find Climate Change and Being Useful," 158–82

"Climate Change: An Evangelical Call to Action" (New Evangelical Partnership for the Common Good), 216–27

Climate Guest Blogger, "'Thinking Big' on Efficiency Could Cut U.S. Energy Costs up to $16 Trillion and Create 1.9 Million Net Jobs by 2050," 258–61

Cole, Luke W., "We Speak for Ourselves: The Struggle of Kettleman City," 88–97

"A Colossal Fracking Mess" (Bateman), 296–306

"The Darkening Sea" (Kolbert), 362–76

Diamond, Jared, 48, 308
    "The World as Polder: What Does It Mean to Us Today," 2–3, 15–28

"Empathy and Climate Change: A Proposal for a Revolution of Human Relationships" (Krznaric), 206–16

"Energy Supply and Use" (National Research Council), 233–53

Epstein, Paul, 116
    "Food Security and Climate Change: The True Cost of Carbon," 147–53

"Find Climate Change and Being Useful" (Cicerone), 158–82
"Finding Nemo on Your Plate" (Wear), 126–29
Fontaine, Emily, "Where Did Our Clothes Come From?," 97–103
"Food for Cars or People: Biofuels a False Solution to Climate Change and a Threat to Food Security" (Shiva), 262–73, 309
"Food Security and Climate Change: The True Cost of Carbon" (Epstein), 147–53
Foster, Sheila R., "We Speak for Ourselves: The Struggle of Kettleman City," 88–97
Friedman, Thomas, 232
    "The Age of Noah: Biodiversity," 273–83

"Gender and Climate Hazards in Bangladesh" (Cannon), 197–205
"Genetically Modified Foods: Harmful or Helpful?" (Whitman), 140–47
"The Genius of the Place" (Pollan), 116, 132–39
"Getting to Know Your Bacon: Hogs, Farms, and Clean Water" (Opperman), 118–21
"Good Old Dirt" (Montgomery), 309–17

Hardin, Garrett, "Tragedy of the Commons," 2, 28–46
Hawkins, Gay, 48
    "Worm Stories," 108–14
"High Tech Trash" (Caroll), 78–87
"How Not to Make Energy Decisions: Lessons from the Battle Over Cape Wind" (Schwartz), 283–88
"How Community-Supported Agriculture Sprouted in China" (Charles), 130–32

"The Illusion of Water Abundance" (Barnett), 337–47
"It Is All About the Framing: How Polls and the Media Misrepresent the Keystone XL [Tar Sands] [Oil] Pipeline" (Barratt-Brown), 253–58

Kempton, Willett, "The Offshore Power Debate: Views from Cape Cod," 288–96
Kolbert, Elizabeth, "The Darkening Sea," 362–76
Krznaric, Roman, "Empathy and Climate Change: A Proposal for a Revolution of Human Relationships," 206–16

Leonard, Annie, 48, 49
    "The Story of Stuff: Bottled Water," 62–78
    "The Story of Stuff: Electronics," 50–61
Leopold, Aldo, 3, 48
    "Thinking Like a Mountain," 12–15
Louisiana Universities Marine Consortium, "About Hypoxia," 331–37
Lozanova, Sarah, "Starbucks Coffee: Green or Greenwashed?," 121–26

Monday Creek Restoration Project, "Upstream Rock Run Coal Mine Remediation," 317–19
Montgomery, David, 3, 308
    "Good Old Dirt," 309–17

National Research Council
    "Advancing the Science of Climate Change," 183–96
    "Energy Supply and Use," 233–53
"Nature: A Major Company Puts a Value on the Environment" (Walsh), 324–28
New Evangelical Partnership for the Common Good, "Climate Change: An Evangelical Call to Action," 216–27

"The Obligation to Endure" (Carson), 4–11
"The Offshore Power Debate: Views from Cape Cod" (Kempton), 288–96

Opperman, Jeff, "Getting to Know Your Bacon: Hogs, Farms, and Clean Water," 118–21

Pollan, Michael, "The Genius of the Place," 116, 132–39
"Putting Farmland on a Fertilizer Diet" (Charles), 328–31

Schwartz, Evan I., "How Not to Make Energy Decisions: Lessons from the Battle Over Cape Wind," 283–88
Shiva, Vandana, 232
  "Food for Cars or People: Biofuels a False Solution to Climate Change and a Threat to Food Security," 262–73, 309
Siegle, Lucy, "Why It's Time to End Our Love Affair With Cheap Fashion," 103–7
Specter, Michael, "Why Sewers Should EXCITE Us," 347–53
"Starbucks Coffee: Green or Greenwashed?" (Lozanova), 121–26
Steingraber, Sandra, "The Case for Gardening as a Means to Curb Climate Change," 320–24
Stiffler, Lisa, "All You Need to Know About Storm Water Runoff," 353–62
"The Story of Stuff: Bottled Water" (Leonard), 62–78
"The Story of Stuff: Electronics" (Leonard), 50–61

"'Thinking Big' on Efficiency Could Cut U.S. Energy Costs up to $16 Trillion and Create 1.9 Million Net Jobs by 2050" (Climate Guest Blogger), 258–61
"Thinking Like a Mountain" (Leopold), 12–15
"Tragedy of the Commons" (Hardin), 2, 28–46

"Upstream Rock Run Coal Mine Remediation" (Monday Creek Restoration Project), 317–19

Walsh, Bryan, "Nature: A Major Company Puts a Value on the Environment," 324–28
Wear, Stephanie, "Finding Nemo on Your Plate," 126–29
"We Speak for Ourselves: The Struggle of Kettleman City" (Cole and Foster), 88–97
"Where Did Our Clothes Come From?," (Fontaine), 97–103
Whitman, Deborah, 116
  "Genetically Modified Foods: Harmful or Helpful?," 140–47
"Why It's Time to End Our Love Affair With Cheap Fashion" (Siegle), 103–7
"Why Sewers Should EXCITE Us" (Specter), 347–53
"The World as Polder: What Does It Mean to Us Today" (Diamond), 2–3, 15–28
"Worm Stories" (Hawkins), 108–14